HISTORICISM, THE HOLOCAUST, AND ZIONISM

STEVEN T. KATZ

Historicism, the Holocaust, and Zionism

Critical Studies in Modern Jewish Thought and History

NEW YORK UNIVERSITY PRESS
New York and London

NEW YORK UNIVERSITY PRESS
New York and London

Library of Congress Cataloging-in-Publication Data
Katz, Steven T.
Historicism, the Holocaust, and Zionism : critical studies in
modern Jewish thought and history / Steven T. Katz.
p.   cm.
Includes bibliographical references and index.
ISBN 0–8147–4616–0
1. Judaism—20th century.   2. Judaism—Doctrines.   3. Holocaust,
Jewish (1939–1945)—Influence.   4. Holocaust (Jewish theology)
5. Philosophy, Jewish.   6. Zionism—Philosophy.   7. Historicism.
I. Title.
BM565.K357   1992
909'.04924082—dc20   91–29416
                                                        CIP

New York University Press books are printed on acid-free paper,
and their binding materials are chosen for strength and durability.

Manufactured in the United States of America

c 10 9 8 7 6 5 4 3 2 1

Book design by Ken Venezio

To *the memory of my mother,*

MARY (MIRIAM) KATZ,

*my teacher, my friend, and a
neverending source of love and encouragement.*

"May her memory be for a blessing."

Contents

Acknowledgments

I would like to thank the following individuals, publishers, and journals for permission to reprint the following material: Professor Wolfdietrich Schmied-Kowarzik, editor of *Der Philosoph Franz Rosenzweig* (Verlag Karl Alber, Munich, 1988), for permission to reprint the article "On Historicism and Eternity: Reflections on the 100th Birthday of Franz Rosenzweig"; Professor Norbert Samuelson, editor of *Studies in Jewish Philosophy: Collected Essays of the Academy for Jewish Philosophy 1980–1985* (Lanham, 1988), for permission to reprint "Jewish Philosophy in the 1980s: A Diagnosis and Prescription"; Dr. Geza Vermes, editor of the *Journal of Jewish Studies*, for permission to reprint my essay "Abraham Joshua Heschel and Hasidism"; Mr. Colin Jones, director of New York University Press, for permission to reprint "1918 and After: The Role of Racial Antisemitism in the Nazi Analysis of the Weimar Republic," from *Anti-Semitism in Times of Crisis*, edited by S. Katz and S. Gilman (1991); Professor Yehuda Bauer, editor of *Holocaust and Genocide Studies*, for permission to reprint "Quantity and Interpretation—Issues in the Comparative Historical Analysis of the Holocaust"; Professor Alan Berger, editor of *Proceedings of the Holocaust Scholars Conference* (forthcoming, 1991) for permission to reprint "Auschwitz and the Gulag: Discontinuities and Dissimilarities; Dr. Dan Cohn-Sherbok, editor of the *Louis Jacobs Festschrift* (1991), for permission to reprint "Defining the Uniqueness of the Holocaust: Preliminary Clarifications and Disclaimers"; Professors Alan Rosenberg and Gerald E. Myers, editors of *Echoes from the Holocaust: Philosophical Reflections on a Dark Time* (Philadelphia, 1988), for permission to reprint

"Technology and Genocide: Technology as a 'Form of Life' "; and Professor N. Waldman, editor of *Community and Culture: Essays in Jewish Studies in Honor of the 90th Anniversary of Gratz College* (Philadelphia, 1987), for permission to reprint "Zionism as an Expression of Jewish Freedom."

Introduction

The present collection brings together essays written over the past decade. Once again, it reflects my ongoing preoccupation with the most important issues in contemporary Jewish thought, in particular, the question of authority and its relationship to historical development, that is, the problem of historicism, the nature and impact of antisemitism in our century culminating in the monumental destructiveness of the *Shoah*, and the meaning of Zionism and its near-miraculous offspring, the State of Israel. Each of these topoi raises difficult and challenging intellectual (as well as existential) conundrums for anyone concerned with the continued vitality of the Jewish People and with the spiritual integrity of Judaism in our time. While I have no illusions about having written the final word on any of these seminal matters, I do believe that the present set of essays does significantly contribute to their conceptual decipherment. Read together with the essays in my earlier volume, *Post-Holocaust Dialogues: Critical Studies in Modern Jewish Thought* (New York University Press, 1983), one can begin to identify the main issues and thinkers within the contemporary Jewish intellectual universe as I perceive them, as well as to comprehend at least the contours of a larger, more synthetic view of contemporary Jewish existence.

It is a great pleasure to thank those who have made the publication of this collection possible. I am deeply indebted to Mr. Colin Jones, director of New York University Press, for his friendship, many acts of kindness, and continued interest in my work. Mr. Niko Pfund and Ms. Despina Papazoglou Gimbel of New York University Press have been a joy to work with on this as on other projects. Assistance of various kinds has been graciously extended to me by Mrs. Phyllis Emdee and Ms. Raihana Zaman of the Department of Near Eastern Studies at Cornell, and is much appreciated. Funding for some of the typing of the essays in this volume was provided by the Jewish Studies Fund at Cornell and the MacArthur Foundation through the Peace Studies Program at Cornell. Lastly, as always, I am happy to acknowledge my immense debt to my children, Shira, Tamar, and Yehuda, and to my wife, Rebecca, for all their sustaining care and love.

1

On Historicism and Eternity: Reflections on the 100th Birthday of Franz Rosenzweig

In honoring Franz Rosenzweig on this centenary occasion, it is appropriate to ask what it is in his work that brings us together. Is this gathering, for all of its special and genuine poignancy, yet another form of war reparations, the honoring of a long-dead Jewish thinker by his native German city nearly 40 years after the *Shoah*, or is it something else? And if something else, what else can it be? That is to say, there are many who would contend that Rosenzweig's philosophical and theological contribution was forever buried in the rubble of Nazism, another minor casualty of Germany's obscene onslaught against the Jewish people. For it can and has been argued, that Rosenzweig's relations to Hegel, to Idealism, to Germany, to the *Galut,* to Christianity, to Zionism, were all so deeply the product of his late 19th–early 20th century German context that the destruction of that *Sitz im Leben* eliminates the viability, the authenticity, the concreteness of his thought. Still more, it is reasonable to suggest that his style is, for all its radicalness, for all its strangeness, for all of its fascination, so thoroughly rooted in the now deeply questionable Germanic philosophical tradition emerging out of Kant and Hegel as to be, in places, nearly unintelligible today. As such, it makes little sense to attempt to extract still usable truths from his peculiar, if original, metaphysical constructions, from his abstruse negations, from his mysterious grammatological proclamations. Let

Originally prepared for the International Congress held in Kassel, Germany, in 1986 in honor of the 100th anniversary of Rosenzweig's birth. Reprinted by permission of Verlag Karl Alber, Munich.

us, contend the critics, move on instead to more certain, less vulnerable, thinkers.

At times, this negative recommendation commends itself to me; but upon studied reflection I am convinced that to follow it would be an error of considerable proportions. And this because, given the absolute centrality of issues relating to history and historicism in all forms of modern philosophical and theological reflection, Rosenzweig still has much to teach us, if only by way of his refusal to capitulate to the dominant historicizing modalities regnant in contemporary conceptual formulations and deconstructions.

I.

History, as reconceptualized in historicist thought, is not only a descriptive category but a prescriptive normative ideology. In the movement from Hegel's *Phänomenologie des Geistes* to Ranke's essays for the *Historisch-Politische Zeitschrift* and to Meinecke's 1936 historicist classic *Die Entstehung des Historismus,* one observes a progressive unfolding of an idea whose power has been felt everywhere in modern intellectual life. Believed to possess almost salvific potencies by some, the historicist idea can be characterized in Dilthey's words as follows:

"Thus historical awareness of the finitude of all historical phenomena, of every human or social situation, the consciousness of the relativity of every sort of belief is the final step towards the liberation of man." [1]

But this affirmation is not without negative and far reaching implications. Thus it is not surprising that in theological circles Christian thinkers from F. C. Baur to Rudolf Bultmann and still more recently W. Pannenberg have wrestled with the skeptical and corrosive implications of this position for Christianity, while Jewish thinkers have engaged the matter not so directly as hermeneutic but rather in the fundamental character of the Jewish theological encounter with modernity which has generated all the reformist movements in Judaism since the Emancipation, ranging from classical Reform to S. R. Hirsch's neo-Orthodoxy (in which the *neo* is all important), to contemporary Reconstructionism.

Let us be more precise about what we are calling historicism, a word used in a variety of differing, at times even antithetical, senses. We are not, first of all, concerned with the political implications of the doctrine as focused upon especially in Karl Popper's several famous polemics.[2]

Nor by historicism do I mean to emphasize Meinecke's concern with the individual, the unique, historical event. Rather, as over-against these usages, the concept is here employed to mean an ideology that: (a) views all events and experiences as in and subject to historical change; (b) views the "truth" as accumulative and open to the future rather than individual and possibly fixed in the past; and (c) holds that to understand an event or experience we need to consider it in relation to, and in the context of, a process of development. Two further corollaries of the notion that we also have in mind when we employ the term are: (a) the claim for the necessarily temporal nature of reason and human judgment; and (b) the claim that authentic knowledge can be arrived at, as it is the product of history, only through a knowledge of history. In addition, two allied, though not necessarily connected factors, also require recognition as part of our attempt to frame an adequate appreciation of the term. The first is the ideology of progress,[3] i.e., the doctrine that we are moving along an upwards path in moral and metaphysical values. This was a major feature of 19th century historicism that, despite the skepticism of Nietzsche and Troeltsch, is still not dead. In the Jewish community this presumption was, and is, a major force in the Reform, Conservative, and Reconstructionist branches of Judaism. The second is the principle that history is subject to certain laws, the position most often associated with the philosophical outlook of Hegel and Marx (and certainly of Marxism).[4]

Under the inspiration of this modern historicist concern as we have just described it, it has become fashionable for scholars to characterize Judaism (as well as the other biblically rooted western religions more generally) as "historical". In contrast, it was Rosenzweig's particular genius, perhaps the consequences of his "uneducated" Jewish sensibility and "raw" encounter with its formative canonical sources, to recognize that Judaism's religious experience cum tradition suggests that historical events *qua* historical events do and do not matter, that Judaism is and is not subject to change, that Judaism can be said to be open to verification in history and that the converse is also a justified conclusion, that Judaism is and is not "this worldly". What this means is that the issues of history and historicity, the claim that Judaism is a historical religion and all that is insinuated by this assertion, need re-consideration.

II.

Rosenzweig, above all others in the contemporary pantheon of Jewish thinkers, was sensitive to the a-historical reality, the meta-temporal normativity embodied in Judaism. Inspired by his fear of the nihilism, the skepticism, the relativism he rightly perceived in historicist postures, he sought to arrest this drift by recalling from "above" non-changing, eternal, verities. In the form of an inventory, I remind you of some of the more important evidences which he called to witness; that is, I wish to provide a brief itemization of those radical *realia* which for Rosenzweig stood over-against, even contradicted, the monolithic, systemic, claims of the historicizing consciousness.

(1) Let us begin with his astonishing, insistent reformulation of the "miraculous". In the second section of the *Star* that Rosenzweig titles *Über die Möglichkeit, das Wunder zu erleben* (On the Possibility of Experiencing Miracles) he fashions a decisive reconstruction of this primal notion. Here he has profound things to say about the complementary relation of miracles to scientific law, and therefore about the relationship of religion (theology) and rational truth, and also through his dense exposition about the development of modern thought and the reasons for its rejection of miracles. But beyond this, and for our present purposes, I concentrate upon the connection he makes between miracles, creation and revelation, i.e., upon the implications of his thought for the understanding of prophecy and redemption. That is, I recall to notice his striking observation that "nothing in the miracle of revelation is novel, nothing is intervention of sorcery in created creation, but rather it is wholly sign, wholly the process of making visible and audible the providence which has originally been concealed in the speechless night of creation, wholly—revelation."[5] Accordingly, by a reasoning we cannot, and need not, recapitulate here, the "miracle", while embodied in the givenness of spacetime, of creation, stands beyond the phenomenal, even beyond the moral and aesthetic, and makes itself present in our existential awareness, our direct intuition, of revelation and redemption. Even philosophers restricted to the historical-temporal must admit the possibility, if not the reality, of such an awareness, of such an address, out of the empirical, to that which lies beyond the empirical. "Where Art Thou", the Divine Address, is the content, arrived at by stages, of the miraculous. A content neither controlled nor addressed by the phenomenal query "Where are you". The miracle is miracle precisely by virtue

of its power to open up for us the connectedness of man, world, and God; an existing interpenetration, a linkage, unstudied by, but not in contradiction to, the natural environment that is the proper subject of scientific inquiry. The singularity of the human "I", the response of the transcendental "Thou", the reciprocity of love, the dialogue of creation and creator, of created being and created being, of covenant and final redemption, all reveal themselves as, at least, possibilities, given this decoding of the real as the locus of the miraculous. And in so doing these possibilities, if still only as possibilities, transcend the false limits of an ardent historicism.

(2) Consider, secondly, certain definitive aspects of Rosenzweig's unique understanding of religion. Here Rosenzweig should be understood as providing *data* not *arguments,* i. e., though I am skeptical of his over-arching synthesis through which he brings these discrete phenomena into a "new thinking", I am quite confident that these elements are beyond the capacity of any strong historicism to assimilate. To be noted are his contentions that:

(a) All historical events are partial and corrupt. As a consequence salvation can only be provided by a metahistorical religiosity.

(b) Creation is a non-temporal logical conception. Its dialectical counterpoint, revelation, is more than historical and provides history's direction and orientation.

(c) The problem of death points out beyond itself, beyond time. As Rosenzweig explains in his comments on "Immortality" in the *Star:*

> "The inevitable growing of the kingdom is not, however, simply identical with the growth of life, and this becomes evident here. For while life wants to endure, it wages a struggle uncertain of issue: that all life must die is a matter, if not of necessity, at least of ample experience. Thus the kingdom may build its growth on the growth of life. But in addition it is dependent on something else, something which first assures life of that immortality which life seeks for itself and which the kingdom must demand for life. Life is assured of citizenship in the kingdom only by becoming immortal. In order to become manifest form, the world thus requires an effect from without in addition to its own inner growth, the growth of life which is precarious because never certain of enduring. This effect affects its vitality in the act of redemption." (*Star,* 224–225)

(d) The reality, the continuity, of the People of Israel challenges all immanent decipherments of the movement of history. Though I do not share his insistence on Israel's more than historical being, all of

Rosenzweig's views on the meaning of Israel's eternity are substantive and insightful. Of this People he writes:

"Time has no power over it and must roll past it . . . Elsewhere past and future are divorced, the one the sinking back, the other the coming on; here they grow into one. The bearing of the future is a direct bearing witness to the past . . . The Patriarchs of old call upon their last descendant by his name—which is theirs. Above the darkness of the future burns the star-strewn heaven of the promise: 'so shall thy seed be'." (*Star*, 298)

One might be rightly cautious of this Rosenzweigian emphasis on "ethnos with God"; but one cannot avoid the fact that it is in keeping with biblical rhythms, and after Auschwitz is both data and doctrine. As such, the imperatives of any Neo-Kantian ethicism, that is, any Hermann Cohen-like interpretation of Judaism and Jewish peoplehood, as over-against this Rosenzweigian ethnicism, should be complementary, not oppositional, and hence reductive.

Here, in the context of an evaluation of Rosenzweig's contentions regarding the eternity of Israel, it should also be noted that even his much criticized understanding of and distance from Zionism is, however open to rebuttal, sensitive to a real issue. Gershom Scholem has already suggested in criticism of Rosenzweig that he "turned Judaism into a Church", by which he meant that Rosenzweig's Judaism lacked the political element. In this sense, according to this national-political criterion, as Scholem correctly perceived, Zionism, and Jewish history more generally, have transcended Rosenzweig. But, and I say this as a Zionist, Rosenzweig sensed the deep and abiding problematic inherent in the Zionist enterprise. That is, he recognized correctly that Zionism is not like other nationalisms, for the State is not absolute in its self-consciousness, rather the State is there only to serve the Jewish people; and is created to solve the historical problems connected with Israel's exilic condition.[6] The internal tensions within contemporary Zionism still reveal that this dilemma abides with repercussive consequences.[7]

(e) History requires, in the strong sense, transcendence, the meta-historical, in order for it to be redeemed from meaninglessness. Without the transcendental there is, ultimately, only that fragmentary meaningfulness which cannot, finally, withstand the primordial chaos, the absurdity that follows upon relativism.

In and through these five elemental "religious" concerns, along with his reading of the miraculous, Rosenzweig, sensitive observer that he was, the defender of that philosophy of experience which he continually made reference to, *erfahrende Philosophie,* raises again "givens" whose decoding pushes back the frontiers, challenges the premises, of any rigorous or narrowly historical argumentation. We need not accept Rosenzweig's ontology of the *Star* as the definitive way of explicating these elemental factors, as the preferred solution to the metaphysical and axiological conundrums that these difficult issues raise, indeed his ontology seems markedly flawed and in parts unbelievable if not absurd, but we do need, even now, to attend to the perennial relevance of those *realia* to which he points as well as to his "counter" reading of the ambiguities of human existence.

III.

Rosenzweig's argumentation raises, in addition, fundamental logical issues to which I would like to call attention, if only schematically. Six related and inter-dependent logico-metaphysical issues require comment at this juncture to push the analysis along.

(1) It is, as Rosenzweig recognized, an inherent—and necessary— feature of historicist reasoning, especially as it is employed in the analysis of theological matters, that it utilizes a questionable form of analogy, of analogical inference, in order to reach its conclusions. The nature of this inference has been helpfully described as follows:

"Theology can take the historical method seriously once again if the principles of research are freed from an ideological anthropocentrism which denies absolutely the dimension of transcendence in reality. The principles of research as such do not necessarily presuppose that history is driven by man rather than by God. Of course, there is an anthropocentric element in historical knowledge as in all human knowledge. All historical knowledge depends on the principle of analogy, that is, approaching what is yet unknown on the basis of what is already known. Distant events of the past are knowable only because the historian finds some connection between them and present-day occurrences with which he is familiar. The principle of analogy has to be applied cautiously, however, lest it lead the historian to a simpleminded reduction of the past to the present, preventing him from learning anything really new or different from history. History would be allowed to reflect or illustrate only what he already knows, nothing more. This would be to repeat the rationalist prejudice of David Hume who said that 'history informs us of nothing new'. The point of the principle of analogy is that by starting with what is familiar and similar, eyes are opened to what is strange, novel, and dissimilar. The historian should press beyond the apparent identities or similarities to the really individual and radically contingent phenomena in historical reality.

Has the historian not all too commonly tried to reduce all phenomena in history to laws in analogy to the natural sciences? Such a view of history seems to be presupposed in Bultmann's statement that the 'historical method includes the presupposition that history is a unity in the sense of a closed continuum of effects in which individual events are connected by the succession of cause and effect ... This closedness means that the continuum of historical happenings cannot be rent by the interference of supernatural, transcendent powers and that therefore there is no 'miracle' in this sense of the word'. Within such a world view, the principle of analogy is likely to be absolutized, leading to a tendency to discover only likenesses, regularities, typical occurrences, and recurrent situations. Theology has no interest in denying these aspects of historical reality, but it is equally committed to a perception of what is special, unique, novel, and unrepeatable. If an event is reported in the tradition, the fact that there is no immediate analogy between it and our everyday experience of reality is insufficient ground for denying that it happened. The historian, the historiographer, to be free from dogmatic prejudices, must inquire further, and recognize the limits of the principle of analogy as well as the possibility that he may never have the means for establishing whether the event really happened.[8]

(2) Historicity, as we have defined the term, and as Rosenzweig understood the notion, *must* employ an immanentist principle of causality, i.e., "every experience or event E is the result of a specifiable cause C, and for every E there is a C". Historicist forms of explanation use words such as "because", "thus", "hence" and "therefore."[9] Accordingly, this line of reasoning raises several significant issues about the kinds of events or data it can legitimately accommodate. Consider:

(a) Most historical explanations fail to meet this test, e. g., what C is responsible for the specific teachings of the Torah, even if we reject revelation? That is, the explanation of historicist causality is almost, except in usually trivial cases, incomplete.

(b) To seek the cause of any discrete event E is different, and radically so, from seeking the cause of all E's, i. e., of the whole. The failure to recognize this leads to fundamental epistemological as well as metaphysical confusions.

(c) Causality is predicated on the assumption of the operation of laws, e. g., the proposition "the kettle boiled when put on the stove", is a species of causal explanation that appeals to the laws of thermodynamics. That is K (kettle) B (boils) when placed on S (stove) because whenever S (stove) Ks (kettles) B (boil) (allowing of course for the interruption covered by another law of the form that the stove must be heated to a certain degree and the kettle must have water in it, etc.). However, what law is predictive of the singular occurrence of Covenant or Exodus? (Other, that is, than having recourse to transcendental descriptions or explanations which invoke God's love and saving nature etc. But such theological statements are metaphysical explanations or doctrinal interpretations, not laws in the scientific sense.) [10]

(3) One needs to be self-conscious, as Rosenzweig repeatedly forces us to remember, about the categorical status of the historicist thesis: it is a *metaphysical* and not (as is so often assumed, at least implicitly) an empirical theory. As such it has to defend itself on grounds other than an appeal to specific bits of historical evidence; it needs to offer a theory of the superiority of the temporalizing, historicizing view of man, transcendence and history as compared to alternative metaphysical options. No version of the historicist thesis, however, has been able to provide such a theory. As such, the historicist method remains exposed, rightly, to serious attack. Heidegger has labored longest and hardest in this vineyard—and we know how limited and unsatisfactory his results are. Here a historical note makes a philosophical point worth reflecting upon. Historicity was introduced into modern metaphysical speculation primarily through the agency of Hegelian Idealism, e. g., Croce in our time was a historicist because he was, to a large extent, an Hegelian (and, conversely, Rosenzweig was an anti-historicist in large measure due to his dialectical polemic against Hegel). However, Hegel's Idealist metaphysical program has been everywhere rejected, yet its historicist component remains a dogma in most quarters. Rosenzweig, in contrast, is one of the few post-Hegelian thinkers to recognize the connection with sufficient clarity and with admirable consistency, to understand that the repudiation of the Hegelian superstructure allows one, with philosophical probity, to question the legacy of Idealist historicism.

(4) Any analysis of the metaphysical implications of the historicist position must recognize the inherent, necessary subjectivism of the enterprise and the curious paradox it generates. The subjectivism, the relativism, emerges from the fact that if one accepts the truth of the historicist principle of truth, then this truth is, necessarily, to be historicized and hence no authentic standard exists for any normative judgment of historical realities, e. g., "Thou shalt not kill" is not a more worthy principle than Hitler's racial laws of annihilation. Historicism, to put the matter

directly, seems incompatible, if consistently applied, with values. This Troeltsch[11] and especially Dilthey already realized, and it was this recognition of the negative consequences of the structural relativism inherent in the historicist modality that Rosenstock-Huessy forced upon Rosenzweig, thereby changing his life.[12] The post–World War I work of philosophers such as Croce and Heidegger, and again lesser historicist thinkers, have given us no cause to alter this skeptical judgment as to the unsatisfactory entailments of holding a historicist position. Indeed, Heidegger's rapturous embrace of Nazism, however temporary,[13] precisely on the grounds of his own philosophical hermeneutic is cause for extreme caution.[14] Hegel's principle that "what is reasonable is real; and what is real is reasonable"[15] already holds within it the transcendence of moral judgment by a metaphysical supercessionism that can only lead to moral anarchy, if called by other names in the Hegelian lexicon of the Spirit. "With Hegel and Croce (and other historicists) Historicism results in a complete amoralism, in the cult of success, in an idolatry of the accomplished fact."[16] It was Nietzsche's genius to reject this claim—a key reason for his adoption of a cyclical theory of history. As he wisely remarked:

"If every success carries within itself a necessity of reason, if every event is a victory of logic or of the idea, let us kneel down quickly and hurry kneeling through the whole scale of success ... History always teaches: 'it once happened', but ethics says: 'you ought not!' or 'you should not have'. Thus history becomes an epitome of factual immorality".[17]

This also applied, as Rosenzweig makes clear, to matters of moral and religious reform, i. e., are we to justify and hence accept all reform in the name of historical change—even if called progress—or rather, ought we to stand over against history with a critical consciousness that dares, in the name of other higher norms, to reject the ultimate reality of the historical and its dictates. While the various modernist movements and thinkers have resisted a complete contextualizing of values, in some, usually moral, areas, though not always even here, there is no clear principle at work to justify this selectivity. That is, it needs to be asked why, if, indeed, morality[18] is not subject to historicizing forces, the same meta-historical or a-historical claims can not be made regarding the truth in relationship to other axiological and metaphysical categories? While if it does extend to other, e.g., religious or metaphysical, domains than the main thrust, the cardinal principle of legitimation, of the modernist ideologies that have had such a powerful influence in reshaping

our contemporary normative sensibility needs rethinking in its fundamentals. It should be made explicit that this criticism is made specifically
against Jewish (and other religious) thinkers—Rosenzweig had Reform
Judaism primarily in mind—who have an interest in maintaining prescriptive values of a religious sort even as they champion historicist
criteria of meaning, verification and truth.[19] In the case of non-theists,
e.g., Sartre or Camus, the objection may have less force, certainly it
would need reconstruction to fit the particularities of their atheistic
existentialism and its "meaningless" universe. Though even Sartre's "ma
liberté est l'unique fondement des valeurs"[20] is troubled by the question,
if not outright contradiction, of why and how freedom becomes the
"foundation for values" in a world that is otherwise absurd.

Rosenzweig recognized that at this point a fundamental paradox
emerges: if truth is the result of the historical process then the Truth,
with a capital T, of the historical process can only be known at its end,
i. e., from a suprahistorical vantage point. And here Rosenzweig's perspective gains the upper hand.

There is also an essential self-defeating entailment embodied in the
historicist mode of argumentation, an entailment that is, in fact, just
another instance of an old and familiar conundrum. If the proposition
"all truth is subject to historicist categories" is true, then there is at least
one truth, namely itself, which is not so subject to historicist requirements. And if this is so then the universal metaphysical claim advanced
by historicism is shown to be contradicted. As Leo Strauss noted: "Historicism thrives on the fact that it inconsistently exempts itself from its
own verdict on all human thought."[21] To make the point of this criticism clear, once there is at least one truth that is independent of historicist requirements then there is at least the possibility that there are
additional truths that transcend the confinement of historicist criteria.

(5) Historicism in its particular application to theological truth insists
that *Transzendenz*, in Jaspers's terminology, or what Heidegger calls
Being (Sein), can only become real for us in certain temporally conditioned ways. Heidegger's thought, which has most consistently and
forcefully advocated this thesis, has been aptly characterized as follows:

"This anticipatory understanding of Being (analogous to Kant's pure categories
of understanding) is possible because the horizons of temporality permit beings
to be (manifest) only in certain ways. Hence temporality is 'receptive' because it
lets the Being of being give itself, *but also 'active' in that it determines a priori
the manner in which this giving can occur*".[22]

But can this ontological *"chutzpah"*[23] be allowed to stand? That is, can we follow Heidegger, and other historicists, as over-against Rosenzweig, in establishing temporality as superior to Being, which we, along with Rosenzweig, prefer to call God? Or, alternatively, must we not, and this is a logical 'must' given the definition of the Jewish God, reject this inversion of *Sein* and *Zeit*—in other words, overturn Heidegger's essential claim, at least in terms of God. Another way of exposing the significance of this issue is by asking the Rosenzweigian question: "Is God subject to the laws and constraints of temporality?"[24] Heidegger, of course, is careful to insist he is agnostic on these questions and systematically refuses to enter into theological conversation. But we must push the issue at the very point at which he stops. The issue is the least logically possible ontological difference between *Sein* and *Dasein*. And, complementarily, a recognition of the distinction between *Dasein* as human existence *qua* immanent temporality and *Dasein* as the locus of the revelation of transcendental reality and hence an alternative temporal modality. Regarding *Dasein* as human temporality, as finitude, as *fundamental anthropology,* the historicist-Heideggerian stance is instructive, if limited even here. But *Dasein* as the 'point' where Being/God discloses Itself or Himself, not for our sake alone but also for, even primarily for, His sake, cannot be so circumscribed. History and time as God's creation created by Him in order to reveal His will and purpose stand in a different relation to the limits of temporality and historicism altogether. One might put it thus: history and time are in the service of God, God is not in the service of time and history.[25] Of course, one has not yet shown *how Sein* (God) and *Dasein* are related and how *Sein* reveals itself in *Dasein,* nor have we attempted this ultimate metaphysical schematization. What we have, however, tried to show is that, as the *Star of Redemption* insists, a new-old understanding of the relationship between time and transcendence is required in order to comprehend the ontological framework upon which a sustainable contemporary Jewish theology can be built.

(6) A further metaphysical dilemma, brought to critical consciousness by Rosenzweig, is the relation of historicity to totality, i. e., can a historicist mode of exegesis and deconstruction account for "totality" either in the specific form of the totality of Jewish History or in the more general form of History *per se;* or again, can it satisfactorily answer basic metaphysical questions regarding the relationship that obtains between the concept of totality and the categories of origins and ends? The

answer seems almost certain to be "no" and, as such, shows once more the inadequacy of the historicist hermeneutic as a complete Jewish interpretive theological schema.

(7) Finally, the relation of history and human nature needs to be considered. The historicist position wants to call into question claims for a non-historical "I", what Kant called the "transcendental unity of apperception", and older philosophers knew as the "self". The critical issues raised by this historicist negation are of the utmost importance for philosophy and theology in general and Jewish thought in particular, as Judaism is the bearer of its own version of this traditional doctrine of a "self" (a "soul" embodied). Were it to be successfully called into question the fundamentals of Judaism, and of Judaism as Rosenzweig understood it, would be shaken it not annihilated.

IV.

To conclude these reflections I would like to offer some brief schematic comments about what Rosenzweig's reading of Judaism still has to teach us.

(1) Rosenzweig's observations as to the immediate, existential poignancy, the profound human meaning, of the Jewish Holy Days, of the traditional religious calendar that, parenthetically, he employs in the *Star* as compared to the more usual Christian calendar, are remarkably insightful. He recognized, for example, that in our faith we *are* contemporaries of Moses and participants in the Exodus, hence the character of the Passover *Seder,* and of all the historical "remembrances" of the Torah. Not only are they past events, but also and always present realities. It is we who are redeemed from Egypt on Passover—or on *Succoth,* we who live in "Booths"—or on *Chanukah* or *Purim,* we who are "saved"—or on *Shevuoth,* we who receive the Torah. Hence the two tenses of the blessings made over the Torah when it is read in the synagogue which remind us that the Torah is, as it were, a new revelation directed to each of us personally every time it is recounted; hence, especially, the "messianic" second half of the *Seder* through which we seek to bring the eschaton; hence the constant invocations in all public rites of *our* state of *Galut* (exile).

Here Rosenzweig's fecund "intuitions" as to the meaning of the liturgical year are also richly suggestive. He reminds us that the weekly repetition of Sabbath, which recalls creation, is not an historical event in any ordinary sense; it is, rather, as the *Chazal*[26] tells us "a taste of eternity in time". The repetitions of *Rosh HaShanah* (the New Year) and *Yom Kippur* (the Day of Atonement), so overwhelmingly important to Rosenzweig,[27] are cyclical, spiritual moments, not only historical occasions. *Shacharith* (the morning prayer service), *Mincha* (the afternoon prayer service), and *Maariv* (the evening prayer service), the three occasions of public (and private) prayer that comprise the daily cycle of prayers, are in time but make little sense in terms of Hegelian, linear, history. It is the recognition of these facts that makes Rosenzweig's patient, if obscure, teachings on time and liturgy, as well as on holiness *(Kedushah),* teachings that point to a level of Jewish existence largely unrecognized by contemporary historicist philosophers, so rich and lastingly significant.

(2) In the dialectic of theological reflection it is not enough, Rosenzweig insists, as contended by the elemental principle of, e. g., Reform Judaism, and a considerable amount of post-Holocaust theology, solely to measure the past by the present; at the same time we are logically obligated by the rhythm of Jewish life to measure the present by the past. This is what it means to take the Bible seriously (consider here Rosenzweig's translation of the Bible in co-operation with Martin Buber and his dialogue with Buber over the principles this involved);[28] this is what it means to think Jewishly (consider here Rosenzweig's study and translation of the poetry of Jehuda Halevi);[29] this is what it means to do Jewish theology as compared to a neutral philosophy of history or philosophy of religion (consider here Rosenzweig's decision to create the *Lehrhaus* rather than accept the university position offered him, as well as his theoretical constructions in the *Star* and his other writings of the 1920's). It needs always to be remembered that Torah, *qua* Torah, has absolute priority over the teachings of those who interpret it. This is what it means to be Torah.[30]

Repeatedly and in different ways, Rosenzweig reminds us that we need to re-assert the value of the biblical and traditional witness even while recognizing the principle of non-coercion in matters of religion and politics. Contemporary man, the type of Jewish individual Rosenzweig was and the type of Jewish individual whom he sought to address, must be free to inquire into and to criticize these canonical inheritances, to interrogate the past from our perspective, to ask difficult, awkward, challenging questions, but at the same time he must make himself and his hermeneutic *vulnerable* to input and challenge from the other, traditional, side. Thus, and specifically, the historicist ideology of change, temporality and evolution must be tested by and open to the alternative view that holds the converse true, namely that the "truth" does not change, in any fundamental way, through time,[31] nor is it subject to temporality as are other forms of human consciousness, and most importantly, and perhaps most challenging in the polemical context of modernity, the claim needs to be seriously entertained that truth, i. e., normative revelation, has been revealed in its finality in the historical past. If the Bible and the Jewish tradition is to 'reveal' all it is capable of revealing, then the modern exegete-theologian has to recognize the possibility that these sources might well say something different than he does, that the tradition may place value where he does not, that it might distribute emphasis differently than do we, that it might even mean by *value* something altogether other than what the contemporary historicist consciousness means by value. That is, the abiding significance of the canonical sources may reside exactly in this challenge to, this reversal of, our contemporary value system. The ordering and structure of *Mishnah,* for example, with its decidedly unmodern emphasis on cult and purity (approximately 40% or more of its contents deal with these matters) is a paradigmatic case in point. Alternatively, the confrontation and selective dismissal of "cult", i. e., references to the Temple, messianism, and related ideas, in 19th century Reform theology instructs us in this regard by coming at it from the radically opposite direction. Given its particular post-Kantian, post-Emancipation, sensibility it was willing to make dramatic concessions to the *Zeitgeist,* to allow no "authority" to reside anywhere but in its own normative schema, with the result that it created a form of Judaism that was not only radically different from any previous form of Judaism but which, as the record of the last two centuries indicates, lacked the spiritual integrity as well as the capacity for inspiring Jewish loyalties and Jewish survival that the more traditional rabbinic forms of Judaism had. By adopting as its own the criteria of modernity, by not insisting on some dialectical, oppositional, independent and abiding Jewish set of values, some peculiarly Jewish axiology, Reform Judaism was unable, in any successful way, to legitimate Jewish particularly, to "resist" modernity and hence to effectively provide a reason for Jewish continuity. Rosenzweig recognized this issue in the clearest and most immediate way, for it was, in his opinion, the cause of the conversion of his friends and family, e. g., of Rosenstock-Huessy and the Ehrenbergs, and even of his own near-conversion. Having translated

Judaism solely in Kantian or Hegelian categories, there seemed little reason for enduring as a Jew. One could be a rigorous apostle of the categorical imperative, and could keep abreast of the evolutionary development of the Absolute Spirit as it made its journey through time, without the decidedly "unmodern" trappings of the Torah. Only if the Torah, only if the *halachah,* Jewish law, taught something else, something not translatable into Kantian, Hegelian or Marxist terms, was it of enduring, contemporary, relevance. Its "relevance" is proportionate to its otherness, to its ability to complement, to oppose, the regnant normativenesses of our, and all, ages.

In contradistinction to this demand, to this Rosenzweigian exegetical principle, that the biblical and rabbinic witness be "antithetical" in a productive, dialogical, manner, the historicist pre-supposition, the historicist form of reading, tends to make one's engagement with the biblical and traditional texts eisegetical and reductive. Through its selectivity, through its method of consistently choosing what fits its preconceived scheme rather than allowing the sources an independent objective status that makes claims on us as well as over-against our hermeneutic, it assures that the Torah can never be more than we are, that the Torah can never be mysterious and uncanny, that it can do nothing but confirm us in our present spiritual and moral position as compared to calling this status, this *status quo,* into question. Over-against this modern reading, as Rosenzweig would have us learn, the biblical (i. e. revelation) or rabbinic text must be allowed to assert *its* normativeness, to impact on our approach to this material; we must not only ask "What does X mean to us given our norms", but also "What do our norms mean in the light of X?" We need to inquire into not only what the biblical history of God's relations with Israel can mean in light of our understanding of history, but also—and centrally—what history might mean (i. e., our understanding of it), given the claims of Covenant and the putative relations of God and Israel. This is to say, the specificity of the biblical-historical moment, in all its oddity, rather than our appropriation of it, demands a primal place in our "response" to it for our "response" is not the first order reality, the theophanous, revelatory event itself is.[32]

(3) Jewish thought, reflecting on Jewish tradition, must reject the notion, stated naively, that Judaism is "a historical religion." Jewish history, as understood from within, as correctly described by Rosenzweig once he grasped the authentic inner structure of Judaism, is not secular, linear, non-teleological history. Its source, according to its own

self-consciousness, is a "miracle", or a series of "miracles", i.e., absolute interruptions of the historical process, e.g., Covenant, Exodus and To-rah, that transcend all explanation in terms of immanent historical causality. This "fact" of its origins negates, if dialectically, the historicity of its phenomenality, that is, its reduction to an immanent historical happening that can be deciphered by a wholly immanent analytic sche-mata, and creates both a special ontological class as well as particular and unique, epistemological and interpretive problems.

I should add, lest my view be misunderstood, that this does not mean, as Rosenzweig thought, that Judaism is peculiarly unhistorical because it is "with God" and that Christianity is historical because it is "on the way" to God. Such a view represents Rosenzweig's uncritical, though transmuted, acceptance of the Christian and Hegelian reading of Jewish history, that reading of Jewish history that argues for its transcen-dence by Christianity and the negation of its world-historical role, even if, at the same time, Rosenzweig, in the *Star of Redemption*, translates this historical-theological negation into a virtue. In opposition to this Rosenzweigian view, I would contend that in order to arrive at an accurate perception and depiction of Judaism, and of Judaism's relation-ship to Christianity, one must begin by rejecting Christian theologizing *vis-à-vis* the Jewish situation after the rise of Christianity, on the one hand, and on the other, note that Christianity's own reality, as well as its theology of history, is no more historical than is Judaism's. Christian-ity too is "unhistorical" and "anti-historicist", as I am here using these terms.

Alternatively, we must also reject the Barthian-like caricature of the nature of Jewish history after the rise of Christianity, and of the relation-ship of Judaism and Christianity as powerfully expressed by Hans Urs von Balthasar in his study *Man in History*. Von Balthasar, in effect, inverts Rosenzweig's polemic in a Christian revisionist reading of consid-erable power. He writes:

"Both events, the philosophical and the theological, are unique. The axial period cannot return. Israel's religion is part of history and, thus, bound to that time (even in its supernatural aspect). An Israel after Christ is not only a theological contradiction; it is also a historico-philosophical one. In order to continue to exist it must somehow detemporalize itself: around the 'letter' of the law or the 'spirit' of wisdom or enlightened Gnosticism. Its institutions, its temple cult, and its priesthood together with its sacrifices are bound by time and cannot return (even in today's state of Israel): thus it can replace its former institutions only by secularized ones. In Qumran the end is already visible.

Yet Israel goes on, ambiguously, without any possible inner development, since on the one hand, it is a 'branch broken off' next to the living Church (Rom. 11,17), and on the other, it is the 'holy root' (Rom. 11,16) on which the Church is grafted. It is as if frozen in this ambiguity and, thus, apparently shares in the lack of development of the Church. But the time form is different: it is determined by the messianic historical development of the Old Testament, but at the same time by the missing out on the messianic Christian message. Hence, Israel will be through all ages the fount of *inner-historical* (and hence anti-Christian) messianisms. It will be a principle of dynamic utopian movements, inspired by a transcending, absolute belief in the *inner* perfectibility of man and the world, *a belief which will always reproach Christianity for having betrayed man and the world to the beyond.* In the contrary accusation of having betrayed the faith of the bible is completed the theological mystery of the mutual 'jealousy' between Jews and Gentiles, the responsibility for which is assigned to God (Rom. 10,19)".[33]

But this characterization, for all its intelligence, is also grossly inaccurate, rooted primarily in the classical Christian theology of supersecessionism rather than any divine necessity. The entire vocabulary of Rosenzweig and von Balthasar, the peculiar shape of the theological and historical problematic as it appears to both of them, each in his own partial and notable way, is grounded in the acceptance of normative Christian notions of the transcendence of Judaism by Christianity, notions that need to be re-considered and reconstituted if an accurate, nonstereotypical, image of Judaism is to be arrived at.

(4) A singular consequence of the centrality, that is the absolute seriousness, with which the tradition read the Torah must be explicitly recalled. It is a commonplace[34] to argue that the Jews, in their recording of biblical history, began the process of historical writing and awareness. For example, the eminent classical historian Moses Finley makes this claim in comparing ancient Greek and Hebrew historiography.[35] But the matter is not so simple. As a corollary to the normative way of comprehending the Bible I have already argued for above, it needs to be noted that the biblical authors after Sinai, if not already after the Abrahamic covenant with its futuristic interests (promises), were not concerned with history *qua* history but rather with the historical occasion, as well as with the totality of history, as the locus of the unfolding of God's promise(s). The nature of God's promise(s) needs to be understood aright: a Divine Promise is *not* uncertain or in doubt. The conditions of its specific fulfillment may not be grasped fully till it "comes to pass" but that it will come to pass is assured, given the Source of the promise. In this, of course, it is radically, qualitatively, different from human

promises. As such history is important only as the medium of the fulfillment of Divine intentions already revealed rather than the "open" future
of, for example, existentialist historiographers or non-teleological historicists. One waits on God's promise(s)—and in accordance with the
Torah, attempts to assist in their fulfillment, i.e., lives one's life according to the regimen of *mitzvot,* but this is predicated on a view of history
as fulfilled telos in light of a Divine guarantee rather than history *per se.*
Historical events are thereby, as Rosenzweig perceived, valorized into
metaphysical moments, and this is their meaning *qua* Judaism. This
entails the paradox that, for example, the destruction of the Temple, the
Galut (the Exile of the Nation), and return, are all, as it were, "accomplished" even before they take place in line with Divine revelation. This
also accounts for Israel's faithfulness, trust and repentance in the face of
catastrophe—for catastrophe is not a random surd in a meaningless
universe but is, rather, a programmed event whose meaning is clear, and
to which the response, *teshuvah,* "return", is also clear. Without this
anticipatory pre-understanding the catastrophe(s) would be overwhelming in its traumatic negativity and Israel, like its ancient neighbors
in the face of national calamity, would disappear from history. Only the
particular unhistorical selfconsciousness here described allows Israel to
survive calamity by interpreting it as, at one and the same time, redemptive history. (Accordingly the rabbinic "response" to 70 was "unhistoric"
compared to the Christian or Roman. Jews rejected history as the final
arbitrator of Truth.)[36]

(5) The corollary of the biblical mentality is the rabbinic indifference
to history. It has often been noted by classical Jewish historians and
talmudists how little historical information one gets in the Talmud,
perhaps the most surprising and instructive example being the nearly
complete silence about the Maccabean revolt which is immortalized in
the festival of *Chanukah.* Or again, in reflecting on this issue, one is
struck anew by how little and how useless is the information one receives
about Jesus, the early Church and later the effects of Constantine's
conversion. Despite its final redaction in the Byzantine era, the Talmud
conducts its affairs, records its version of "history", as if Christianity
didn't exist.[37] This should cause modern Jewish theologians at least to
pause in their mad rush to accent history as *the* criterion of Jewish value.
Despite impassioned modern attempts to impute to the *Chazal,* the sages
of the Talmudic and post-Talmudic era, an historical consciousness,
even the embrace of a *Wissenschaft des Judentums*[38]—like principle of

historical evolution, the matter is properly analyzed otherwise. The *Chazal* did *not* employ history as a theological category that *legitimates* change. Historical cataclysmic transformations might force changes in the Jewish theological polity but the *justification* for these changes was not *history*. Here two elements need to be carefully reviewed. First, actual historical events, e.g., and most important of all, the destruction of the Temple, were responded to by the *Chazal* in light of their previous philosophy of history which saw history as theophanous and providential. Present events, no matter how devastating, were only another instance of the rule of Divine punishment and salvation, and faith in future salvation was as certain as the reality of the present destruction.[39]

If anything, what the *Chazal* seem to have done as a result of 70 C.E. was to place the contemporary events in an inherited theological mould with the effect of even more profoundly denying the significance of history rather than providing it with a new prominence. The emphasis of the *Chazal* was on adopting and applying the inherited dialectic of sin and *teshuvah* to their own generation so as to encourage the necessary *teshuvah* which, in their *Weltanschauung,* would trigger the eschatological happenings that they believed would overturn their exilic condition. Sin and *teshuvah* were ontological, as well as volitional and psychological, determinants that regulated the intercourse of "above" and "below" and hence effectively determined the course of "history", and Israel's status. After 70 C.E.[40] the *Chazal* adopted, carried forward and heightened the earlier biblically rooted ideological stance that history as the flow of everyday events had little significance[41] in comparison to a theology of *mitzvah* that had as its aim the re-establishment of Divine-Israel, i.e., covenantal, dialogue that would, in turn, reverse the alienation of man from God created by disobedience and thus, concomitantly, the exilic circumstance which was nothing other than the instantiation of the power of sin. Torah observance was the instrument of this renewed encounter, and Torah observance is essentially a non-historical regimen, e.g. *Kashruth* (kosher food and dietary rules), *Kedusha* (rules of holiness), *tzitsith* (law of "fringes" on a garment), or again, *tashlich* ("casting away of sins"), *mezuzah* (door "signs"), *lulav* (palms) and *esrog* (citron), all predicated on a "brit" (a covenant) that is "unhistorical" though in history and a cyclical calendar of Sabbath, *Rosh Chodesh* (the new month) and recurring festival observances set in a larger cyclical frame of sabbatical and jubilee years.[42]

For us this rabbinic corpus, this rabbinic *Weltanschauung* contains an acute warning as Rosenzweig knew, and as he sought to teach us to see again: if we are to do *Jewish* theology we need first to discover what is normative in Jewish tradition and then to ask how it applies to our circumstances.

(6) This recognition leads naturally to a consideration of the issue of the relation of *halachah* (normative Jewish Law) and *history*. In reviewing the whole range of *halachic* concerns in preparation for analyzing this issue here, I was struck, as never before, by how unconnected and unconcerned with anything resembling an historical interest the *halachah* is. I have already alluded above to the *halachah* (the legal requirements) of Sabbath, e.g., *melakhah* (work) and *issur melakhah* (prohibition of work), as well as the *halachic* requirements of the festivals, the sabbatical year and jubilee cycle—all of which set in place a temporal frame that is non-linear and non-historical. Then too, the details of *halachic* practice connected with the *Chagim* (the festivals) is strikingly a-historical. For example, the High Holy Days' customs of *kapparot* (custom of atonement); the blowing of the *Shofar* (ram's horn); fasting; *viddui* (confession of sins); *teshuvah* (return); and *tzedakah* are all fully indifferent to historical matters. Again, the *Succot* festival practice of *lulav* (palm) and *esrog* (citron) as well as the general ritual practices of *tefillah* (prayer) and *kiddush* (sanctification) are in no way defined by any historicist concern. Then again, the laws of personal status and personal behavior: *brit milah* (circumcision); *mikveh* (ritual bath); *taharot ha-mishpachah* (family purity laws); *mamzeruth* (bastardy); *kiddushin* (marriage); *avelut* (mourning); *tefillin* (phylacteries); and *kashruth* are regulated by and respond to non-historicist principles. Then there is the entire civil jurisprudence of *Baba Metzia* and *Baba Kamma*,[43] the laws of the *Shomer* (the watchman) and the rules of *chazakah* (property acquisition by transformation). All this Rosenzweig, though not a trained halachist, understood—perhaps precisely because he had no "Jewish education" of the sort usually acquired, in passing, by individuals of his class and time to falsify his sensibilities.

In trying to bring these brief remarks on *halachah*, history and Rosenzweig to a reasonable closure I am a acutely aware that I have not fully explored the many central issues this interpenetrating set of factors raises nor have I fully assimilated the import of my own comments on this theme. I am, however, certain that one must now stand back and think again about the interconnections that do exist between these various elements, especially the relationship of history and *halachah*. Clearly the nexus is neither simple nor direct, with a host of mediating principles intervening in whatever reciprocity does exist. However, how one gets from contingent historical transformations, that is by what principles of reason and legal correctness one moves from specific historical changes to the legitimation for *halachic* modification is now a far less clear, far more problematic, process to me than ever before. Assuredly not all historical alterations justify *halachic* revisions, either specifically, i.e., particular *halachot*, or generally, i.e., the whole *halachic* structure. But then, which historical events do legitimate change, however this is mediated within the *halachic* system, i.e., what is the "quality" of the historical reality that legitimates *halachic* change? The answer to this foundational question is not at all obvious; nor have various Jewish modernist movements and theologians who have used historical developments to call for, and justify, *halachic* transformations given, as far as is known to me, a sound explanation for satisfying the logical and theological criterion by which such an answer could be convincingly arrived at.

V. CONCLUSION

In attempting to think through the contours of a truly contemporary Jewish philosophical stance one continually runs up against the unavoidable demands of modern historicist thought in one form or another. In responding to this massive post-Hegelian legacy one returns again and again to Rosenzweig's fertile, radical questioning of the entire historicist enterprise for inspiration and direction. Though one is usually more confused after reading Rosenzweig than one was before reading him, the resultant confusion is not the consequence of metaphysical unimaginativeness nor again of overall logical incoherence,[44] but rather the outgrowth of having moved, of having been moved, to a far more fundamental level of reflection.

In a special way, Rosenzweig raises to consciousness as no other thinker the problematic, the closed premises, of European thought since the *Phenomenology*. His own suggestions for going beyond the old to the "Neue Denken", the new thinking, may not be fully persuasive; indeed his positive, systemic teaching is highly suspect. Yet his creative genius for subjecting the consensus position to vigorous interrogation, his passion for truth, his philosophical probity and existential integrity, his recognition and reclamation of elements of the Jewish tradition rejected by modernity for its own reasons, his unwillingness to settle for things in time when he could reach for eternity, are programmatic and existential lessons to us still. On this 100th anniversary of his birth we honor him best not by becoming Rosenzweigians, an intellectual impossibility, but by making his suspicions of the orthodoxies of modern European thought our own.

NOTES

1. W. Dilthey, "Plan der Fortsetzung zum Aufbau der geschichtlichen Welt in den Geisteswissenschaften", in *Gesammelte Schriften,* Vol. VII (Leipzig, 1927), p. 290.
2. See Karl Popper, *The Poverty of Historicism* (London, 1957); and even more his classic, if problematic, *The Open Society and Its Enemies* (London, 1959).
3. On this idea see R. Nisbet's *The Idea of Progress* (Cambridge, 1980).
4. This, of course, is the point of attack for Popper's critique of historicism. But not all "historicism" is committed to this principle.
5. Franz Rosenzweig, *The Star of Redemption,* trans. by W. W. Hallo (Boston, 1972), p. 111.
6. For a fuller discussion of some, though only some, of the fundamental issues this notion of Zionism raises, see my essay "Zionism as an Expression of Jewish Freedom", chapter 12 in this volume.
7. I have analyzed the most pressing of these concerns in my essay "Criteria for a Contemporary Zionist Ideology", reprinted as chapter 11 in this volume.
8. Carl E. Bradten, *New Directions in Theology Today,* Vol. 11 (Philadelphia, 1971), pp. 44–45.
9. See M. Murphey, *Our Knowledge of the Historical Past* (Indianapolis, 1973), p. 102.
10. This argument, in essence though in a different form, was already introduced by Solomon Steinheim in his criticism of Moses Mendelssohn's effort to interpret the meaning and implications of revelation. See his *Die Offenbarung nach dem Lehrbegriffe der Synagoge, ein Schiboleth* (Frankfurt a. M., 1835); and his *Die Glaubenslehre der Synagoge als exacte Wissenschaft* (Leipzig, 1856).
11. See E. Troeltsch, *Der Historismus und seine Probleme* (Tübingen, 1922).
12. For more on Rosenstock-Huessy's influence in this direction on Rosenzweig consult Eugen Rosenstock-Huessy, *Judaism despite Christianity* (Alabama, 1969). See also more generally on Rosenzweig's turn away from relativism Nahum Glatzer, *Franz Rosenzweig* (New York,1973).
13. Recent work suggests, in fact, it was more deeply rooted than heretofore thought and not "temporary" at all.

14. Heidegger's relationship to Nazism is a hotly debated topic. Whatever his apologists say, however, his early defense and embrace of Hitler is a matter of public record. Moreover, and especially tragic, i.e., morally offensive, was the fact that in the three post-war decades that Heidegger continued to live, he never publicly acknowledged his error, if he indeed saw it as an error, and never made any real public acknowledgment of his role in 1933 and 1934. For more on this issue see David Novak, "Buber's Critique of Heidegger", *Modern Judaism*, Vol 5, No. 1 (May, 1985), pp. 134–136; Hannah Arendt's apologetic defense in her essay "Heidegger at Eighty", in *Heidegger and Modern Philosophy* (New Haven, 1978), p. 302; W. J. Richardson, "Heidegger and God—and Professor Jonas", *Thought*, Vol. 40, No. 156 (Spring 1965), p. 39; Emil Fackenheim, *To Mend the World* (New York, 1982), p. 166ff.; Michael Wyschograd, "Heidegger: The Limits of Philosophy", SH'MA, Vol. 12, No. 231; George Steiner, *Martin Heidegger* (New York, 1979), which also contains a brief bibliography of further, earlier works on this controversial subject; Victor Farias, *Heidegger et le Nazisme* (Paris, 1981), published in English translation by Temple University Press (Philadelphia, 1989); Richard Rubenstein, "Heidegger and the Jews", *Modern Judaism*, Vol. 9, No. 2 (1989), pp. 129–196; and Jean François-Lyotard, *Heidegger et les juifs* (Paris, 1988).
15. Hegel's *Philosophy of Law* as cited by A. Stern, *Philosophy of History and the Problem of Values* (The Hague, 1962), p. 159. See his entire discussion on "Historicism, Natural Right and Values", pp. 138–181.
16. Ibid., p. 160.
17. Friedrich Nietzsche, "Vom Nutzen und Nachteil der Historie für das Leben", in *Gesammelte Werke* (Munich, 1922), p. 298f.
18. Usually a specifically Kantian form of morality is employed in modern discussions. And the Kantian aversion to history is well known.
19. Rosenzweig, it must be remembered, was a severe critic of Reform Judaism as he knew it.
20. Jean-Paul Sarte, *L'Etre et le Néant* (Paris, 1949), p. 76.
21. Leo Strauss, *Natural Right and History* (Chicago, 1953), p. 25. Attempts to refute this argument seem to me singularly unsuccessful, e.g., R. Frondizi, "Are Truth and History Compatible?" in H. G. Gadamer (ed.), *Truth and Historicity* (The Hague, 1972), pp. 29–34; and more significantly Hans-Georg Gadamer's own reply in *Truth and Method* (New York, 1975), p. 482ff.
22. Michael E. Zimmerman, *Eclipse of the Self* (Athens [Ohio], 1981), p. 107f. My italics, for emphasis, of the last two lines.
23. The Yiddish term for "arrogance".
24. This is one of the entailments of Rosenzweig's "empiricism" in the opening sections of the *Star*. That is, God's "givenness" is not reducible either by historicist or anthropological efforts in this direction.
25. Heidegger's late work, that attempts to substitute ontology for anthropology, seems to be the result of his recognition, however partial, of this truth.
26. The recognized sages of Jewish tradition are known by the acronym *Chazal*.

27. Because of his own "conversion" experience on Yom Kippur 1913 that led to his decision to remain a Jew. His own description of the spiritual meaning of Yom Kippur can be found in *Star,* Part III. On this experience of 1913 see also N. Glatzer, *Franz Rosenzweig* (New York, 1973), pp. XVI–XX and p. 25ff.
28. Cf. their joint study, *Die Schrift und ihre Verdeutschung* (Berlin, 1936).
29. Franz Rosenzweig, *Jehuda Halevi. Zweiundneunzig Hymnen und Gedichte* (Berlin, 1926).
30. The contemporary deconstructionist view that a text is really no more than its interpreter, its interpretation, is confused on many levels and its adaptation as a form of biblical exegesis an absurdity that altogether loses sight of the revelatory claim that individuates the biblical, as compared to other, texts.
31. Rosenzweig's debate with Buber over the "Law" is an excellent example of his sensitivity, as compared to Buber's, to the biblical text and its demands. Note, for example, their correspondence published in Nahum Glatzer (ed.), *On Jewish Learning* (New York, 1965). For a more detailed criticism of Buber's position consult my essay on "Martin Buber's Epistemology: A Critical Appraisal", in Steven Katz, *Post-Holocaust Dialogues: Critical Studies in Modern Jewish Thought* (New York, 1983), pp. 1–51. Buber's tendency to treat historical sources very loosely is also critically discussed by me in detail in connection with his interpretive retelling of Hasidic materials in my essay on "Buber's Misuse of Hasidic Sources," in *Post-Holocaust Dialogues,* pp. 52–93.
32. This is why deconstructionist accounts of revelation are so unsatisfactory.
33. Hans Urs von Balthasar, *Man in History* (London, 1968), p. 172f. (Italics have been added by me for emphasis.)
34. See, for example, M. Darcy's remarks in his *Meaning and Matter of History* (London, 1959), pp. 220–221.
35. M. I. Finley in *History and Theory,* Vol. 4, No. 3 (1965), p. 294ff.
36. So the Talmudic dictum in response to the destruction of the Second Temple in 70 C.E.: "On the Day the Temple was destroyed the Messiah was born."
37. Other, that is, than as a minor Jewish heretical group, and even then the material on Christianity is extraordinary oblique and scanty.
38. For a fuller discussion of this immensely influential 19th century Jewish scholarly school consult Salo Baron's, *History and Jewish Historians* (Philadelphia, 1964); Michael Meyer's *Ideas of Jewish History* (New York, 1974); and recently, Ismar Schorch's article on the "Wissenschaft des Judentums", in the new *Encyclopedia of Religion* (New York, 1986), edited by Mircea Eliade.
39. In our time a similar theology finds expression in the explanation of the Holocaust as merely a repetition of this pattern of sin and punishment. It is the preferred explanation, in fact, of the extreme right-wing Orthodox Jewish community. For more details see my essay on "Jewish Theological Responses to the Holocaust", in the new *Encyclopedia of Religion* (New York, 1986).

40. In this response they were, of course, drawing on elemental older pre-70 C.E. notions. To treat the rabbinic response after 70 C.E. as if it were totally innovative is to misunderstand it altogether. The destruction of the First Temple in 586 B.C.E. and much else in pre-70 Jewish history had prepared the grounds, and provided the resources, for the formulations made at Yavneh (post-70) and beyond.

41. This is one of the key sources of Rosenzweig's own views on Jewish a-historicity after 70 C.E., though he gives it his own special character as a consequence of his unique post-Hegelian revisionist agenda.

42. Of course, I here oversimplify the complexities of the rabbinic tradition both in the immediate aftermath of the Roman Wars and later throughout the medieval and early modern period. But I feel this procedure is justified not only because of the space limits under which we are working, but also because there is a genuine need to emphasize the elements with which we are presently concerned, given both Rosenzweig's position as well as the general scholarly presentation of this material that tends to emphasize, incorrectly in my view, rabbinic discontinuity with pre-70 C.E. Judaism as compared to its continuity.

43. Two tractates of the Talmud that deal with civil law.

44. Though, of course, there is much that is logically incoherent in *The Star of Redemption,* a fact which we should neither forget nor minimize.

2

Jewish Philosophy in the 1980s: A Diagnosis and Prescription

The new beginning represented by the creation of this Academy is a significant event of which I feel privileged to be a part. The dialogue that fuels philosophical creativity requires a community of shared interest and support—and these promise to be provided by the sustained experience of our work together. Though in the end philosophical ingenuity is an individual gift, this gift needs to be nurtured and encouraged. It is not accidental that moments of philosophical novelty are almost always the result of a stimulative environment where issues are "in the air" and many minds are all seeking their solution, each nourishing the other.[1] Therefore, I have every confidence that all of us will benefit from the dynamic milieu that is certain to be generated by this Academy.

This significant effort comes none too soon, for Jewish philosophy since World War II has not been an area of great creativity. By and large it seems to be working out the final "death gasps" of the dominant prewar existentialism of Buber and Rosenzweig. However, adding philosophical footnotes does not produce works of vitality; especially when the "texts" being footnoted are themselves, by the standards of historical significance, of minor consequence to begin with. I think it fair to summarize the situation this way: one cannot name a single Jewish philosophical monograph of real novelty and continuing importance, with perhaps the exception of some of Heschel's work, written since the

A lecture given at the inaugural meeting of the Academy for Jewish Philosophy in Philadelphia in June 1980. Reprinted by permission of the Academy for Jewish Philosophy and the University Press of America, Inc.

1930s. This paucity is all the more notable in light of the dramatic revolution in Jewish life during this period, i.e., the Holocaust and the rebirth of a Jewish commonwealth. One is particularly struck, in reviewing the literature, how philosophically limited the philosophical corpus generated by and reflecting on these two events has been.[2] It may well be that we are too close to these events, contemporaries and near contemporaries, and thus unable to see them with the requisite distance, *sub specie aeternitatis,* that philosophical reflection and interrogation requires; but whatever the reasons the results are, so far, unimpressive.

The work we have begun today, however, holds out the promise of a more vigorous future—let us hope its promise is realized. Yet, merely to speak of a brighter future is not enough. To translate this optimism into solid accomplishment, to actualize the possibilities for Jewish thought in our era requires the clarification of a number of fundamental issues. And it is to these that I propose to direct the remainder of my remarks.

1. REVELATION

Insofar as Jewish philosophy *must* emerge out of the concrete conditions of the Jewish religious experience, that is out of the interaction of God, Israel, and Torah (however these notions are defined or redefined aside for the moment), one category becomes central: revelation, i.e., the manifestation of God in the midst of His people, the means by which God makes known His will and concern, His demands and providence. Yet, at the same time as one acknowledges the centrality of revelation one notes its problematic character. Of all the classic doctrines of Judaism, none has been rendered so difficult to maintain as this one. Stemming, I would contend, not so much from a Humean-like empiricism that denigrates revelation on the grounds of its anthropomorphism, i.e., God "speaks," but rather as a consequence of the profound impact of biblical criticism coupled with the dominant secularism fed by its "twin" historicism, claims to revelation are more than suspect. Certainly traditional claims to "Torah mi-Sinai", in its literal modality, are met with incredulity by all but the most orthodox; I use the term "most orthodox" advisedly, because even many who are orthodox in terms of their religious behavior, i.e., who are "shomer mitzvoth," would not defend the classical orthodox claim, though they would not deny it in public either.

In this sceptical, critical sense Spinoza is the first truly modern Jew and the *Tractatus* the first "Modern" Jewish theology. The impact of this trend on the various theological movements in Judaism is readily apparent: Reform, Conservative, Reconstructionist, as well as Buberian and Rosenzweigian "nondenominational" existentialist revisions, are all predicated on the correctness of the criticism of the traditional model of revelation. The Buber-Rosenzweig model of revelation as "non-content dialogue" is aimed at steering a dialectical course through this overwhelming difficulty: on the one hand acknowledging the merits of the "Higher Criticism" and therefore rejecting traditional claims for the Torah, while on the other hand arguing for God's reality and hence the reality of revelation, even if in ways not open to the biblicist and historicist critique. That is, God as the *Eternal Thou* who reveals "Presence Alone" is *not* rejected, i.e., His reality is not even touched by discussions of the human and historical character of the Bible, attributes of the biblical text readily conceded by, e.g., Buber. Rather, in contradistinction to more traditional approaches, this dialogical model has the great merit of shifting the debate to altogether different philosophical areas, while not being forced into the corner of rejecting the results of modern biblical and historical scholarship. Thus the fundamental ontological claim as to God's reality is advanced and protected, while the debate about human admixture in the *ex post facto* testaments to revelation is not unreasonably foreshortened. Hence the positive value and wide influence of this hermeneutic in modern Jewish, as well as non-Jewish, e.g., Bultmann and his school, thinkers. However, this gain is itself paid for at a great price; and in the end a price too high to pay. The cost has to be measured on two levels. On the technical philosophical level the dialogical model is logically incoherent, while on the Jewish level it is more than problematic.

As regards the philosophical decipherment, consider as paradigmatic, and for purposes of clarification, Buber's classic account of dialogical revelation. For Buber *I-Thou* dialogue is really only another name for "revelation." This is not surprising within Buber's terms of reference. As he structurally equates, as a basic premise of his entire enterprise, the God-man relation with *I-Thou* relation, analyzing it on the same lines and applying the same criteria, it is to be expected that he should understand the nature of what transpires between man and God, what has traditionally been called "revelation," in much the same way as he understands what transpires between man and man. When it is assimilated to this intersubjective dialogical model, "revelation" is denied all "content" and therefore, of necessity and by design, it cannot be claimed that God is a legislator or revealer of anything resembling the doctrines of positive religion. In *I and Thou* Buber gives us the following intriguing description of "contentless" revelation:

Man receives, and he receives not a specific "content" but a Presence, a Presence as power. . . . Man can give no account at all of how the binding in relation is brought about, nor does it in any way lighten his life—it makes life heavier, but heavy with meaning. Secondly, there is the inexpressible confirmation of meaning. Meaning is assured. Nothing can any longer be meaningless. . . . But just as the meaning itself does not permit itself to be transmitted and made into knowledge generally current and admissible, so confirmation of it cannot be transmitted as a valid Ought.[3]

Furthermore, God is the "Thou who can, by its nature, never become an *It*";[4] that is, He is a being who escapes all attempts at objectification and transcends all description. The *Eternal Thou* can never be treated as one particular among many particulars, one thing among many things. Nor can God be known through "experience" because "experience" yields only *It* not *Thou*. God cannot be "known" outside the committed existential act of relation. All attempted philosophical theologies based on any and all forms of theological empiricism or deductive metaphysics that attempt to "prove" God's existence must always fail because God can only be addressed, not defined. "A conceptual apprehension of the Divine," Buber argues, "necessarily impairs the concrete religious relationship."[5]

Buber, as we can see, places great emphasis on "responding" to the address of the *Thou* and to the two-sidedness of dialogical encounter. But he has misconceived the essential character of "Address" and "Response," so that his emphasis on the "sincerity" or "authenticity" of this existential act becomes a caricature. "Address" and "Response" are not simply intelligible given data of experience, even dialogical experience. There are no direct uninterpreted dialogical "facts" that are totally unrelated to the categorical range of our objective conceptual understanding. The claim to the contrary rests on a mistake—and, it should be noted, is itself a confused and concealed metaphysical claim. What we call "facts" are to some necessary extent always a function of our conceptual and linguistic schema. There must be forms and rules, at least internal dialogical forms and rules, according to which Buber's utterances make sense. The very notions "Address" and "Response" are intelligible only within the particular universe of discourse Buber employs. "Sound" has to be organized and shaped to be "Speech," and

"Speech" has to be channelled through complex and highly structured interpretive schemata to be understood as "Address," even if these terms function only as metaphors for Buber. Metaphors also require structure to obtain meaning. Likewise "Response" calls for ordering principles and conceptual structures in regard to both that which we claim to experience as "Address" and in expressing and giving shape to our reply.

The Buberian emphasis on and assertion of dialogical immediacy, stressed so forcefully by him as the means of short-circuiting such conceptual, cognitive, and interpretive activities and all their attendant logical and philosophical difficulties, is not helpful in dealing with the issue, simply because it reduces the situation to a ghostlike image of its true, more complex self. Buber's position loses sight of the fact that when one wants to talk meaningfully of "Address" or "Response" one has to recognize the objectivity requirements involved in these sorts of activities, i.e., one has to know to and with whom one is in relation and who one is "Addressing" and to whom one is "Responding" in order to know what to say or how to act. I address my wife and respond to her quite differently from the way in which I address or respond to other women with whom I do not live and with whom I have not chosen to link my future. Likewise in respect to the *Eternal Thou*, I address God in prayer because I believe Godlike things about Him and respond to his address in unique ways for the same reason. I do not pray to my dean or respond to the address of the president in the way that I do to the *Eternal Thou*. If I thought of God differently or "interpreted" my encounter with him differently, I would pray to him differently or perhaps not at all. We have no clearer example of this than in the differing interpretations given by Buber and traditional Judaism to their respective God-Idea. For example, Buber does not set much store by prayer or ritual while traditional Judaism does, and again, the biblical God is understood by the tradition primarily as a lawgiver, while for Buber this is something he cannot be. Moreover, at this point Buber's constant invocation of revelation as the revelation of "Presence" alone merely starts the discussion, it does not end it. The meaning of the "Presence" of the *Eternal Thou* is dependent on the meaning of *Eternal Thou*. We cannot merely shout "presence" and leave the table. The sense of "Presence", and indeed of Buber's revelatory paradigm *Ehyeh Asher Ehyeh* (Ex 3:14), is contextual and embedded in the concrete existential and historical situation. Again, the meaning of the revelation is dependent on, among other things, something as basic as the rules of Hebrew grammar governing the future tense of the verb "to be." Also, it is not enough to assert that revelation understood as "Presence" means "event" and not content, and that all talk of logic and criteria is therefore out of place, for an "event" is also something that has to be made sense of and is clearly grounded in the conditions of our experiential life.

Likewise, any satisfactory account of what it is to be a person will involve bodily criteria and objectivity concepts, and any convincing account of the *Eternal Thou* will involve similarly identifying predicates that are appropriate to His ontological status. Among other considerations there is the fundamental one that, unless there are such criteria, how would we be able to differentiate in our ascription of the predicate *Thou* between one person and another person? How would I know I was having a *Thou* relation with my wife rather than with my neighbor's wife or, for that matter, with my neighbor's husband, if all physical criteria were absent from *I-Thou* relations and from all saying of *Thou?* The same sort of problem exists in identifying God as the *Eternal Thou*, as we shall see shortly.

Buber, of course, wants to avoid empty abstractions and so insists on "meeting," i.e., dialogue, as the "empirical" ground of his position. At first glance this claim gives Buber's thought a decidedly concrete existential "look." But the issue for Buber is more problematic than it appears for, despite his intentions, the question is whether Buber can maintain his existential claim that dialogue is true meeting with an Other when he insists that this encounter is aspatial, atemporal, wholly nonsensual, and nonexperiential in all the ordinary senses. Can there be any residue of substantial meaning left in the motions of "meeting," "encounter," "Other," and "Thou" when all experiential and empirical content is denied them. Or again, can Buber's original intuition that we must understand our basic and most important relations to nature, other people, and God in *personal* terms be maintained when the terms "person," "personal," and "personality" are divorced from all behavioral or material predicates. To say "I encounter a Thou," when none of the ordinary limiting conditions and experiential concepts apply, is to utter a pseudomeaningful proposition because we cannot understand what sense is being claimed for the words "encounter," and "Thou." What seems to be the case is that Buber's use of "encounter," "meeting," "Thou," etc. is at best metaphorical and analogical, dependent on the non-metaphorical use of these concepts in ordinary discourse, and that Buber's usages retain a descriptive appearance because of the covert

retention of attachments which have been overtly rejected in his dialogical presuppositions. However, even this may be giving away too much
to the philosophy of dialogue, for one has finally to ask whether we can
properly understand an encounter to which no predicates apply even as
a metaphor or analogue of ordinary encounters, or whether Buber has
gone so far with his negative stipulations that even the notion of a
metaphor or analogue is saying more than it is permissible to say. And
in any case, this metaphorical route seems closed to Buber, who explicitly tells us that *"Thou* is no metaphor."[6] As Buber uses the term,
however, it can hardly be a definite description. This sort of difficulty is
seen to be particularly acute in ascribing *Thou* predicates to God, i.e., as
the *Eternal Thou,* as all such predicates that are ascribed to things in
this world are tied to experiential conditions obtaining as a minimum
yet constitutive feature of such ascriptions. Yet in God's case none of the
ordinary experiential conditions obtain. In what sense then is God a
person, even the Absolute Person, the *Eternal Thou,* and in what sense
is it legitimate to predicate the personality of the Divine?

On the Jewish level Buber's account of revelation, as I have argued at
length elsewhere,[7] necessarily causes a subjectivism that empties the
Jewish historical past, Jewish tradition, and Jewish community of any
value and reduces the Torah to, at best, irrelevance. The latter happens
because dialogical models of revelation cannot grant the Torah any
objective content or authentic authority. Acceptance of the Torah as a
norm is replaced by subjective choices about what one feels attracted to,
what "speaks" to the individual in his or her situation, what the self
decides is authentic for itself.

The significance of this criticism is that it requires, on the part of
nonorthodox, i.e., the majority of both modern Jews and Jewish thinkers, as well as orthodox thinkers who acknowledge the force of historical
scholarship in the area of biblical studies, a different yet still coherent
model or account of God's relation to Israel past and present. How God
makes His will known to mankind, if indeed He does—which itself is
one of the key issues of the debate, the proponents of the nonpropositional account negating this claim as to the revelation of Divine Will
though not of Divine Presence—needs to be coherently described and
defined. My own view is that some sort of propositional model is required, for without it there can be no viable sense to the concept of
Torah and mitzvot that does not collapse under its own subjective
weight. Moreover, though a propositional model may, at first, seem

difficult to accept, it is both plausible, at least theoretically and logically, while seemingly being a theological necessity. This is true on the logical level because, if one accepts the existence of God—a claim which is, in actuality, the major difficulty—believing that He is capable of revealing Himself and His will in some form of "speech" must, of necessity, be believable. That is, it is a possibility entailed by His "omni" predicates and perfection. To believe in God and deny the possibility of His "speech" is to "swallow the camel and strain at the gnat."[8] Theologically, opting for a propositional model is a requirement because it alone will provide grounds for a sustainable notion of covenant and even more for meaningful interpretations of the reality and significance of Torah and mitzvot.

This is not to argue that this need for a propositional model will bring it into being. It may well be a theological chimera forever to be sought without satisfaction. And I am perfectly prepared to admit this hermeneutical possibility. However, this neither makes its establishment less necessary nor, and I stress this, does it justify other unsatisfactory models in the absence of a satisfactory one. Thus, I commend to each member of the Academy individually as well as to the group collectively that we take up the inquiry of what would constitute a sound doctrine of propositional revelation for our time—if such is possible.

II. ONTOLOGY

This somewhat sustained, by no means unambiguous, comment on revelation leads to a second, related area of the utmost significance which we in the Jewish philosophical world have avoided: ontology.

This is to say, we have, for a variety of reasons—some good, some bad—positively eschewed metaphysical investigations. In part, again, this is one of the mixed blessings of the existentialist inheritance, those grand dissemblers who denied they were involved in metaphysical debate, as if "existence," "being," "becoming," "authenticity," "historicity," "subjectivity," and "truth" were not metaphysical concepts. While denying metaphysics they did metaphysics and therefore their impassioned denial led not to the transcendence of metaphysical enquiry but to poor, sloppy, metaphysical conjecturing. There is no avoidance of the metaphysical—ontological concern: the only question is how well we do it.

In place of smuggling our ontological commitments in by the back door we need to let them in, after they are carefully scrutinized, by the front. As Jewish philosophers we have to be willing to take a stand on "what there is," i.e., on the existence of God, His character and attributes, His relations to Israel (covenant) and the nations; the ontic status of the Torah, of men and mankind, of the soul, sin, and salvation. Of all religious traditions modern Judaism seems most onticly agnostic, but this ontic agnosticism cannot sustain Jewish belief, Jewish practice, or continued Jewish identity. It cannot answer the pressing query, "Why be a Jew?" If metaphysical commitments and talk of transcendence in some form or other, i.e., in whatever modality is appropriate, are the monumental embarrassment they seem, let us be honest and stop the charade![9] If they are not, then let us take them "out of the closet" and confront their meaning and implications directly. Given our agenda for this initial meeting I will refrain from making any specific recommendations in this area and I will resist the temptation to single out specific metaphysical propositions or entities for description, defense, or descontruction. Instead, I will content myself with the more general recommendation that we attempt to bring the entire metaphysical issue back into the center of our deliberations.[10]

Toward the accomplishment of this broader end, however, I feel it is not inappropriate to make two further structural comments at this juncture. First, there is a real need for us to offer some image of the "whole," that is, not only to discuss a particular answer to a particular problem, e.g., the Holocaust or the various negations of the Torah, but rather to situate these individual concerns in a more complete *Weltanschauung*. Whether successful or not, Rosenzweig and Kaplan, of all twentieth-century thinkers, seem to have understood this imperative best. Since 1945, however, we have generally avoided these larger schematic issues. Heschel was working toward it, but too impressionistically and obliquely; Buber eschewed it despite the generality of his overly simplistic dialogical typology of *I-It* and *I-Thou;* Baeck, Soloveitchik, (Arthur) Cohen, Borowitz, Schweid, Schwarzschild, Heschel, Fackenheim, Berkovits, and still others have not even attempted such a constructive program. The only radical or novel metaphysical doctrine of the postwar years is, paradoxically, Richard Rubenstein's "pagan naturalism." But, as I have argued at length elsewhere,[11] this will not serve as a Jewish theology for our time as it is "Jewishly" inauthentic and logically indefensible.

Secondly, the reasons for this unsatisfactory situation are, of course, tied in some considerable measure to the larger philosophical environment of our era. In previous generations theologians and Jewish philosophers had confidence in particular metaphysical theories, e.g., Philo in Platonism; Saadia in Kalam; Maimonides in Aristotelianism; Krochmal in Hegelianism, and the like. More recently Buber was a Kierkegaardian-like existentialist; Rosenzweig a "left-wing" Hegelian; Hermann Cohen a confirmed neo-Kantian; Kaplan a Durkheimian and a pragmatist. Since World War II all of these philosophical orthodoxies are under attack and it is a fair summary of the present philosophical environment to suggest that it is as uncertain about metaphysical issues as are we. Put differently, our malaise is predicated on theirs.[12]

Having diagnosed the cause of the illness, what are we to do? Here I have an epistemological and ontological proposal that I also believe anticipates the next movement of philosophical enquiry—we need to work toward a realist ontology that will help us out of our present difficulties. Kantianism, *the* dominant philosophical spirit of the last two centuries, is in any form, and let me assert this as clearly as I can, incompatible with a viable Jewish philosophical outlook. As a consequence, any Jewish philosophy that begins from a "Kantian" base, e.g., a belief in the subjectivity of space-time, and knowledge as knowledge only of the "appearances" of things as they are, will collapse under its own constructs.[13] Thus, neo-Kantianism à la Cohen or Soloveitchik is not capable of providing the ontological structure we require, nor again is existentialism which accepts Kant's basic dualistic position as correct and then tries to work out the subjective implications of Kant's delimitation of the parameters of the knowable. If the self *creates* the world it inhabits, then the only result can be an unacceptable subjectivism, a knowing only of "appearances" or the "appearances" of "appearances." No amount of neo-Kantian tinkering will preclude this epistemic inevitability, no illusory Husserlian phenomenological intuitions will provide access to the "real," no existentialist substitutions in the direction of the dogma that "truth is subjectivity" and "subjectivity is truth" will help, in fact, to establish the reality of God and the world.

This Rosenzweig already saw, if dimly, and hence his call for a "radical empiricism," the label he attached to his own work. The only way out of the conundrum is a radical rejection of the main trunk of the modern philosophical tradition, i.e., a rejection of Kantianism, which is equivalent to a rejection of Idealism, whether of a so-called "critical," or "transcendental," or "subjectivist" variety. Unless the world is ordered and the "furniture" of the world is really there, and we can know both the order and nature of this "furniture," there is no possibility of anything but "situation theology" and "situation ethics," i.e., indefensible bias; or again, Kierkegaardian-like "leaps" that are no longer philosophical but which rather inhabit an altogether different theological orbit. Having said this I want to be understood: I do *not* have, yet, a defense of a realist ontology that I, or anyone else, will be satisfied with. However, I recognize that the present Kantian inheritance is a disaster—and it is this recognition that I want to drive home. The present philosophical generation, for the most part, seems not to recognize the necessarily negative consequences of Kantianism, in one or another of the forms we all inherit it, and hence continues to construct its efforts on foundations of sand.

III. LANGUAGE AND LOGIC

Insofar as we are reviewing the needs of our discipline in more comprehensive areas, our third concern must be the interconnected areas of language and logic. Modern Jewish philosophers, with the exception of Buber's pronominal approach,[14] have made almost no contribution to the modern debate about religious language and the impact of logical considerations on theological discourse. And even Buber's remarks are so unsystematic and contradictory that his best insights are cancelled by their being situated in the larger Buberian dialogical context. More generally, existentialist influence on modern Jewish thought has had a deleterious effect on its reflections about language and logic: it has created the impression that theologians could talk in "paradoxes" and write in grand, vague, contradictory generalizations and still communicate what they wished to. This is a serious mistake. What are "paradoxes" to the man who utters them are usually just illogical and contradictory statements to the people who hear them (unless one can provide a rule for which is which). In order for theology to be a public enterprise open to rational discussion and debate, the rules of logic and the nature of language must be understood and respected by Jewish philosophers as they are by everyone else. Otherwise Jewish philosophy is reduced to the making of statements that have little cognitive content, and that serve more as personal and biographical utterances, of which we have all too many in modern Jewish thought, than meaningful theological statements that inform us about the world, about God, and about God's relation to mankind. If there are special sorts of theological or philosophical discourse that are immune to or transcend ordinary syntactic, grammatical, and logical laws, this has to be shown. If Jewish philosophers have a special dispensation to use language "oddly," then the grounds of this dispensation have to be made evident. It is not sufficient warrant to make such claims as if they were self-authenticating; they are not. A perusal of the inventory of mutually contradictory things that have been said at one time or another to be "self-evident" will reveal the utter hopelessness of this epistemic gambit. We have to stop ignoring what modern linguistic philosophy has to teach us and become its student, just as much as we must learn what there is to learn from continental philosophy.

Jewish philosophers also have an obligation to consider the entire related area of theological and philosophical epistemology in order to come to a better understanding of just what the proper function of language and logic is in terms of their interests. I will not expand on this epistemological requirement in detail except to say that epistemological investigation is both basic and nearly untouched by post-1945 Jewish thinkers. We all continue to use inherited epistemic models that are inadequate, e.g., the extremely influential Buberian dialogical account that is insupportable or the neo-Kantian which is also flawed as already noted. The call I have already made for a realist ontology requires, necessarily, a fresh epistemological approach.

IV. HISTORICISM AND PSYCHOLOGISM

Historicism and psychologism are the two most widespread as well as potent ideological trends within modern intellectual life. While both contain truths not to be ignored, neither is to be granted a privileged position as philosophy's censor. Instead, one has to know when they have something valid to contribute as well as when they go beyond their competence and become examples of bad metaphysics masquerading as pseudoscience. Freud's writings on religion and Jung's "intellectual Disneyland" are the best-known examples of the latter, while much Jewish Reform theology as well as the majority of liberal Protestant theology culminating in Troeltsch and Ritschl are examples of the former, as are various forms of Hegelian, neo-Hegelian, and Social Darwinian writings. The technical philosophical problems raised by historicism especially are of the utmost interest. For reasons of space I will not enter into a more detailed discussion of this issue and refer readers instead to my arguments in the opening chapter in this volume, pp. 1–26. However, I would like to make one further comment dealing specifically with the functionalist hermeneutic employed, almost without exception, by the various social scientific and historicist models of explanation. On my view such functional approaches are circular and therefore lack logical force. Hempel's[15] studies of the logic of functional analysis leave little doubt as to their tautological character. They ultimately explain nothing. Hence their favored status in modern approaches to religion, e.g., Freud's claim that religion functions to satisfy psychological needs; or again Durkheim's and hence Mordecai Kaplan's argument that it functions to fulfill social requirements, is to be rejected. Here the imperative regarding methodological sophistication comes to the fore.

I am cognizant that I have dealt with the most pressing modern problem, historicism, too briefly. It deserves detailed review. My present remarks and those referred to in chapter 1 on Rosenzweig, are intended only as a first move, an indication that I recognize this topic as a central one that requires detailed analysis.

V. TORAH AND MITZVAH

Except for the orthodox, and even in this camp problems exist, the fundamental ideas of Torah and mitzvah have little resonance in contemporary Jewish philosophy. In part this is due to several factors already discussed. Firstly, there is the reductionist approach introduced, if unwittingly, by those who favor a nonpropositional hermeneutic in these matters as a way of responding to the historicist challenge; secondly, our abdication of metaphysical discourse is of consequence; thirdly, there is the historicism of our age; and finally biblical criticism has taken a heavy toll. There are, however, two further consequential factors to be considered—one external, one internal. The former is the influential Kantian critique of heteronomy that is a hallmark of modern rationality— yet which is not self-authenticating and in considerably more need of philosophical defense than is usually noted. The still more important internal factor is this. Modern Jewish thinkers and modern Jewish ideologies have continually attempted to define or explain Torah and mitzvah in a subtly, and sometimes not so subtle, reductionist fashion. By this I mean they have, continuing while at the same time distorting a well-established medieval philosophical penchant where *ta'amei ha-mitzvot* (reasons for the mitzvot) is concerned, attempted to explain or justify these categories, Torah and mitzvah, in terms of something other than themselves. For example, the meaning of the Torah is said to equal: historical lessons, ethical truths, social norms and communal solidarity, nationalism, health (Kashrut), philosophical truths, etc. Hence Torah and mitzvah are valued because they embody and stand for some other value. We do not keep the mitzvah for the sake of the mitzvah but for ethical or other reasons. While often an appealing substitution, this approach fundamentally shifts the focus in ways detrimental to an understanding of Torah and the practice of mitzvot. This occurs because such an interpretive procedure establishes other values, e.g., moral or social, or other realms, e.g., the historic, as the values or criteria of worth and thus necessarily diminishes the ultimacy of Torah, e.g., not Torah but ethics is absolute.

This criticism, it should be explicitly noted, is not incompatible with, nor in contradiction to, the further presumption that the mitzvot are "true," "good," and "valuable." For their "truth," "goodness," and "value" is a *given,* insofar as they are said *a priori,* to be God's ways: "The precepts of the Lord are right, rejoicing the heart; the commandments of the Lord are pure, enlightening the eyes" (Ps 19:9). By definition, God would not demand evil or falsehood, the nonvaluable or meaningless—but this is all stipulative. As a *secondary* explanation, one can refer particular mitzvot to specific instrumental values, e.g., ethics or wisdom, but this explanatory modality must be recognized for what it is: secondary and nonessential—something other than that which is constituted by an *a priori* presumption of truth and value. And again— it needs to be understood that the actual explanation of *every* mitzvah in instrumental terms is not required for their maintenance, for their primary role is relational, not utilitarian; existential and ontological, not pragmatic or functional. Moreover, where instrumental reasons can be found for mitzvot, e.g., ethical values in the prescriptions to avoid murder or theft, social values in rules of marriage and legal systems, historical values in terms of the education of the Jewish people away from idolatry, rational values in Torah study, these are all to be considered *additional,* important reasons for the mitzvot, i.e., above and beyond their intrinsic revelatory significance and their capacity to facilitate dialogical reciprocity.

In the *Guide of the Perplexed* Maimonides criticizes what may appear to be the position I have just advocated. He argues:

There is a group of human beings who consider it a grievous thing that causes should be given for any law; what would please them most is that the intellect would not find a meaning for the commandments and prohibitions. What compels them to feel thus is a sickness that they find in their souls, a sickness to which they are unable to give utterance and of which they cannot furnish a satisfactory account. For they think that if those laws were useful in this existence and had been given to us for this or that reason, it would be as if they derived from the reflection and the understanding of some intelligent being. If, however, there is a thing for which the intellect could not find any meaning at all and that does not lead to something useful, it indubitably derives from God; for the reflection of man would not lead to such a thing. It is as if, according to these people of weak intellects, man were more perfect than his Maker; for man speaks and acts in a manner that leads to some intended end, whereas the Deity does not act thus, but commands us to do things that are not useful to us and forbids us to do things that are not harmful to us. But He is far exalted above this; the contrary is the case, the whole purpose consisting in what is useful for us, as we have explained on the basis of the (Scriptural) dictum, for our good always, that He might preserve us alive, as it is at this day (Dt 6:24).[16]

Let me therefore say another word on this matter. There is no denying that I do not share Maimonides' faith in Aristotelian rationality, its scope and limits. In many ways, as a post-Kantian, post-Einsteinian man I have more faith in reason, especially technological reason, than he. Alternatively, after Kant on the one hand, and the Holocaust on the other, I have less faith in, if also a different sense of, rationality than he. Given this starting point, one can make, in fairness, the following observation: Maimonides more successfully than anyone before or after him made the case for the rationality of all the mitzvot and their utilitarian value, in the broad sense. How far he succeeded in this is perhaps his outstanding philosophical achievement, and gives one pause in these matters. And to the degree that any given Maimonidean explanation in instrumental terms is convincing I have no difficulty, on what I have called the secondary level, in accepting his view. Still more, I can agree with him vis-à-vis his absolute *a priori* precondition: the Torah as God's revelation is true and purposeful, etc.

Where I cannot follow him, nor do I think anyone else should follow him is, first, in making the criterion of usefulness[17] both absolute and primary;[18] and secondly, and related, as regards his misunderstanding of what is entailed by the *a priori* precondition of his (and my) analysis. That is, to claim that the entire Torah is the result of God's wisdom does not mean we know in what way God's wisdom is operative in every biblical statute or ordinance. Though we may seek to comprehend God's wisdom in every way possible,[19] it is not necessary that we gain such understanding in order to maintain the meaningfulness of the

Torah and the regimen of mitzvot, nor again are we required to insist that all Divine wisdom manifest itself instrumentally. Phrased differently, to argue for *mitzvot shimmiyot* (mitzvot for which we can find no utilitarian reason) is not necessarily to argue, as Maimonides suggests, that God is imperfect and man more rational than his Creator. Or again that these *mitzvot shimmiyot* are totally devoid of meaning or usefulness.[20] We too, of necessity, given the logic of biblical monotheism, presume God's wisdom and goodness and hence the wisdom and goodness of the Torah; but this presumption neither assumes that all God's ways are intelligible to us, that *we* have to understand all God's ways, nor again that the only values the mitzvot can have are what we take to be rational or pragmatic. Rather, they all have as their end covenant and communion, and then some, in addition, have secondarily other significant values, e.g., moral or social as well. This view, of course, alters the sorts of rationalistic translations required by a Maimonidean approach. I should add, lest any misunderstanding arise, this analysis does not impugn the importance of the secondary purposes adduced, e.g., morality, etc., nor does it discourage the rational examination of the Torah for *ta'amei ha-mitzvot,* etc., or the *a priori* rationality of the Torah as a whole.

The "translation" hermeneutic that I have called Maimonidean and criticized seems, moreover, to lose sight of at least two essential Jewish "truths" that are imperative to protect. Firstly, that the Torah and the mitzvot are, according to Jewish tradition, *God's way* to God. This is their primary value and significance. It is this fact that obviates all modern and premodern distinctions between ethical versus ritual mitzvot and makes all mitzvot of equal value as ways to His Presence.[21] As a consequence, as Saadia already noted in Treatise III of his *Book of Beliefs and Opinions,* and Maimonides notwithstanding, it is precisely the *mitzvot shimmiyot,* for which no extrinsic justification can be given (which does not mean they are irrational but rather that we do not know the reason for them, though presuming God's attributes means presuming they have a reason or reasons) that should be considered from one point of view the most acutely Torahanic, i.e., we would not have them but for the Torah, and hence it is they which are peculiarly defining of Judaism.

This seems especially true in the post-Christian, post-Muslim age when the ethical commandments of the Torah are claimed as the common property of all three faiths, not to mention the other religions of the world and righteous atheists as well. Certainly Judaism demands morality, but to be moral is not in itself to be a Jew. The "righteous gentile," whether a Buddhist or Marxist, Christian or Taoist, Hindu or atheist, remains a "righteous gentile." And he may, as the Talmud tells us, reach a higher station of sanctity in God's sight than many a Jew, for Judaism does not claim and knows of no monopoly on salvation. Yet he is not a Jew; he does not practice Judaism. Conversely, this is not to denigrate the moral or to be misinterpreted as an ethicsless Judaism; rather it is to argue that Judaism seeks a communion with God, recognizing that the God of Israel may well be found only through the world, rather than through an ethical system *per se*. It is this perspective that legitimates[22] "And keep my statutes [Hukkim]," (*Leviticus* ch. 17; 4) understanding *Hukkim* as acts of obedient devotion in the service of a loving relation, that opens up the entire reality of Torah to the Jew as the dialectical nexus it is: God's movement toward Israel and Israel's response to God.[23] Only such a nonreductionist conceptual schema allows for the totality of organic Jewish life, allows for the recognition that religion is not derivative or functional in its etiology, and legitimates the authenticity of the Jewish past as well as the wholeness of the Jewish *Weltanschauung*. Only such a characterization allows for the completeness of the human reality, for the fullness of Israel's historic and social-existential being, for a nonschizophrenic directive as to which actions bring the individual into God's Presence. All permissible actions, done as mitzvot, are the mediative vehicle of transcendence.

Secondly, the Maimonidean and like accounts compromise the ontic status of the Torah and its mitzvot. The *Chazal* spoke of the "creation of the Torah before the world,"[24] by which they meant to suggest that it is a part of the fabric of reality, not merely a social instrument or pedagogical device. Precisely here we have something to learn from the kabbalistic tradition. In it the Torah is *not* valued because it is a metaphor or allegory[25] that stands for something else; rather its value lies precisely in its *not* being anything else. Its *holiness*, as the meaning of *kadosh* indicates, is its difference and separation from everything else and its unique ontic status *per se*. With regard to the detail of the mitzvah this is particularly important—no other action or thought can take its place, nor again is it merely a metaphor for other domains of action or concern. Rather, the mitzvah is the reality; it is the expression of reality in a way that is nontransitive. I would add as well in a more contemporary idiom that the reality of the mitzvah is irreducible, for the essence of the mitzvah resides in its specific occasion, i.e., the action of the mitzvah creates the operative and significant onticity[26] with which Judaism is concerned. The elemental fact is not some static "reality" that can be conjured or contemplated from many perspectives; rather, the "real" is the dynamic creation brought into being by *mitzvot ma'asiyot* (the doing of mitzvot). Thus, the logic, as well as the ontology, of the mitzvah is structural rather than substantial. That is to say, the ontic uniqueness of the Torah and its mitzvot—which creates its holiness— lies precisely in this: it brings men into relation with God, nothing else.

I am aware that these remarks generate a good many difficulties[27] in their own right, especially as regards the areas of morality and natural law on the one hand and the renewed metaphysical emphasis on the other. I have no illusions regarding this. Yet, it seems philosophically imperative to attempt two things at the present juncture: to reestablish the rationale for commitment to Torah and mitzvah as meaningful, indeed, the most meaningful, aspects of Jewish life and thought; and, secondly, to provide a new way of understanding their meaning that is, at one and the same time, not reductive but affirmative of their connection with the transcendent. Hence, the mitzvah, the commandment, is not disparaged as futile heteronomous action, but rather as the establishing of a relationship to the commanding Presence who gave the Torah and prescribed the regimen of mitzvot. Alternatively, if it proves impossible to do this, as well it might, then the fate of Jewish philosophy as a significant Jewish enterprise is called into question.

VI. HALACHAH

Because we are Jews, mention of Torah and mitzvah immediately also requires consideration of the character and status of *halachah*. This consideration is a methodological and philosophical demand if not a religious one, for the *halachah* has been the main expression of Jewish thought and spirituality over the centuries and its study and development has historically been the major vehicle of and for Jewish theology. More than in philosophical tracts or kabbalistic commentaries, more than in midrashic ruminations, biblical exegesis, poetry, or philology, the Jewish mind as well as the Jewish soul has expressed itself first and foremost in *halachic* reflection, disputation, and resolution.

To refer to the *halachah*, however, raises several related issues, each of which is an integral part of the project that is Jewish philosophy in the 1980s. The first issue is simply competence in *halachic* sources. I would argue that no one can be a fully satisfactory Jewish philosopher if he is not also, at least, a competent talmudist.[28] The reason is this: such a thinker is out of touch with the most important Jewish spiritual resource next to the Bible. And even with regard to the Bible none of us today are Karaites. All of us, even those who are no longer committed to the *halachah,* stand as heirs, whether we desire it or not, of the rabbinic tradition. It is the rabbinic version of Torah and Judaism that defines the Torah and Judaism to be accepted or rejected by us: "mega-leh panim batorah shelo k'halachah" (do not interpret Torah contrary to halachah). On the other hand, this is not to confuse the issue and argue that rabbinics is Jewish philosophy *per se.* It is not; rather, it is to assert that rabbinics provides much of the data for Jewish philosophizing as well as an authentic (perhaps the only authentic, which is something we will have to discuss) standard of Jewish practice and ideology. Certainly it was the standard of Jewish authenticity until the period of Emancipation, while today its problematic character is perhaps the Jewish philosophical issue *par excellence,* i.e., what is to be the standard of authority that governs Jewish life in our time.

Secondly, unless one is familiar with the details of the *halachah,* all discussions of "Jewish" sensitivities, values, norms, and beliefs are inauthentic and misdirected because they are, at best, marginal as well as partial. What is distinctively *Jewish* can only be ascertained through familiarity with the *halachic* tradition. There are, of course, other "data," sources and sensitivities to be factored in, but the *halachic* element is a necessary minimum condition. For example, can one speak of the *Jewish* view on any issue of contemporary concern, ranging from theodicy and salvation, to abortion, sexual morality, DNA research, and the religious role(s) of women, if one does not know the history of these concerns in the *halachah?* All such ungrounded discourse is absurd; there is nothing "Jewish" about it. Moreover, it is not just the case-by-case details that should instruct us. Consider, for example, the structure and weighing of the *Mishnah,* one-third if not more of which is concerned with ritual purity in a direct form, i.e., the last two of its six orders are *Kodashim* and *Tohorot* respectively, a fact that should sensitize us to the realization that Judaism is not to be reinterpreted and scaled down into Kantian morality or Durkheimian sociology. This unusual (by modern standards) *mishnaic* orientation alerts us to the fact that a more complex ideology is at work in the *halachah* than is usually understood and hence a more complex understanding of Jewish tradition, its contents, values, and parameters is required of us.

In reflecting on the *halachah's* role in Jewish philosophy it is appropriate to add a comment on the use of *aggadah* as a source for Jewish philosophy and theology. That it is a prime source, as Maimonides already made clear,[29] is beyond question; what is at issue, however, is how it is to be used. Max Kadushin[30] and more recently Emil Fackenheim,[31] among others, have championed its usage as the most important classical data on which to draw in constructing contemporary Jewish philosophical positions. This recommendation, however, is fraught with danger. First, whatever its merits it must not replace the *halachah* as the *primary* source tradition. Secondly, such theorizing from the *aggadah* is almost always, as it must be, overly selective. Hence, the classical principal consistently cited in the responsa: "Do not rule on the basis of aggada"[32] is full of warning for us. There are no short-cuts for Jewish philosophy to be found in the midrashic inheritance, though this rich treasure is a repository of Jewish resources to be mined by us—but with care.

One further corollary with regard to *halachic* competence also calls for comment: methodology. The *halachah* is as much a method as it is a series of legal prescriptions. That is, as in philosophical argument, what is as important as one's conclusion is how one reached it. A *halachic* conclusion is only as persuasive as the soundness of its *halachic* procedure. This recognition is of considerable significance, especially in our time when various groups within the Jewish community all lay claim to speak in the name of, and out of, the *halachic* tradition, yet quite clearly disagree on what this tradition is, how it operates, and what it can be made to sustain by way of contemporary transformations of Jewish thought and practice. The winter 1980 issue of the quarterly *Judaism* devoted to "Jewish law" is a recent, straightforward example of the confusion that reigns. For example, what is the legal principle involved in the oft-cited *Prozbul,* and what does it and what does it not justify in the way of modern *takkanot?* I want to emphasize that, at least, on the initial level of methodological discussion, there is no requirement that one be committed to the *halachic Weltanschauung.* Rather, the only necessity is that those who seek to enter into dialogue with the *halachah,* even with the intent of changing or destroying it, have a logical obligation to know what it is. This requirement flows from a concern with method, not *emunah* (faith).

VII. THE HOLOCAUST

The Holocaust raises all the important issues, or rather the most important issue relevant to maintaining belief in God, i.e., theodicy. Over the last thirty years, Jewish thinkers of all persuasions and none have attempted to "explain," "account for," and "respond" to Auschwitz in a wide variety of ways. I do not think it unfair to conclude that, despite the intensity of the invested passion and the sincerity of the commitment, none has proven completely convincing nor philosophically adequate. This is in no way surprising, given the immensity of the occurrence. Yet, the "sting" will not go away and Jewish philosophy will need to continue to wrestle with its problematic, trying to form ever-more complete as well as cogent "responses." In order to do this, moreover, we will have to do at least two things: We will have to learn the details of Jewish history both past and present so as to be able to understand the historical reality of the Holocaust, its similarities to and differences from previous national calamities, and whether and in what sense it is "unique" or not, and whether this "uniqueness" does or does not matter for Jewish philosophy. Secondly, we will have to absorb and locate this history in a philosophy of history—something also pressingly relevant in relation to the discussion of Zionism. Here we need to confront the metaphysical dimension raised by classical claims that history reveals God's providence. And again, in connection with a philosophy of Jewish history we need to explore a host of multifaceted arguments, ranging from those connected with what Bultmann would label "demythologizing" to those regarding the meaning of past events in terms of contemporary history, covering laws, miracles, and the like. In short, we need to enter into one of the thorniest of philosophical subjects. Yet, there is no escaping this requirement; even Rosenzweig had to take up the issue, despite his view of the post-70 C.E. Jewish transcendence of history. In fact, he is one of the two interesting, richly suggestive, if profoundly wrongheaded, modern workers in this genre, Krochmal being the other. In the end, both Rosenzweig and Krochmal are overcome by the Hegelian burden they carry, but they understood, as part of the positive Hegelian inheritance, the seminal issues that need confronting. Alternatively, there is not a single sustained work in this genre in all post-1940 Jewish philosophy. We must change this.

The absence of any progress in the philosophy of Jewish history has also stymied any creative philosophical exploration of the meaning of Zionism.

VIII. THE REBIRTH OF A JEWISH STATE

It is remarkable that there is not even one major post-1948 work ema-nating either from the diaspora or Israel, that offers a satisfying Jewish philosophical account of Zionism and Jewish nationalism. Yet, at the same time, what kind of success can one claim for any contemporary Jewish philosophy if it does not "account" for the most central issue in modern Jewish life: the State of Israel?

The complete array of issues that come under this rubric are too numerous to discuss here in detail, e.g., the reevaluation of the meaning of "religious" and "secular" in a Jewish state; the "religious" value, if any, of a state; the eschatological, nomocratic, and theocratic dimensions of such a state; the obligations, if any, of diaspora Jewry to the state; what changes in Jewish life and *halachic* practice are legitimated by the state; and the list goes on. Conversely, what are the philosophical implications of following Yeshayahu Leibowitz's[33] view that the state has no intrinsic Jewish value at all? All these questions are of urgent philosophical, not to say, practical concern.

IX. PLURALISM

The vexing issue of pluralism provides our final substantive category. Modern Jewish life is singled out by its diversity, a diversity much broader in range than even that of the *Bayit Sheni* (Second Temple) period. The philosophical question raised by this historical reality is, can and should Jewish philosophy legitimate this pluralism? If so, how? And if not, what are the consequences of this negation? Christian thinkers have been trying to construct a philosophical foundation for intra-Christian dialogue, e.g., Orthodox, Catholic, Protestant, etc.; ought we do the same in terms of the present reality of Jewish denominationalism, or should we reject such attempts as temporizing evasions? And if we reject such attempts, will Jewish philosophy degenerate into the most unsavory sort of theology by label, heresy-hunting, the hurling of the "ban" and mutual disrespect, an unappealing prospect intellectually and perhaps even more significant, suicidal in terms of the larger Jewish agenda. Alternatively, can this be accomplished without appeal to the "lowest common denominator"? I confess to near despair over this topic. Then again, there is also a pressing question concerning Jewish—non-Jewish pluralism. Can we, may we, come to a more sophisticated understanding of the *theological legitimacy,* the *spiritual authenticity* of other religions?

CONCLUSION

The nine elements enumerated are certainly not exhaustive; many additional problems confront the construction of a viable, persuasive, intellectually satisfying, Jewish philosophical position in our time. Increasingly, for example, the issue of "secularism," which has been on the docket since the Emancipation, will come to the fore. That is, how does one do Jewish philosophy in a secular pluralistic universe? This and other difficulties must be confronted sooner or later as part of an organic, holistic Jewish philosophy. In sum, Jewish philosophy today does not lack for an agenda. Whether we are equal to its demands is the challenge before us.

NOTES

1. In our own century one can cite such examples as the extraordinarily fruitful encounter of Wittgenstein with Russell, and earlier of Russell with G. E. Moore, J. M. Keynes, and A. N. Whitehead. Or again, on the continent, of H. Cohen and the Marburg neo-Kantians with Heidegger or in Jewish circles of Baeck and Rosenzweig with H. Cohen and then later of Rosenzweig with Buber. The history of philosophy is full of similar examples, e.g., Socrates and Plato, Plato and Aristotle, Leibnitz and Spinoza's response to Descartes, Kant's influence on Hegel, Schelling, and Fichte. The University of Berlin in the first quarter of the nineteenth century, the Harvard Philosophy Department in the first quarter of the twentieth century, Oxford in the 1950s and 1960s.
2. For more details see, for example, my article, "Jewish Faith after the Holocaust: Four Responses," in *The Encyclopedia Judaica Yearbook* (1976), pp. 92–105; and the series of studies on contemporary Jewish thinkers presented in my *Post-Holocaust Dialogues: Critical Studies in Modern Jewish Thought* (New York, 1983).
3. *I and Thou,* (New York, 1937), p. 110f.

4. Ibid., p. 112.
5. *The Eclipse of God* (New York, 1952), p. 14.
6. *I and Thou*, p. 112.
7. S. Katz, "Martin Buber's Philosophy: A Critique," (a precis of a paper) in *The A.J.S. Newsletter* (January, 1975); idem, "Martin Buber's Concept of Revelation," *Fifth World Congress of Jewish Studies* (Jerusalem, 1977); and in detail in my forthcoming study of Martin Buber to be published by New York University Press in its *Modern Masters Series*.
8. Parenthetically, this same logical argument applies to the acceptance of miracles.
9. For example, how can we go on with *tefillah* (prayer) and ritual, Mordecai Kaplan's illogical "reconstructions" notwithstanding. For more, see the debate between A. J. Heschel and E. Kohn with Kohn defending a version of Kaplan's naturalism held at the Rabbinical Assembly in 1953 and recorded in the *Proceedings of the Rabbinical Assembly of America,* Vol. XVII (1953). See also A. J. Heschel's later paper on the need for prayer in *Conservative Judaism,* Vol. XXVI (Fall, 1970), and Louis Jacobs's useful discussion of prayer in modern Jewish theology in his *A Jewish Theology* (London, 1974), ch. 13.
10. It is with sound judgment that Maimonides begins his *Mishneh Torah* with a decidedly metaphysical assertion:

    The fundamental principle and pillar of all science is to know that there is a First Being who has brought everything that exists into being. ("Fundamentals of the Torah," ch. 1, 1)

11. See my article on "Richard Rubenstein, The God of Israel and the Logic of History," in *The Journal of the American Academy of Religion* (September, 1978), pp. 313–350, reprinted in my *Post-Holocaust Dialogues,* pp. 174–204.
12. One is here reminded of A. N. Whitehead's remark, "the rejection of metaphysics is one of the sicknesses of our age."
13. I have discussed this subject in more detail in a paper entitled "Martin Buber's Epistemology: A Critical Appraisal," reprinted in my *Post-Holocaust Dialogues,* pp. 1–51.
14. Rosenzweig and Heschel were also sensitive to many of the essential issues, but their positive contributions to solving the difficulties raised by modern philosophers and logicians was not of the same magnitude as their awareness of the problematic.
15. See his paper on "The Logic of Functional Analysis," in C. Hempel, *Aspects of Scientific Explanation* (New York, 1965), pp. 297–330. As this applies to religious theories, see also Hans Penner's essay, "Creating a Brahman," in Robert Baird (ed.), *Methodological Issues in Religious Studies* (Chicago, 1975), pp. 55–59.
16. Maimonides, *Guide* III, 31.
17. In the *Guide* III, 26, he wrote: "all laws have causes and were given with a view of some utility." It should be noted that the Sages seem to specifically

locate the superiority of Israel's acceptance of the Torah in its avoidance of such practical considerations, i.e., where the other nations "calculated" whether to accept or reject the Torah, Israel replied, *"Na'aseh ve'nishmah"*; for more on this point, see *Sifre*, Beracha, ch. 21, and cf. also Rav J. Soloveitchik's discussion of this issue in his essay "Mt. Sinai—Their Finest Hour," in Rabbi A. Besdin (ed.), *Reflections of the Rav* (Jerusalem, 1979).

18. Unless we define "useful" as including relation to God. If we do that the difference between Maimonides and myself disappears. However, I do not believe Maimonides can be read in this way without distorting his intent.

19. Here one needs to become involved in the technicalities of Maimonidean exegesis. Cf. what Maimonides wisely states in his discussion of the rationality of the mitzvot in *the Guide* III, 6. One can recognize in this nuanced discussion an attempt by Maimonides to protect the details of the Torah, and hence the Torah itself, from the destructive tendencies embodied in a totally, ruthlessly, rationalistic (not to be confused with rational) approach. The issue, however, now becomes where to draw this line.

20. See note 18 above.

21. Cf. R. Shneur Zalman of Liadi, *Tanya*, ch. 7 (London, 1973), p. 428. Also see *Sifra* 93d.

22. *"And My statutes shall ye keep,* i.e., such commandments to which Satan objects, they are [those relating to] the putting on of *sha'atnez*, the *halizah* [performed] by a sister-in-law, the purification of the leper, and the he-goat-to-be-sent-away. And perhaps you might think these are vain things, therefore Scripture says: I am the Lord, i.e., I, the Lord have made it a statute and you have no right to criticize it."

23. "Prior to the giving of the Torah, heaven and earth were two totally separate things, but once the Torah was given, earth went up to heaven and heaven came down to earth" (*Pesikta de Rav Kahana*, ed. S. Buber).

24. See *Hagigah* 13B and *Gen. R.* 8, 2.

25. The widespread view that Kabbalists view the Torah in its most essential modality as "allegorical" is a mistake. I have discussed this issue more fully in my paper, "The Conservative Character of Mystical Experience," in S. Katz (ed.), *Mysticism and Religious Traditions* (New York, 1983), pp. 3–60. See also *Zohar* III, 152a and G. Scholem's comments on the Torah in his *Kabbalah* (New York, 1975).

26. The word "onticity" is almost a Heideggarian-like locution and for this I apologize. However, its meaning is, I believe, apparent and should cause no confusion regarding my meaning.

27. Even if others disagree I hope my remarks will cause them to rethink the issues before us. If there are disagreements over the interpretation of Maimonides, as I am sure there are, let us *please* ignore them for the moment and concentrate on the philosophical rather than the historical issues I am trying to raise in these remarks, as this is not intended as an essay in Maimonidean scholarship.

28. This is why Maimonides has always been, and continues to be, the paradig-

matic Jewish philosopher, whether one agrees with his philosophical views or not, while Buber, for example is not.

29. Cf. Maimonides, *Commentary on the Mishnah, Sanhedrin,* and *Guide,* "Introduction." See also I. Twersky's important remarks on this theme and its influence in his *Introduction to the Code of Maimonides* (New Haven, 1980), pp. 11–12 and note 15, p. 12.

30. See, for example, Max Kadushin, *The Rabbinic Mind* (Chicago, 1964), and his *A Conceptual Approach to the Mekilta* (New York, 1969).

31. Cf. E. Fackenheim, *God's Presence in History* (New York, 1970).

32. See Maimonides, *Guide,* "Introduction"; *Ozar Ha-Geonim, Berachot,* I, 131.

33. See his *Judaism, A Jewish People and The State of Israel* (in Hebrew), (Tel Aviv, 1976); and his essay entitled "State and Religion," in *The Jerusalem Quarterly,* No. 14 (Winter, 1980), pp. 59–67.

3

Abraham Joshua Heschel and Hasidism

braham Joshua Heschel is now a twice famous name in the annals of
Hasidism. It belonged to the beloved early sage, Abraham Joshua
Heschel of Apt (d. 1825) and to his great-grandson, our late contemporary Abraham Joshua Heschel (d. 1972). If one believed in the kabbalistic doctrine of *gilgul* (transmigration of souls) one might argue that the
soul of the first Abraham Joshua had reappeared in the body of the
second, but perhaps the more reasonable doctrine of *yiches,* noble family
tradition, is sufficient to begin to account for the latter's greatness.
Stemming as he did from two major Hasidic dynasties, Heschel was a
complete product of the Hasidic milieu of Eastern Europe with all its
richness and diversity. As a consequence, he was in a unique position to
combine an authentic relationship to Hasidism with a profound sensitivity for the more general state of the Jew and Judaism in the modern
world. This sensitivity is manifest in his many seminal essays and monographs on all aspects of the Jewish heritage. No area of Jewish study was
alien to him and he published important papers on Kabbalah, Jewish
Philosophy (both medieval and modern), Rabbinics, Biblical Studies and
Hasidism. Moreover, he not only studied Torah but lived it: the roster
of activists in almost every major campaign of Jewish or humanitarian
concern since the 1930s has included his name.[1] In this chapter we shall
concentrate on one aspect of Heschel's achievement, his contribution to
our understanding of Hasidism.

Reprinted by permission of the *Journal of Jewish Studies.*

I

A Passion for Truth,[2] Heschel's posthumously published study of Reb Mendl of Kotzk (1787–1859), brought his Hasidic interests into the center of the public eye. It confirmed in a major way, especially as it was his last work and so received unusual publicity, that Heschel not only had his biographical roots in the Hasidic context but that he was also a foremost interpreter of this eastern European Jewish folk movement. However, to those familiar with his life's work, this late study was no surprise, for they had come to know and to respect Heschel's expertise as a master-student of the subject, uniquely equipped to make the subject his own. To fully understand Heschel's contribution and the significance of his final monograph on the Kotzker, one has to start with his earlier studies in this area rather than with his last scholarly testament.

Raised as a child in the Hasidic environment of Eastern Europe, Heschel first knew Hasidism from the inside. This biographical element is of key importance because it forever protected Heschel from a too eisegetical, too extraneous, too non-Hasidic interpretation of the relevant material. One especially sees the significance of this biographical factor when one compares Heschel's situation with that of Martin Buber, the most famous of all modern interpreters of Hasidism. Buber was neither the product of a Hasidic home nor of a Hasidic childhood, coming to the study of Hasidism only in his twenties. Buber never was a *hasid*,·i.e., he never belonged to any Hasidic community and certainly never took upon himself the main acts of Hasidic piety, adherence to a Rebbe, and the *halachah*. Although in some ways Buber saw himself as a Hasidic Rebbe, and certainly this was also how many of his disciples viewed him, this posture was inauthentic.[3] Heschel was different. Having been raised among the Hasidim of Poland, having been taught Hasidism in the traditional fashion of the Hasidic community, having been a *Hasid* in the authentic sense of devotion to Rebbe and Torah, Heschel was from the outset constrained in fundamental ways from idiosyncratic errors of judgment and excesses of subjectivity. His Hasidic sages and their teachings represent real products of actual Hasidic life rather than romanticized abstractions, appealing as such abstractions might be.

On the basis of this solid biographical foundation, which however, by itself is *not* adequate grounds for serious scholarly contributions, Heschel built his Hasidic research. Over a period of 30 years Heschel's academic concern with Hasidism was reflected in a steady stream of publications in Hebrew, Yiddish and English. Among these publications, and far from a complete bibliography, one should take note of the following papers: "A Cabbalistic Commentary on the Prayerbook";[4] "The Eastern European Era in Jewish History";[5] "Rabbi Phinehas of Koretz";[6] "The Mystical Element in Judaism";[7] "Rabbi Gershon of Kuty";[8] "Rabbi Mendel mi-Kotzk";[9] "Rabbi Nahman of Kossov, Companion of the Baal Shem",[10] "Rabbi Yitzhak of Drohobitsch";[11] and "Unknown Documents in the History of Hasidism".[12] In addition, Heschel wrote two book-length studies on Mendel of Kotzk, one in Yiddish (in 2 vols.) entitled, *Kotzk: The Struggle for Truth*,[13] and one in English which we have already referred to, *A Passion for Truth*.[14] Lastly, there is his warm study of Jewish life in eastern Europe entitled, *The Earth Is the Lord's: The Inner Life of the Jew in East Europe*.[15]

Each of these studies is a mine of information wedded to insight regarding the Hasidic movement. In their individuality each makes a real contribution to its subject. Moreover, from a close study of these documents taken collectively something of further interest emerges that sheds additional light on each of the studies taken separately. It becomes clear that Heschel was not only engaged in random piecemeal work on this or that Hasidic sage but rather, he was involved in a systematic study of the earliest and most important phase of Hasidism. Taken as a whole, Heschel's studies are actually an exceedingly thoughtful attempt to build up a broad picture of the original historic Hasidic environment through the study, first, of the Baal Shem Tov's most important companions, and then, presumably, culminating in a study of the Baal Shem Tov which would serve as the central hub that would tie all these separate spokes together. Unfortunately, Heschel did not live to complete the treatment of the Baal Shem Tov which was to provide the unifying focus for the totality of his Hasidic reflections.[16] The closest thing we have to this unifying understanding of the Baal Shem Tov is the still fragmented and partial reflection on the Besht in the opening section of *A Passion for Truth*.

II

Before passing directly to consideration of Heschel's last study, however, a brief comment on his other monograph, *The Earth Is the Lord's* may prove helpful in setting the larger context for our analysis of *A Passion for Truth*. We treat *The Earth Is the Lord's* first as it can be dealt with more economically, being already a classic though only just a quarter of a century old.

Written in Heschel's unique evocative rather than descriptive style, intended to move the reader to investigate his own situation as well as to learn the record of history past, *The Earth Is the Lord's* chronicles the inner struggle for survival of Polish Jewry. Essential for Heschel in this chapter of Jewish history is the inner dimension, the striving for intimacy with God, what the Hasidim stressed in the mystical doctrine of *devekuth* and which Heschel holds activated all eastern European Jewish existential concerns.[17] Heschel conveys not only the facts but also the spirit of this way with great success. He captures, too, the mystery at its root, for Heschel knows of the other-worldliness that is at the heart of Hasidism. Subtly presented yet inestimably significant, Heschel is clear on the essential point: "The Hasidism have always maintained that the joys of this world were not the highest one could achieve."[18] He correctly sees their dialectical alternation between this world and the world to come and quite properly speaks of their "fanning in themselves the passion for spirituality, the yearning for the joys of the world to come."[19] The recognition of this other-worldly dimension reflects Heschel's authentic insight. While in some respects Heschel wants to make Judaism into an existentialism, and some features of his Hasidism are not immune from this temptation as becomes clear especially in *A Passion for Truth*, he generally knows the boundaries of legitimacy where this existentialist interpretation is concerned.

In this respect it is instructive to compare Buber's views with Heschel's, for though Buber was a major influence on Heschel's thinking in general as well as on his study of Hasidism in particular, a careful reading of the two men's presentations of the relevant material will reveal marked differences. Buber, who was in love with this world, cast Hasidism into the role of a paradigmatic this-worldly, dialogical, pansacramental community. In Buber's presentation, despite the talk about God, the centrality of divine-human relationship and the use of the imagery of the kabbalistic doctrine of the "sparks" and their "redemption," the authentic element of transcendental mystery so central to Hasidism is lost. It is lost because it is not coupled to the deep Hasidic other-worldliness that desires to overcome our world and that finds expression in such cardinal Hasidic doctrines as that of *bittul ha-yesh* (annihilation) and the like. Buber's Hasidism, for all its splendour, is largely a this-worldly existentialism in Jewish dress. Alternatively, Heschel's Hasidism is something radically different, being closer to the authentic mood of Hasidic piety. The price Heschel pays for this authenticity is that his vision remains grounded in its specifically Jewish milieu as the Hasidim themselves intended. There is not even the attempt, which supplies the motive power for Buber's entire enterprise, to liberate Hasidism from its Jewish context, claiming to find in it some spiritual-dialogical panacea for modern man's spiritual malaise. Instead Heschel, in his opening paragraph, writes in full Hasidic flavour: "Hasidism banished melancholy from the soul and uncovered the ineffable delight of being a Jew." A concomitant feature of this accurate, fully Jewish emphasis is Heschel's proper recognition of the foundational role played by the *halachah* and *mitzvot*. Certainly the emphasis with regard to the *halachah* is on *kavvanah* (religious inwardness or intention) and rightfully so for this orientation is a distinguishing mark of Hasidic religiosity, but this inwardness is not stressed at the price of correct observance or of trying to portray the Hasidim as antinomians of one sort or another. Rather, Heschel's true sense of the Hasidic theological rhythm allows him to catch both the inner and outer aspects of Hasidic observance.[20] He is able to write: "it is incumbent upon us to OBEY our father in heaven, but God in turn is found to take pity on His children.[21] Buber could not have written this line.

III

We are now in a position to consider the volume that inspired this chapter, *A Passion for Truth*.[22] This is a very personal book, written in a personal way. Yet though it begins in subjectivity, or more correctly, in subjective response to certain men and ideas, its ambition is to go beyond subjectivity and to use subjectivity as a means for achieving truth —both intellectual truth and truth on the level of existential concern. It is a work that unites the different strands of its author's interest in things Jewish, Hasidic and theological, and molds them into one mosaic history. Being so many things it is not easy to review its contents or to evaluate it: to evaluate it only as history or theology would be to miss a large part of its point, but to review it merely as *credo* would be to do injustice to author as well as to audience.

As to its genesis in its author's biography there can be no doubt. In the "Introduction" Heschel confides to his reader the Hasidic influences on his childhood. He tells of being especially influenced by two Hasidic masters, one of whom, the Baal Shem Tov (1700–1760), is the greatest in the history of the movement, while the other, Reb Menachem Mendl of Kotzk, the Kotzker (1787–1859), is the strangest. Between these two, with their opposing *Weltanschauungen,* Heschel lived, sometimes following the way of Mezbizh, sometimes the way of Kotzk.

"I was taught about inexhaustible mines of meaning by the Baal Shem; from the Kotzker I learned to detect immense mountains of absurdity standing in the way. The one taught me song—the other silence. The one reminded me that there could be a Heaven on earth, the other shocked me into discovering Hell in the allegedly Heavenly places in our world."[23]

One is tempted to speculate that more of his earlier years were spent in Mezbizh, while the older he got the more he resided in Kotzk. This speculation is prompted by this, his last effort, which is clearly more a product of Kotzk, though not just of Kotzk alone.

Though the work begins in biography it does not remain there. In the very first section of the book Heschel attempts to provide in broad strokes the distinctive features of "The Two Teachers." Having drawn his two images, however, the differences between the two are not presented as matters of personality or particular outlook but are used as the medium through which to present two alternative religious life-styles. It is as if Heschel were using these Zaddikim to portray "types" of piety, with each differing as to his understanding of Judaism's essential elements: God, Israel and Torah. While the Baal Shem Tov is the paradigm of love, the Kotzker is the model of truth. Where one is joyous, the other is somber. Where one feels the nearness of God, the other finds the presence of God a distant goal to be struggled for—usually with little success. Where one sees God in 'all things great and small,' the other finds the world an impediment to be overcome on the way to God. Where one is open to all men, finding divinity in each, the other seeks only the select few capable of especial acts of self-discipline leading towards transcendence. Where one stresses emotion, the other teaches discipline. Where one sees harmony between body and spirit, the other sees antagonism. Where one sees harmony between nature, man and Creator, the other sees tension. Where one is an optimist, the other is not. Where one is infused with wonder and exaltation, the other teaches self-reflection, sobriety, severity. Where one sees only the good, the other sees mostly the evil. Where one seeks ecstasy, the other stresses contrition. Where one sees meaning, the other senses absurdity. Where one knows God primarily as Father, the other is awe-struck at God as Judge. Regarding the two one recalls the well-known tale: When asked where God dwelled the Baal Shem answered, everywhere; the Kotzker (answered), where he is allowed to enter.[24] In comparing the two Heschel writes: "The former began with grace, the latter with indignation. A light glowed in Mezbizh; a fire raged in Kotzk."[25]

That Heschel sees these two spiritual titans not only as individuals but as models is supported by a comment he makes in the course of his treatment of the notion of "Faith." He reminds us that:

"In the history of Hasidism we come upon *two types of faith*: one is intimate, personal attachment to God, the other is self-centeredness overcome . . . The first is a promise, the second a challenge. The first is nurtured by wonder, song, poetry; the second initiates a process of self-scrutiny and alertness that can never end; there silence is the only refuge."[26]

From what he has already told us about the ways of Mezbizh and Kotzk it is clear that the former way is that of the Baal Shem Tov, the latter the way of Reb Mendl. It was Reb Mendl who taught that faith meant simply, "to disregard self-regard."[27]

Heschel's attempt to fashion a phenomenology of religious types in this work, despite its unsystematic, aphoristic appearance, becomes still clearer when one takes into account the second section of the book which deals with the unlikely comparison of "The Kotzker and Kierkegaard." Only someone with theological imagination would suggest such a comparison, if for no other reason than that most people who know something about the Kotzker are unfamiliar with Kierkegaard and vice versa. Moreover, those who find inspiration in one are usually separated from finding theological sustenance in the other as a result of dogmatic, confessional differences. Hasidim and Protestant fundamentalists alike will no doubt take offense at this comparison, yet Heschel, a student of both the Danish Protestant and the Polish Zaddik, is not daunted, knowing full well the risks. Heschel goes so far as to speak of a "striking similarity of their concerns" and of "so impressive an affinity between them."[28] In what lies this parallelism? Heschel locates it in what he calls "depth-theology," i.e., both struggle with the same human problems that emerge from the existential situation of man *qua* man—problems that 'transcend' or rather 'precede' 'secondary' problems of confessional religion, nationality, education or class. And to these shared existential problems they give a common human reply, though each clothes it in different images and speaks in different vocabularies. "To many people,"

Heschel suggests, "the inner life is a no-man's land. To Kierkegaard and the Kotzker, it was of the deepest concern."[29]

For Heschel, Kierkegaard and the Kotzker represent a similar *form* of religiosity, not, of course, in their doctrinal beliefs but in their existential relation to the world and its Creator. Heschel attempts to flesh out this claimed similarity by recounting the teachings of Kierkegaard and the Kotzker. By way of comparison Heschel argues that both men insisted on the fundamental premise that life was not given but made; that it was man's unique challenge to make a life out of the possibilities that lay open to him. "He who thinks that he is finished," insisted the Kotzker, "*is* finished," and the Danish sage would wholeheartedly agree. Authenticity in life has to be won: only the commonplace, the mediocre, the trivial come easily. Both agreed that man had to establish his individual identity over against "the crowd." Kierkegaard gave pointed expression to this concern in his now famous description for his existential hero: "the single one." Each man lives and each man dies *alone*. We are all individuals responsible for making ourselves—or, more often, for undoing ourselves. The "single one" must start with honest knowledge of self; with the will to interrogate the very roots of his or her own soul in order to cast out all hypocrisy, all deceit, all evil that finds a warm, safe haven there. Even, one might almost say especially, religious faith can be a sham, a deception: "The problem is not whether to trust God but whether to trust one's acceptance of God."[30] For Kierkegaard as for the Kotzker religious integrity begins in self-examination. Moreover, religious integrity requires total commitment. Kierkegaard expressed his rejection of all compromise in matters religious in his oft-repeated phrase "either/or." One cannot serve both God and another. One cannot be a faithful servant and an idolator simultaneously. Likewise, the Kotzker stressed that "God is either of supreme importance or none."[31] According to Heschel, this radical honesty allied to the demand for total concern leads both men to come to see that the decisive dimension of authentic religiosity lies in a quintessential subjectivity. The *how* of an action is the categorical concern over the *what*. Subjectivity here means the total re-orientation of one's personality, the transformation of one's essential self, the renewed—indeed passionate—dedication of one's being to one, and only one, goal. Understood in this way subjectivity provides the motive power for all spiritual renewal. Even truth cannot be found without it, for truth in the highest sense is not propositional knowledge

but existential certitude which mirrors ontological realities. For Kierkegaard and the Kotzker, man does not know the truth, he lives it.

Reb Mendel teaches the almost absolute power of the human will and
Kierkegaard concurs. Both challenge those who would be their true
disciples to question all inherited orthodoxies, not necessarily in order
to overthrow them but rather in order to make them truly their own.
Both realized that this enjoined a struggle with all establishments and a
conscious decision to eschew all majorities: truth is one thing that is
impervious to majority votes as well as to majority mores. Both preach
a desired alienation from the world and the limitation, if not complete
sublimation, of one's sensuality. Both teach the spiritual necessity of
solitude and poverty. "Discard the world," the Kotzker exhorted, "money—
Pfui!"[32]

Having set out this typological dichotomy between the Baal Shem
Tov and Kotzker-Kierkegaard, these *two types of faith,* what follows?
Of what significance is the Heschelian exercise in religious phenomenology? Is it merely intended as a historical description of academic interest
or are we meant to learn something more from it? To this question there
are three answers. The first is a simple yes to the concern for historical
information. Heschel *is* trying to write history in a broad yet clear sense.
Secondly, Heschel is trying to construct a description of two different
yet legitimate kinds of religious behaviour. The first is the way of the
Baal Shem Tov, the other the way of Reb Mendl. One way is suitable
for some men and for *some* times, the other for other men and *other*
times. I stress the importance of the times in which one lives because it
appears that Heschel came to the conclusion that *our* time favors the
way of Kotzk. More on this below . . . The third answer to our question,
that is both a corollary of the second as well as an independent line of
thought, is actually already contained in the description of the way of
Kotzk given above. Truth is something to be lived. Kierkegaard and the
Kotzker intend to teach not by doctrine but by example, and Heschel
likewise. We are introduced to the Kotzker not primarily in order to
study his life but to change our own. Heschel intends, through the
medium of the investigation of Kierkegaard and Reb Mendl, to evoke a
subjective response from his readers. He is concerned to do what his two
mentors were concerned to do: to throw the reader back on himself. The
ultimate aim is not to teach us about Kotzk or Copenhagen but about
each of us here and now. Where Kierkegaard used pseudonyms and

paradoxes to force the reader back into his own subjectivity, so Heschel uses the images of Kotzk and Kierkegaard to do likewise. The real subject of the work is not meant to be the Kotzker or Kierkegaard, and certainly not Heschel, but ourselves, the readers.

Moreover, the use of Reb Mendl and Kierkegaard as intermediaries creates a distance between Heschel and ourselves that allows him to express sentiments, especially severe critical judgments of our genera-tion, that might have proven difficult in the first person. Heschel can cajole, encourage, interrogate and rebuke us without our taking offence or getting upset at him, thus finally missing the point which is at the center of his challenge: change your lives. The whole form of Heschel's presentation insinuates its purpose. The form is meant, first, to turn us away from an interest in Heschel, then away from concentration on the Baal Shem Tov, the Kotzker and Kierkegaard respectively, leading finally back towards ourselves through an act of introspection. From such introspection self-revelation is generated that leads to *teshuvah*—and then and only then is it possible to begin to pursue that distant ideal which we do not possess but which we can avoid seeking only at the price of our own authenticity: Truth. In the interpretation of this book what is ideally revealed is the interpreter. In this sense the book is only the means of providing the reader with an opportunity for reflecting on his own unique life situation relative to the divine imperative. It is a mirror through which we are able to see ourselves. The Kotzker, Kier-kegaard and Heschel do *not* want to be *gurus*, they want only to provide the occasion for each man's reflection, inwardness and authentic search for the transcendent.

Let us return for a moment to the implication of our second reply above—that Heschel seems now to find more affinity with Kotzk than Mezbizh. This conclusion will, I think, surprise the faithful readers of Heschel's earlier works. It surprised me. Yet it seems an unavoidable judgment which is made, nonetheless, with some reticence, as I am hesitant about speculating about another philosopher's state of mind. Let us, therefore, first review the non-speculative 'hard-evidence' for this conclusion. Besides the remarks in the last chapter of Heschel's work entitled "The Kotzker Today" that will be treated below, there are quite a number of passages throughout *A Passion for Truth* that lend them-selves to our interpretation. One of special significance reads:

"In times of balanced living, the Kotzker's repeated cries to look within and to practise continuous self-inspection may be both unbearable and unnecessary.

Yet in today's disintegrating world, where all inwardness is externalized, our inner selves face a wasteland. We may sense a new relevance in such a call."[33]

Here Heschel does two things: he recognizes that in other historical circumstances there are other legitimate ways beside that of Kotzk towards the inseparable goals of personal authenticity and relation to God. One might argue in reply that to the truly sensitive man, say for example the Kotzker, there do not exist "times of balanced living," all such balance being illusory and the projection of dishonest men. But this matter aside, it is clear that Heschel knows there is more than one way towards God. Yet, and this is the second, more important, element in his remark, *our* age is an age that responds most effectively to the way of harsh self-criticism and constant introspection propounded by Reb Mendl. Heschel, whose earlier works reflect a vision drawn from the Baal Shem Tov, "of song, of joy, of closeness to God," now sees the world in new, darker shades. Heschel, to whose earlier works one could rightly apply the description used of an earlier Jewish sage—"the God-intoxicated philosopher"—now seems aware of quite another, altogether more absurd dimension of human existence. The mountains of absurdity that confront us are recognised as the dominant features of our landscape. Now the world takes on the characteristics of Eliot's wasteland and Heschel no longer sees only the grandeur of nature and history. There is here a new depth in Heschel that reflects a changed awareness of the seriousness of the modern human predicament. Though Heschel tries to respond in somewhat the same way as he had in his earlier writings—after all, he always remained a man of great faith—one must recognize that even the old answers are now presented more cautiously, in fragments rather than monographs, in flashes of insight rather than philosophical treatises, because Heschel now lives with the world's dark-side in a way that is new for him.

The note of unexpected disillusionment that one begins to hear becomes more pronounced as the monograph proceeds. It coincides especially with Heschel's treatment of the Kotzker's withdrawal from active life in 1840, after which he lived for the next twenty years in seclusion, only rarely breaking his self-imposed exile to come among his Hasidim and then usually in such fury as to only further distance himself from them. Heschel chronicles this period with success, a success that one senses is, at least in part, generated by an empathy Heschel feels for the Kotzker's predicament. Did Heschel perhaps feel a subterranean biographical parallel with the cause of Reb Mendl's retirement: "Reb Mendl had sought men whose hearts were of steel but discovered that most of them had stultified ears. He had been misunderstood by his closest friends . . ."[34] And is this personal element present again in Heschel's speculation that perhaps the Kotzker's disillusionment came as a result of "the realization that truth was a derelict . . . or the thought that ultimately God Himself was responsible for the inherent falsehood of human existence."[35] This latter reflection would be daring for any Jewish thinker, for Heschel it is revolutionary. These remarks of Heschel's appear to be more than historical recollections alone in that they mirror, while also accounting for, Heschel's pre-occupation with the Kotzker late in life. It would seem that Heschel, heretofore the follower of the Baal Shem Tov, the ardent gladiator for human rights, the streetmarcher for black equality with Martin Luther King, the leader of the Jewish battle for survival in Russia and *Eretz Yisroel,* the fiery prophetic opponent of the Vietnam tragedy,[36] is now overcome by the lack of progress in so many areas of his most committed concern. Heschel, like the Kotzker, looked out at the world a second time and realized that it met neither the requirements of Divine righteousness, nor human majesty. The haunting question he attributes to Reb Mendl may, in fact, be his own haunting question: "Is God Himself responsible for the inherent falsehood of human existence?" Even to ask this question is to traverse the conceptual parameters of the Heschel of *God in Search of Man*[37] and *Man Is Not Alone.*[38] In *Man Is Not Alone,* under the heading of "Doubts", Heschel felt confident to write: "Search for God begins with the realization that it is man who is the problem; that more than God is a problem to man, man is a problem to Him."[39] In this last work, however, Heschel's heretofore unswerving optimism gives way to a new sense of the seemingly intractable absurdity that confronts man in history. Here God, too, is a problem: "Is God Himself responsible for the inherent falsehood of human existence?" The way of Mezbizh has led to the way of Kotzk.

These "hints" of malaise in Eden become still more direct in the penultimate chapter of the book entitled appropriately enough "The Kotzker and Job." The problem of *Job,* that is, the problem of evil, is seen to be the mystery which consumed the Kotzker's last twenty years. "He was tormented," Heschel suggests, "by the ever-present enigma: why did God permit evil in the world?"[40] According to Heschel this concern manifest itself in protest. Protest even against God! "Though he cloaked his accusations in silence for the most part, occasionally he would shout out biting words!"[41] The Kotzker is here a faithful rebel but a rebel nonetheless. He is overwhelmed by the power of Satan in the world and he wants to know why God permitted it. Likewise, Heschel too seems ready to call God before the *Beth-Din*. Applauding the spirit of the Kotzker he goes so far as to council his contemporaries: "In the Jew of our time, distress at God's predicament may be a more powerful witness than tacit acceptance of evil as inevitable."[42] Like Reb Mendl, Heschel seems to have grown troubled with God Himself. In fact, so troubled is Reb Mendl that he even dares to question the existence of God: "Could it be that the palace (the world) has no lord?" If Heschel is to be believed, Reb Mendl dared to consider radical disbelief (though one suspects that neither the Kotzker nor Heschel really went this far). Similarly, Heschel seems, as expressed through the subject matter of this last work, to have entered a phase of more radical and more honest uncertainty that recalls to mind Tennyson's lines: "There lives more faith in honest doubt than in half the creeds." The strength of this radical doubt finds powerful expression: "So many of us are haunted by the ugly futility of human effort, the triumph of brute force, of evil, of man's helpless misery. Is not any form of hopefulness false, unreal, self-deceiving?"[43] In the entire earlier corpus of Heschel's work one will not find such an evocative indictment of life's possible meaninglessness.

As with the Kotzker, however, this mood of despair does not lead to denial. It does not go in the direction of, say, Camus' atheism, for despite its sense of grievance at the injustice of the world's governance it maintains its ability to believe: to believe precisely *despite* the world's absurdity. Rather than negate doubt, here doubt is held as part of the dialectical alternation of a mature faith. In this, too, Reb Mendl is Heschel's guide-cum-model and, as Heschel would have it, the model for us all. Heschel sees a "leap of faith" as the legitimate way beyond the absurdity we encounter. Fraught with danger as this way is, Heschel nonetheless holds firm to his belief that it is an authentic way over the abyss of meaninglessness that seems to open before us on all sides. Though this gambit raises severe philosophical conundrums we need to consider below, let us for the present follow Heschel, Reb Mendl and Kierkegaard as they perform the spiritual gymnastics of their "leap of faith."

In what does this "leap" consist for the Kotzker and Heschel in a specifically Jewish context? Heschel offers the very Jewish—authentically Jewish, not ersatz Jewish—reply: "All searching for rational meaning must yield to the reality upon which Judaism is built: to live is to obey."[44] The effective significance of such a move is that it replaces the *standards of value* that allow for the growth of the notions of absurdity and meaninglessness with alternative values which do not—this is a *logical* 'do not'—allow for the construction of these concepts. This is to say, one replaces the anthropocentric basis of value with an *a priori* theocentric one in which the commanding God who reveals His will in Divine Imperatives is posited to be all-good, all-wise, "omni-everything" in the classical vocabulary. In this way we solve the problem of absurdity by the *a priori* declaration of the world's meaningfulness through the stipulated existence of an all-wise, all-good, all-powerful Creator whose will brings the world into being and whose will is to be obeyed not questioned. Belief in this Creator removes all doubts, for it is *a priori* certain that all semblance of absurdity comes not from God but from our misunderstanding. God is in His heaven and all is right with the world. Heschel does not, of course, put the case or its implications in this logico-analytic form. Instead for him it is a matter of existential decision. He writes: "We must disregard self-regard in thinking about God, we must transcend our sense of values in evaluating the enterprise of living. In faith we can accept that there is *meaning beyond* absurdity."[45] In the specifically Jewish context this argument takes the form of faith in the absoluteness of the Divine imperative as revealed in Torah. This is what Heschel means by the category of obedience. It is to obey the Will of God in faithfulness. In such a way we transcend the uncertainty of charting our life's course by the arbitrary dictates of finite wills, overcoming thereby the primary source of the seeming uncertainty, nay absurdity, of life. God's Will is the sole solid basis for dedicated action, action which is secure in the grounds of its own meaningfulness. Heschel attributes the structure of this movement of religious faith to the Kotzker and Kierkegaard. It also sounds very Kantian—an influence at work subterraneously in Kierkegaard and Heschel. We believe because we need belief to salvage meaning from its nemesis, meaninglessness.

Having posited God in faith, meaning is now safe. "We encounter meaning beyond absurdity in living as a response to an expectation. Expectation of meaning is an *a priori* condition of our existence."[46] The logic of this assertion is not unassailable. In fact, it is not even a logical argument though stated as one. Rather it is a confession of faith.[47] As a confession of faith, however, it is evidence of *at least* the meaning Heschel found, and that he claimed the Kotzker also found, in order to sustain him in the face of the world's absurdity. Moreover, what is particularly impressive about it as a confession of faith is its total commitment. It is a religious position unalloyed by compromise. God wills, man does! To try to make God over in human form, to try to fit Him into *our* standards, into our conceptions so that we can understand His ways, is to *reduce* God to the limit of our imagination. This conceptual direction Heschel insists we avoid. As a consequence the outstanding feature of the Kotzker's faith is his willingness to believe despite his inability to understand. Heschel specifically cites Buber's position as an instance of religious reductionism, contrasting it to the total commitment of the Kotzker:

"Martin Buber's declaration: 'Nothing can make me believe in a God who punishes Saul because he did not murder his enemy' must be contrasted with the Kotzker's statement 'a God whom any Tom, Dick, and Harry could comprehend, I would not believe in.' "[48]

This is a decidedly non-modern view—yet as much as it is out of tune with the modern consciousness it is decidedly in tune with the biblical *Weltanschauung*. It neither tries to understand God, nor does it forsake God because it fails to understand Him. It does not try to reduce God to Kant's ethical imperatives or the like, yet it always insists on God's justice. It insists that though we may not understand God's transcendental way we can be certain that it is the way of Truth.

We gain here an 'answer' to Job's situation—not an answer that *explains* anything but an answer that assures of meaning in the face of seeming absurdity. And absurdity—Job's senseless suffering—is the real challenge of this biblical work. Job, and like him the Kotzker and Heschel, learn that though we do not understand God's way this does not invalidate it. In the midst of suffering, God, as if out of the whirlwind, reveals Himself and this revelation guarantees that though we don't understand we can believe. "There is a King in the Palace." The threat that life is "a tale told by an idiot signifying nothing" is now cancelled. The Presence of God, even the inscrutable, mysterious Presence of God, is the surety that there is meaning. In this approach we are asked to realize the polarity at work; there are two very different sides from which to adjudge the fate of the cosmos: God's and Man's. What appears absurd from our perspective is meaningful from His. This is Spinoza's solution, *sub specie aeternitatis,* and the solution of all men of faith in the face of the world's, now only apparent, meaninglessness. "Be in a hell of a mess and survive on faith," the Kotzker taught.[49]

The transcendental position being advanced here is summed up by Heschel as persuasively and as briskly as one has ever seen it put. I quote his summary:

"To be overwhelmed by the transrational majesty of God one has to accept the risk of not understanding Him. The incompatibility of God's ways with human understanding was, according to the Kotzker, the very essence of our being . . . 'For my thoughts are not your thoughts, and your ways are not my ways . . .' (Isaiah 55:8).

If we maintain that God's ways and man's ways are mutually exclusive, that man is incapable of understanding God, then the impossibility of our comprehending His ways *a priori* excludes the possibility of finding an answer to the ultimate question."[50]

What follows this statement of Heschel's starting position is a series of time-honored, classical apologetic moves in defence of God and the vindication of His justice. The most fundamental of these, woven anew in Heschel's special poetic language, is the argument that evil comes, at least in part, as a consequence of the need for freedom. Without freedom, so the claim goes, man could be neither saint nor sinner, nor could the possibility of performing truly righteous acts, acts rich in meaning, exist. The very existence of real freedom which allows for the exercise of human majesty necessarily entails the possibility that this freedom might be abused. Moreover, its abuse is something God Himself must countenance if the conditions of free action are not to be seen to be violated by their Divine Author, thus transforming the concept of freedom into a charade. "If truth were manifest and strong, man would lose his major task, his destiny to search for it."[51] Detailed comment on the philosophical coerciveness of this and like arguments is withheld for another more fitting occasion. What can be said here is that these traditional defences of theodicy are given a fresh feel in Heschel's hands—though ultimately they are still persuasive only to those who already believe.

The final section of the discussion of "The Kotzker and Job" ends on a particularly Heschelian note: "Man's responsibility for God." This theme, associated with Heschel's writing from the time of his early work on the *Prophets*,[52] through his major philosophical treatises such as *Man Is Not Alone*, and *God in Search of Man*, is introduced as part of the analysis of the Kotzker's understanding. It is clear that here there may be a bit of Heschelian eisegesis, though there is some support for it in the brief corpus of *Kotzkeriana* we possess, as well as in Hasidic theology more generally. God's fate in the world, the argument has it, is in man's hands. Mysteriously, God has tied His destiny to that of men so that what men do affects God just as what God does affects men. This, Heschel insists, is the essential meaning of God's covenantal relation with Israel. The covenant between God and man binds their fates together. This Jewish, especially kabbalistic, emphasis shifts the burden of history and the source of evil in history in complicated ways back onto man's shoulders.[53] The earlier, new Heschelian emphasis on God's responsibility for history, stated in the previous sections of *A Passion for Truth,* now gives way to the older Heschelian emphasis on human action and its reverberations in the Heavenly court. "In the light of God's mysterious dependence upon man," Heschel argues, "the problem of anthropodicy and theodicy cannot be separated . . . Why does the God of justice and compassion permit evil to exist? is bound up with the problem of how man should aid God to see that His justice and compassion prevail."[54] The theology embedded in this view is as suggestive as it is problematic. At one and the same time it recognizes the need to keep man and God together, to hold that somehow history does make a real difference to God and is not just divine sport—while it also raises seemingly insuperable philosophical problems relating to anthropomorphism, epistemology and "God-language." A thorough analytic review of the entire character of this line of thought is required—but not here. For the present we want only to try to understand Heschel's enterprise. Accordingly we will conclude this discussion of Heschel's final chapters with Heschel's own moving *apologia* for God and man in the face of the world's evil.

"Life in our time has been a nightmare for many of us, tranquillity an interlude, happiness a fake. Who could breathe at a time when man was engaged in murdering the holy witness to God six million times?

And yet God does not need those who praise Him when in a state of Euphoria. He needs those who are in love with Him when in distress, both He and ourselves. This is the task: in the darkest night to be certain of the dawn, certain of the power to turn a curse into a blessing, agony into a song. To know the monster's rage and, in spite of it, proclaim to its face (even a monster will be transfigured into an angel); to go through Hell and to continue to trust in the goodness of God—this is the challenge and the way."[55]

We are now in a position to see how well Heschel succeeded in his three goals of (a) providing a historical picture of the Baal Shem Tov and, more especially, of the Kotzker; (b) constructing a phenomenology of religious types; and (c) fulfilling his existential-theological ambition of aiding his readers to find meaning in their own lives in the face of all the obstacles to this end. It is clear that the emphasis in *A Passion for Truth* is on the latter two concerns and the latter parts of the book deal almost exclusively with the subject of our own existential situation, "the search for our own eternal happiness," as Kierkegaard might say. Indeed, the historical picture presented is certainly inadequate, needing to be supplemented by, among other things, the more concrete types of scholarly investigations into the historic origins of Hasidism that Heschel's already referred-to technical studies represent (and that is also found in the two-volume Yiddish work *The Struggle for Truth*). Yet at the same time, the image drawn of the Besht, the Kotzker and Kierkegaard is not historically *in*accurate and does provide a broad, rough historical framework in and through which to understand the philosophical discussion that flows from the sketched historical skeleton. In defense of this arrangement and weighting of material it must be recognized that the book is not meant to be just, or even primarily, a historical discussion of its subject. Thus, even if weak in its treatment of the relevant historical detail, with regard to its other ideological motivations and existential goals the book succeeds—insofar, that is, as the type of phenomenological and existential position that Heschel adopts can be said to be successful at all. The final sections on theodicy, on "Job and the Kotzker," are especially intriguing in light of these concerns, as well as being particularly open to rigorous interrogation from an analytic point of view. The strength of Heschel's religious sensitivity as well as the fundamental conceptual problematic of his thought both surface to a significant degree in this final attempt to work out the "meaning beyond absurdity."[56] In that the book raises essential issues and treats them in a suggestive, even intriguing, manner which has the power to provoke us to further reflection, Heschel can be said to have accomplished a large part of what he set out to do when he decided to write *A Passion for Truth*.

IV

Criticism of Heschel's position, especially as articulated in *A Passion for Truth,* has been purposely eschewed in this paper. This avoidance of criticism is not due to total agreement with Heschel's views but is rather the consequence of the critical judgment that whatever reservations one has (and this author has many) about Heschel's Hasidic investigations and his reflections thereon, this corpus of material nonetheless constitutes a contribution of first-rank importance to the available literature. It is particularly valuable as an antidote to the prejudices of *Wissenschaft* ideology, whose influence is still felt in many quarters and also as a corrective to the enormously influential, though distorted image of Hasidism presented by Martin Buber. As such, Heschel's work deserves to be studied and assimilated before it is subjected to a more detailed and, where necessary, negative critical scrutiny.

NOTES

1. For details of his variegated achievements see Steven T. Katz, (ed.), *Jewish Philosophers* (New York, 1975), pp. 207–215.
2. *A Passion for Truth* (New York, 1973).
3. For detailed criticism of Buber's understanding of Hasidism see G. Scholem, "Martin Buber's Hasidism: A Critique," in *Commentary*, Vol. 22 (October, 1961), pp. 305–316, and reprinted in Scholem's *The Messianic Idea in Judaism* (New York, 1971), pp. 228–250. Consult also R. Shatz-Uffenheimer's critical essay in *The Philosophy of Martin Buber*, ed. P. Schilpp and M. Friedman (Illinois, 1967), pp. 403–434; and Steven T. Katz, "Martin Buber's Misuse of Hasidic Sources," in *Post-Holocaust Dialogues* (New York, 1983), pp. 52–93.
4. Published in *Studies in Memory of Moses Schorr*, ed. by L. Ginzburg and A. Weiss (New York, 1944), pp. 113–126 [in Hebrew].
5. Published in *Yivo Annual of Jewish Social Science*, Vol. 1 (New York, 1946), pp. 86–106. This article was also reprinted as the "Introduction" to Roman Vishniacs, *Polish Jews: A Pictorial Record* (New York, 1947), pp. 7–17.
6. Published in *Alei Ayin: The Salmon Schocken Jubilee Volume* (Jerusalem, 1948–52), pp. 213–244 [in Hebrew].
7. Published in *The Jews*, ed. Louis Finkelstein (New York, 1949), Vol. 1, pp. 602–623. Available now in a paperback from Schocken Books (New York, 1971), Vol. 2 (of 3), pp. 155–177.
8. Published in *Hebrew Union College Annual*, Vol. 23 (1950–51), Part 2, pp. 17–71 [in Hebrew].
9. Published in *Hadoar*, Vol. 39, No. 28 (June 5, 1959), pp. 519–521 [in Hebrew].
10. Published in *The Harry A. Wolfson Jubilee Volume*, ed. Saul Lieberman et al. (New York, 1965), pp. 113–141 [in Hebrew].
11. Published in *Hadoar Jubilee Volume*, Vol. 37 (1957), pp. 86–94 [in Hebrew].
12. Published in *Yivo Bletter*, Vol. 36 (1952), pp. 113–135 [in Yiddish].
13. *Kotzk: The Struggle for Truth*, (2 vols.) (Tel Aviv, 1973) [in Yiddish].

14. *A Passion for Truth* (New York, 1973).
15. *The Earth is the Lord's* (New York, 1950); paperback edition (New York, 1963).
16. Heschel's most extensive, though still fragmentary, reflections on the Baal Shem Tov are found in Part I of *A Passion for Truth*.
17. A. J. Heschel, *The Earth Is the Lord's* (New York, 1950), p. 80.
18. Ibid., p. 80.
19. Ibid., p. 89.
20. See here Heschel's remarks in ibid., p. 90.
21. Ibid., p. 84. For a fuller critique see my essay "Martin Buber's Misuse of Hasidic Sources."
22. I shall not review Heschel's two-volume Yiddish study of the Kotzker entitled *Kotzk: The Struggle for Truth* (Tel Aviv, 1973) separately. The first volume of this Yiddish work covers much the same material as *A Passion for Truth*, while volume two recounts the history of the Kotzker's heirs and contains important and interesting material on the development of Hasidism in the 19th century. In general this Yiddish work is more scholarly in nature.
23. *Passion,* p. xiv.
24. Ibid., p. 33.
25. Ibid., p. 15.
26. Ibid., p. 192 (my italics).
27. Ibid., p. 192.
28. Ibid., pp. 85–86.
29. Ibid., p. 87.
30. Ibid., p. 94.
31. Ibid., p. 95.
32. Ibid., p. 176f.
33. Ibid., p. 127.
34. Ibid., p. 233.
35. Ibid., p. 233.
36. Heschel was a very early opponent of the Vietnam War and Co-Chairman of the anti-war group *Clergy Concerned about Vietnam.*
37. *God in Search of Man* (New York, 1956).
38. *Man Is Not Alone* (New York, 1951).
39. Ibid., p. 83.
40. *Passion,* p. 263.
41. Ibid., p. 268.
42. Ibid., p. 269.
43. Ibid., p. 287f.
44. Ibid., p. 287.
45. Ibid., p. 288, italics in original.
46. Ibid., p. 290.
47. There is a serious philosophical issue at stake here which I hope to take up at some future time.
48. *Passion,* p. 292f.
49. Ibid., p. 295.

50. Ibid., p. 295.
51. Ibid., p. 296.
52. A. J. Herschel, *The Prophets* (New York, 1962).
53. For more on these Kabbalistic views see G. Scholem's *Major Trends in Jewish Mysticism* (New York, 1954); idem, *Kabbalah* (New York, 1974); idem, *On the Kabbalah and its Symbolism* (New york, 1965). See also I. Tishby, *Torah ha-Rah ve-ha-kelipah be-Kabbalat ha-Ari* (Jerusalem, 1968) [in Hebrew]; and I. Tishby's *Mishnat ha-Zohar* (Jerusalem, 1957) [in Hebrew], now available in an English translation under the title *The Wisdom of the Zohar*, 3 vols. (Oxford, 1989).
54. *Passion*, p. 298.
55. Ibid., pp. 300–301.
56. The title of the next-to-last section of "The Kotzker and Job" in *A Passion for Truth*, p. 244f.

4

1918 and After: The Role of Racial Antisemitism in the Nazi Analysis of the Weimar Republic

Post-1918 Europe was a breeding ground for conditions in which racial theory and political reality converged. The final coalescence of these two vectors after 1933 was neither "fore-ordained" nor "historically inevitable," but rather, one of the fecund possibilities that a traumatized and exhausted post-war Europe generated. The forces and personalities that could have acted to prevent this victory, that could have brought about some other scenario, failed the test, leaving Nazism, and its phantasmagoric racial doctrines, victorious.[1] The causes of this devastating eventuality lie inherent in the fact that from 1918 to the *NSDAP* seizure of power, German political and social life was caught up in a series of crises and contradictions, eight general elections between June 6, 1920 and March 5, 1933[2] being symptomatic of the instability that plagued Weimar and from which it could never extricate itself. The consequence of these unsettled circumstances was the radicalization of German life in all its public modalities, necessarily including those affecting the Jewish community,[3] and not least the formulation and articulation of various types of antisemitism. The conservative and more restrained style of the Wilhelmine period now gave way to an era of unbridled polarization of expression and action on both the left, e.g., Eisner's revolution,[4] and the right, e.g., the Kapp Putsch of 1920,[5] and again Hitler's failed 1923 Putsch. In this environment racial antisemi-

Reprinted by permission of New York University Press.

tism, in particular, was given a new and uncontrolled life.[6] And it is with its character and manifestation that we shall concern ourselves for the remainder of this chapter.

To advance our understanding of this obscene, yet powerful phenomenon, it is essential to analyze four repercussive historical *topoi.* They are: (a) the defeat of 1918 and Jewish behavior in World War I; (b) the Versailles Treaty and the conditions of the peace; (c) the stereotype of the Jew as revolutionary; and (d) the caricature of the Jew as supranational capitalist.[7] On the face of it this limited but inclusive list, except for those particulars created by the war, contains a by-now standard conservative indictment of "the Jews." However, in the transformed context of 1918 and after, each of these polemical elements stands under the ominous shadow of an ever more virulent racialism. "Blood mixture and the resultant drop in the racial level," Hitler would write in the 1920s, "is the sole cause of the dying out of cultures; for men do not perish as a result of lost wars, but by the loss of that force of resistance which is contained only in pure blood."[8]

I. THE DEFEAT OF 1918

A large segment of German society, especially among those who had fought in the war, could not assimilate the stark reality of defeat.[9] German national chauvinism, allied with individual and class egotism, made it impossible for considerable sectors of the populace to admit that weakness which the defeat represented.[10] Therefore, to account for the disaster that had occurred, this community required another, alternative explanation, and they found one readily at hand.[11] The nation had been betrayed from within by leftists,[12] unpatriotic profiteers, pacifists and, above all (and overlapping with the other categories), the Jews.[13] It was the Jews, the disloyal aliens *par excellence,* who, with the aid of their corrupt leftist puppets, had consciously administered the fateful "stab in the back" which had undermined Germany's ability to wage a successful war.[14] This despite the remarkable, even disproportionate enthusiasm German Jews had showed for the war, and their major participation in it. Eighty thousand Jews had served in the Kaiser's army, a tremendous patriotic effort given the size of the total German Jewish population which numbered just over 500,000.[15] Moreover, of those who served, 12,000 had died and no fewer than 35,000 had been decorated,[16] while at home Jews like Rathenau and Haber played major roles in the organization of the war economy. Yet all this was forgotten, even impugned. A German soldier reports his quite typical view of the reasons for the defeat:

The way the war ended we simply could not understand. I was resigned to the disloyalty of the Poles (which I had encountered during the war) but could never grasp how Germans could let us down. Today I know better. There were people who once called themselves Germans and now pledge loyalty to another people if necessary. They taught our German brothers lies and hatred. They stabbed our soldiers in the back. The German Siegfried found his murderer . . .

Captivity [in a POW camp] is death and freedom means life, or so I thought in those days. But I soon noticed the chains slung around our poor people and recognized our slave-masters. The first official to meet me at home was a Jew who talked very fast and praised the blessings of the revolution. I replied with hard and bitter words but was not yet completely aware of the role of the Jews. Years of observation and, at last, reading my "Führer's" book *Mein Kampf* fully opened my understanding for the fateful mole-like activity of these corrupters of the earth.[17]

The terms of the Peace following upon this humiliating defeat saddled the Weimar Republic with a burden it could not carry, not least a "guilt by association" in the minds of many who, illogically, held the Republic to be the result of the war betrayal and its aftermath. According to this logic, the Republic was the creation of those same leftists[18] and Jews[19] who acted with nefarious intent in 1918 and before. As a consequence, the post-war leadership inherited a political debt which eventually helped overwhelm it, while making it vulnerable almost from its inception. Over and over, every national issue became a "Jewish" issue, every motion or proposal, especially if prompted by actions taken by the allies, became an act of "International Jewry." For example, when the Dawes Plan was accepted by the Reichstag with the support of President Ebert, Ludendorff railed: "This is a disgrace to Germany. Ten years ago I won at Tannenberg. Today they [the Weimar liberals and allies] have won a *Jewish Tannenberg*."[20] This cant was symptomatic of the politics of the anti-republican camp. All right-wing parties, i.e., from the *Deutschnationale Volkspartei*[21] rightwards, would exploit this putative Jewish connection, this vulnerable element within the immature democratic structure, until Weimar's final collapse. As early as 1919, the *Deutschnationale Volkspartei* had called for the rejection of "the predominance of Jewry in government and public life, which since the revolution [of 1918] has become increasingly ominous. The influx of aliens [eastern Jews] across our border is to be cut off."[22] In exploiting this sensitive issue, however, no one was as strident or as successful as Hitler. For him, while the German army and the Kaiser had made specific tactical errors, the real cause of the defeat of 1918 lay in the racial degeneracy that overtook the Kaiserreich in its final phase.

> The deepest and the ultimate cause for the ruin of the old Reich was found in the non-recognition of the race problem and its importance for the historical development of the people. For events in the lives of the nations are not expressions of chance, but, by the laws of nature, happenings of the urge of self-preservation and propagation of species and race, even if the people are not conscious of the inner reasons for their activity. . . .
>
> If we let all the causes of the German collapse pass before our eyes, there remains as the ultimate and decisive cause the non-recognition of the race problem and especially of the Jewish danger.
>
> The defeats in the battlefield of August, 1918, would have been easily bearable. They were out of proportion to the victories of our people. Not the defeats have overthrown us, but we were overthrown by that power which prepared these defeats by robbing our people systematically, for many decades, of its political and moral instincts and forces which alone enable and entitle people to exist in this world.
>
> The old Reich, by inattentively passing by the question of the preservation of the racial foundations of our nationality, disregarded also the sole right which alone gives life in this world. Peoples which bastardize themselves, or permit themselves to be bastardized, sin against the will of eternal Providence, and their ruin by the hand of a stronger nation is consequently not an injustice that is done to them, but only the restoration of right. If a people no longer wants to respect the qualities which Nature has given it and which root in its blood, then it has no longer the right to complain about the loss of its worldly existence. . . .
>
> All really important symptoms of decay of the pre-war time ultimately go back to racial causes.[23]

Is it imperative to understand Hitler's argument correctly, to locate his perversion of the truth properly. For his biocentric contention embodies and gives voice to not only or even primarily a radical political critique of Weimar and the traitorous clique of 1918 peacemakers, but rather and more elementally expresses his primordial conviction that political behavior was an epiphenomenal manifestation of one's racial nature. The disaster of 1918 was not properly analyzed as a political error or as the effect of a failure of national will, but rather as the "catastrophic consequence of a moral and ethical poisoning."[24] The language of deconstruction is not social and political, nor again economic and class directed, but biographical.[25] Race, "blood," was the decisive arbiter. "Heroically our people won the war," Hitler declaims. "It took four and a half years to poison our people to the point that it defeated itself." And again, "How could a people that waged such heroic battles lose its national spirit all at once? Through moral contamination by the Jews."[26] It was in this sense that he saw himself as a "servant of the German people against the mortal enemies of our people, against Jewish blood—and race poisoning."[27] He declared that "to dispose of the evil mushroom [Jewry] . . . the evil must be grasped by its root." That is, "solving the Jewish problem is for us National Socialists the core problem. This problem cannot be settled by tenderness, but in view of the enemy's fearful weapons only by brachial violence."[28]

If at the beginning of the war and during the war, twelve or fifteen thousand of these Hebraic corrupters of the nation had been subjected to poison gas such as had been endured in the field by hundreds of thousands of our very best German workers of all classes and professions, then the sacrifice of millions at the front would not have been in vain. On the contrary, twelve thousand scoundrels eliminated at the right moment and a million orderly, worth-while Germans might perhaps have been saved for the future.[29]

It was only thus that Germany could "efface the poison outside and inside of us" which would make recovery possible.[30] This racial analysis was believed by its proponents to explain the present malaise and the source of national humiliation as could no other. Still more importantly, having revealed the nature of the disease only the Nazi party could propose the correct therapy.[31]

II. THE VERSAILLES TREATY

The Versailles Treaty, whether rightly or wrongly, was an unexpectedly harsh blow to Germany. "No subject," Gordon Craig has correctly observed,

agitated the textbook writers more or gave them a better excuse for oblique attacks upon the Republic than the Versailles Treaty. This was inevitable, for there were few Germans who were not left aghast when its terms were revealed. Having placed their faith in the American President and convinced themselves, by an extraordinary feat of wishful thinking, that the decisions made at Paris would be guided by the spirit of reconciliation that he had expressed in the speech announcing the Fourteen Points, they were outraged to discover that the victors intended to apply that older principle of settlement, *vae victis*. Most indignant, naturally, were those who had least cause to complain, the people who had luxuriated in the most grandiose dreams of conquest and material acquisition during the war. But even more reasonable persons, who had expected the terms to be severe and had even believed that their country deserved to be punished, were shocked by what appeared to them to be the Entente's flagrant violation of their own declarations (for example, in their plundering of Germany's colonial empire), of the facts of history (in their attribution of exclusive responsibility for the war to Germany and its allies), and of the rules of economic reason (in the horrendous load of reparations that the war-guilt clause was intended to justify), and were left incredulous by their apparent lack of interest in the question whether Germany was to become a viable democracy or not (else why would they heap these indignities upon the new Republic?).[32]

And, of course, in the treaty conditions[33] lay many, though by no means all, of the difficulties never overcome by the Republic.[34] How could such a monstrous, purposely demeaning[35] treaty, unconnected with the real military situation, have been negotiated? Who would have accepted such a "syphilitic peace?"[36] Certainly not a "true German." Again it was the *Dolchstoss*[37]—the betrayal. Candidates for this role were not hard to conjure; a familiar list was paraded out with "the Jews" at the top, cited especially as manipulators of the Republic and as its chief beneficiaries. Indeed, this contended linkage, this putative Jewish influence, even domination, was fatal for the Republic. Already as early as the election of 1920 this association began to take its negative toll, with the right-wing parties successfully exploiting it in their campaign rhetoric to undermine the electoral support of the three pro-Weimar parties whose share of the vote fell to that of a minority position with only 43.6% and 206 out of 459 parliamentary seats. By contrast, the right-wing, anti-Republican parties gained 33% of the vote and 157 seats and the anti-Republican left 20% of the vote and 87 seats.[38] This lamentable outcome provided a deeply wounded basis for Republican government.[39]

Once the Church had used "the Jews" as the symbol of antithesis and negativity; now this was the fashion of all segments of German society opposed to the treaty. Typical is this description of events given by a German soldier returning home:

The partisan squabbles took an even greater hold of the people. The Jews had laid such a foundation and they had managed to prepare all this inner corruption behind the facades. Wherever you looked, wherever you went to talk to people, you found Jews in the leading positions.

And so I was seized by such a tremendous hatred that once, in 1922 at a war invalid's meeting, I launched into the open struggle against the Jews without realizing in my innermost mind the consequences to which their regime would take us. I began to search. I bought books that threw some light on the Jewish way of life and its goals. I studied Freemasonry and discovered that, according to the documents handed down, this terrible war had long been prepared and planned. Although they tried to tell us that the war was our fault, I suddenly realized that it was all a game of intrigues, a net of lies without equal in world history.[40]

Still more significant, Hitler never forgot nor forgave the signing of the Versailles Treaty. Paradigmatic of his unwavering feelings in this regard is his *völkisch* commentary of 1923: "The Versailles dictate is the death sentence for Germany as an independent state and as a *Volk*."[41] And again in *Mein Kampf:*

While the international world Jewry slowly but surely strangles us, our so-called patriots shouted against a man and a system which dared, in one corner of the earth at least, to free themselves from Jewish-Masonic world embrace and oppose a nationalistic resistance to this international world poisoning . . .[42]

By this last phrase—"international world poisoning"—Hitler means to refer to "Jewish control" over Britain, Europe, Russia of course, and even America—except for "a single great man, [Henry] Ford"[43] (at least in the first edition of *Mein Kampf,* before Ford recanted his antisemitic nonsense in the face of a Jewish boycott of his Model T).[44] A control most especially exercised along racial lines:

[One] must open [their] eyes on the subject of foreign nations and must remind them again and again of the true enemy of our present-day world. In place of hatred against Aryans, from whom almost everything may separate us, but with whom we are bound by common blood . . . it must call external wrath upon the head of the foul [Jewish] enemy of mankind as the real originator of our sufferings. It must make certain that in our country, at least, the mortal enemy is recognized and the fight against him a gleaming symbol of brighter days, to show other nations the way to salvation of an embattled Aryan humanity.[45]

The Treaty of Versailles is seen, as is here evident, not as a political contract between nations, but as a declaration of racial war by Jews against Aryans. To evade its deadly intent, to overturn its funereal ambition, mere political transformations are inadequate; only a racial revolution will suffice. *"Today it is not princes and princes' mistresses who haggle and bargain over state borders,"* i.e., it is not a simple national struggle but rather, *"it is the inexorable Jew who struggles for his domination over the nations."*[46] This biological line of thought, this racial meditation on the rise and fall of nations, of mastery and servitude, is again clearly expressed in *The Secret Book* of 1928. There, reflecting on the implications of the Versailles Treaty, Hitler observes:

In opposition to the present bourgeois conception that the Treaty of Versailles has deprived our people of arms I can reply only that the real lack of weapons lies in our pacifistic-democratic poisoning, as well as our internationalism, which destroys and poisons our people's highest source of power. For the *source of a people's whole power does not lie in its possession of weapons or in the organization of its army, but in its inner value which is represented through its racial significance, that is the racial value of a people as such.*[47]

And the unmistakable meaning of this genetic-normative axiom is this:

Blood mixing and lowering of the race are then the consequences which, to be sure, at the beginning are not seldom introduced through a so-called predilection for things foreign, which in reality is an underestimation of one's own cultural values as against alien peoples. Once a people no longer appreciates the cultural expression of its own spiritual life conditioned through its blood, or even begins to feel ashamed of it, in order to turn its attention to alien expressions of life, it renounces the strength which lies in the harmony of its blood and the cultural life which has sprung from it. It becomes torn apart, unsure in its judgment of the world picture and its expressions, loses the perception and the feeling for its own purposes, and in place of this it sinks into a confusion of international ideas, conceptions, and the cultural hodge-podge springing from them. Then the Jew can make his entry in any form, and this master of international poisoning and race corruption will not rest until he has thoroughly uprooted and thereby corrupted such a people. The end is then the loss of a definite unitary race value and as a result, the final decline.[48]

Fate played a cruel trick on the Jewish people in this unhappy circumstance; it placed Walter Rathenau, self-hating Jew yet Jew nonetheless to all the antisemites,[49] in the position of German Foreign Minister in 1922, decisive "evidence" that Weimar was a *Judenrepublik*. ("The sudden outbreak of *Judenkoller* tends to occur," Peter Merkl's study shows, "most often among respondents complaining about the new Weimar leaders or about social disintegration in 1918.")[50] Whether rightly[51] or wrongly,[52] Rathenau felt himself honor bound, on behalf of Germany, to abide by the terms of the treaty:

We Germans are obligated by our signature, by the honor of our name that we have placed under the treaties. We will fulfill and we will go to the limit of our ability in order to preserve the honor of our name, which stands affixed to the treaties, and we recognize their binding character even though they do not express our wishes.[53]

This support of the agreement was held as little short of treasonous by the vocal antisemitic nationalist and rightist groups both within and without the Reichstag. General von Rabenau would express this broadly when, after Rathenau's murder, he wrote "The nomination of this ethnic alien [was] a sharp challenge to those Germans mindful of their race."[54]

The assassination of Rathenau[55] would not, of course, prevent the French from occupying the Ruhr in 1923[56] as a consequence of Germany's failure to abide by its treaty obligations,[57] but it could be manipulated to keep alive the myth of betrayal.

And why were the Jews so inclined to betray Germany? Because of Jewry's racially motivated supranational, conspiratorial loyalties, of which more below, bred of biological rather than national allegiance. The truth, of course, was decidedly otherwise. Jews in the disputed territories in the east, assigned to Poland, and in the west assigned to France, continued their fierce loyalty to Germany. In the eastern districts in particular, Jews spared no efforts in order to maintain their connection to Germany, including joining in the underground free-corps units that fought to keep these areas German. When polled in the League of Nations plebiscites they overwhelmingly voted to remain part of Germany, and when this did not happen many, at great personal cost, emigrated to Germany territory.[58] In this behavior, it should be added, they replicated a by-now nearly century-old pattern according to which Jews tended to favor Prussian rather than Polish rule. For example, after the 1848 revolution Jews in Poznan and related regions, mindful of Polish antisemitism, pogroms and the exploitive nature of the *szlachter* (Polish aristocracy), sided with the pro-German nationalists.[59] Tragically, all these, and other, profound and purely motivated expressions of that German-Jewish symbiosis[60] so real to most German Jews were ignored, and then ploughed under by the racialist bands that eventually won the day.

III. JEWS AS REVOLUTIONARIES, MARXISTS AND BOLSHEVIKS

Closely allied to the charge of Jewish defeatism and disloyalty was the accusation that Jews were revolutionaries of one left-wing variety or another whose sworn purpose was to undermine the established order and its values, replacing them, in turn, with a "Jewish" form of government which would invert the economic and power relations between Aryans and Semites. The significance of this issue was made real by the revolutionary events in Bavaria in November 1918, the leaders of which would forever be known as the "November Criminals" in the jargon of the right, and credited with the defeat of 1918 and much more. Begun in naval circles in Kiel,[61] the revolutionary mood spread to Munich, where a coalition of left-wing groups, led by the socialist Kurt Eisner, took power on November 8, and to Berlin, where a national republic was declared on November 10, and an armistice with France agreed on November 10 and signed on the eleventh.[62] This, in turn, unleashed a civil war between factions of the extreme Communist[63] left and a coalition of the republican right,[64] finally resolved with the defeat of the Communists in 1919, that radicalized and divided German society along political lines as never before.[65] In the eyes of those on the right, this division was the work of the Marxists and Jews (the two being more often than not interchangeable) who were intent on destroying German culture as they knew it.

This stereotypical reaction reflected a peculiar amalgam of empirical evidence and paranoia. The hard data were supplied by the reality of events in 1918–1919 Germany as well as the legitimate fears generated by the Bolshevik revolution[66] of 1917. For, was not Eisner a Jew, Liebknecht and Rosa Luxemburg Jews, Landauer and Kautsky Jews?[67] Again was not Zinoviev, Trotsky, and for many Lenin, a Jew? One of the Abel interviewees reports: "When in 1918 the Marxist revolution broke out . . . the Spartakists dressed as sailors, raged and destroyed everything . . . they were headed by Jews."[68] Paranoia was sparked off because the Eisner-Spartakist action was seen as conforming to, and confirming, a mythic paradigm of Jewish-Marxist world revolution and eventual domination. In this Eisner and his colleagues supposedly mirrored and replicated the age-old pattern of Jewish revolutionary behavior.[69] Hitler's fantasies on this score, indebted as they were to Rosenberg and Eckart, and the *Protocols of the Elders of Zion,* knew no bounds. For example, his account of the Exodus from Egypt was based on the notion that the Jews were expelled for preaching revolution, while the Jew Paul "virtually invented Christianity in order to undermine the Roman Empire . . ." Likewise, Hitler argued, "the Old Testament already provided the pattern of the Jewish assault upon the superior, creative race, a pattern repeated again and again down the ages."[70] With this ancient, inherent design revealed, the racial critics argued, the November revolutionaries were now unmasked, their eternal, undeviating nature and their degenerative purpose exposed. And Hitler's rancid imaginings were not his alone. Eckart could refer assuredly to "the Christian-Kosher-butchering dictatorship of the Jewish world savior Lenin";[71] the *Deutsche Völkischer Shutz-und-Trutz Bund* could disseminate in good conscience a German translation of the *Protocols,* resuscitate charges of ritual murder, and reissue Rohling's slanderous *Talmud-jude;*[72] older popular novelists like Arthur Dinter and Gustav Freytag[73] could find a new audience exploiting the theme of Jewish racial-sexual pollution of Aryan women; and Theodore Fritsch could continue to issue ever-new editions of his rabidly antisemitic *Handbook*. At the same time, the police, courts,[74] army,[75] schools, churches and universities[76] could all fall back on the idiom of racially inspired subversion. Consonant with this shrill racist mythology the *Münchener Beobachter* of October 4, 1919, in rhetoric now typical of the extreme right-wing press, could report on contemporary revolutionary events as follows:

[These are] dreadful times in which Christian-hating, circumcised Asiatics everywhere are raising their bloodstained hands to strangle us in droves! The butcheries of Christians by the Jew Issachar Zederblum, alias Lenin, would have made even a Genghis Khan blush. In Hungary his pupil Cohn, alias Bela Kun, marched through the unhappy land with a band of Jewish terrorists schooled in murder and robbery, to set up, among brutal gallows, a mobile machine gallows and execute middle-class citizens and peasants on it. A splendidly equipped harem served him, in his stolen royal train, to rape and defile honorable Christian virgins by the dozen. His lieutenant Samuely has had sixty priests cruelly butchered in a single underground room. Their bellies are ripped open, their corpses mutilated, after they have been plundered to their blood-drenched skin. In the case of eight murdered priests it has been established that they were first crucified on the doors of their own churches! The very same atrocious scenes are . . . now reported from Munich.[77]

Revolution and the chaos it unleashed were uniquely the work of the Jews. Hitler, employing this explanatory archetype, perceived the Russian revolutionary situation and its immensely destructive consequences wholly in racial terms. "Here Fate itself seems desirous of giving us a sign," he writes.

By handing Russia to Bolshevism, it robbed the Russian nation of that intelligentsia which previously brought about and guaranteed its existence as a state. For the organization of a Russian state was not the result of the political abilities of the Slavs in Russia, but only a wonderful example of the state-forming efficacy of the German element in an inferior race. . . . For centuries Russia drew nourishment from this Germanic nucleus of its upper leading strata. Today it can be regarded as almost totally exterminated and extinguished. It has been replaced by the Jew. Impossible as it is for the Russian by himself to shake off the yoke of the Jew by his own resources, it is equally impossible for the Jew to maintain the mighty empire forever. He himself is no element of organization, but a ferment of decomposition. The giant empire in the east is ripe for collapse. And the end of Jewish rule in Russia will also be the end of Russia as a state. We have been chosen by fate as witnesses of a catastrophe which will be the mightiest confirmation of the soundness of the folkish theory.[78]

Still more generally, writing in 1928, Hitler declaims, "The economic conquest of Europe by the Jew was pretty much completed around the turn of the century, and now he began to safeguard it politically." This means, according to the governing biocentric logic, the "attempt to extirpate the national intelligentsia . . . in the form of revolution." Everywhere in Europe, beginning with his successful campaign in Russia, the Jew has the same subversive design, assisted by "Marxism, democracy and the so-called Christian center" which are, in reality, only the Jew's "shock troops"[79] in this struggle for domination. Given this awesome association of Jews, Bolshevism and left-wing revolution, Hitler's description of the meaning of National Socialism is apt and chilling: "[The aim of National Socialism] is very brief: Annihilation and extermination of the Marxist worldview."[80] A prescription which for Hitler meant, certainly, the Marxist-Jewish worldview. Should there be any doubt about this intimate, inseparable association in his perverted deciphering of world events, I recall, from many possible examples, his continuous, and for him necessary and inescapable, linkage of Jews and Marxism. Thus in his rabid remarks in *The Secret Book* regarding "the Marxist defilers of culture . . . in the South Tyrol . . . [who] have let the theater sink to the level of a brothel, into sites of demonstrated race defilement . . . [who] let German literature sink into mud and filth," he concludes his diatribe by suggesting that these Marxist culture corrupters have "surrender[ed] the whole intellectual life of our people to international Jewry."[81] Similarly, in *Mein Kampf* he moves effortlessly from "the Social Democratic Press . . . directed predominantly by Jews" to "this type of Marxist press production";[82] while again in *The Secret Book* the fateful connection is drawn: "The end of the Jewish world struggle . . . will always be a bloody Bolshevization."[83] Ever and again in his rhetoric it is the fault of the Jewish-Marxists, the "Jewish-God-denying Marxists,"[84] and their subservient minions.

The real as well as distorted association of Jews with the extreme revolutionary left was enough to poison the more authentic collaboration of Jews with moderate socialist parties such as the *SDP (Sozialdemokratische Partei Deutschlands)* in which they did play a considerable role. It is estimated that 10% of the *SDP* Reichstag representatives during the Weimar period were Jews.[85] To the antisemite, however, such nuanced distinctions regarding alternative and quite varied socialist affiliations were irrelevant, while to the mass of uninformed citizens the connection of Jews and Marxism was only further reinforced by the perception of Jewish involvement in socialist politics. It should, however, be noted that, in contradistinction to this prejudiced construal, the actual reality was that Jews as a group overwhelmingly voted for centrist parties.[86] Even during and after the Depression this pattern, in general, remained constant.

Yet, truth aside, the grotesque stereotype of the revolutionary Jew was fixed: he was the embodiment of negativity, he destroyed the political order, exploitatively manipulated the world economy for selfish gain, eroded the foundations of true morality, opposed God and His Church, sexually corrupted all peoples, created internal social strife and caused civil war, worked to invert the natural order, sought to impose the base on the noble, the ignominious on the ideal and above all attempted to racially poison the nations of the world, thereby guaranteeing his own victory. Should he triumph, however, his conquest would be illusory for, given his parasitic and necessarily destructive nature, ultimately he must consume even himself. "If with the help of his Marxist creed," the future Führer tells his Weimar audience, "the Jew is victorious over the peoples of the world, his crown will be the funeral wreath of humanity and this planet will, as it did millions of years ago, move through the ether devoid of men."[87]

IV. THE "SUPRANATIONAL" JEW

The putative racial distinctiveness of the Jew, given the governing and immutable postulates of the racial analysis of nationality and national history, made it impossible for the Jew to be seen as a loyal, integrated member of any state. His racial destiny, the genetic and meta-genetic imperatives to which he was subordinate, demanded his transcendence, or subscendence, of national parameters at the same time that they required that he work for the exploitation of all political entities in his own self-interest. In this ontological necessity rooted in blood lies the ground of his alliance with revolutionaries and revolution, though it extends even beyond the Marxist-Revolutionary category. For according to the logic of extreme racial antisemitism, the Jew's meta-political nature is a telling symptom of his normative standing outside the ordinary universe of obligations and rights normally imposed by national criteria and definition. Not belonging to any polity (other than that of the Jewish people), the Jew feels no obligations to any civic morality, and thus, conversely, he exists outside the accepted realm of human rights. Accordingly, the human transactions between the Jew and others are ethically anachronistic, with the consequence that the juridical and ethical premises that otherwise apply to intergroup relations do not obtain in the case of political relations with Jews and the Jewish community. Recognizing this, the Jew-hater seeks to reverse the entire process of emancipation that has occurred since the French Revolution, the erroneous axiomatic basis of which is the human equality, the fundamental anthropological sameness, of the Jew. "A rational antisemitism," Hitler would therefore write, "must lead to the systematic legal fight against and the elimination of the prerogatives of the Jew. . . . Its ultimate goal, however, must unalterably be the elimination of the Jews."[88]

This call for disemancipation was, of course, not invented in its generality by the antisemites of the Weimar era. What the post-1918 generation did witness, however, was a deepening of the political exclusiveness envisioned by such a program as a consequence of the new emphasis on the racial nature of this heretofore largely socio-political question. When the *Judenfrage* was thus transformed into a meta-biological issue, its very character was transmogrified to such an extent that it eventually fed, after many unexpected and unpredictable turns, a genocidal rather than a national-exclusivist (i.e., one that favored disenfranchisement and expulsion) teleology. Ahaseurus, according to classical Christian anti-Judaism, had to wander, had to be made to wander, but his life was inviolate and his journey could end through his adoption of the true faith. By contrast, Hitler and the racial ideologues of the right after 1918 spoke in a new and different idiom. On the one hand they repeated the slogans about legal disenfranchisement, e.g., the *NSDAP* Party Program of February 24, 1920, called for the end of all Jewish gains in civil status achieved since Emancipation as well as the deportation of the Jews under certain conditions, while, on the other hand, they also spoke far more ominously about "eliminating the Jews altogether."[89] This extremism found voice because Jewish racial corruption could not be warded off simply by keeping it at arm's length, or even by some mysterious process of "conversion," for race, especially the assault of microbial racial infection, could not be neutralized by expulsion nor rendered harmless by dunkings in the baptismal font. "With the Jews there can be no bargaining, but only the hard either-or."[90]

Above all, it needs to be understood that, from the Hitlerian perspective, the Jewish assault on the nations of Europe was racial rather than national in character and victory came not through conquest but through pollution. A polluted people becomes weakened and thereby enslaved, genes not armies decide the fate of the world. In this light

the highest purpose of the folkish state is its care for the preservation of those racial primal elements which, by providing culture, create the beauty and dignity of a higher humanity. We, as Aryans, are therefore able to imagine a state only as the living organism of a people *[Volkstum]* which not only safeguards the preservation of that people, but which by a further training of its spiritual and ideal abilities, leads it to the highest freedom.[91]

In speaking here of freedom Hitler, as ever, is not referring to the freedom of the individual but rather to that of the state and to its primordial basis the *Volk*. Understanding this, one is able to comprehend the pseudo-organic meaning he attributes to the state: "The German Reich, as a State, should include all Germans; it has not only the task of collecting from the people the most valuable stocks of racially primal elements and preserving them, but also to lead them, gradually and safely, to a dominating position."[92] By comparison, "the final goal," Hitler writes of Jewish racial supranationalism, "is denationalization, is sowing confusion by the bastardization of other nations, lowering the racial level of the highest, and dominating this racial stew by exterminating the folkish intelligentsias and replacing them by members of his own race."[93]

Going still further, it must be understood that for Hitler, and here we summarize a more complex conceptual deconstruction of the metaphysical dogmatics of Nazism,[94] the Jews are not merely human enemies, but incarnations of the principles of darkness and chaos that transcend all that is human and virtuous and thus their transcendence of the nation, that structure through which men give form to their lives and through which they protect their racial purity, is in keeping with their inner and essential nature. As such, their supranationalism, their "internationalism," is reflective of the metaphysical *Kampf* between the "human," the racially pure, most authentically represented by the Aryan, humanity's highest fruit, and the non-human Jew. "If our people and our state become victims of these bloodthirsty and avaricious Jewish tyrants of nations, the whole earth will sink into the snares of this octopus."[95] The Jew is external, systematically and naturally alien, not only to Germany or France, to this nation or that, but to all nations, all units of human fellowship, all circles of noble and "pure" blood. It is for this reason, predicated on this ontological decipherment of Jewish supranationalism, that the stakes are so high in the Aryan-Semite encounter: "if Germany frees herself from this embrace [of the octopus], this greatest of dangers to man may be regarded as broken for the whole world." [96] Israel is not only another human competitor and her potential victory means not only economic exploitation, colonial oppression and political domination; rather, and far more serious, with all the gravity of a pathogenic catastrophe: "Judah is the plague of the world." [97] And why is Jewry such a dire threat? Because she encourages in her own self-interest "Blood mixing and lowering of the race. . . . For this reason internationalmindedness [read Jews] is to be regarded as the mortal enemy of these [noble racial] values." [98] Or put differently, the nation ideally emerges from the *Volk,* while the Jew, in the name of the nation, would destroy the *Volk* through miscegenation.

In pursuit of his ends the Jew's assault on nations [and *Volk*] takes, in addition to the manifestations of revolution and induced chaos, two additional, significant forms. The first is as economic exploiter, a theme with particular resonance in inflation-ridden and then depression-bound Weimar. The second is as degenerator of culture, the all-powerful destroyer of the virtuous and sublime. The theme of economic corruption needs little elaboration; its untruth has been made a cliché, but it is no less decisively destructive for that. Neither did it matter that in fact the German Jewish community was seriously impoverished by the same economic gyrations that caused havoc within the population at large. The number of upper-middle-class Jews, for example, judging by the tax register, dropped nearly 50% during the 1920s. In 1912, 10.6% of Berlin Jews earned over 5,000 marks a year; in 1924 this number had fallen to 5.8%, while the number of Jews with incomes under 1,200 marks jumped from 73.3% of the Jewish population to 83.6%. In addition, the Berlin Jewish community alone was forced to open nineteen soup kitchens and seven shelters for the homeless. [99] Donald Niewyk has also pointed out that "signs of [economic] decline within the Jewish middle class were by no means confined to the years of inflation and depression" but continued throughout the later years of the Weimar era. [100]

Nonetheless, though the hyperinflation destroyed the lives of Jews and non-Jews alike, this indiscriminate economic victimization proved an enormously effective tool for antisemitic propagandists. Both in 1923 and then even more importantly after 1930, inflation, wedded to the other deep civic and political dislocations of the Weimar era, caused a social vertigo in which people lost their sense of place and order, finding eventual re-equilibrium only in Nazism's preachments about righting the existing economic and related wrongs. The national trauma of defeat and Versailles, the sense of shame and national weakness exposed and betrayed by "the Jew," were the enemy that Nazism, above all other parties, consistently attacked with unsparing, single-minded vehemence. Where inflation generated uncertainty, Hitler promised fiscal and political certainty; where economic chaos threatened all security, Hitler pledged to solve the economic crisis and provide security; where society appeared to be devolving, Hitler spoke of social coherence; where Weimar was the new, the urban, the "un-German," Hitler promoted the old, conservative virtues (or so it appeared), the agrarian-*völkisch* style, the true Germanic manner; where a near-chiliastic sense of doom, even annihilation settled over large segments of the populace as their financial independence and life-long savings eroded, Hitler appeared as a savior possessed of heavenly secrets through which the kingdom could be achieved;[101] where Germany was passive before its enemies, Hitler encouraged direct action; where 1918 and after were the fault of the new exploitative master-class, the Jews, Hitler made a commitment to return things to their proper order—Aryans on top, Jews on the bottom. Anomie,[102] individual and collective, monetary and normative, was the consequence of this many-sided disarray, while National Socialism believed itself, and made others believe, it was the re-integrative antidote.

It is not accidental that Nazi electoral popularity was directly related to the degree of economic uncertainty felt among Weimar's citizenry. Between 1924 and 1928, relatively prosperous and secure years for the Republic, the Nazis' share of the vote, as that of right-wing parties in general, continually diminished while the Social Democratic Party, the party most deeply committed to the Weimar Republic, prospered. In 1928 the *SDP* elected its first Chancellor in eight years and saw its popular vote increase by over one million, while the *NSDAP* saw its share of the electorate drop to 810,000 votes, a mere 2.6% of the vote.[103] In contrast, the Depression reversed this trend, pushing the Nazi vote to unprecedented heights. In the election of September 1930 they gained 107 seats, 6,410,000 votes, or 18.3% of the vote, and this count rose to 230 seats in the July 1932 elections. Alternatively, as the economy improved in the fall of 1932 Nazi popularity declined and by

November 1932, they had lost two million votes and 34 seats,[104] a negative trend that continued through the remainder of 1932.[105]

According to Nazism's sovereign mythology, international Jewry manipulated the economies of countries for their own gain, while they avoided the pain associated with local economic catastrophes by being supranationalists. That the real causes of German economic disarray lay elsewhere, namely in the vast governmental overexpenditures that exceeded government income by over thirty million reichmarks[106] between 1920 and 1923 was of no consequence, for the republican leadership was, in any case, Jewish. But if the Nazis' explanation of the inflation was altogether deficient, it nevertheless had the "positive" virtue that it seemed to make the crisis less the consequence of large and impersonal forces and more the product of intelligible and manageable elements, "The Jews," that every person could understand. It also made for a simple cure: eliminate the Jews. The immediate concrete expression of this rationalization, of this diagnosis, was the large "pogrom" in the Jewish quarter of Berlin on November 5–6, 1923. The same (il)logic applied during the Great Depression, only more so.[107] In this series of crises the eternal semitic enemy stood ready as a convenient explanation.[108]

The second meaningful aspect of the Jew's supranationalism, his corrosive impact on culture, though less significant to the average German, was also trumpeted across the land. The fluid, often vibrant and creative, certainly original, culture of Weimar was seen as shockingly debased and "un-German" by the cultural mandarins of the right.[109] To them, its experimentation and novelty were a sign of moral[110] and aesthetic decay. And the role of the Jews in the ferment was not lost on friends and foe alike. Walter Laqueur's summary of Jewish participation is succinct as well as accurate:

Without the Jews there would have been no "Weimar culture"—to this extent the claims of the antisemites, who detested that culture, were justified. They were in the forefront of every new, daring, revolutionary movement. They were prominent among Expressionist poets, among the novelists of the 1920s, among the theatrical producers and, for a while, among the leading figures in the cinema. They owned the leading liberal newspapers such as the *Berliner Tageblatt*, the *Vossische Zeitung* and the *Frankfurter Zeitung,* and many editors were Jews too. Many leading liberal and avant-garde publishing houses were in Jewish hands (S. Fischer, Kurt Wolff, the Cassirers, Georg Bondi, Erich Reiss, the Malik Verlag). Many leading theatre critics were Jews, and they dominated light entertainment.[111]

Rather than appreciating this creativity, the despisers of Weimar culture viewed all these developments with genuine alarm. To the anti-semites they represented another form of the Jewish virus, of the Jewish racial attack on all that was orderly, vigorous and healthy in traditional German life. "The metropolis began its race-annihilation work. . . . A race chaos of Germans, Jews, and anti-natural street races was abroad. The result was mongrel art."[112] As a being devoid of the higher human characteristics, certainly barren of desirous virtues, the Jew is incapable of producing authentic, ennobling spiritual products. "Culturally," Hitler argues, the Jews' "activity consists in bowdlerizing art, literature, and the theatre, holding the expressions of national sentiment up to scorn, overturning concepts of the sublime and beautiful, the worthy and the good, finally dragging the people to the level of his own low mentality."[113] At the same time, this materialistic racial shallowness makes him envious of the high innovativeness of others. He is therefore the enemy of all aesthetic and cultural greatness. And this negative vulgarizing proclivity has its roots in racial soil: "to turn upside down the most natural hygienic rules of a race. The Jew makes night into day; he stages the notorious night life and knows quite well that it will slowly but surely destroy . . .";[114] and again, "Blood mixture and the resultant drop in the racial level is the sole cause of the dying out of old cultures."[115]

With this contention the biological circle comes full turn: every decrepitude, every vice, every degeneracy political, economic, and cultural has one cause, racial decay, one causal agent: "The Jews." And this in a period of political fluidity when the *NSDAP* was still a minority party, distant from the mechanisms of power, those mechanisms which when controlled in totalitarian fashion drive the ideological to become still more absolute and extreme in the absence of sufficient resistance. Fed by the reality of power, the theoretical becomes more, not less extreme in the actuality of its implementation.[116] This is true not only of Nazism, but also of Stalinism, Maoism, Castroism and the Cambodian regime of Pol Pot, among many possible examples. For us this means that racial antisemitism, raised to previously unprecedented heights in Weimar, would know still more unrestrained expression and incomparable genocidal reality in the years of Nazi political control. And even before this final, deadly transformation of the political landscape of Germany and her allies, this racial perspective would have scored a notable success in setting a good deal of the political agenda—even for those in the political center and left. The universally heightened sensitivity to Jewish issues caused by the unrelenting propaganda of the extreme right forced the shape of political debate into contours constructed out of, even if opposed to, this racial program. In this way the racists of the Weimar era can already be seen to have achieved a lasting victory, for they had succeeded in undermining the *givenness* of Jewish emancipation and Jewry's collective participation in a modern pluralistic Europe.[117]

NOTES

1. It needs to be emphasized that in the discussion that follows, the focus is on a typological account of the roots and nature of Weimar and more specifically Hitlerian antisemitism. As such, it over-emphasizes this factor in Weimar life to a certain degree. To correct this historical distortion, i.e., to properly situate our analysis in its historical context, it must be noted that the outright antisemitic parties never garnered more than 8% of the total vote during the life of the Weimar Republic prior to 1930.

2. Koppel Pinson, *Modern Germany* (New York, 1955), p. 419.

3. On the demographic profile of Weimar Jewry, consult Eric Rosenthal, "Trends in Jewish Population in Germany, 1910–1939," *Jewish Social Studies*, Vol. 6 (1944), pp. 233–74; Esra Bennathan's essay on "Die demographische und wirtschaftliche Struktur der Juden," in Werner E. Mosse and Arnold Paucker (eds.), *Entscheidungsjahr 1932; Zur Judenfrage in der Endphase der Weimarer Republik* (Tübingen, 1966), pp. 87–131; and Donald L. Niewyk, *The Jews in Weimar Germany* (Baton Rouge, 1980), pp. 11–42. Peter Gay, *Freud, Jews and Other Germans* (New York, 1978), calls attention to the demographic growth of the Ostjuden in Germany in the first quarter of the twentieth century. In 1900 there were approximately 11,000 Ostjuden in Berlin out of a total Jewish population of 92,000. This figure increased fourfold in absolute terms and doubled in percentage terms by 1925 when Ostjuden numbered 43,000 out of a Berlin Jewish population of 172,000 or 25.4% (p. 172).

4. R. H. Lutz, *The German Revolution, 1918–1919* (Stanford, 1922); Gerhard A. Ritter and Susanne Miller (eds.), *Die deutsche Revolution 1918–1919* (Frankfurt a. M., 1968); Allan Mitchell, *Revolution in Bavaria, 1918–1919: The Eisner Regime and the Soviet Republic* (Princeton, 1965); Gordon Craig, *Germany 1866–1945* (New York, 1978), pp. 396–414; and David W. Morgan, *The Socialist Left and the German Revolution: A History of the German Independent Social Democratic Party, 1917–1922* (Ithaca, 1975).

5. Robert Waite, *Vanguard of Nazism: The Free Corps Movement in Germany, 1918–1923* (Cambridge, 1952); Johannes Erger, *Der Kapp-Lüttwitz Putsch. Ein Beitrag zur deutschen Innenpolitik 1919–20* (Düsseldorf, 1967); G. Craig, *Germany*, pp. 429–32; and John W. Wheeler-Bennett, *The Ne-*

mesis of Power: The Army in Politics, 1918–1945 (London, 1953), pp. 60–82.

6. There are a number of valuable narrative histories of this era from which I have benefited: Gordon Craig, *Germany 1866–1945;* Koppel Pinson, *Modern Germany* (New York, 1955); Erich Eyck, *A History of the Weimar Republic,* 2 Vols. (Cambridge, 1962–1965); Albert Schwartz, *Die Weimarer Republik* (Konstanz, 1958); Hajo Holborn, *A History of Modern Germany* (New York, 1969); Donald L. Niewyk, *Jews in Weimar;* and Ferdinand Friedensburg, *Die Weimarer Republik* (Berlin, 1946).

7. Of course, for racist thinkers like Hitler all these, and many other phenomena, are just the outward expression of more deeply rooted racial laws.

8. Adolf Hitler, *Main Kampf* (German edition, Munich, 1941), p. 296.

9. P. Merkl's evidence, based on the Abel interviews (cf. Theodore Abel, *The Nazi Movement: Why Hitler Came to Power* [New York, 1966]), puts this figure at 46% of veterans, *Political Violence under the Swastika* (Princeton, 1975).

10. K. Pinson, *Modern Germany,* p. 414, notes that "not a single school text in Weimar Germany presented the true story of German defeat in 1918." As a consequence, this resentment at Allied and "fifth columnist" behavior, as well as at the Weimar Republic for "agreeing" to exist on such terms, was passed on to successive generations of young Germans which in turn made "high school and universities . . . focal centers for the rightist nationalist movements" among both students and faculty. On education in Weimar, see also G. Craig, *Germany,* pp. 421–24. This issue has been helpfully analyzed in the important works of Wolfgang Kreutzberger, *Studenten und Politik 1918–1933: Der Fall Freiburg-im-Breisgau* (Göttingen, 1972); and R. H. Samuel and R. H. Thomas, *Education and Society in Modern Germany* (London, 1949). The importance of these facts is brought home by the Abel interviews which reveal that 50% of politicized activist Nazi youth in the 1920s reported "having had a völkisch or Nazi teacher or conflict with Jewish fellow students" at school, P. Merkl, *Political Violence,* p. 277. On the opposition to Weimar in the universities, see W. Laqueur, *Weimar: A Cultural History 1918–1933* (London, 1974), pp. 183–223. Laqueur describes the majority of professors "as reactionary *tout court,* the minority was *vernunftrepublikanisch,* pro-republican because they accepted it as a political necessity, rather than out of instinct or deep moral conviction" (p. 184).

11. Note the responses of early Nazis to the defeat as reported in P. Merkl, *Political Violence,* pp. 144–88.

12. It should be noted that the German Communist Party also railed against the "chains of Versailles": see K. Pinson, *Modern Germany,* p. 417.

13. Jews were already singled out in this respect by the 1916 War Ministry census carried out in order to check on the rate of German participation in the war. On this issue, see the early study by Franz Oppenheimer, *Die Judenstatistik des Preussischen Kriegsministeriums* (Munich, 1922); Egmont Zechlin, *Die deutsche Politik und die Judem im ersten Weltkrieg* (Göttingen, 1969), pp. 524–37; and Werner Angress, "Das deutsche Militär und die

Juden im Ersten Weltkrieg," in *Militärgeschichtliche Mitteilungen,* Vol. 19 (1976), pp. 77–146. In respect of this issue it is surely ironic, as Robert Waite points out, that Hitler's Iron Cross First and Second Class, earned during the war, was only granted to him as a consequence of the strenuous effort made on his behalf by his adjutant, Hugo Gutmann, who was Jewish. R. Waite, "Hitler's Antisemitism," in B. Wolman (ed.), *The Psychoanalytic Interpretation of History* (New York, 1971), p. 195.

14. See P. Merkl's *Political Violence,* p. 169; and also pp. 213–14.
15. The official German count gives 539,000 Jews in Germany in 1910, 0.92% of the population.
16. Figures given in Hugo Valentin, *Antisemitism: Historically and Critically Examined* (New York, 1936), p. 109.
17. P. Merkl, *Political Violence,* p. 166.
18. I purposely use this general and vague term, rather than identifying specific left-of-center political parties, because this is how Hitler and the right-wing parties used it. The unspecific abstraction served better.
19. Peter Gay calls this connection to the fore by reminding us that "Hugo Preuss, the architect of the Weimar constitution, was a symbol of revolution; as a Jew and a left-wing democrat, he had been kept out of the university establishment for all his merits, and now he, the outsider, gave shape to the new republic, *his* Republic." *Weimar Culture* (New York, 1968), p. 17. Then again, the flag of the Republic was accused by nationalists of containing "the yellow stripe of Jewry." Cited in E. Eyck, *History of Weimar,* Vol. 1, p. 190.
20. Cited by E. Eyck, *History of Weimar,* Vol. 1, p. 315.
21. On the *Deutschnationale Volkspartei,* see the monograph by that title by Werner Liebe (Düsseldorf, 1956).
22. Quoted in W. Liebe, *Deutschnationale Volkspartei,* p. 115.
23. *Mein Kampf,* pp. 388 and 452–53.
24. Ibid., p. 252.
25. E. Jäckal observed this same phenomenon in *Mein Kampf:*

    In the antisemitic passages one is struck, first of all, by a very peculiar vocabulary. Here is a catalogue from Volume One of *Mein Kampf* as it appears there in the sequence of pages: The Jew is a maggot in a rotting corpse; he is a plague worse than the Black Death of former times; a germ center of the worst sort; mankind's eternal germ of disunion; the drone which insinuates its way into the rest of mankind; the spider that slowly sucks the people's blood out of its pores; the pack of rats fighting bloodily among themselves; the parasite in the body of other peoples; the typical parasite; a sponger who like a harmful bacillus, continues to spread; the eternal bloodsucker; the peoples' parasite; the people's vampire. Almost all of these expressions derive from the realm of parasitology; the Jew was isolated from the rest of human society, and the use of language suggests the methods of his elimination. (Jäckal, *Hitler's Weltanschauung, A Blueprint for Power* [Middletown, 1972], pp. 58–59)

26. Cited by R. Binion, *Hitler among the Germans* (New York, 1976), pp. 36 and 39. This theme was an *idée fixe* of Hitler's which never changed. Thus

in 1941, in his table talk with Himmler, he reminded him "that race of criminals [Jews] has on its conscience the two million [German] dead of the first world war and now hundreds of thousands more" (p. 87).

27. Cited by R. Binion, *Hitler among the Germans,* p. 24.

28. In *Mein Kampf* (English edition, trans. R. Manheim [Boston, 1943]; henceforth cited as E.T., p. 800), he would demand that "some day a German national court will have to sentence and to execute some ten thousand of the organizing and thus responsible criminals of the November treason."

29. *Mein Kampf* (E.T.), p. 984.

30. Cited by R. Binion, *Hitler among the Germans,* pp. 26, 27, 28.

31. Hitler's extremism was, of course, not yet acceptable generally and would also have to wait its turn, which was not too long coming.

32. G. Craig, *Germany,* pp. 424–25.

33. These are well summarized by K. Pinson:

> For the average German, irrespective of political party, and reconciled though he might have become to the restoration of Alsace-Lorraine to France and Eupen and Malmédy to Belgium, the Treaty of Versailles was an "instrument of subjugation." It had turned over German territory and German population in the east to Poland, a nation traditionally regarded by Germans as beneath contempt; it created the "impossible" Polish corridor which divided the German Reich in two and cut off the "hallowed" soil of East Prussia from the rest of the Reich. Measured in terms of the resources of Germany before the war, the treaty meant the loss of 13 per cent of its territory, 10 per cent of its population, 100 per cent of its colonial domain, about 15 per cent of its arable land, 74.5 per cent of its iron ore, 26 per cent of its hard coal assets, 68 per cent of its zinc, 17 per cent of its potato yield, 16 per cent of its rye, and 13 per cent of its wheat. To top all that, the Treaty of Versailles meant the complete demilitarization of Germany and the military occupation by the Allied powers of 6 per cent of its remaining domain. (K. Pinson, *Modern Germany,* pp. 424–25)

34. This was argued very strongly, for example, by Ludwig Zimmermann, *Deutsche Aussenpolitik* (Göttingen, 1958), pp. 474f. But cf. the useful review of the evidence by Erich Matthias, "The Influence of the Versailles Treaty on the Internal Development of the Weimar Republic," in Anthony Nicholls and Erich Matthias, (eds.), *German Democracy and the Triumph of Hitler* (New York, 1971), pp. 13–28. See also E. Eyck, *History of Weimar,* Vol. 1, pp. 80–128.

35. It was not accidental that the peace conference began on January 18, the anniversary of the founding of the German Empire, in the same Hall of Mirrors where the victorious Germans had issued the proclamation of Empire fifty years earlier, while June 28, the signing date, was the date of Archduke Ferdinand's assassination. J. Fest, *Hitler* (New York, 1973), p. 82.

36. *Völkische Beobachter,* April 6, 1920.

37. In addition to the recurrence of this theme in *Mein Kampf* and Hitler's early *Reden,* see also Hermann Göring, *Germany Reborn* (London, 1934), pp. 19–20; the interviews in T. Abel, *The Nazi Movement;* and P. Merkl's two

volumes, *Political Violence* already cited and *The Making of a Stormtrooper* (Princeton, 1980).
38. Electoral figures summarized from V. R. Berghahn, *Modern Germany* (Cambridge [England], 1982), p. 74. Consult also on the entire question, Karl Bracher, *Die Auflösung der Weimarer Republik* (Villengen, 1960³). The results of the Weimar elections are closely analyzed by Alfred Milatz, *Wähler und Wahlen in der Weimarer Republik* (Bonn, 1965). For the election of 1920, see pp. 29–39.
39. For more on the lasting effects of the defeat of 1918 on Nazi ideology and practice, see the interesting essay by Tim Mason, "The Legacy of 1918 for National Socialism," in A. Nicholls and E. Matthias (eds.), *German Democracy and the Triumph of Hitler*, pp. 215–39.
40. P. Merkl, *Political Violence*, pp. 511–12. See also, as a related indicator of such sentiment, Joseph Goebbels, *Der Angriff* (Munich, 1935), and again Hermann Göring, "Wahrt das Recht des Volkes," *Völkischer Beobachter*, Sept. 11/12, 1932. Göring laments: "The destruction of Carthage was as nothing compared to the shameful peace of Versailles."
41. *Mein Kampf*, p. 454.
42. Ibid., p. 465.
43. Ibid., p. 639.
44. Henry Ford's antisemitism is intelligently and fairly discussed by Leo Ribuffo, "Henry Ford and *The International Jew*," *American Jewish History*, Vol. 69 (June, 1980), pp. 437–77.
45. *Mein Kampf*, p. 640. Emphasis in original.
46. Ibid., p. 651. Emphasis in original.
47. Adolf Hitler, *The Secret Book* (New York, 1983), pp. 27–28. Emphasis in original.
48. *The Secret Book*, pp. 28–29.
49. See G. Craig's description of the role Rathenau's Jewishness played, *Germany*, pp. 441–42. Also, for more on this issue, note the sources listed in Craig, *Germany*, pp. 441–42, note 18.
50. The objective truth was vastly different. Jews were still approximately 1% of the total population, in 1925 there were 568,000 Jews out of a total population of 63,181,000, or 0.90%. Intermarriage was rampant, reaching 24% in 1929. Economically Jews were overwhelmingly middle-class, only 2% were, despite antisemitic propaganda, bankers or stockbrokers. For the detailed breakdown of Jewish demographic and economic life in Weimar, see Esra Bennathan, "Die demographische und wirtschaftliche Struktur der Juden," in W. Mosse and A. Paucker (eds.), *Entscheidungsjahr 1932*, pp. 87–131. They were considerably overrepresented in the white-collar professions; 16% of Germany's lawyers, 10% of her doctors, 3% of her university teachers, 5% of her journalists and 4% of her creative artists were Jews. I summarize here the discussion of Karl A. Schleunes, *The Twisted Road to Auschwitz* (Urbana, 1970), pp. 38–41. In addition, and very important, Jews did not "control" the press, over 50% of which was owned by Alfred Hugenberg, chairman of the right-wing *DNVP*, Hitler's coalition partner in

1933. The quote from Peter Merkl's work is from his *Political Violence*, p. 559.

51. K. Pinson defends the Versailles Treaty as being as good as could be expected under the circumstances and not unduly harsh by prevailing standards, e.g., the German treaty of Brest Litovsk with Russia, *Modern Germany*, p. 423.

52. Discussed by Arno J. Mayer, *Politics and Diplomacy of Peacemaking: Containment and Counter-Revolution at Versailles, 1918–1919* (New York, 1967); and G. Craig, *Germany*, pp. 424ff.

53. Cited in K. Pinson, *Modern Germany*, p. 429. See also on this entire issue, David Adler, *Walter Rathenau and the Weimar Republic: The Politics of Reparations* (Baltimore, 1971). It is also not irrelevant to this matter that Alfred Rosenberg had publicly linked Rathenau to Bolshevism and Bolshevism to World Jewish power in his 1922 pamphlet *Pest in Russland*.

54. Cited by E. Eyck, *History of Weimar*, Vol. 1, p. 215.

55. G. Craig, *Germany*, p. 444, note 27, censures David Adler, *Walter Rathenau and the Weimar Republic*, for "over-emphasizing" antisemitism as the motive for Rathenau's murder. It appears to me that Craig is wrong in this judgment, given the virulent attack upon Rathenau *qua* Jew. After all, the right had cited, "Knallt ab den Juden Rathenau/die Gottverdammte Judensau," while right-wing groups sang "Schlagt tot den Walter Rathenau / Die gottverfluchte Judenau." Cf. also E. Eyck, *History of Weimar*, Vol. 1, pp. 211F. Consider also as paradigmatic here, i.e., the turning against the Jews as traitors who could become "scapegoats" for Germany's defeat, Ludendorff's memoirs, *Kriegsführung und Politik* (Berlin, 1922), in which he decries "the Supreme Government of the Jewish People who work hand and hand with France and England." The role of the *Protocols of the Elders of Zion* in the thinking of Rathenau's murderers, i.e., of Rathenau as one of these Elders, as described by them at their trial, also strongly suggests that Rathenau's Jewishness was central to his assassination. There is an important discussion of this connection in Norman Cohn, *Warrant for Genocide* (New York, 1969), pp. 141–48 and 178–79. For details, see also Eyck's summary, *History of Weimar*, Vol. 1, p. 214. The political careers of Hilferding and Heilmann, two Jewish ministers in later Weimar governments, are also instructive on this point. Recently, Henry Pachter, "Walter Rathenau: Musil's Arnheim or Mann's Naphta?" in his *Weimar Studies* (New York, 1982), pp. 171–88, also called attention to the ironic role the *Protocols* played among those who wanted Rathenau to serve as Foreign Minister, hoping that as one of the *Elders* he could influence the reparations treaty, p. 171. Pachter also writes (p. 186): "He was murdered not because of what he stood for but because of what he was—for being Jewish." Alternatively, one must acknowledge how common political murder in early Weimar was. One fair estimate suggests that there were 376 political murders between 1919 and 1922, 354 committed by the right, George Mosse, *The Final Solution* (New York, 1978), p. 183.

56. G. Mosse, *Final Solution*, pp. 175–76, calls attention to the importance of

the use of black troops in the 1919–1920 French occupation and the role they played in enflaming racial concerns and hatreds in Weimar Germany. The Jews, not unexpectedly, were accused by the right, of causing this "disgrace," of waging a "Negro-Jewish" war on Germany. This issue is also explored in more detail in Keith L. Nelson, "The Black Horror on the Rhine: Race as a Factor in Post-War I Diplomacy," *Journal of Modern History*, Vol. 42, No. 4 (December, 1970), pp. 606–28. The French were careful *not* to repeat this experiment in 1923 when no black soldiers served in the occupation of the Ruhr.

57. Such obligations were continually attacked by the right as turning Germany into little more than a slave-labor colony or the victorious allies. See, e.g., Hitler's remarks in his *Reden* (Würzburg, 1962–63), Vol. 1, pp. 7–8, (ed.) M. Domarus; and Alfred Rosenberg, *Der Mythus des 20. Juhrhunderts* (Munich, 1930), p. 1, for the repetition and exploitation of this theme.

58. These events are described more fully in D. Niewyk, *Jews in Weimar*, pp. 109–10.

59. These events, and the circumstances surrounding them, are analyzed by Hans Schmidt, *Die polnische Revolution des Jahres 1848 im Grossherzogtum Posen* (Weimar, 1912), pp. 150–52; on the Jewish issues, see A. Heppner and J. Herzberg, *Aus Vergangenheit und Gegenwart der Juden und der jüdischen Gemeinden in den Posener Landen* (Koschmen-Bromberg, 1909), pp. 851–52. A useful review of the nationality question in Poland is now available in William W. Hagen's, *Germans, Poles and Jews: The Nationality Conflict in the Prussian East, 1772–1914* (Chicago, 1980), pp. 109, 116–17.

60. A classic defense of this thesis is presented by Hermann Cohen, "Deutschtum und Judentum," in his *Jüdische Schriften*, 2 Vols. (Berlin, 1924). The classic critique of this position has been offered by Gershom Scholem in his essay, "Wider den Mythos vom deutsch–jüdischen Gespräch," in his collected essays, *Judaica*, Vol. 2 (Frankfurt, 1970), p. 7ff.

61. The events leading up to this rebellion are described by Daniel Horn, *The German Naval Mutinies of World War I* (New Brunswick, 1969), and in more summary fashion by G. Craig, *Germany*, pp. 398–400; and K. Pinson, *Modern Germany*, pp. 355–57.

62. For a full review see A. Mitchell, *Revolution in Bavaria;* and G. Ritter and S. Miller, *Die deutsche Revolution;* briefer reviews are found in G. Craig, *Germany*, pp. 400–402; and K. Pinson, *Modern Germany*, pp. 357–65.

63. Cf. Eric Waldman, *The Spartacist Uprising of 1919 and the Crisis of the German Socialist Movement* (Milwaukee, 1958).

64. On this coalition, see Harold Gordon, *The Reichswehr and the German Republic 1919–1926* (Princeton, 1957); G. Waite, *Vanguard of Nazism;* G. Craig, *Germany*, pp. 402–12; K. Pinson, *Modern Germany*, pp. 366–91; and F. L. Carsten, *The Reichswehr and Politics, 1918–1933* (Oxford, 1966).

65. A description of the major political groups and their views on the *Judenfrage* and relationship to antisemitism is provided by D. Niewyk, *Jews in Weimar*, p. 43–81.

66. "In Russian Bolshevism we must see the attempt undertaken by the Jews in the twentieth century to achieve world domination," *Mein Kampf*, p. 960.

67. See Hitler's speech of November 1928 on the "November Criminals"; "The Jewess Rosa Luxemburg"; and "The Jew Kurt Eisner." The Jewish presence in revolutionary councils was, of course, a reality. See, e.g., on Ludwig Marum and Ludwig Haas, two Jews in the Baden revolutionary government of 1918, John Peter Grill, *The Nazi Movement in Baden, 1920–1945* (Chapel Hill, 1983), p. 30. One should also recall the role of Paul Hirsch in the Prussian revolutionary government and that of George Gridnauer in Saxony, while the role of Luxemburg, Liebknecht and Eisner requires no further comment. For a detailed biography of Luxemburg, see Gilbert Badia, *Rosa Luxemburg, Journaliste, polémiste, révolutionnaire* (Paris, 1975); while on Liebknecht, see Helmut Trotnow, "The Misunderstood Karl Liebknecht," *European Studies Review*, Vol. 5, No. 2 (1975), pp. 171–91; and Enzo Collotti, "Karl Liebknecht e il Problema della Rivoluzione Socialista in Germania," *Ann. dell'Instituto Giangiacomo Feltrinelli*, Vol. 15 (1973), pp. 326–43. Note also the reporting of these events in serious papers such as the *Augsburger Postzeitung* and the *Münchener Neueste Nachrichten*, not to mention the gutter journals of the extreme right. On the entire issue, see Werner Angress, "Juden im politischen Leben der Revolutionszeit," in W. Mosse and A. Paucker (eds.), *Deutsche Judentum in Kreig und Revolution* (Tübingen, 1971), pp. 137–315.

68. P. Merkl, *Political Violence*, p. 146. See also Merkl's statistical breakdown on the attribution of "causes" of the revolution to specific groups, p. 289.

69. The role of the *Protocols of the Elders of Zion* is very important here.

70. J. Fest, *Hitler*, p. 211, based on Hitler's remarks to Dietrich Eckart while in Landsberg Prison.

71. Cited in J. Fest, *Hitler*, p. 132.

72. G. Mosse, *Final Solution*, pp. 182–83. On the circulation of the *Protocols* in post-1918 Germany, consult N. Cohn, *Warrant*, pp. 130ff. See also on the Schutz-und-Trutz Bund, Uwe Lohalm, *Volkischer Radicalismus: Die Geschichte des Deutschvölkischen Schutz-und-Trutz-Bundes* (Hamburg, 1970), throughout.

73. The irony here is notable in that it was Freytag who, in 1869, defended Jews against Wagner's attack in the journal *Die Grenzboten*. In reply to Wagner's antisemitic call, Freytag wrote of the Jews that "in no area are they predominantly representatives of a trend which we must hold socially injurious." "Der Streit über das Judentum in der Musik," *Die Grenzboten*, No. 22 (1869), reprinted in G. Freytag's *Gesammelte Werke*, Vol. 16 (Leipzig, 1898), pp. 321–26. Quoted from Alfred D. Low, *Jews in the Eyes of the Germans: From the Enlightenment to Imperial Germany* (Philadelphia, 1979), p. 338. See his entire discussion of "Freytag vs. Wagner," pp. 338–39. In the *Mitteilungen des Vereins zur Abwehr des Antisemitismus* for 1895, a letter is recorded from 1892 indicating that Freytag married a Jewess and even supported her son's (his stepson's) Hebrew instruction at home.

74. See D. Niewyk's careful study of Weimar courts. He reminds us that, of course, not all, or even most courts were under the sway of radical antisemitism. However, such attitudes did exist, and were both actualized in specific instances, and agitated for all the time by the racial antisemites. For a full discussion, see D. Niewyk, "Jews and the Courts in Weimar Germany," *Jewish Social Studies,* Vol. 37 (1975), pp. 99–113; and his summary in idem, *Jews in Weimar,* pp. 74–77. See also Thilo Ramm (ed.), *Die Justiz in der Weimarer Republik: Eine Chronik* (Neuwied and Berlin, 1968); Ambrose Dozkow and Sidney Jacoby, "Anti-Semitism and the Law in Pre-Nazi Germany," *Contemporary Jewish Record,* Vol. 3, No. 5 (1940), pp. 498–509; and Heinrich Hannover-Druck, *Politische Justiz 1918–1933* (Frankfurt a. M., 1966), pp. 263–73. An indictment of the right-wing sympathies of the courts is provided by P. Gay, *Weimar Culture,* pp. 20–21.
75. The character and significance of antisemitism in the German army during the Weimar era has been briefly summarized by D. Niewyk, *Jews in Weimar,* pp. 77–78.
76. The issue of the enormous rise in student antisemitism is deciphered by Hans Peter Bleuel and Ernst Klinnert, *Deutsche Studenten auf dem Weg ins Dritte Reich* (Gütersloh, 1967); Michael H. Kater, *Studentschaft und Rechtsradikalismus in Deutschland 1918–1933* (Hamburg, 1975); W. Kreutzberger, *Studenten und Politik 1918–1933;* Jürgen Schwartz, *Studenten in der Weimarer Republik* (Berlin, 1971); and Michael S. Steinberg, *Sabers and Brown Shirts: The German Students' Path to National Socialism, 1918–1935* (Chicago, 1973).
77. Cited in J. Fest, *Hitler,* p. 95.
78. *Mein Kampf,* pp. 654ff.
79. The material quoted and the two lines quoted above are from *The Secret Book,* pp. 214–15. See also Hitler's views on Bolshevist Jewry vs. England, pp. 158–59 and 175 of *The Secret Book.*
80. Cited in J. Fest, *Hitler,* p. 92. See also the role the "Jewish Conspiracy Theory" played in the maturing thought of Himmler in Bradley F. Smith, *Heinrich Himmler* (Stanford, 1971), pp. 74–75.
81. *The Secret Book,* pp. 185–86.
82. *Mein Kampf,* p. 61.
83. *The Secret Book,* p. 213.
84. Ibid., p. 58.
85. See on the *SDP* D. Niewyk, *Socialist, Anti-semite, and Jew* (Baton Rouge, 1971); and idem, *Jews in Weimar,* pp. 25–27.
86. As analyzed by P. B. Weiner, "Die Parteien der Mitte," in W. Mosse and A. Paucker (eds.), *Entscheidungsjahr 1932,* pp. 289–321.
87. *Mein Kampf,* p. 249 (E.T., p. 269).
88. Hitler's memo of Sept. 16, 1919, Ernst Deuerlein (ed.), "Hitler's Eintritt in die Politik und Die Reichswehr," in *Vierteljahrssheft für Zeitgeschichte,* Vol. 7 (1959), p. 204.
89. However, one must not read full-blown genocidal intentions into these early post-war phrases.

90. *Mein Kampf* (E.T.), p. 269.
91. Ibid., p. 595.
92. Ibid.
93. Ibid., p. 325.
94. See, as a very preliminary study, my essay, "Hitler's 'Jew': On Microbes and Manicheanism," *Proceedings of the Ninth World Congress of Jewish Studies* (Jerusalem, 1986), Vol. 3, pp. 165–72.
95. *Mein Kampf* (E.T.), pp. 324–27. Of course, Hitler's use of traditional theological notions was only propaganda.
96. See Hitler's remarks on Jewish influence in Britain and Italy in *Mein Kampf* (E.T.), pp. 622ff. Thus he continually ascribed British opposition to "Jewish influence," e.g., late in the war he "confessed": "I myself have underrated one thing: the extent of Jewish influence on Churchill's Englishmen." H. R. Trevor-Roper (ed.), *The Testament of Hitler* (London, 1960), p. 30f. Reading Bernard Wasserstein's indictment of British action (and inaction) during the *Sho'ah, Britain and the Jews of Europe* (New York, 1976), makes one realize how preposterous this notion is.
97. *Mein Kampf* (E.T.), p. 906.
98. Cited by E. Jäckal, *Hitler's Weltanschauung,* p. 57.
99. Cited from D. Niewyk, *Jews in Weimar,* p. 18.
100. Ibid., p. 19.
101. P. Merkl, *Political Violence,* pp. 498ff. calls this "Adolf Hitler's Big Lie." Alternatively, James Rhodes, *The Hitler Movement: A Modern Millenarian Revolution* (Stanford, 1980), has elaborated on this theme at length under the term, borrowed from Michael Barkum, *Disaster and the Millennium* (New York, 1974), "The Disaster Syndrome," pp. 31–42.
102. The important observations of William Kornhauser, *The Politics of Mass Society* (Glencoe, Ill., 1959), are opposite here.
103. These figures are provided by Fred Weinstein, *Dynamics of Nazism* (New York, 1980), p. 60; and J. Fest, *Hitler,* pp. 259–332.
104. See G. Craig, *Germany,* pp. 562–63.
105. Goebbels thus wrote in late 1932: "The year 1932 was one long succession of bad luck. . . . The past was difficult, and the future looks dark and troubled; all prospects and hopes have vanished." Quoted by F. Weinstein, *Dynamics of Nazism,* p. 62.
106. For details consult Gustav Stolper, *German Economy, 1870–1940* (New York, 1940), pp. 81ff; G. Craig, *Germany,* pp. 448–56; K. Laursen and J. Pederson, *The German Inflation of 1923* (New York, 1969); and R. J. Schmidt, *Versailles and the Ruhr* (London, 1968).
107. The impact of the Depression on German Jewry is described by Ernst Hamburger, "One Hundred Years of Emancipation," *Leo Baeck Yearbook,* Vol. 15 (1970), p. 32; D. Niewyk, *Jews in Weimar,* pp. 18–19; and Hans Joachim Bieber, "Anti-Semitism as a Reflection of Social, Economic and Political Tension in Germany, 1880–1933," in David Bronson (ed.), *Jews and Germans from 1860 to 1933* (Heidelberg, 1979), pp. 33–77.

108. And there was much to explain when, e.g., unemployment moved from 1,899,000 in 1929 to 3,076,000 in 1930, 14% of the work force, and then to over 5.4 million by February 1932, 10% of the total population. For more on these economic conditions, see G. D. Feldman, *Iron and Steel in the German Inflation* (Princeton, 1977); A. Ferguson, *When Money Dies* (London, 1975); F. Graham, *Exchanges, Prices, and Production in Hyperinflation Germany* (Princeton, 1930); and L. E. Jones, "Inflation, Revaluation and the Crisis of Middle-Class Politics," *Central European History*, Vol. 7 (1974), pp. 143–68.

109. For the manifestation of the same sort of sentiment among the common folk, see P. Merkl, *Political Violence*, p. 173.

110. For a more detailed excursus on the Nazis' claimed moral decline in Germany after the war, and the Jews' central role in it, see J. Rhodes, *Hitler Movement*, pp. 92–95.

111. W. Laqueur, *Weimar; A Cultural History*, p. 73. See also, on the Jewish involvement in Weimar cultural and artistic life, Istvan Deak, *Weimar Germany's Leftwing Intellectuals* (Berkeley, 1968); K. Pinson, *Modern Germany*, pp. 457–66; P. Gay, *Weimar Culture;* K. Bullivant (ed.), *Culture and Society in the Weimar Republic* (Manchester, 1978); Wolfgang Rothe (ed.), *Die deutsch Literatur der Weimarer Republik* (Stuttgart, 1974); and Walter Fahnders and Martin Rector, *Linksradikalismus und Literatur: Untersuchungen zur Geschichte der sozialistichen Literatur in der Weimarer Republik* (Hamburg, 1974), 2 Vols. Also of interest in this connection is the role of the Jews in left-wing intellectual circles, e.g., Walter Benjamin, Georg Lukács, and the various members and activities of the *Institut für Sozialforschung*, begun in Frankfurt in 1923. For more details on Lukács, see Istvan Meszaros, *Lukács' Concept of Dialectic* (London, 1972); and for the Frankfurt school, see Martin Jay, *The Dialectical Imagination: A History of the Frankfurt School and the Institute of Social Research 1923–1950* (Boston, 1973), and Susanne Petra Schad, *Empirical Social Research in Weimar Germany* (Paris, 1972), pp. 76–96.

112. A. Rosenberg, *Mythus*, cited in Robert Pois (ed.), *Race and Race History and Other Essays* (New York, 1970), p. 149.

113. *Mein Kampf*, pp. 273–74.

114. See Hitler's entire bizarre discussion of the "ills" that plague German society and the role of the Jews in this crisis, *Mein Kampf* (E.T.), pp. 327–64.

115. Cited in J. Fest, *Hitler*, pp. 140 and 210. Hitler here tapped a deep feeling among Germans, and especially those who joined the *NSDAP*, as is clear from the Abel data.

116. Herein lies the fallacy of so many, both inside and outside Germany, who thought once Hitler came to power, "reality" would force him to moderate his "rhetoric," which was no rhetoric but his deepest belief, on the *Judenfrage*.

117. This is increasingly true even for left-wing parties. On this issue, see

G. Mosse, "German Socialists and the Jewish Question in the Weimar Republic," *Leo Baeck Yearbook,* Vol. 16 (1971), pp. 123–34; Bela Vago, "The Attitude towards the Jews as a Criterion of the Left-Right Concept," in B. Vago and G. Mosse (eds.), *Jews and Non-Jews in Eastern Europe* (New York, 1974), pp. 21–50; and G. Mosse, *Final Solution,* pp. 185–88.

5

Quantity and Interpretation—Issues in the Comparative Historical Analysis of the Holocaust

The comparative analysis of the Holocaust with other major historical tragedies turns on three issues at the very least. First, matters of definition and method; secondly, matters of fact; and third, matters of interpretation. In this paper I propose to suggest a definitional and methodological approach to the vexing comparative issue based on a summary review of a number of relevant comparative cases. My carefully chosen cases, all widely referred to in the literature without adequate analysis or nuance, are of two sorts. The first set of putatively parallel examples is drawn from the vast pre-Holocaust, pre-20th century historical experience of persecution and mass death and is comprised of: (1) the medieval witchcraft trials; (2) the destruction of North American Indians; and (3) the data provided by Black Slavery. The second set derives from the exact same context as the *Shoah*, i.e., the Second World War, and consists of three cases known to all readers of this volume. They are: (1) the murder of Europe's Gypsies by the Nazis; (2) Second World War casualties inflicted upon Europe's homosexual population; and (3) lastly, the statistical evidence of casualties suffered by the major national groups of Eastern Europe under Nazi domination.

The one assumed 'premise' employed in this paper is the definition of physical genocide which, based on a revision of the United Nations

This is a revised version of the paper presented at the 'Remembering for the Future' Conference held at Oxford University, July 10–13, 1988. Reprinted by permission of Pergamon Press PLC.

105

Convention on Genocide, is understood to be 'acts committed with the intent to physically destroy a national, ethnical, racial or religious group'.[1]

I. THE MEDIEVAL WITCH CRAZE (AND MEDIEVAL ANTISEMITISM)

To begin our substantive analysis let us start with the odious witchcraft persecutions of the late medieval—early modern period.

The 'witch' is an ancient and widely attested phenomenon. Our interest is concentrated, however, only on the late medieval and early modern history and theory of witchcraft (up to 1700) as it emerged out of a number of different, earlier, less developed traditions regarding heresy, *maleficium,* sorcery and devil worship (sabbats), all of which came to the fore in response to, and as a consequence of, medieval Christian fears and medieval Christendom's doctrines. The witch, like the Jew, was an enduring protagonist, a palpable challenge to the Church and to that society which rotated around, and which received its orienting sense of direction and equilibrium from this fixed center. As such, witches, as Jews, needed to be rooted out, their threatening presence confined, before they were able to express their infectious, transcendental antagonism, before they succeeded in undermining the delicate fabric of communal and personal life. Those same merciless, unifying forces that impacted negatively on Jews and Judaism, i.e., the doctrine of the state and social order as the mystical *Corpus Christi,* a doctrine that makes society's defenders God's instrument and society's 'enemies' God's enemies, underwrote and animated the increasingly organized determination to free Christendom of the evil of witchcraft. There can be no co-existence between the radiant, saving community founded by Christ Jesus and the dark, subversive hell overseen and choreographed by Belial. This belief, expressed in the ritualized enmity of the anti-witch crusade, recycles, as does anti-Judaism, older, constant, mythological certainties, but it does so with a new uncompromising, systematic insistence that translates itself into structural, i.e., institutional, forms whose very purpose is confrontational, violent, often deadly.

Given that the witch willfully, knowingly rejects heaven, and is consumed by an unremitting desire to obliterate Christian society, the Church, in self-defense, is legitimately entitled, even required, to take all necessary, harsh but licit steps to frustrate these evil designs. Use of force, both in the form of judicial torture and then lawful death, was allowed in order that the witches, recognizing the absolute sinfulness of their espousals, repent of their impieties and hence redeem, by this holy reversal, his or her soul. Yet despite the statutory legitimation, conjoined with the requisite theological convictions, before 1200 witches were rarely killed in any case, while until the early 15th century witches were generally treated according to the more universal canons appertaining to heresy, i.e., witches, as heretics, were given an opportunity to recant their betrayal of God and repent, only a second or even a third offense bringing a sentence of death, usually by fire. After 1375–1400, in consonance with the closing of Christian society, the climate of judicial as well as clerical opinion became more severe. As a consequence the witch craze accelerated, as society increasingly feared their presence so, dialectically, they became increasingly present, while, reciprocally, as a result of this hardening of attitude, witches were liable to be judicially killed even for a first offense, a penalty more severe than that which continued to govern the punishment of heretics. This growing legal stringency was accompanied by a dramatic increase in the use of, and reliance upon, torture to prove charges of witchcraft. The significance of this development cannot be overestimated, for who would not confess to a pact with the devil after days, even weeks or months, of relentless torture, of unimaginable cruelty the likes of which escape the power of linguistic conveyance.

This extremism, this polarization of intellectual attitudes, seems plausibly to have been the consequence of the fear, real and imagined, that the mystical *Corpus Christi* was being attacked, even dismembered. That is, the transfiguring drive towards unity entailed, should reality, or at least the perception of reality, not conform, a great fear: the dread of the victory of the Antichrist. The declining security of Jews in the 15th and 16th centuries and of witches in the 15th century forwards are both related to this absolute conceptual precondition, Christian unity, and its threatened dissolution. Already in the 15th century there was an increasing disintegration of that idealized harmony to which Christendom aspired and the witch craze was one of its consequences, though the significance of the growth of the Inquisition as an independent, self-perpetuating bureaucracy should also be noted but not exaggerated as is more usually the case. (Though this, too, i.e., the strengthening of the Inquisition, is in some considerable degree, also a corollary of the developing social malaise.) Inquisitors empowered to find heretics and witches found heretics and witches, though they did not create, *ex nihilo,* witchcraft.

The theoretical construction of witchcraft which we have offered to this point is incomplete because in its abstractness it has not yet connected the discussion concretely to the primary group targeted as witches: women. To understand witchcraft as a historical phenomenon one has to recognize that it received much of its thrust from the dialectical metaphysics of misogynism. That is, to elucidate the full meaning of witchcraft both as mendacious doctrine as well as lamentable reality one is required to investigate, to encounter, the acute existential predicament confronted by the other crucial overlapping, 'outsider' group of interest in this context, women. Women were the abiding 'community' that sustained witchcraft through the centuries. This concern is decisive, in particular, when one seeks to evaluate, finally, the inevitable question of the comparability of medieval antisemitism to witchcraft, and both these medieval realities to the *Shoah.* For, as shall be seen, the ambiguous, alternating status of women will, ultimately, lead not only to judgments of commonality with medieval antisemitism but also to judgments of non-commonality, and still more significant will make the actual fate of women *qua* witches radically different from the fate of Jews under Hitler.

The medieval conception of women shares much with the corresponding medieval conception of Jews. In both cases a perennial attribution of secret, bountiful, malicious 'power,' manifest as a fearsome numinal quality, is made. Women were anathemized, and closely aligned with witchcraft, because of the enduring, grotesque fears they generated *vis-à-vis* their putative, though loathsome, abilities to control men and thereby coerce, for their own ends, male-dominated Christian society. Whatever the social and psychological determinants operative in this abiding obsession, there can be no denying the consequential reality of such anxiety in medieval Christendom. Rooted in theological traditions of Eve and Lilith, women are perceived as incarnations of inexhaustible negative influences; not quite quasi-literal incarnations of the devil as were Jews, women are, rather, their ontological 'first cousins' who, like the Jew, emerge from the 'left' side of being. But the situation is still more complex than this charged negative stereotyping would at first suggest for, in the case of women, both their sociological circumstances and their theological status is more diverse and ramified than is that of the Jews. As to the sociological determinants, more will be suggested below in the course of our discussion. As to the theological attitudes, let it suffice to recall that there is in the canonical corpus the prototype of the Virgin Mary as well as of Eve—a duality largely absent from the Jewish mythic circumstance—and to whose life-saving implications we shall return.

Historically, the most salient manifestation of the unreserved belief in women-power and women's evil is evidenced in witchcraft. Though there were male witches, when the witch craze took hold and became a mass phenomenon after 1500 it was predominantly aimed at female witches. Indeed one suspects that the development of witch-hunting into a mass obsession was possible only when directed primarily at women. Jean Bodin, one of the 16th century's leading intellectuals and witch-hunters, wrote: 'It is clear from the books of all who have written on witches that for every male witch there are fifty female witches . . . [this is due to their] bestial cupidity'.

The description of women so far presented is accurate—to a point. But it fails to be a true portrait because it ignores altogether the two-sided ideology governing the real position of women in medieval society. The truth comes into focus only by recognizing that the woman as witch, as sorcerer, as numinous being was juxtaposed, and profoundly mediated, by a whole series of countervailing institutions whose purpose was to fully, intimately, integrate women into the social fabric in a 'non-terrifying' way. Women, in effect, are perceived to lose their indecency, their ontic negativity, by entering, by being absorbed within, various structures whose very existence is due, from the perspective of the self-understanding of the church, to their ability to assure just such a trans-mutational result. From wild, sensual, free, castrating and devouring creatures of natural and supernatural power, women become domesticated, sexually subordinated, by entering into societal arrangements meant to insure just this austere transformation. So the institution of the family, i.e., of wife and mother and economic partner in nearly every trade and task, and the institution of the nunnery, with its idealized sublimation of female sexuality for non-married women, come into being and have their sacred function. These new, civilizationally defined, roles act to neutralize women's inherently anarchic libido, to subdue the undesirable.

Crucially important is the fact that the natural affection attendant on the roles of mother, wife, and daughter, and the ideological legitimations offered by such roles as that of nun caused two elemental substantive consequences: (a) the role and understanding of women in medieval society was pluralistic, i.e., women were not reduced solely to the status of 'alien', 'outsider', witch; and (b) most women, having been benignly incorporated or reincorporated in the community, were not charged, persecuted or executed as witches or sorcerers. That is to say, the elemental structural arrangements of Christian society were intended, functionally, to establish the bases for an overtly non-aggressive, male dominant *modus vivendi* between the sexes, and this, for the most part, it did successfully. This is so *even* at the height of the witch craze, i.e., between the 1480s and the 1650s, during which the vast majority of women (protected by their role(s)) were not directly touched by the mania.

Only when we understand these competing, often antithetical depictions of women can we fully comprehend the actual nature of the relation of women and witchcraft on the one hand and its *differences* from medieval (and modern) antisemitism on the other. For what distinctly emerges from a close study of the witch trials is that it was preponderantly those women who did not fall into these 'regulative' and domesticating patterns who were charged with witchcraft. Spinsters, widows, unmarried women, eccentrics, peasant women to the degree that the lower classes represented a folk culture, a primitive sexuality no longer tolerated by a post-Lutheran world, and independent women were the primary targets for accusation because they were not immunized by entry into (or being in) some acceptable socially constructed prophylactic or transformatory process, some elemental relationship of dependence upon a man, thus their 'natural' propensities, i.e., their inherent mental weakness and lustiness, made them particularly suitable objects of seduction by the devil. It is surely no accident that the witch mania escalated at exactly the same time, the late 15th century, that Europe was beginning to go through a period of rapid and intense social transformation which changed, even destroyed, those very social mechanisms—family, nunnery and chivalric ideal—that had been the primary vehicles for 'protecting' women, both peasant and high born, from themselves and the devil. As regards the family, especially the lower-class family, the late 15th and 16th centuries saw a shift of population to urban centers with a corresponding decline in the existing family-unit arrangement. Sex roles, as social roles in general, now began to be more autonomous, fluid and open-ended. In addition, there was a significant increase in the age of marriage and rate of unmarried persons. The unprecedented pressures of urban living, the forceful pressures of proto-industrialization, the nascent re-organization of society along freer, capitalist lines in keeping with the requirements of the market place, cast a long shadow in undermining the traditional patriarchal family (even as the demand that patriarchal domination be reinforced was being heard)—for many the equivalent of civilized society itself.

We can now come to the point. Conceiving of witches *per se* as outsiders in the Christian commonwealth is unarguably correct, but when one correlates the role, the status of witches, with the far more polyvalent and ambiguous role of women in medieval society, then the issue of the outsider becomes much more limited and even anomalous. By comparison, Jews were always, *per definitionem,* outsiders to something approaching, though not yet reaching, the maximal degree. (Only in the modern period would the Jew reach the maximal condition as outsider; this is *the* paradox of the Jewish situation in the modern era of emancipation and political citizenship.) Whereas Christianity worked hard to create mechanisms to integrate women and to encourage love between Christian men and women in authorized institutions, most notably the family, leaving the woman *qua* outsider as a small minority, in the case of the Jew it did just the opposite. Increasingly, and at every turn, as Christianity gained an ever-tighter and more monopolistic control of society it took new steps, or reinforced older ones, to displace the Jew from normal human relations with his Christian neighbor. No mediating social avenues or institutions existed to domesticate, to culturally ingest the Jew other than the traumatic one of conversion. While women could be idealized and typologized as nun, wife, mother, virgin, lady—the Jew in late medieval Christendom was always and only Jew. Papal policy, though consistently molded to protect Jews, also intended to enforce Jewish 'servitude', to make manifest in the existential reality of Jewish lives their apostate, reprobate status.

The meaning of this difference can be seen clearly through examination of the demographic statistics pertaining to witch-hunts. Extreme caution is required in making these calculations, for the relevant estimates vary by a magnitude of at least 300, that is estimates that range from 30,000 up to 9 million witches put to death between 1480 and 1700 are cited in the literature. A widely used figure around which a certain 'consensus' has formed is that of 200,000, 'conservatively estimated', by R. H. Robbins. However, Robbins' calculations are open to question on methodological grounds. His estimate is very haphazardly arrived at. 'The most reliable suggestion', he writes, 'is that of George L. Burr, who estimated a *minimum* of 100,000 men, women and children burned in Germany alone. One might double this figure for the whole of Europe'. But this casual doubling procedure will not do, both because Burr's specific estimates for Germany may well be too high, and, secondly, because the suggested method of doubling this figure almost certainly provides an excessive total for the remainder of Europe. My scepticism concerning Burr's calculations is predicated on the careful review of the trial evidence from Germany, the epicenter of the drama, by Kieckhefer for the period before 1500 and Midelfort for southwestern Germany during the height of the witch trials, 1562–1684. Kieckhefer's review yields a picture of sporadic and minimal witch-hunting that claimed, at most, several thousand witches before 1500. Even more significant, Midelfort argues that only 3229 people (2527 Catholics and 702 Protestants) were killed between 1561 and 1670 in southwest Germany. These relatively low figures suggest that previous estimates for Germany may have been excessive. This conclusion is supported by Henri Hiegel's tabulation of only 638 accusations and 484 executions in the German-speaking section of the Duchy of Lorraine between 1580 and 1632. Similarly, for the rest of Europe, less than 1000 witches were burned in England, while Guido Bader's investigations provide a figure of 5417 executions (Bader thinks it was probably higher, but lacks documentary evidence) in Switzerland between 1400 and 1700. Even lower figures for Switzerland are now carefully documented by Monter, who estimates 396 individuals were executed in the Swiss territories of the Republic of Geneva (68 persons), Canton of Zurich (74 persons) and the Canton of Lucerne (254 persons) between the Reformation and the end of the Swiss witch trials. Added to this are 102 deaths in the Catholic area of Basel, 80 in Ajorie, 20 in St. Ursanne and 53 in Fribourg. In Scotland the numbers range from estimates of 3400 to 4400, while in the Channel Islands there were 66 executions out of 144 persons tried. In France governmental restraint limited the number of 'victims' to no more than a few thousand. Given these figures, it is difficult to arrive at the total of 100,000 for the remainder of Europe, excluding Germany, that Robbins, and others, assume. Perhaps this tendency to demographic exaggeration is explained by the impact such events had, i.e., their historical significance and psychological impression was, rightfully, disproportionate to their actual numbers. It is also probably due to not allowing for the very high rate of sentences other than execution, e.g., public penances, various devotions, public lashings, limited jail terms and banishment, in witch trials, i.e., there were far more trials than executions. The 20 witches burned in Salem is a good example of this magnifying phenomenon. *A fortiori,* the extreme claims of scholars like Matilda Joslyn Gage that 9 million witches were burned, a claim, unfortunately, used widely by contemporary feminist authors, is without any basis in fact. What this means is that Europe, partly because of its bifocal vision of women, and the accompanying Christian morality thereof, and partly for institutional reasons, never translated its own instinctually negative image of women into an active, all-encompassing, non-reciprocal, policy, *even during the two centuries of the witch craze.*

In defense of this all-important judgment consider the demographic factors from a second perspective. If one assumes, conservatively, an average European population of 55 million throughout the 15th, 16th, and 17th centuries, evenly divided by sex, and then assumes a birth rate equivalent to producing a new generation every 20 years, then over the nearly 200 years of the witch craze 550 million people (ten generations) lived, at one time or another in Europe, half of whom, or 275 million, were women. Of these 275 million women, less than 200,000 (and in all likelihood, less than 100,000) were executed for witchcraft. If, that is, one divides this total of 275 million women and 200,000 total witches by our ideal 20 year 'generation', over two centuries, i.e., does not bother to allow for variations decade by decade that did occur, then one would have a profile that looks like this: in each generation there were 27½ million women, 20,000 (or less) of whom were executed for witchcraft, i.e., less than $\frac{1}{13}$th of 1 per cent of the female population ($\frac{1}{26}$th of 1 per cent if one uses the figure of 100,000). Moving from this unnuanced mathematical constant, and examining periods of particular intensity, one still arrives at no more than $\frac{2}{10}$ths of 1 per cent of the female population executed in any decade. These figures explain why, though having much in common ideologically with antisemitism, medieval views of feminism and anti-feminism, are to be considered ultimately asymmetrical with medieval anti-Judaism, and produce extraordinarily different results. Medieval anti-feminism, the most notable expression of which is the witch craze, is (a) not genocidal, i.e., not gynocidal; and (b) not fully commensurate with medieval antisemitism. Secondly, in regard to our overriding question, there is no valid comparison to be made between either medieval antisemitism, or, now, and even more so, medieval anti-feminism and the reality of the Holocaust. In comparison to the *Shoah* of the 20th century, that consumed approximately 65 per cent of potential victims in 4 years, 6 million persons, these medieval phenomena, especially those relating to women, belong to lesser and altogether qualitatively different magnitudes of violence, as well as to separate intentional and ideological matrices.

Parenthetically, let me add that a similar analysis for the medieval era of the Albigensian Crusade, and later the French Catholic persecution of the Huguenots, often erroneously cited in comparative analyses of genocide, will yield similar results, i.e., they will reveal a radical discontinuity with the Holocaust.

II. NORTH AMERICAN INDIANS

The fateful, catastrophic encounter of European civilization with the indigenous peoples of the Americas is one of the most tragic meetings in all of human history. Inherently asymmetrical, this contact has entailed not only immense socio-economic and geo-political transformations for the native population but also enormous, transfiguring despoliation. On grounds of the erosion of population, their collective tragedy parallels, even exceeds, that of European Jewry. The specific delineation of the circumstance depends on what demographic base one begins with, and many different numerical bases have been suggested, but in any and all cases, it can be concluded without fear of contradiction that many millions of Indians were killed. Consider, for starters, one carefully arrived at composite estimate that will convey something of the vast, obliterative proportions of the demographic chaos. In their study of the 16th century Mexican Indian population, Sherburne Cook and Woodrow Borah posit a base population in the central Valley of 16.8 million Indians in 1532, declining to less than half that number, 6.5 million in 1548, and then down to only 2.65 million Indians by 1568, while for Mexico as a whole they estimate a pre-conquest population of approximately 25 million in 1519 declining to under 7.5 million by 1550 and dropping unbelievably to approximately 1 million in 1605. In percentage terms, this is a decline of over 95 per cent in less than a century. Likewise, in the same vein, composite profiles for the territory that is now the United States range between older estimates which suggested a pre-European population of 1 million, plus or minus 10 per cent, and newer calculations that suggest a population as high as 3.3 million, with a subsequent loss ranging from a low estimate of 60 per cent (on the basis of 1 million as the original base) to over 85 per cent on the 3.3 million base. Similarly, and here let one specific example stand for many, it is estimated that in 1769 the Native American population of California numbered approximately 250,000, while by 1880 it had declined to 20,000, largely due to changed socio-economic conditions, and the diseases that accompanied them, associated with the discovery of gold.

Moving from the specific to the general level again, several well-known recent estimates for the Americas (the Hemisphere) as a whole, have suggested an Indian population of approximately 80 million (or higher up to 112 million) on the eve of European arrival (35–40 per cent in North America), a figure reduced by 7⁄8ths to approximately 10 million in the latter half of the 16th century, i.e., after 50–75 years of destructive encounter. If these constructs are accepted as being within any reliable parameters—and though open to revision, they appear to be so within an acceptable range of statistical error of 50 per cent either way—the depletion of the indigenous peoples in the first century of European domination in the Americas must be apprised as representing the very greatest demographic carnage in human history. In statistical terms, only Stalin even approaches the death trail of Cortés and his Conquistadoran colleagues, and even at that, Stalin's record finally comes in a distant second both in absolute terms, and even more in relative ones, for his average base population was larger than that of the American Indians, i.e., the Russian population at his death was not very different than it had been when he came to power, as compared to the Indian population which declined precipitously over the course of the 16th century.

Given these statistics, we must say unequivocally that if numbers alone constitute uniqueness, then the Jewish experience under Hitler was not unique. Let us, therefore, turn our phenomenological investigation, insofar as we seek to illuminate the matter of comparability, from demographic issues to consider the quite different topic of the 'intention' behind the white man's subjugation, enslavement and murder of the Indian. Did the European intend, that is to ask, this demographic catastrophe? Even more specifically, more tellingly, did he intend that this violent, problematic collision of worlds result in genocide?

The decisive evidence for the absence of any genocidal intentionality in the population catastrophe that overtook the Native Americans is provided by, derived from, the axial role played in these macabre events by disease. All serious students of the demographic annihilation of the

Indian are agreed that its overwhelming cause was unintended disease that produced vast epidemics in, e.g., 1545–1546 and again in 1575–1576, and smaller, though still considerable epidemics on a regular basis both earlier and later, e.g., in the southeastern area of the United States where in the 16th century the population was decimated in a few years and in New England where various pathogens may have claimed up to 30–40 per cent of the Indian population in the years 1616–1620.

To understand the meaning of such events one must recall that the Europeans themselves lacked the medical knowledge either to cause or, more importantly, to abort such plagues, as is demonstrably revealed in the regular series of such outbreaks which ravaged European populations until the 20th century. Once infectious agents were set loose, the populace, given the state of medical ignorance, was impotent in halting their spread. This inability to retard the effects of epidemic illnesses in Europe is evidenced to by the fact that even the most conservative modern estimates of the death toll during the Black Death in 1346 put the loss in that one year alone at 25–35 per cent of the total population. Between 1346 and 1377 the population of England is estimated to have declined 40 per cent, from 3,700,000 to 2,200,000, while for Europe as a whole the population declined from approximately 76 million to 50 million. Some individual mortality rates are particularly striking: In the Dominican monastery of Montpellier, only 7 of 140 Friars survived; in the monastery at Maguelonne, only 7 of 160. Between May and August 1346, 26 per cent of all Cardinals of the Church died. Rank was no defense: The son of the Byzantine Emperor died in three days in Constantinople; Leonora, Queen of Aragon, Princess Maria of Aragon, the Count and Countess of Ribagorce, King Alfonso XI of Castile, Edward III's daughter Joan of England, two successive Archbishops of Canterbury, all died from the Plague. It is important to recognize, moreover, that the Plague did not disappear after 1350 but recurred in various locales for the next half-century; in France and Germany in 1357–1362; in Poland in 1360–1361; in Aquitaine in 1361 and 1375; in Germany again in the 1380s; and then at intervals in Florence in 1371, 1374, 1390, 1400 and 1418. Josiah Russell's careful reconstruction of medieval English population statistics suggests that the first round of the Plague in 1346 killed 25 per cent of the population, the second round of 1360 killed 22.7 per cent, the third round of 1369, 13.1 per cent and the fourth round of 1375, 12.7 per cent. A century later an epidemic would again overtake Europe. In 1456–1460, 15 per cent of England, France and the Netherlands died. In the middle of the 16th century a similar pattern would again impact catastrophically on European populations.

This evidence indicates that the devastating recurrent pattern of epidemic disease as experienced by the American Indian in sixteenth century Mexico was by no means exceptional, though as virgin soil epidemics they were extreme manifestations of the phenomenon. Indeed they were 'typical' of the impact that European pathogens had on newly infiltrated areas as is attested, for example, by the vast devastation among the Guanche in the Canary Islands that followed the arrival of the Spanish in the 15th century. God 'sent among them la peste', a contemporary Spaniard wrote, 'which in a few days destroyed three-quarters of the people'. Though this estimate may be on the high side, recent studies suggest it is not high by much.

It is also apposite to note that such demographic erosion cut both ways, e.g., European loss in Africa due to disease was immense as is revealed in the mortality rates (in some cases 500 per 1000 per annum and more) among white slavers, merchants and soldiers stationed in Africa. When English prisoners were, for a short period, exiled to Africa, Edmund Burke described it as a death sentence. Even blacks returning to Liberia were not immune to its deadly environmental consequences. 'In the first year of the Province of Freedom, Sierra Leone, 46 per cent of the whites died, but so did 39 per cent of black settlers'. And this pattern continued: 'In Liberia between 1820 and 1843, 21 per cent of all immigrants, presumably all or almost all of them black or mulatto, died during their first year of residence'. A similar circumstance operated in reverse among whites born in areas such as New Zealand and Australia who then returned to England without European immunities. Likewise in Australia, British seamen infected the aborigine population with smallpox among other diseases and as many as 33 per cent of the native population may have died in the first contact period as a result. Throughout the 19th century the aborigine population would be repeatedly reduced by these alien pathogens.

The mortality rate among early white settlers in the New World also reveals a similar pattern of succumbing to various maladies, e.g., by 1626 the white population of Virginia had grown since 1607 to 1232, but in order to achieve this figure, 8000 other European settlers had already died. Even in our century infectious disorders are the great killer, for example, the Spanish flu of 1918–1920 killed more people than the armies of Europe had lost in the First World War. And as late as 1952,

99 per cent of the Eskimo population came down sick and 7 per cent of the Eskimo population of the region died when measles was introduced into Ungava Bay, while the Kreen-Akores lost 15 per cent of their people in the early 1970s when first contacted by whites and introduced to the common influenza germ.

The staggering erosion of the North American Indian population due to disease, that is viewing pandemics as the prime agent of Indian mortality in the 16th and 17th centuries, there having been no less than 14 to 17 epidemic outbreaks between 1524 and 1600, finds incontrovertible support in the following figures: While the contemporary Conquistador historians estimated a 50 per cent mortality rate from smallpox in 1520–1524, the most recent, highly detailed and technically sophisticated analysis has estimated that 75 per cent of the native Mexican population fell in this first major smallpox epidemic. Assuming a base Mexican Indian population of 25 million, using Cook and Borah's estimate, this would mean an unintended loss as a direct consequence of this initial encounter with European pathogens of 18.75 million individuals. No Conquistador, or Spanish king, made, or had to make, any willful negative decision *vis-à-vis* the inhabitants of the New World; merely by their arrival the Europeans, according to blind, mechanistic, natural biological laws, doomed the majority of Mexico's population. And it was this biological assault, above all else, that simultaneously not only eliminated the Indian peoples but also made the European conquest possible. If Cook and Borah are correct, and there is every reason to believe they are, within the bounds of accepted statistical error, the nearly 97 per cent destruction of the indigenous Mexican population was primarily (i.e., more than 90 per cent), the consequences of the activity of the mindless forces of disease. In relation to other causes of population reduction, 'the effect of diseases . . . was, therefore, approximately, five [to ten] times as great as the effect of physical assault, warfare and homicide'.

These lachrymose details are recalled in order to emphasize that it was essentially disease unaided, i.e., disease *per se,* along with the sociological dislocations it created, for example, the breakdown of the food chain, as well as the more general disruption of Indian family and communal life, that was the prime agency of death.

On the basis of this review of the statistical data, only a fraction of which has been cited, of the toll exacted by disease in the decimation of the Indian population we can draw two fecund conclusions relative to our broader conceptual concern. First, it is now beyond argument that physical genocide—meaning intentional corporate physical annihilation—was not the purposeful program of any of the pre-1776 Colonial Empires. When, and as often, mass death occurred, it was almost without exception caused by microbes not militia, unintentionally rather than by design, even occurring in opposition to the will of the white empire-builder or settler.

Certainly the fatigue, the hunger and the psychological dilemmas attendant upon white conquest reduced the ability of the native population to withstand the heretofore unencountered pathogens. Yet this negative assistance does not alter the unintentional character of the spread of these infectious visitations, or the meaning to be ascribed to colonial policy. The comparative data we have considered, plus much additional data on the spread of epidemics in this era in other areas of colonial conquest, makes this abundantly clear.

Moreover, in contradistinction to those who would overemphasize the non-pathogenic causes of Indian decline, it needs to be understood that it is highly likely that the most widespread and demographically significant epidemics were the very earliest ones, e.g., those of 1519–1521 and again the one of 1524, which occurred prior to any full-scale Conquistador program of enforced labour and related abuses, yet which claimed an estimated one-third of the population. In contrast, by the 17th century, the Indian population stabilized and even began to grow, even though it was now under the full control of the imperial system. The reason for this demographic reversal is, once again, a matter of biology: only those Indians with resistance to white diseases were now reproducing among themselves and with Europeans thereby producing a population far more, though far from fully, resistant to European pathogens.

Secondly, as if to confirm this conclusion drawn relative to the pre-United States era, if we consider the demography of Native Americans after their destiny became inextricably linked with that of the United States we again discern the non-genocidal, though cruel and profoundly uncaring, policy of white society. Though all figures on Indian demography between 1775 and 1900 are highly provisional, most scholars concur in estimating the Native American population in the Revolutionary period in the area of 450,000–550,000, declining by the end of the first century of American control to *ca* 275,000–300,000. In the special 1890 census of Indians, the government counted 248,253 Indians in the country. However, thereafter, due to: (a) improved medical knowledge in general; (b) the continuing development of immune systems among the Indian population; and (c) new efforts by the U.S. government and various other interested parties, for example, and most significantly, compulsory smallpox vaccinations in Indian schools begun in 1907, the Indian population grew to 265,683 by 1910; 332,397 in 1930; and all the way back to 792,730 according to the 1970 census; being today well over 1.5 million and growing very rapidly.

III. BLACK SLAVERY

During the 16th to 19th centuries, 9½ to 15 million blacks were enslaved. These statistics, however, only tell us about the quantity of slavery as an institution, they do not yet tell us anything about its character. And it is its character that primarily concerns us.

Here economic factors are, though not unmediated, decisive. That is, the institutions, the configurations, the human relationships (both between black slaves, as well as between whites and blacks), the 'morality' of this 'peculiar institution' were defined, first and foremost though not solely, by financial considerations. From the systemic forces that initially lead to their capture until their death, slaves cannot avoid being defined by the economic equation in which they play a crucial, if mainly passive, part. Ponder the chain of happenings, the network of structures and motives, that now re-create the lived reality of the captive. Begin with that first link in the entire slave trade, the act of enslavement which was the product of mercenary considerations by the slave's fellow African captors. As 'enemies' were worth more alive than dead, African tribal warfare, which now regularly included expeditions solely for the procurement of slaves, was pursued according to a strategy of capture: defeated tribes, rather than being murdered, became *a* if not *the* main source of supply for the slave trade both inside Africa and for the export market. Consider that simultaneously whites, especially the Portuguese, British and French, with assistance from the Dutch, created a large fleet to transport blacks, valued not as individuals but according to a measure known as the *Pezas de India* that computed their worth on the basis of their labor capacity, because transporting and trading in blacks promised considerable profits (whether such profits were realized or not). And then remember the obvious fact that blacks, in turn, were exported and redistributed in those areas where their efforts could be translated into gains for their owners. And finally, while enslaved, the character of their lives, their work regimen, their food, clothing and shelter, their mating patterns, their childhoods, their maturity, the possibility of their being sold again, were the end result of largely economic, if not altogether economically rational, factors, compromised by various moral, political, religious and cultural elements.

What these unsentimental, calculating conventions indicate, what this functional cycle gauged by the calibrations of profit and loss has to teach us, can best be exposed by beginning our detailed deconstruction with the 'Middle Passage', that fateful journey by ship which brought the slaves to the New World. These crossings were filled with terror. Over-crowded, roughly treated, modestly fed and cared for, exposed to disease and seasickness, blacks endured these sailings, in many ways the worst segment of the entire experience of slavery, with a grim fortitude. And their fatal consequences were considerable, as the mortality rates indicate. In the 16th century, estimates of loss in transit seem to have averaged 20–25 per cent. This high casualty rate appears to have continued until the 17th century, as the recorded statistics of the Royal African Company which reveal a loss in transit of 23.6 per cent between 1680–1688 indicate. These statistical parameters are also reinforced by studies of the Nantes slave trade between 1715 and 1741 which yields a rate of 22.2 per cent of slaves lost in transit. Likewise for the Brazilian trade in the 16th and 17th centuries, an average mortality rate during the crossing of 16 to 20 per cent has been proposed. These percentages dropped, on average, in the 18th century when it is estimated that: there was a 15 per cent loss in transit in both the British trade between 1701 and 1761 and the Portuguese trade between 1761 and 1810; a 13 per cent rate of decrement for French ships; and a 12.3 per cent decline for the Dutch ships. It should also be noted that while the British trade experienced only half its earlier erosion, i.e., 7.5 per cent, after 1761, the average mortality rate in transit for the European trade as a whole after 1760 was in the vicinity of 10–12 per cent. Our estimate of an overall 15 per cent decline for the Portuguese trade is supported by Goulart's analysis of the Brazilian trade, for which he suggests a 10 per cent loss in transport in the 18th and 19th century.

Though these Middle Passage mortality rates are smaller than the popular wisdom would have it, averaging on my calculation for the entire trade over 275 years, and allowing for increased quantities after 1800 when the loss experience was lower, 13–17 per cent, when one figures that this trade involved between 9½ to 15 million individuals, the loss of life in transit is somewhere between 1,200,000 (i.e., 13 per cent of 9½ million at a minimum) and 2,600,000 (i.e., 17 per cent of 15 million at a maximum). And it is here, with the invocation of this ghastly memory, this monumental carnage, that the determination to compare slavery and the *Shoah* appears most compelling.

But one must look beyond the absolute numbers, the raw 'body count', if the dialogue concerning comparability is to be more than an actuarial enterprise. In alluding to the meta-mathematical level we mean to indicate the requirement that the dynamic nuances, the defining reciprocities, inherent in each empirical texture not be lost. For example, consider comparatively the conceptually preeminent matter of causation. 'Why did 13 to 17 per cent of the black cargoes not reach their destination? Were there repeated instances of mass murder aboard the vessels that carried them or is some other explanation, some other decoding, of the frightful circumstance required?' The subversive answer to this question, that is the reply that forces a reconsideration of the naive claim for comparability, is that these slaves, despite their dying, were not murdered. The captains and crews who worked this inhumane journey were not *Einsatzgruppen*. Upon close inspection one recognizes that, abhorrent as the Middle Passage was, the great majority of the deaths that occurred were humanly unintended, unplanned and assuredly undesired. As with the decimating epidemiological impact of European settlers on Native Americans, as well as the repeated devastating impact of epidemics on European populations, so, too, disease was the main killer of black slaves. Anstey summarizes the British experience in these terms: 'losses on any scale nearly always stemmed from an epidemic of dysentery, measles or smallpox as exacerbated by deficiency of provisions and hygiene, and the protraction of the voyage'. Similarly, Gaston Martin's figures for the Nantes trade support this conclusion decisively, i.e., they indicate that approximately 88 per cent of slave loss in transit was directly due to disease. If one takes these statistics as representative in percentage terms for the trade overall, then one can attribute over 80 per cent of deaths in passage to disease. More specifically it was dysentery, yellow fever, other 'fevers', and such communicable ailments as measles and especially smallpox, that were the main killers. The very high mortality rates on individual slaving voyages were almost always due to the uncontrollable outbreak of one or another of these communicable diseases. It is, of course, necessary to recognize that other factors such as food (quality and quantity), weather, shelter, seasickness, over-crowding, physical violence and the duration of the trip, which contributed to the presence of scurvy and amoebic dysentery, as well as food and water shortages that took time to develop, were significant insofar as they made it more or less possible, in certain instances, to resist disease. However, in the overall adjudication of causes these many elements must be considered as secondary to the purely uncontrollable pathogenic factor. And, on reflection, this should not surprise us. Given the regnant economic rationality governing the entire enterprise, this identification of irresistible epidemic disease as the primary cause of death makes sense, i.e., it accords with a prudent desire to keep slaves alive. So too does the practice of innoculating slaves for smallpox once this technique became available at the end of the 18th century.

That these black mortality rates were unplanned is confirmed, as it were, by the corresponding mortality rates among white slavers. For those who were resident in Africa up to one year, the mortality rate, due to local deadly microbes, was at least 50 per cent, while the mortality figures for the white crews that served on slave ships sailing from Nantes between 1748 and 1792 are approximately the same as for the slave population carried on these voyages. Likewise, British crews in the 1780s show a loss due to disease of approximately 22–23 per cent. Generalizing from this and related evidence, Curtin concludes that 'the death rate per voyage among the crew was uniformly higher than the death rate among slaves in transit at the same period. These data are so consistent and regular in this respect that this can be taken as a normal circumstance of the 18th century slave trade'.

Even more interesting in trying to properly understand, in attempting to conceptualize, the wider implications of the slave loss rate in the Middle Passage are the parallel statistics for European immigrants to the Americas in the 18th century. Though the relevant data are far less comprehensive than those which exist in regard to slavery, there is reason to believe that such immigrants experienced

very high epidemic rates in this period. Thus in 1710, 10 ships carrying German immigrants to Philadelphia experienced a 25 per cent mortality rate . . . Other quite small samples . . . also report mortality rates of between 15 per cent and 20 per cent.

Though these figures may need marginal adjustment for age and sex distribution, their implications for our analysis of slave crossings during the 17th and 18th centuries are clear.

For us, in terms of our overall project, the importance of this collection of largely statistical evidence is this: the black death rate during the Middle Passage, appalling though it was, was not the result, the fatal consequence of, intentionally malicious, premeditatively murderous, treatment. Every slave who died was a loss for the slaver, a defeat for the slave system.

This pecuniary self-interest of the slaver was clearly expressed in legislation governing the manner of slave shipments, i.e., the limits placed on the number of slaves that could be transported on any one ship relative to its total tonnage. The Portuguese already in 1684 legally limited the carrying load to approximately 2.6 to 3.5 slaves per ton, the relevant legislation including this explanation of its rationale: 'If in a decked ship in which there are portholes through which the negroes can easily receive the necessary fresh air, then capacity below decks should be 7 adults for every two tons; not having said portholes, the capacity should only be 5 slaves per two tons below decks'. Similar legislation, predicated on a like mixture of utilitarian and moral intent, was enacted by the British in the 18th century. It was in everyone's interest to keep blacks alive, indeed to see them increase so as to maximize their commercial profitability. Accordingly, captains of slave ships and ships' surgeons were paid a bonus for low mortality rates.

The repercussive role of the logic of survival operative in the domain of New World slavery is generally attested throughout the system. Slaves tended to have more deaths than births in the sugar cultivating areas, such as Jamaica and northeast Brazil in the 17th and 18th centuries, due to the nature of the very heavy work encouraged by the technology of sugar production, the excessive ratio of men to women in these areas, and the calculation that it was cheaper to buy slaves than breed them. In many other areas there was a rise in black population through natural increase. This fact is most especially in evidence in the southern colonies of the future United States, where, over the centuries, the black population advanced, through natural increase, ten-fold. Parts of Brazil and Argentina also experienced significant native-born slave growth, as did Cuba, Montserrat, St. Kitts, Nevis and Antigua after 1807. The situation also improved after 1807 in Granada, St. Vincent, and St. Lucia, though overall it was still negative, i.e., more deaths than births. Even Jamaica by the 1840s and Barbados after 1810, with the increase in available black women due to a changed attitude towards the economics of breeding vs. import, experienced an improvement in the demographic situation. And even when there was, as in a number of locations, a net decrease in black slave population, the decrease was very gradual, especially when allowances for ageing and other processes, including dramatic variations due to epidemic outbreaks within the parameters of natural mortality, are factored in. For example, in the 18th century British sugar islands in the Caribbean, mortality rates averaged 10–40 per 1000, e.g., Jamaica between 1703 and 1721 had a decrease of 1.2 per cent per annum, while in Cuba between 1774 and 1817, and Puerto Rico (all the way up until 1845), the decrease was only 0.5 per cent per annum. The data for the 19th century reveal a similar pattern, e.g., in Cuba between 1817 and 1826 the evidence suggests a drop of only 0.7 per cent per year, and between 1827 and 1840 only 0.5 per cent. It is also to be observed that the mortality rates for slaves in, for example, Jamaica in the 18th and 19th century are not any higher than they were for the white, free population of London and other urban areas in this same period. While earlier, for example, in Virginia white mortality rates were so high that 15,000 new immigrants between 1625 and 1640 added less than 7000 to the ultimate total population.

There is one additional, elemental consideration that we need to factor into these demographic statistics so as to arrive at a true understanding of their significance: the relative scarcity of black women among the slave population. The scarcity of black slave women obviously reduced the birth rate and hence eliminated the counterbalancing forces operative in a more standard population sample. This factor distorts the meaning of the raw growth—decline figures, i.e., not unusual cruelty, but lack of reproduction, accounts for a great deal, if not all, of the loss in population akin, to take an extreme analogy, to what occurs in monastic communities over time. Of course, the converse to this argument is that, unlike monastic environments, the sexual imbalance that existed among slaves was involuntary and another symptom of the cruelty of the system which saw masters prefer the importation of black males over the importation of black females for economic reasons. However, this view has now been called into question by Herbert Klein and others who have shown that the relative absence of women in the slave exporting trade was not due to any sexual preference, motivated by price or labor needs, nor again by the New World system as a whole, but was due rather to the simple availability of female slaves in the African market. Female slaves were not as generally available for export, being kept back for use within Africa.

Slavery, then, and this applies to Roman and medieval forms of slavery as well as New World slavery, for all its inherent immorality and barbarity represents a different form of evil, a wholly other phenomenological reality, than that incarnated in Auschwitz.

IV. GYPSIES UNDER THE NAZIS

The first and most important comparative case emerging out of the context of the Second World War that requires our close attention is, of course, that of the Gypsies. It is regularly argued that the sinister Nazi contrivance towards the Jews has a direct, even exact, or nearly exact, parallel in the Nazi design towards Gypsies. Thus, the Nuremberg Tribunal linked the two groups together in its indictment of German War Criminals. The Court charged that the prisoners had 'conducted deliberate and systematic genocide . . . particularly Jews, Poles and Gypsies'. The essential rationale for this contended linkage is the presumption that in both circumstances, i.e., of the Jews and Gypsies under the Nazi regime, the ideological justification governing their treatment was the same, i.e., racial inferiority and hence the resultant practical policy applied was synonymous. But this presumption of commonality is not correct: neither the pertinent ideology, racial and otherwise, nor the horrific results of the translation of metaphysics into pitiless action was equivalent, though the specific outcome in *both* instances was abominable and beyond any moral legitimacy. Because of the widespread belief to the contrary, however, a closer analysis of the comparative data is required.

The most elemental consideration towards which attention must be directed for arriving at a correct understanding of the comparative issue revolves around the Nazi self-understanding of their onslaught against the Gypsies. And here, the more one searches into this self-understanding, the more one comes to realize that the Nazis were confused and uncertain about the status of Gypsies in essential ways, as compared to their self-assurance about the transcendental negative status of Jews. On the one hand, the Nazis sought to classify the Gypsies by race, to see their collective transgression as biologically determined, and to persecute them accordingly as inferior non-Aryans. The first specifically anti-Gypsy ordinance of late 1938, for example, states: 'Experience gained in the fight against the Gypsy menace and the knowledge derived from race-biological research have shown that the proper method of attacking the Gypsy problems seems to be to treat it as a matter of race'. Thus, too, the Gypsy 'research work' carried out at the *Bekämpfung des Zigeuner-wesens* and again at the *Rassenhygienische und bevölkerungsbiologische Forschungstelle* under Dr. Robert Ritter was concerned with the racial character of the Gypsy 'menace'. In this biocentric assault, in this fatality of blood and descent, lies the similarity to the Jewish fate. But even here, where no exegesis seems required, seminal, that is life-and-death, differences assert themselves. For whereas the Nazis classed all Jews as racial *'Untermenschen'*, as necessary begetters of cosmic and natural pollution, and hence properly annihilated, they recognized a primal distinction between pure, i.e., Aryan, Gypsies and impure, i.e., non-Aryan, Gypsies. This absolute distinction had evident, life-defining consequences to which we shall return. On the other hand, and elemental, Nazi policy towards the Gypsies was not only predicated on the category of race, but also on the altogether different notion of asocials. Thus, the 1937 *Law against Crime* specifically links Gypsies with, for example, beggars, tramps, prostitutes and the like who show 'anti-social behaviours'. Likewise, in the concentration camps, though forming a distinct subgroup, the Gypsies generally wore black identification patches indicative of asocials. (Until they reached the concentration camps, Gypsies were not required to wear special identifying marks on their clothing, as compared to the requirements covering the Jewish use of the yellow star.) It is interesting in this connection to note that 'Gypsy Travellers' who were *not* Gypsies were also hounded by the Nazis under various ordinances, and some were even sterilized under the 1933 laws, eliminating them as a presence of any consequence by 1938, while the few that remained were sentenced to camps as *asocials*. That is to say, race was not the only or decisive factor in consigning Gypsies and those who shared their life style to concentration camps. The treatment received by Fellow-Travellers supports the argument that the *asocial* motive was a potent element in the actual historic context. Alternatively, the mixed, fluid, uncertain character of the situation is seen in the different settlement legislation of 1939 that allowed Travellers to continue to travel while not allowing Gypsies to do so. The juridical-ideological confusion as to the racial and/ or criminal depravity of the Gypsies is also evidenced in official memoranda, as, for example, that of 1938, which refers to Gypsies in these terms: 'Because the Gypsies have manifestly a heavily-tainted heredity and because they are inveterate criminals who constitute parasites in the bosom of our people, it is fitting to . . .' This document provides lucid proof of the hermeneutical rule that where more than one explanation is proffered, one convincing explanation is absent. The significance of the asocial modality, of the overzealous drive for public order, is also evidenced, if negatively, by the exemption from deportation of Gypsies who have been regularly employed for five years.

This lack of a monolithic, insistent, clairvoyant racial policy towards the Gypsies accounts, in all likelihood, for the differing fates suffered by Jews and Gypsies under Nazi control. This vital difference, this lack of explanatory singlemindedness, transmuted the Nazi assault against the Gypsies into a mediated confrontation that blunted a considerable part of the deadly fury which potentially could have been brought to bear against the Gypsies but wasn't, as compared to the unmediated impulse which compellingly strove against the Jews. This moderating intercession, this lack of genocidal consistency, is revealed in a considerable number of Nazi actions. Consider, first of all, the Nazi-created anomalies based on the asserted distinction between pure Aryan and impure non-Aryan Gypsies already referred to. As a consequence of this bifurcation, while many Gypsies in Germany and Poland were being rounded up after 1943 for deportation, Himmler himself was intervening to save the 'German' Gypsy Sinti and Lalleri tribes, about 10 per cent of the total Gypsy population, even over objections from such personages as Bormann and Goebbels. Second, we find regulations governing the exemption from deportation for, take note: 'Rom Gypsies and part Gypsies still serving in the army or who have been released with decorations or wounded . . .' Third, according to the deportation orders of 27 April 1940, Gypsies married to Germans or with a father or son in the forces, or those who owned land, or were of foreign nationality were exempted. A similar order, listing various additional exemptions, was issued by Himmler on 29 January 1943. Though it has been suggested that these exemptions and related procedures 'compare with similar arrangement for Jews', this contention is inaccurate, particularly as there were no Jewish fathers or sons serving (knowingly) in the Nazi armies, nor again were 'pure' Jews ultimately exempted from any aspect of the murderous system. Fourth, while Gypsies as late as 1942 and after were released, under certain conditions, from camps such as Maidanek, the same cannot be said for Jews. Fifth, Gypsies continued to serve in the regular

Nazi army as late as 1943 as well as in reserve units of the territorial army. Nothing comparable exists on the Jewish side. Sixth, on 27 March 1943, a law was passed that declared pure Gypsies exempt from both forced labour and military service, while part-Gypsies were required to serve in the second reserve.

The difference between the treatment of Gypsies and Jews in the various occupied countries is even more telling. For example, in February 1943, the Jews of Brest-Litovsk were liquidated, while 'the Gypsies were put in their houses in the ghetto'; in France the Vichy government's attitude towards Gypsies was far more benevolent than its attitude towards Jews, 90,000 of whom perished. In Italy Gypsies were conscripted into Mussolini's army for service in Yugoslavia and Albania and elsewhere—no Jews were so conscripted! In Greece there are no reports of Nazi persecutions of Gypsies as compared to the fate of Greek Jewry, which was sent off to Auschwitz, where 77 per cent died. The same anomaly existed in Romania, where Gypsies continued to serve in the army while 300,000 Jews were being murdered.

In the East a similar discrepancy existed. For example, when the *Einsatzgruppen* were killing *all* Jews encountered in Eastern Europe, the German authorities issued orders on 24 March 1943, and repeated them in November 1943, that hereafter Gypsies who were of a 'non-migratory' status and hence a 'non-criminal' element, who could prove a two-year period of residence in the locale in which they were identified, were to be exempt from execution. Again, in Latvia, Gypsies were drafted into the Wehrmacht, while those of Eastern Galicia and Lwow were generally spared.

Lastly, and the most salient fact of all, were the differing policies established at Auschwitz for Jews and Gypsies. The essence of this programmatic difference at Auschwitz can fairly be described as, and correctly attributed to, a fundamental governing distinction between a genocidal vs. a non-genocidal schema. The gas chambers are the logical consummation, the literal teleology, of Nazi anti-Jewish racial manicheanism. The same cannot and ought not be said of Nazi anti-Gypsy pieties. The black identification triangles worn by Gypsies at Auschwitz (and Buchenwald and earlier at Dachau and Ravensbrück) indicative of *asocial* rather than racial criminals, meant that in a hierarchical cosmos defined by racial criteria they all did not have to die. Even Kenrick and Puxon, despite their strong desire to conflate the Jewish and Gypsy situation in order to magnify the Gypsy tragedy, are forced to describe the system relative to Gypsies operative at Auschwitz as follows:

According to Broad, a member of the SS staff, the camp authorities received a telegram from Berlin just as the camp was opening saying the Gypsies should not be treated the same as Jews. We cannot say for certain on the basis of existing knowledge that the Gypsies were sent to Auschwitz to be killed. Those unfit for labour were not gassed on arrival and only a few Gypsies worked during the first months, so there was no policy of 'Annihilation through work'. Also the Gypsies in other camps were not transferred to Auschwitz.

This essential, asymmetrical, dissociative reading of Auschwitz practice is, moreover, supported by Commandant Höss's own testimony on the matter.

Important for substantiating the argument for a meaningful distinction between the Nazi treatment of Jews and Gypsies is the evidence supplied by the markedly dissimilar rules governing the fate of women, especially pregnant women and children in the two communities. To be a pregnant Gypsy woman, or an infant, did not mean, as was the case with pregnant Jewish women and infants, certain, near-instant death. No order, no overriding national or metaphysical imperative required such victims. Infant mortality rates among the Gypsy newborn in the camp were high, but it was not an ontic necessity that, as with Jewish infants, they be total. This is not to suggest that the Gypsies were treated any way but brutally at Auschwitz, but at the same time, their treatment, however obscene, and their fate, however cruel, was qualitatively different, at once less ritualistic, less uncompromising, less categorical, *on orders,* than that of the Jews. This is evidenced pellucidly if we compare the mad, sanctioned rush to kill Jews, to eliminate every vestige of Jewish blood from active human history, at Auschwitz in 1943 and 1944 with the relative neglect, that is the life-saving indifference to the Gypsy population of the camp in this frenzied climactic period of its existence. While up to 10,000 Hungarian Jews were being murdered daily at Auschwitz in the spring and summer of 1944, the *total* number of Gypsies deported to Auschwitz between February 1943 and July 1944 was approximately 22,500, and even of these a fair percentage survived because the SS had their murderous gaze distinctly fixated on the Jews.

It is apposite to note in this context, in addition, that the two relatively large 'operations' against the Gypsies at Auschwitz, during which 1700 Gypsies from Bialystok were gassed in March 1943 and 1042 were gassed on 25 May 1943 (again over 950 of whom were from Bialystok, the remainder from Austria) were due, in at least large if not full measure, to reasons of communicable disease. Both 'actions' are accounted for in the sources as the consequence of 'suspected typhus cases', and there is reason to believe that this was, in fact, the motivation behind these two special odious events. This recognition, of course, in no way legitimates these heinous crimes, but it does indicate that the rationale behind it was not that of a blanket policy of genocide. Relevant, too, is the deportation from Auschwitz, with the intention of keeping them alive, of approximately 4300 Gypsies to such concentration camps as Buchenwald, Flossenburg and Ravensbrück, when the special Gypsy camp at Auschwitz was eradicated between April and August 1944. In this period, coincidentally, vast numbers of Jews were being brought to the camp with the express purpose of murdering them. Though approximately 4000 Gypsies were exterminated when the Gypsy camp was liquidated, this number represents less than 17 per cent of the total number of Gypsy inmates who were incarcerated in Auschwitz at the time. Comparing these Gypsy statistics in quantity and percentage of victims to the over 1 million Jewish inmates who died at the camp, representing a rate of over 90 per cent of those who arrived there, and comparing them as well to the 58,000 Jews who were force-marched to other camps when Auschwitz was wholly liquidated in mid-January 1945, most of whom died during these forced marches, reveals the incontrovertible gap between the intended fate of the two peoples. To so argue is not intended to minimize the terrible fate, or the individual suffering, of the over 200,000 Gypsies who were murdered by the SS, including 5000–15,000 at Chelmno, thousands in medical experiments, thousands more at Maidanek, Bergen Belsen, Ravensbrück, Sobibor, Treblinka, Neuengamme, Belzec as well as Auschwitz, but it is to distinguish their collective, national odyssey from that of the Jewish people.

The only defensible conclusion, the only adequate encompassing judgment to be drawn from this mass of evidence is that in comparison to the ruthless, monolithic, meta-political, genocidal design of Nazism *vis-à-vis* Jews, nothing similar, for all the enacted, obliterative, malevolence, existed in the case of the Gypsies. The ambiguous, even paradoxical, features of Nazi policy in the latter case is reflected in the grim statistics of the tale. Of an estimated 936,000 Gypsies in Nazi-occupied territory, 219,700 are estimated to have been annihilated, i.e., 23.5 per cent, as compared to the more than 85 per cent of Jews who fell under Nazi control. In the end, it was only Jews and the Jews alone who were the victims of a total genocidal onslaught in both intent and practice at the hands of the Nazi murderers.*

V. HOMOSEXUALS DURING THE SECOND WORLD WAR

In recent years a group, heretofore essentially unstudied, has been added to the list of Hitler's victims: homosexuals. Largely, if not exclusively, through the publicity surrounding the play *Bent,* the Nazi persecution of gays has become the focus of serious discussion. Certain supporters of the homosexual cause have gone so far as to assign them the preeminent 'outsider position in the Nazi hierarchy, lower even than the racial antagonism engendered by the Jews'. For example, in *Bent,* the playwright has one of the two main protagonists survive by 'trading up' his pink badge worn by homosexuals for a yellow star of David. In addition, enormous demographic claims have been made regarding the extent of homosexual repression, incarceration and annihilation.

The variegated background facts are these: (1) Soon after the Nazis' accession to power, a significant number of homosexual men were rounded up and imprisoned in concentration camps. (2) In May 1933 the Nazis burned the holdings of the Magnus Hirschfeld Institute of Sexual Science in Berlin. (3) In 1934 (30 June) Ernst Röhm, the leader of the paramilitary SA, was murdered on Hitler's orders, the 'justification' offered being his homosexuality. (4) Between 1933 and 1945 laws against homosexuality were written and acted upon, especially Paragraphs 175 and 175A of the Criminal Code. (5) A special 'Reich Centre for the Fight against Homosexuality and Abortion' was established on 10 October 1936, under the jurisdiction of the Criminal Police. As a consequence of these legal enactments and political persecutions, there were, on average, 10,000 convictions per year for homosexuality in Germany during the Nazi era according to official court records. Thus, at its simplest, there were 120,000 convictions over a dozen years. This count, however, reveals only a fragment of the tale, for only a small fraction of those convicted were sentenced to concentration camps, and fewer still to death camps. For example, in 1937 Himmler exempted 'the incarceration of an actor or an artist on the ground of unnatural vice' except where Himmler's 'express permission' was obtained. Further edicts is-

---

* Further valuable discussion with colleagues at the 'Remembering for the Future' Conference has both reinforced the argument here and indicated that the various demographic estimates might be subject to some revision as new evidence comes to light.

sued by Himmler also required the offenders, if actors, be caught 'in the act'. Again, to bring order into the proceedings, and reduce the number of people sent to jail or camps, the Reich Minister of the Interior issued a clarification on 14 December 1937, that only repeat offenders be incarcerated (on a fourth criminal offense or someone who had already served six months in jail). Again, in 1940, Himmler singled out multiple offenders.

All these factors considered, a careful review of the concentration and death camp figures, where available, suggests that only a small number of prisoners were imprisoned for their sexual preference. It has been conservatively estimated, based on the extant concentration camp records, that 'the total number of officially defined homosexual prisoners ever incarcerated in the camps was about 10,000 (but it could be as low as 5000 or as high as 15,000)'. Some additional homosexuals were incarcerated under the *Führer* Decree of October 1939 dealing with 'the elimination [of] harmful influences of the alien parts of the population which represent a danger to the Reich and German Volk Community', and possibly, though records are unclear, under the Hitler decree on euthanasia. But even allowing for these matters the number of homosexuals deported to death camps or killed elsewhere in the Reich remains small.

There is evidence to suggest that in the 1930s homosexuals were often assigned, along with many other groups, the most arduous work assignments, but this practice gave way after 1939, and especially after 1941, with the explicit formulation of anti-Jewish genocidal policies. In addition, there is abundant documentation to indicate that the gays often brought out a special, sexually perverse sadism on the part of the SS and their collaborators. As a consequence, for that relatively small percentage of homosexuals who were sent to camps, the percentage of those who died, with allowance for different mortality rates in different camps and at different periods, seems higher than for political and other non-Jewish prisoners. At the same time, however, it should be noted that the records indicate that 13 per cent of all homosexual camp inmates were reprieved and released. This again points away from any imputation of genocidal assault on the gay population.

In sum, it has been estimated that 60 per cent of those imprisoned for homosexuality died in the camps. Translated into a numerical total, this suggests (based on an estimate of 10,000 homosexual inmates) that 6,000 homosexuals died *cum* homosexuals as a consequence of Nazi persecution. This figure, however, is remarkably modest, when one considers Himmler's own estimate of the number of homosexuals in Germany in the 1930s. 'When we assumed power in 1933', Himmler asserted in February 1940, 'we were also confronted with homosexual organizations. Their registered membership was 2 million: conservative estimates of experts lead us to conclude that there are 2 to 4 million homosexuals in Germany'. If Kinsey's estimate that 4 per cent of any general modern population is gay is correct, then Himmler's estimate was plausible, allowing for all the ambiguity in such projections, based on a total German population of approximately 50 million, not to speak of the hundreds of millions in occupied Europe from the English Channel to Leningrad, from Norway to North Africa.

Given this demographic estimate, the number of gays killed, while deplorable, inexcusable and brutal, translates into a small fraction of less than 1 per cent. As in the case of the perverse persecutions of witches in the medieval era, we here move in a terrain of barbarism, prejudice, sadism and sexual repression and expression, yet not one which was in any sense genocidal.

VI. POLISH AND UKRAINIAN LOSSES DURING THE SECOND WORLD WAR

Should one object that the losses experienced by the Poles and Ukrainians (and Russians) during the war contradict any claim for the uniqueness of the *Shoah,* let it be explicitly recognized that the vast casualties suffered by these national groups are of a completely different order from those experienced by the Jews, or even the Gypsies, and, accordingly, properly fall outside any analytically precise discussion of genocide. Certainly millions of Slavs (and Russians) died at the hands of the Nazis, but the ultimate Nazi intent toward both groups was not genocide, but enslavement. After destroying their leadership and educated classes, the Nazis intended to turn these people into a permanent underclass, a modern type of helot, an enduring exploitable, primitive colonial empire. For all the real anguish and suffering of these Eastern European peoples, regarding which estimates of loss ranging up to 10 million have been proposed, those who would, for whatever reason, conflate their experience to that of the Jews during the period 1941–1945 either do not know the facts or do not care to know them. This is not said to denigrate or reduce the immensity of the tragedy lived through by these groups. It is, however, stated without equivocation in order to maintain our phenomenological distinction between physical genocide and other forms of mass despoliation and demographic reduction.

The point of maintaining this distinction is revealed in considering, for example, Polish casualties under Nazi control. Of a pre-war Polish population of approximately 29 million, including 3.3 million Jews, approximately 3 million Christian Poles were estimated to have been killed during the war, 600,000 of whom died while fighting in defense of Poland either in the national army during the initial invasion or later in resistance movements during the occupation. Excluding the percentage lost through direct military action (600,000), the percentage of non-Jewish Poles killed is somewhat less than 10 per cent, as compared to the death rate of over 90 per cent for Polish Jews. The statistical disparity in the death rate between the two groups does not suggest or support claims for a genocidal Nazi blueprint in Poland.

The Nazi policy in Poland was aimed at destroying the national leadership so the masses could be colonized and enslaved. And this is what actually took place, not genocide. If one compares the demographic impact of the Nazi destruction of the Polish 'elite' with similar destructive strategies in the many cases of political domination and colonialism one can easily find in the apposite historical sources, one will recognize a common pattern. The Polish losses in the war years of occupation were, as noted, approximately 10 per cent, a figure not radically dissimilar from, and in many cases, less than, relevant comparative instances of 'internal colonialism', in the broad sense of that term. Moreover, this figure does not justify extravagant claims about the Nazis employing an overly broad definition of 'elite' in the Polish context (*contra* Lukas). Lukas' own figures, in fact, prove that the 'elite', within quite acceptable parameters for the meaning of this term, was uniquely targeted for elimination. Thus, for example, at war's end, Poland had lost '45 per cent of her physicians and dentists, 57 per cent of her attorneys, more than 16 per cent of her teachers, 40 per cent of her professors, 30 per cent of her technicians, and more than 18 per cent of her clergy'. These figures speak for themselves when one compares them to the very small percentage of, for example, Polish farmers or artisans murdered by the Nazis. Nor again, would anyone disagree that the Nazis sought to implement a thorough program of cultural genocide and economic despoliation in Poland in order to assure their future control.

The situation elsewhere in Eastern Europe was much the same as that in Poland. In the Ukraine, which suffered even greater overall losses than Poland during the war, the conclusion to be drawn *vis-à-vis* Nazi policy is the same as for Poland. The total population of pre-war Ukraine is estimated at 40 million, of whom upwards of 6–7 million are thought to have been killed. However, a more refined breakdown of these aggregate numbers indicates that of the total of 6–7 million Ukrainian losses 900,000 to 1 million were Jews, while of the remaining 5–6 million (approximately) victims, 1.5–2.5 million died in direct military situations (this tally may well be too conservative) leaving a residue of 3.6–4.5 million non-Jewish civilian casualties out of a total non-Jewish population of 39 million, i.e., approximately 9–11.5 per cent of the population. Again, the pattern of Nazi destructive activities centered on the elite, with the aim of permanently enslaving the leaderless masses. As Wytwycky has correctly observed, 'The Ukranians were never slated for total annihilation, as were the Jews and Gypsies [*sic*]'.

Likewise, in Belorussia the total population was 10.5 million before the Nazi invasion in the summer of 1941, including Jews. Of these, 2.3 million people are estimated to have been killed. Of these, 250,000 were Jews, and approximately 1 million people were lost in direct military action, leaving 1 million to 1.4 million civilian casualties. This, once more, translates into roughly 13.5 per cent of the non-Jewish population.

In none of these Eastern European locations do we witness a desire to replicate a program of genocide.

VII. CONCLUSION

This analysis summarizes in very schematic fashion a highly variegated, historically diverse, chronologically and geographically diffuse set of empirical circumstances. All share the fact that they are cited as cases of genocide comparable to the *Shoah;* some by virtue of their size, their massive loss of human life; others by virtue of their sharing in the racially driven context of Nazism. But all, on closer inspection, as we have shown, are to be fundamentally distinguished from the Holocaust even when they reveal horrifyingly large casualty figures. That is to say, the statistics are never sufficient in drawing the fundamental normative conclusions we seek, but they are not irrelevant either. In every case the 'how' or 'what' needs to be balanced by the 'why' for a definitive, defensible, conclusion to emerge. And this applies, of course, to the many apposite cases, for example the Gulag, the mass-murder of the Armenians by the Turks in the First World War, and the tribal and colonial wars in Burundi, Nigeria, Indonesia, Vietnam and Cambodia, that would need to be considered in any complete comparative taxonomy of mass murder and genocide. If nothing else, it is my hope that this chapter will have provided enough hard evidence and sound argument to persuade all scholars to be more judicious, more exact, more precise, in their comparative decipherment of Auschwitz, and in the conclusions they draw from such comparisons.[1]

NOTES

1. In keeping with the Conference format of this essay, all source notes, other than this one, have been excluded. Full documentation on all these and other cases will be found in my forthcoming three-volume, *The Holocaust in Historical Context* (tentative title), to be published by Oxford University Press beginning in 1992.

6

Auschwitz and the Gulag: Discontinuities and Dissimilarities

S cholars and others have, for various reasons, been likening Auschwitz and the Gulag since the 1940's, and the comparison has
become "canonical" since its powerful employment by Hannah Arendt
in her *Origins of Totalitarianism,* first published in 1951.[1] Today this
linkage is again at the center of the historical and normative discussion
due to its vital role in the "Historical Debate" generated in Germany by
the obscene nationalist apologetics of Ernest Nolte and his supporters.[2]
But is this accepted historical piety correct? I think not. In contradistinction to Arendt and Nolte,[3] and others, I want to argue that the usual
analogies drawn between these two evil phenomena are largely and
essentially misleading, even fundamentally incorrect.

Before proceeding, however, let me be very clear about what I am and
what I am not saying. The difference that I will argue for is not moral—
that one environment was more evil than the other (though this may
also be the case)—but phenomenological, that is that the two contexts
were created by, organized through, and employed in and for vastly
different purposes, with nearly wholly different regulative ideologies. In
their design, empirical facticity, intentionality and teleology they are
radically alternative forms of manipulation, violence, and death. Both
Auschwitz and the Gulag perpetrated monstrous acts of inhumanity and
it is the recognition of this fact that leads to the intuitive assertions
regarding their commonality. But on other than ethical grounds, and the
unsparing moral condemnation of both, the comparison is misleading.

Reprinted by permission of Edwin Mellen Press.

That is to say, the awareness of this primal ethical similarity must serve as the beginning of a conversation, not its conclusion, if we are not to lapse into intellectual barrenness, into that type of conceptual sterility that is a corollary of an inability to make necessary, if hard, distinctions. And it is to the making of such repercussive phenomenological discriminations as a moral obligation, as a debt to the truth, that we must now turn, inquiring in what way the Gulag is comparable to Auschwitz, in what way is it not.

I

The intriguing, not altogether transparent exposition of the larger social-historical contexts out of which Nazism and Stalinism respectively grew is where we must begin.[4] Nazism emerged out of the turmoil of the post–World War I years, out of the inability of Germany to admit its own responsibility for defeat, out of the lack of viable democratic traditions in Germany, exacerbated by the inherent weaknesses of the Weimer state,[5] and out of the economic chaos created by the combination of reparations required by the Versailles Treaty and the "Great Depression." Yet it occurred in a highly modernized, technologically and culturally advanced society.[6] By contrast, Stalin came to power in the wake of a violent revolution wrought by an ideological, urban minority whose achievement of political control was in direct violation of those very Marxist theories in whose name it seized power. The revolution and Stalin's eventual triumph occurred in a society that was generally backward[7] and underdeveloped in every sense and, importantly, that was accustomed to harsh autocratic government maintained by force, secret police agencies, and detention camps, chronicled so powerfully by Dostoevsky.[8] A society without any tradition of political freedom or human rights. It was, perhaps, therefore not altogether unexpected that Bolshevism should, once it had seized political power, replace one menacing dictatorship with another.[9] Certainly the revolutionary leadership was not averse to the use of force to maintain itself as the Kronstadt uprising and its suppression showed.[10] Or again as the coming into being of the Checka revealed. Indeed Lenin seems to have felt such repression was a necessary condition for the maintenance of a proletarian revolution.[11] Thus, the ground for a bureaucratic, centralized, dictatorial, if not murderous regime was established,[12] to be exploited to its full potential for evil, as well as transmuted in unprecedented[13] ways, by Lenin's successor, Comrade Stalin.

Stalin, with his immense energy, uncanny cunning, total unscrupulousness, and eccentric psychology, which included considerable native intelligence, would exacerbate, in central areas even recreate and transmogrify through a quantitative radicalness, all existing problems.[14] His parochial Russian nationalism[15] would bring him into conflict with Russia's minorities; his uncompromising drive towards rapid industrialization would produce the terrible, ravaging collision with the peasants (not only the wealthy kulaks); and his egomaniacal hunger for absolute power would cause his paranoic fear of any and all holders of power, no matter how marginal or delimited, within the state and lead thereby to the many bloody party and army purges that mark his tenure as leader of the Soviet Union.[16] Together these factors, always combined with his heightened political instincts and total lack of political morality, would sweep away all real and imagined opposition, leaving him not only the undisputed ruler of Russia, but the greatest murderer, in quantitative terms, history has every known.[17]

Of great importance is the fact that the historical context, the political culture and socio-economic realities, out of which Stalinism emerged and in which it functioned, was markedly different[18] from that of Nazism. In Nazi Germany, because of its virulent antisemitic legacy (shared with most of Europe), and, even more, due to its own contemporary ideological constructions which led to genocide, the Jews were singled out for "metaphysical," i.e., racial and Manichean, reasons. There was, neither in 1933 nor subsequently, any fundamental political or economic[19] gain in persecuting them, despite much widespread misunderstanding to the contrary. In Russia the Terror was, in contrast, a function of politics and economic policy (industrialization) plus Stalin's mental instability— a murderous quirkiness[20] he shared with Hitler.

Put another way, Hitler could have pursued all the dominant goals in his political revolution, e.g., national renaissance, *lebensraum,* even the disemancipation of western Jewry, without the "final solution"—assuming for the moment that killing Jews *per se* was not his major goal, as it seems finally to have been.[21] In contrast, Stalin could not have succeeded in his push towards rapid collectivization and the transformation of the fundamentals of the Soviet economy as part of the overall socialist reconstruction of Russian society without a direct clash with the peasantry as well as a deadly collision with the remaining elements of the pre-revolutionary socio-economic structure that still survived.[22] He could, of course, have taken a different tack on economic policy, as Lenin and others had thought the better course, but once he decided on radical socialization and industrialization, or as he might argue in his own self-defense, with some modest justification, once these policies were forced by events upon him, extensive, pervasive conflict was inevitable. Isaac Deutscher has sensitively described the inherent confrontation in these terms:

> It would be easy for the historian to pass unqualified judgement on Stalin if he could assume that in his fight against Bukharin, Rykov, and Tomsky he pursued only his private ambition. This was not the case. His personal ends were not the only or the most important stakes in the struggle. In the tense months of 1928 and 1929 the whole fate of Soviet Russia hung in the balance.
>
> On the face of things, the opening of the crisis was so undramatic as to appear irrelevant. The peasants had failed to deliver a few million tons of grain to the towns. Prosaic as the event was, there was real drama in it. In refusing to sell food, the peasants had no clear political motives. They did not aim at the overthrow of the Soviets, although some of the politically minded elements among the well-to-do peasantry hoped for such an ending. The mass of the peasants was driven to apply that peculiar form of "sabotage" by economic circumstances. Most of the small farms did not produce more than was needed to feed their owners. After more than ten years the agricultural upheaval of 1917 was now taking its revenge. The splitting up of large estates into tiny holdings had given the Bolsheviks the support of the peasantry in the civil war; but in consequence the productivity of farming, or rather its capacity to feed the urban population, deteriorated. The big farmers, on the other hand, demanded high prices for food, prices intolerably burdensome to the townspeople; and they also pressed for further concessions to capitalist farming. Stalin was, indeed, confronted with a most complex dilemma. If he yielded more ground to the peasants he would dangerously antagonize the urban working classes, which, on the whole, now again stood behind the Government, especially after the Government had about 1927, succeeded in rebuilding industry to its pre-war condition. But the refusal to yield to the peasantry also entailed the threat of famine and unrest in the towns. The problem demanded a radical solution. If the Government had begun to curb the big farmers and to encourage gradual collectivization earlier, as Trotsky and Zinoviev had counselled, it might not have needed now to resort to drastic emergency measures in order to obtain bread. As things stood, Stalin acted under the overwhelming pressure of events. The circumstance that he was not prepared for the events precipitated him into a course of action over which he was liable to lose control.[23]

Survival, economic and national, not ontological fantasies, was the key determinant. The contextual consideration of the terror in Russia suggests that Stalin was confronting, to some degree at least, real[24] enemies both politically and in class terms during the 1920's, and possibly up until 1934–36.[25] By contrast, the Jews of Germany (and Europe) were not, except by definition, an authentic, political "enemy."

Still more, despite scholarly claims to the contrary,[26] Stalinism is not a complete *novum* in Bolshevik (and earlier Russian) tradition; it is, for all its radicalness, even recognizing its innovativeness, intimate with the Russian past. Not so the Nazi death camps. Auschwitz was unpredictable before it occurred, while having occurred it is not accounted for, nor explained, by precedents, despite the many terrible anti-semitic precedents that do exist. A student of Czarist coercion and Leninist ideology would not be totally surprised, as the vast secondary literature proves, to encounter the phenomenon of the Gulag, though its sheer magnitude would still ravage one's sensibilities. By contrast, no study of pre-1933 German or modern western European history would suggest, or *ex post facto* explain, Treblinka and *Einsatzgruppen*. Looking back one can find "roots," but no amount of such "backward looking" historiography is sufficient to the reality. What occurred not only so exceeds what was "predictable," but in its qualitative dimensions is so discontinuous with its immediate pre-history as to represent its antithesis. The uncompromising, revolutionary evil of Auschwitz, as compared to the massive, unceasing, primitive immorality of the Gulag, therefore conjures a different mood, a dissimilar cognitive response. The Holocaust remains always "beyond comprehension," an event as much revealed as mysterious, much as we must insist that it be open to scholarly investigation and ordinary rules of historical and philosophical enquiry. It is these very qualities that lead to the constant temptation—*to be resisted*—to remove it altogether from history. By contrast, the Gulag generates rage and dread, anger and sorrow, but not mythification. One is prepared, alas, to find it all too believable.

II

It may be that this impression, this disjunctive response, rests ultimately on the assimilability of the Gulag to two not unfamiliar historical categories, penal detention and slavery, that mix together in a particularly bitter way to create the Stalinist camps. Penal institutions, including the use of special incarceration centers for political "dissidents," is an all too common historical phenomenon.[27] For example, the Nazi use of internment camps from 1933, e.g., Dachau, for political enemies such as

Communists and liberals, is a parallel occurrence belonging to this general history and need not detain us.[28] The same may be said of the schematic role and temporal evolution of Czarist prison institutions into Bolshevik ones. Dostoyevsky's *The House of the Dead* leaves us no innocent illusions on this subject. The relation of Stalin's Gulag to the normative structures of slavery,[29] however, requires a closer, adequately nuanced look. The basic, compelling comparability of the two oppressive configurations lies in their purposeful, aggressive exploitation of human labor, i.e., both are rooted in and maintained by specific economic and social needs that are held to be best met by unfree labor.[30] Stalin's policy of the forced acceleration of industrialization was "aided"[31] by reducing a significant percentage of Russia's population into, effectively, "slaves," if by another name. Through this coercive labor policy, rooted in the Czarist past,[32] the inmates of the camps were made to provide crucial cheap labor for all forms of Soviet industrialization, ranging from the mining of raw materials to the building of transportation networks.[33] Representing, at its peak, on some accounts, more than 1/6th[34] of the adult male population, this "enslaved" group comprised the largest single industrial working class in Russia. Moreover, this captive class was able to be set tasks that were: (a) necessary to the economy as a whole, yet which were situated in places where labor on the free market would have been very costly to procure;[35] and (b) that could be accomplished by the calculated substitution of a large work force in place of expensive machines, machines that could only be procured through foreign currency that the Soviet Union did not have.[36]

What requires particular recognition is that this slave labor system was not created as the result of the devastation wrought by the First World War, nor the consequences of special short-term problematics, aberrations, in the life of the Stalinist regime, though the numbers of such workers did vary from period to period. Rather, and unmistakably, it was inherent, as Solzhenitsyn has so dramatically emphasized, in the very fabric of Stalinism *per se*.[37] The abiding constitutive excess which was a dominant feature of Stalinism was predicated upon, enacted within, an already grotesque, authoritarian order. Not only in the Gulag empire, but throughout the Soviet economy coercion was the norm after 1929. The brutalities of agricultural collectivization form an essential ingredient in our schematic deconstruction, and to them must be added the extensive re-organization of (regular) industrial labor in 1930 that led, for example, in December 1938, to the system of industrial passports and in October 1940 to the introduction of severe penalties for lateness, absenteeism, and curtailment of the workers' freedom in job selection.[38] Even more significant, analogous in intent to slave labor, is the system of State Labor Reserves[39] established by Stalin in October 1940 which, in effect, created large-scale pools of young, *unfree* industrial workers. According to this scheme, as many as 1 million male teenagers, the majority off the farms, would be "drafted" into technical industrial apprenticeships deemed necessary by the State economic planners. After a training period lasting between 6 months and 2 years, depending on the job for which he was being prepared, the young man would be assigned a task to which he was legally bound for 4 years. In this way a novel method of industrial serfdom was instituted. The Fourth Five-Year Plan called for 4,500,000 such recruits, a major percentage of all industrial employees. And, as in the Gulag, such unfree labor was expected to provide, in particular, 70% to 80% of the new workers in the heavy industries, e.g., coal-mining, the mining of ferrous metals, and machine building.[40] In this sense, then, the Gulag can be identified as the end point of a spectrum of Soviet labor exploitation rather than as a discontinuous and radical alternative to the "normal" Stalinist social order.

Upon reflection it becomes unarguably clear that those who project a mythical "Stalinism without excess" are twice deluded, once because the notorious extremes were the very stuff of Stalin's regime, and secondly, because the excesses were built into a normative, abiding structure that, in and of itself, was barbarously abusive. Hitler, or perhaps more precisely Himmler and Speer,[41] would create, during the war, a somewhat comparable slave empire comprised of captured prisoners of war, overrun Slavic peoples, and even citizens of conquered countries in western Europe, not to mention the industrial complexes utilizing Jewish labor at Auschwitz and elsewhere. However, Hitler's use of slave labor, whatever its overall qualitative comparability to Stalin's, differed with respect to the expropriation of Jewish labor. Jewish manpower resources were not utilized as slave labor, either in the classical or Stalinist sense,[42] but rather as, in Ferencz's telling phrase, "less than slave [labor]," i.e., the German intent was not to foster economic efficiency, or substantive production gains, but instead, sought to establish the disutilitarian equation that balanced labor utilization with necessary guarantees that Jewish workers be worked to death in a very specific, highly inelastic period of time.[43] Stalin's system, in contrast, theoretically at least, and more often than not in practice, was predicated on a fixed period of forced labor. The dominant concern of the regime was the realization of the labor quotas, while at the same time being callously, cynically *indifferent* to the survivability of its prisoner labor force. Whether Kolyma workers lived or died was a matter of little moral or practical import, aside from its bearing on productivity, to Stalin or the camp bureaucracy. If inmates could survive under the prevailing execrable conditions, well and good, but their individual fate was not primary—*neither that they survive nor that they die.* In the main, during most of the Stalinist era the Gulag was uncaring vis-à-vis the majority, its state-dictated attitude towards its wards expressed in a sceptical, perverse disinterest in their particularity. Without doubt there was in the organization of the Gulag much malice, sadism, and murder. Brutality was normal, the norm brutal. What was absent, however, was a specific, unambiguous national policy of mass murder. Despite the high death toll in the Gulag, with the exception of that exceptional year 1938, the major causes of death in this environment were corollaries of the dolorific natural conditions and the official attitude of unconcern that had the impact of ramifying the negative consequences of the ecological habitat. No less a critic of Stalin's Camps than Robert Conquest has summarized these circumstances in the following terms:

Previous years [pre-1938] had seen, on occasion, massive casualties. But these had been due to inefficiencies in supply, attempts to carry out assignments in impossible conditions, and in fact—if in exaggerated form—the normal incompetence and brutality of Soviet life. When the difficulties could be overcome, conditions, as we have seen, were tolerable. But above all, prisoners were not subjected to lethal conditions on purpose.[44]

Even in that cruelest of years, 1938,[45] when Stalin and his new chief henchman for the Kolyma region, Major Garanin, ordered an unprecedented wave of shootings, increased every manner of abuse, and saw to it that conditions went from bad to unbearable, even then, for the entire year, the whole Kolyma district witnessed "only" 40,000[46] shootings, i.e., planned, directly sponsored, intentional, official murders.[47] And, even now, 1938, executions were still coupled to work quotas[48]—and generally unconnected to any other ideological or normative category, e.g., kulaks, old Bolsheviks, or Jews. This is not to argue that Stalin's new ferocity towards the Gulag's population did not take its considerable, if more oblique, toll during this year. Figures are uncertain, but estimates ranging from 200,000 to 400,000 deaths caused by cold, starvation, and overwork are commonly accepted. For this one year, under these exceptional conditions, the Gulag approached Auschwitz *asymptotically.* Asymptotically because even in this worst of years the Gulag did not operate under the same equation of life[49] and death as did Auschwitz. The priorities of labor versus death, of productivity versus dehumanization, did shift towards a heretofore unprecedented near equality; yet, even at its nadir, the demands of life, even if translated and reduced to economic units, still had at least equal weight.[50] In this matrix exploitation and annihilation certainly became too casually contraposed, while the original dominant economic drive saw itself paralleled by a corrupt desire to debase, even destroy, many of the Camp inmates. However, even amidst this rueful re-evaluation of purposes, at no time was the equation so wholly inverted that death was all; the highest, supreme, unchallenged good. Moreover, and elemental to the Nazi vs. Gulag comparison, the Gulag killed people distributively, i.e., taking its toll on all groups, singling none out for "special treatment."[51] Then again, the powerful streak of harsh realism in Stalin's perception of life caused him to recognize the need for "compromise" between actual economic requirements and the primitive desire to "punish" real or imagined enemies, while his Marxist-Leninist ideology allowed for such mediation. Alternatively, Hitler's severe biocentric "idealism" encouraged no comparable compromise on the Jewish question, while his immolating racial metaphysics permitted none.

As a consequence, Himmler's SS empire manifested no such mediating dispositions, nor did it represent similar, primarily utilitarian priorities, at least not where the *Judenfrage* was concerned. In this arena it was primordially committed not only to Jewish submissiveness, to the exploitation of frightfully controlled Jewish labor, but also, and more rudimentarily, to the unenigmatic biological extinction of each and every Jew trapped within its parameters. Hitler and his Aryan elite were neither sceptical about nor disinterested, *contra* the controlling rationality of the Gulag, in the fate of "their" Jews—they were, rather, passionate advocates of the universal imperative that all Jews *must* die. Under no conditions, no matter how economically advantageous their efforts and no matter how politically co-operative Jewry proved itself to be, could it be left to survive. *Mere* Jewish survival was the active enemy. Compared to 40,000 shootings in total in the Kolyma in 1938, 10,000 Jews a day died at Auschwitz in 1944.

III

The Gulag was not Auschwitz. Why it was not lies in the differences between the reigning ideologies, let us better call them mythologies, held by the two regimes in question. Nazism was a novel, peculiarly deadly amalgam of racial, Social Darwinian, and Manichean elements that reified the Jew not only as a biological inferior and the enemy of all positive values, but still more importantly as the paradigmatic temporal manifestation of nothing less than the principle of cosmic negativity *per se*. Conversely, Hitler was the supreme contemporary positive incarnation of the Spirit, its principal medium in the world, the prophetic leader of the struggle for that racial purity that translated itself into the advance of civilization, an advance that simultaneously assured certain victory over the metaphysical forces of universal darkness. It is here that the *Führerprinzip* becomes so consequential, with its meta-legal, meta-ethical legitimacy and authority. All positive restraints, either moral or jurisprudential, must—by definition—give way before the incontrovertible will of the Führer. He, and he alone, discerns the opaque but compelling signs of destiny and leads the *Herrenvolk* accordingly.

Marxist-Leninist-Stalinist ideology parallels this mythic political dogma to a considerable extent, in particular through its heightened self-consciousness of itself as the avant-garde of the uncompromisable historical struggle for existential emancipation from class tyranny. Marx and his many, diverse heirs were convinced that they had discerned, in the materialist dialectic, the root principle of historical change, and accordingly were, in history's primordial struggle for human liberation, on the side of the angels. "The Marxist doctrine," Lenin pronounced, "is omnipotent because it is true."[52]

More technically described, Marxism-Leninism-Stalinism can be said to share, allowing for its own particular ideologically reconstructed analysis of key categories and concepts, two of the three principal metaphysical dogmas of Nazism: (a) a variant form of Manicheanism; and (b) its own special totalitarian rendition of Social Darwinism. Its Manicheanism manifests itself in its definition of the class struggle as an unbounded, yet determinate war between the inherently "progressive" forces of history and those that are "reactionary," that is, those that oppose the emancipation and autonomy of the proletariat. Marx's revolutionary conceptual breakthrough was his "discovery" of the universal motivating principle of this conflict, the economic dialectic of material productive forces, which allowed him, armed with this "gnosis," to unlock the inner, heretofore secret, code of history's unfolding. Through such knowledge the Marxist can learn how to assist the virtuous, proletarian masses in overcoming their execrable, tyrannical antitheses, thereby ushering in the socialist equivalent of the "Kingdom of God." Such inspired goals demand a war, for all its terror, "making no concessions whatever to the accursed heritage of serf-ownership, asiatic barbarism and human degradation" and "creating conditions in which it will be impossible for the bourgeoisie to exist, or for a new bourgeoisie to arise" (Lenin). This avowed ruthlessness is legitimate because it is directed against a robber class, which manifests far more despotic behavior, and because it brings into being a pristine order, which produces nothing less than a new form of man as well as an unprecedented mode of egalitarian society. Predicated on a changed distribution of power, the concern of this revolutionary transformation is nothing less than a wholly reconstructed socioeconomic order. Socialist Manicheanism, hence, requires a concrete political struggle for control of the state apparatus that creates, modulates, and distributes influence between classes.

In this challenging context, the revolutionary elite—the Party[53]— leads the remorseless assault against all, including liberal-democratic,[54] anti-proletarian forces. It absorbs all power, brooks no opposition in either theory or practice, and thereby gathers the necessary strength to liquidate the malevolent structures of the class enemy as well as to foment the revolutionary struggle from above. The Party is wholly justified by its revolutionary ethic, which aligns with historical necessity to demand that it transform the masses even while they seem unprepared for this apotheosis. It is in this criss-crossed way that the dialectic of organizational structure and ideology becomes realized: the Party—the bureaucratic vehicle—compellingly implements and rigorously supports the revolutionary Marxist-Leninist synthesis, while the encompassing ideology reinforces the enacted Party-organizational structure and its legal superstructure as reflected in juridical formulations such as the notorious Article 58 (on treason to the Fatherland) of the 1926 RSFSR Criminal Code.[55] It is also through this complex interweaving of form and doctrine that the Party legitimates its terror ideologically, as morally required for capturing the future. "Morality," Lenin would assert at the Third Komsomol Congress, "is that which serves the destruction of the old exploiting society."[56] This strident redefinition also authorizes the monopoly of power exercised by the revolutionary elite—the Party and its leadership. Through their peculiar "awareness" of the *Truth,* as well as of the mechanisms by which it works itself out in space-time, they possess the higher ethical right to total power. "People who were really convinced of the fact that they had advanced knowledge," Lenin asserted, "would be demanding not freedom for the new views alongside the old views, but the replacement of the latter by the former."[57] The Party has now been justified, in the context of this class conflict, as the ruthless agent, if and as required, for carrying through this revolutionary purge of bourgeois elements, indeed of all oppositional groups whether of the right or left, whether of the aristocratic or the middle class.

To this degree then there is a formal as well as structural parallelism between Nazism and Bolshevism, with both asserting their claims and coming to power on the basis of a party machinery outside of, and putatively superior to, the state apparatus.[58] In each case the Party justified itself as the spear-carrier of historical laws, as the embodiment of the Spirit. Moreover, each attributed to its leadership[59] special powers. "The revolutionary leadership," argued Lenin, "[is] rule that is unrestricted by any laws."[60] Hitler would agree. As a result, a war against ideological enemies, in the case of Nazism against its racial protagonists, in the case of Bolshevism its class opponents, was not only defended but recommended as a moral imperative. Yet for all the conceptual, mythic, logical, and bureaucratic similarities between these two immensely powerful world crusades, the defining difference between them must also be recognized.

The defining difference between Nazism and Stalinism resides in the seminal fact that each system understands its Manichean manifesto, its energizing first principles, in radically disparate ways. Given the economic basis of Marxist-Leninism, the imperative is to annihilate an oppressive class regime; the real opponent is a "false" exploitative labor-economic system. The class enemy is an enemy by virtue of the place he occupies in the deformed socioeconomic arrangement. "Our policy is a class policy," Stalin reminded the Central Committee. "He who thinks that one can conduct in the countryside a policy that will please everybody, the rich as well as the poor, is not a Marxist but an idiot . . ."[61] Accordingly, the visionary ambition is to alter the reigning organizational arrangements of society, thereby eliminating the regressive, enervating economic superstructure, and hence the structural immorality of existing political models. Such far-reaching social renovations entail one further, cardinal transposition as well: to eliminate the offending *status* of one's class enemy, that is, to dissolve the very notion of class and hence, necessarily, that of enemy *qua* enemy. Such fundamental repositioning, of course, might require terror on a grand scale, as evidenced, for example, in the protracted and painful war against the kulaks, for the bourgeoisie will not give up its privilege easily or willingly. The intent of such official violence, ideally, however, is not to attack the kulak *qua* being but to transform the power structure that corrupts both the bourgeoisie and the proletariat alike. (This is why at least 65 to 70 percent of the kulaks survived!) Ideologically, even for Stalin, *reeducation, not* physical extermination, is the consummate goal. Bolshevism declares an uncompromising war against the class enemy *qua* class enemy, against his class status; it does not declare an unlimited, annihilatory war against his person *qua* person. In this, Bolshevism manifests a conversionary doctrine and militant zeal analogous to that of the classic Catholic approach to the conversion of Jewry (or perhaps still closer to that of Islam towards Pagans). Reeducated, the former bourgeoisie can take its rightful place in the "workers' paradise," just as a converted Jew can become a fully equal member of Christian society, even a "Prince of the Church."

By comparison, Nazism does not merely apply its vengeful Manichean passion against an alternative economic class or sociocultural status, but against an opposing, assertedly biological givenness—that is, Semite versus Aryan. Given the fixed strategic construction of this binary opposition, it cannot take on the character of a war of status versus status— a collision that does not necessarily deny the essential humanity of the other—for, unlike class conflict, racial conflict does not allow for the conceptual or juridical separation of person and status. A Jew by status, defined biologically, is also necessarily a Jew in person. This, and precisely this, is the intended sting of racial claims—no reeducation, no conversion, no alteration in either status or person is possible. Hence, whereas Stalinism sought "confessions"[62] of wrongdoing, of ideological heresy, of "wrecking," as a required if not always successful prologomenon to social or political rehabilitation, Nazism sought no "confessions," no repentance, from Jews—for it allowed no possibility of their social (i.e., racial) rehabilitation. In this elemental sense, Nazism pushes the primordial struggle fundamental to cosmic-historical progress to a deeper level than Marxism—to biological rather than economic-cultural determinants. As such, Marxism-Leninism-Stalinism has programmatic alternatives open to it that Nazism does not possess. Race, as the primary, immutable determinant of the Manichean cosmology, demands a total war different *in kind* from the revolutionary clash entailed by Marxist-Leninist metaphysics.[63] This intrinsic dichotomy defines the qualitative incongruity between Stalin's Gulag[64] and Hitler's Auschwitz.

The instructive case against which to test these deconstructive meta-ideological observations on ideology is, of course, that provided by the treatment of the kulaks. On the one hand, their tragedy makes clear that all theoretical considerations of individual versus corporate categories, as well as all related questions of mediating moral restraints, were settled by Stalin in a most immoral "corporatist" fashion. For Stalin they were an identifiable segment within the overall population for whom belonging to a collective "category"[65] was to be all-consequential. Yet the actual nature of their appalling dismemberment as a "class," which meant such vast human suffering for millions of peasants, provides evidence that Stalin's onslaught against them was different in kind from Hitler's campaign against Jewry. Consider that: (a) Stalin explicitly chose to murder only a minority of the kulaks, though he could have murdered them all; and (b) the main assault, for all its severity, was against a "contingent," "socially alien"[66] identity, the nature of which was, by definition, subject to change.[67] Whatever neurotic fears energized and accompanied this convulsive anti-peasant policy, there can be no reason to doubt that what was elemental in this unstinting war was the kulaks' economic—that is, class—loyalties, loyalties that had to be broken down[68] for the general good to prevail according to the dominant socialist consensus. (Stalin was *not* alone in holding this view, which was *the* view of almost the entire Bolshevik elite, including Trotsky,[69] differences existing only as to how best to accomplish this policy.)[70] The desired alteration in the kulak's collective class consciousness, and correspondingly the kulak's status as a "class enemy," were to come about through forced collectivization. I estimate that 88 percent of the Russian peasantry, at a minimum, survived Stalin's class war against them in the 1930s. This loss rate of 12 percent or less indicates massive suffering but not a state-dictated, state-actualized policy of physical genocide based on criteria of socioeconomic "class."

IV

In pointing out the sociological, historical, economic, and ideological factors that operated distinctively and disjunctively in the Gulag and

Auschwitz we have no desire to relativize one at the expense of the other, or to deny the immense evil of both. However, evil comes in many forms and it is the task of scholarship, distasteful as it might be, to study these variegated forms and to recognize differences as well as similarities between them. When one looks closely at the Gulag and Auschwitz in all their destructive complexity, one cannot but be profoundly aware of how very dissimilar they are.

NOTES

1. Hannah Arendt, *The Origins of Totalitarianism* (New York, 1951; revised edition New York, 1966).
2. Fuller details of this debate are provided by Charles Meier, *The Unmasterable Past: History, Holocaust, and German National Identity* (Cambridge, 1988); Rudolf Augstein (ed.), *Historikerstreit: Die Dokumentation der Kontroverse um die Einzigartigkeit der nationalsozialistischen Judenvernichtung* (Munich, 1987); and Peter Baldwin (ed.), *Reworking the Past: Hitler, the Holocaust, and the Historians' Debate* (Boston, 1990).
3. In mentioning these two individuals together I do not mean to equate Arendt's employment of this connection with that of Nolte.
4. The particulars of the Nazi onslaught against Jewry will be described and analyzed exhaustively in my forthcoming three-volume study of the *Holocaust in Historical Context* (tentative title) to be published by Oxford University Press beginning in 1992.
5. On the growth and importance of antisemitism in the Weimar Republic, consult my essay, "1918 and After: The Role of Racial Antisemitism in the Nazi Analysis of the Weimar Republic," chapter 4 in the present volume.
6. The many complex issues of the post-1918 situation in Germany will be analyzed in much greater detail, especially as they bear upon questions of German and Nazi antisemitism, in Vol. III of my forthcoming study, *The Holocaust in Historical Context*.
7. For example only 33% of the population could read in 1920. See, for more, Jean Elleinstein, *The Stalin Phenomenon* (London, 1976), pp. 15–16.
8. Note especially his *The House of the Dead* (1861–62). See also David J. Dallin and Boris Nicolaevsky, *Forced Labor in Soviet Russia* (New Haven, 1947), pp. 299–305; and particularly Richard Pipes' extreme view of the origin of and continuity between the Soviet police state and its Czarist predecessor, *Russia under the Old Regime* (New York, 1974). The work of Solzhenitsyn is, of course, relevant here as well.
9. We note that the White Russian army and its short-lived terror was not very much different. Consider, for example, the pogroms in the Ukraine that caused thousands of casualties. It was a case of terror on the right and terror on the left. For fuller analysis of the Ukrainian situation see James Mace,

Communism and the Dilemmas of National Liberation, National Communism in Soviet Ukraine, 1918–1933 (Cambridge, 1983); and J. Borys, *The Sovietization of the Ukraine* (Edmonton, 1980).

10. The entire Kronstadt experiment has been described in the recent excellent study by Israel Getzler, *Kronstadt 1917–1921: The Fate of the Soviet Democracy* (Cambridge [England], 1983); and the earlier work by Paul Avrich, *Kronstadt, 1921* (Princeton, 1970).

11. Cf. Lenin's 1917 essay *Can the Bolshevites Retain State Power?* For discussion of the early history of the Checka and GPU (Secret Police) see Ronald Hingley, *The Russian Secret Police: Muscovite, Imperial Russian and Soviet Political Security Operations 1565–1970* (London, 1970); Boris Lewytzkyj, *Die rote Inquisition: Die Geschichte der sowjetischen Sicherheitsdienste* (Frankfurt a.M, 1967); Simon Wolin and Robert M. Slusser, *The Soviet Secret Police* (New York, 1957); and Elleinstein, *The Stalin Phenomenon,* pp. 20–29. Reference should also be made to Solzhenitsyn's treatment of, and quotation from, Lenin in the *Gulag Archipelago.*

12. On the meaning of the Civil War for later Soviet policies, see Sheila Fitzpatrick's interesting essay, *The Civil War as a Formative Experience* (The Wilson Center, Washington, D.C., 1981). Cf. also on this important issue Ronald Gregor Suny, *The Baku Commune 1917–18* (Princeton, 1972); David Lane, *The Roots of Russian Communism* (Assen, 1969); Robert Service, *The Bolshevik Party in Revolution, 1917–1923: A Study in Organizational Change* (New York, 1979); T. H. Rigby, *Lenin's Government, Sovnarkom 1917–1922* (Cambridge, 1979); and Sheila Fitzpatrick, *The Russian Revolution* (Oxford, 1982).

13. There can be no doubt that Stalinism, in its use of mass murder, transcends the Czarist past. Czarist policy was oppressive in the extreme, but judging by all available statistics *not* murderous to any marked degree as A. Solzhenitsyn points out in his *Gulag.* In the 50 years before the revolution the Czarist regime, with all the provocation of the anarchists and other revolutionaries, executed less than 15,000 individuals. See also on this issue R. Conquest, *Kolyma* (New York, 1979), pp. 229–230.

14. This claim, of course, depends on how one understands the relation of Stalin and "Stalinism" to previous events in Russian history, both Czarist and Bolshevik, an issue too complex to enter into in detail here.

15. Stalin's Russian nationalism represented something very different from Lenin's attitude to other nationality groups. The brief encouragement of minority national identities under Lenin (d. 1924) and for a brief period thereafter, e.g., the brief flourishing of Ukranian, Armenian, Muslim, Tatar, and Yiddish culture, was soon eclipsed by a militant, homogenizing Russian cultural imperialism.

16. On these purges, see Robert Conquest, *The Great Terror: Stalin's Purge of the Thirties* (New York, 1960), and the additional sources cited in the next note.

17. For a more detailed investigation of this highly complex problem see, among many relevant sources, Robert Conquest, *The Great Terror;* idem, *Kolyma;*

idem, "Forced Labor Statistics: Some Comments," *Soviet Studies,* Vol. 34, No. 3 (July 1982), pp. 434–439; idem, *The Harvest of Sorrow: Soviet Collectivization and the Great Famine* (New York, 1986); Iosef G. Dyadkin, *Unnatural Deaths in the USSR, 1928–1954* (New Brunswick, 1983), to be used with care, cf. the review by Michael P. Sacks in *Slavic Review,* Vol. 43, No. 1 (Spring, 1984), pp. 119–120; Frank Lorimer, *The Population of the Soviet Union: History and Prospects* (Geneva, 1946); Mikhail Heller and Aleksander Nekrich, *Utopia in Power: The History of the Soviet Union from 1917 to the Present* (New York, 1986); Jerry Hough and Merle Fainsod, *How the Soviet Union Is Governed* (Cambridge, 1979); Moshe Lewin, *Russian Peasants and Soviet Power* (Evanston, 1968); Robert A. Lewis et al., *Nationality and Population Change in Russia and the USSR: An Evaluation of Census Data, 1897–1970* (New York, 1976); and Murray Feshbach, "The Soviet Union: Population Trends and Dilemmas," *Population Bulletin,* Vol. 37, No. 3 (August, 1982), pp. 3–44.

The most intense debate on the issue has been carried out since 1981 between Steven Rosefielde who favors very high mortality estimates for the Stalinist era ("Collectivization, Gulag forced labour and the terror apparatus that sustained the Stalinist system appear to have claimed the lives of 21.4 to 24.4 million adults and 7.2 to 8.0 million children. An additional 14.4 million unrealized births [projected births in a normal situation] unrelated to the war may also be included in this inventory, bringing the total population deficit attributable to Stalin's forced industrialization policies to 43.8 to 46 million people; figures more than double the 20 million civilian and military casualties incurred during the war," in "Excess Mortality in the Soviet Union," [full bibliographical citation below]) and S. G. Wheatcroft who has been aggressive in defending much lower estimates. For the acrimonious dialogue between these two see Steven Rosefielde, "The First 'Great Leap Forward' Reconsidered: Lessons of Solzhenitsyn's *Gulag Archipelago,*" *Slavic Review,* Vol. 39, No. 4 (December, 1980), pp. 559–587; Stephen G. Wheatcroft and R. W. Davies, "Steven Rosefielde's *Kliuvkva,*" *Slavic Review,* Vol. 39, No. 4 (December, 1980), pp. 593–602; Steven Rosefielde, "An Assessment of the Sources and Uses of Gulag Forced Labor 1929–1956," *Soviet Studies,* Vol. 33, No. 1 (January, 1981), pp. 51–87; Stephen G. Wheatcroft, "On Assessing the Size of Forced Concentration Camp Labour in the Soviet Union, 1929–56," *Soviet Studies,* Vol. 33, No. 2 (April, 1981), pp. 265–295; idem, "Towards a Thorough Analysis of Soviet Forced Labour Statistics," *Soviet Studies,* Vol. 35, No. 2 (April, 1983), pp. 223–237; Steven Rosefielde, "Excess Mortality in the Soviet Union: A Reconsideration of the Demographic Consequences of Forced Industrialization 1929–1949," *Soviet Studies,* Vol. 35, No. 3 (July, 1983), pp. 385–409; idem, "Excess Collectivization Deaths 1929–1933: New Demographic Evidence," *Slavic Review,* Vol. 43, No. 1 (Spring, 1984), pp. 83–88; Stephen G. Wheatcroft, "New Demographic Evidence on Excess Collectivization Deaths: Yet Another *Kliuvkva* from Steven Rosefielde," *Slavic Review,* Vol. 44, No. 3 (Fall, 1985), pp. 505–508; and Steven Rosefielde, "New

Demographic Evidence on Collectivization Deaths: A Rejoinder to Stephen Wheatcroft," *Slavic Review,* Vol. 44, No. 3 (Fall, 1985), pp. 509–516.

A further evaluation of the issues discussed by Rosefielde and Wheatcroft, favoring Wheatcroft's position in general, can be found in Barbara A. Anderson and Brian D. Silver, "Demographic Analysis and Population Catastrophe in the USSR," *Slavic Review,* Vol. 44, No. 3 (Fall, 1985), pp. 517–536. In this context one should also read Stephen Wheatcroft's two complementary papers, "Famine and Factors Affecting Mortality in the USSR: The Demographic Crisis of 1914–1922 and 1930–33"; and "Famine and Factors Affecting Mortality in the USSR: The Demographic Crisis of 1914–1922 and 1930–33, *Appendices,*" both published in the Soviet Industrialisation Project Series, pamphlet numbers 20 and 21, University of Birmingham, Birmingham, England. The basic work done in Russia has been that of B. Urlanis, whose major demographic studies are, unfortunately, still not translated.

18. Hannah Arendt's attempt in *The Origins of Totalitarianism,* and the derivative efforts of those many others who have followed her lead, to portray Stalinism and Nazism as two forms of a common political reality called "Totalitarianism" is seriously flawed and leads to more distortion than illumination in the final analysis of these two movements.

19. The "economics" of anti-semitism are complex, but I would argue that economic justifications are "bad reasons for what people believe on instinct." Jews did *not* control the German national economy as the anti-semites claimed, and their purge would not "free" the economy in any appreciable way.

20. Robert Tucker has described both Stalin and Hitler as "warfare personality" types, a category he defines as follows:

The warfare personality shows paranoid characteristics as psychologically defined, but what is essential from the standpoint of our discussion is that it represents a *political* personality type. The characteristically paranoid perception of the world as an arena of deadly hostilities being conducted conspiratorily by an insidious and implacable enemy against the self finds systematized expression in terms of political and ideological symbols that are widely understood and accepted in the given social milieu. ("The Dictator and the Totalitarian," *World Politics,* Vol. 17, No. 4 [July, 1964], pp. 555–583)

21. See his "Last Testament," for example.

22. The intimate relationship between modernization and conflict in the Stalinist era has been amply studied. Among the more reasoned analyses are N. Valentinov, *The NEP and the Party Crisis* (Stanford, 1971); Cyril E. Black, (ed.) *The Transformation of Russian Society: Aspects of Social Change since 1861* (Cambridge, 1967); Alex Inkeles, *Social Change in Soviet Russia* (New York, 1971); E. H. Carr and R. W. Davies, *Foundations of a Planned Economy, 1926–1939,* 3 Vols. (New York, 1969–71); Nicholas Lampert, *The Technical Intelligentsia and the Soviet State* (New York, 1971); Alexander Ehrlich, *The Soviet Industrialization Debate, 1924–1928* (Cam-

bridge, 1960); and R. V. Daniels, *The Conscience of the Revolution: Communist Opposition in Soviet Russia* (Cambridge, 1960). On the economic situation under NEP see V. N. Bandera, "The New Economic Policy (NEP) as an Economic System," *Journal of Political Economy*, Vol. 71, No. 3 (June, 1963), pp. 265–279.

23. Isaac Deutscher, *Stalin: A Political Biography* (New York, 1949), pp. 317–318.

24. "Real" does not mean I approve, nor that Stalin was the "good" guy and the enemies the "bad" guys. It means only that Stalin had cause to be concerned with, for example, Trotsky and his faction on the one hand and the peasants on the other.

25. See A. Ulam, *Stalin*, (New York, 1972), p. 295, for more on this issue.

26. Consider, for example, the argument of S. Cohen, "Bolshevism and Stalinism," in his *Rethinking the Soviet Experience: Politics and History Since 1917* (New York, 1985). See also Robert Tucker's revisionist thesis in the same general direction, though much more subtly and dialectically stated, and therefore also perhaps embodying a more profound contradictoriness, "Stalinism as Revolution from Above," in Robert Tucker (ed.), *Stalinism: Essays in Historical Interpretation* (New York, 1977), pp. 77–110.

27. The history and character of such penal institutions has been described in Michel Foucault's interesting, but limited, *Discipline and Punish: The Birth of the Prison* (New York, 1977); U. R. Q. Henriques, "The Rise and Decline of the Separate Systems of Prison Discipline," *Past and Present*, Vol. 54 (1972), pp. 61–93; and George Ruschke and Otto Kirchheimer, *Punishment and Social Structure* (New York, 1939).

28. It should, however, be remembered that so-called "concentration camps" are to be clearly distinguished from Death Camps, i.e., places created primarily, if not solely, to kill people, e.g., Treblinka and Auschwitz. The existence of industrial complexes at these Death Camps should not be misunderstood, i.e., as mitigating their overall genocidal charge, for all their Jewish workers were scheduled to die as part of the process.

29. The salient, complex comparative questions raised by the historical institution of slavery will be taken up in detail in Vol. I (Roman Slavery) and Vol. II (Black Slavery) of my forthcoming study, *The Holocaust in Historical Context*.

30. A sad story with many earlier chapters. One such abuse which is paradigmatic of many is that of sixteenth- and seventeenth-century galley slavery, on which see Paul Bamford, *Fighting Ships and Prisons: The Mediterranean Galleys of France in the Age of Louis XIV* (Minneapolis, 1973).

31. I use this term in quotation marks in light of the counter-claim advanced in many, and in particular, more recent studies, particularly of the agricultural sector, that contend that this policy was counter-productive even on the basis of strict economic rationality. For myself, I am not altogether convinced by these arguments against the strictly economic benefits of this activity which, vis-à-vis industrialization, seem positive and real. It seems to me that, while this collectivized labor was not efficient, when all elements

are factored in it did produce modest results, which were exaggerated enormously by Stalin and the ruling elite. This, however, of course, does not mean that I would agree that this was the best way to achieve such results.

32. The use of criminal proceedings and institutions to assure needed labor is an old policy, not only in Russia but elsewhere in Europe.

33. A full list of camps and the type of work carried on in them is given in D. Dallin and B. Nicolaevsky, *Forced Labor in Soviet Russia*, pp. 58–72.

34. All demographic statistics provided in this chapter are provisional and the subject of great scholarly debate. For an introduction to the problematic aspects of this basic issue see: Dallin and Nicolaevsky, *Forced Labor in Soviet Russia*, who give a figure of 5–6 million slave workers in 1937 and 8 million "slave" workers in 1941; Steven Rosefielde, who provides very high estimates of 8 million Gulag workers in 1937, 10 million in 1940, and 12–15 million in 1946–50 in "An Assessment of the Sources and Uses of Forced Labor, 1929–1956," *Soviet Studies*, No. 1 (January, 1981), pp. 51–87; Stephen Wheatcroft concludes that "some four to five million is the maximum number of concentration camp labourers who could have existed in 1939," in "On Assessing the Size of Forced Concentration Camp Labor in the Soviet Union, 1931–1956," *Soviet Studies*, No. 2 (April, 1981), p. 286 —the entire essay covers pp. 265–295; idem, "Towards a Thorough Analysis of Soviet Forced Labor Statistics," *Soviet Studies*, No. 2 (April, 1983), pp. 223–237; R. Conquest, *The Great Terror;* and idem, "Forced Labor Statistics: Some Comments," *Soviet Studies*, No. 3 (July, 1982), pp. 434–439. Conquest seems to put the figure of slave laborers at 8 million or above, *Great Terror*, Appendix A. On Soviet manpower note, in addition, Warren W. Eason, "Forced Labor," in Abram Bergson and Simon Kuznets (eds.), *Economic Trends in the Soviet Union* (Cambridge, 1963), pp. 38–93; N. S. Timasheff's much lower estimate (2.3 million) of forced labor in 1937 in his "The Post War Population of the Soviet Union," *The American Journal of Sociology*, Vol. 54 (1948), pp. 148–155; and N. Jasny "Labour and Output in Soviet Concentration Camps," *Journal of Political Economy*, Vol. 59, No. 5 (October, 1951), pp. 405–419, who gives a lowish figure of 3.5 million Gulag workers in 1941.

35. More details in support of this view can be found in Roy Medvedev, *Let History Judge*, (New York, 1973), p. 394.

36. Dallin and Nicolaevsky, *Forced Labor in Soviet Russia*, pp. 88–90, discuss this issue more fully. Also note the comments of Robert Conquest, *Kolyma*, p. 39; and the observations of A. Ciliga, *Sibérie, terre de l'exil de l'industrialisation* (Paris, 1960).

37. It may well be that part of this problematic is structural, i.e., it is part of the larger problem of trying to reform Russia on the basis of a Marxist theory ill-suited to the industrial and agrarian realities of Russia in the 1920's. Ulam suggests: "One cannot find out from Marx how to build socialism in a prevailingly agrarian society, any more than one can learn how to build a nuclear reactor by reading the works of Newton," *Stalin*, p. 294.

38. This labor re-organization and its implications are analyzed by Solomon M.

Schwarz, *Labor in the Soviet Union* (New York, 1952), pp. 209f. This issue (and relevant sources) was called to my attention by Barrington Moore, Jr., *Terror and Progress in the USSR* (Cambridge, 1954), pp. 54–55.

39. On this program see Harry Schwartz, *Russia's Soviet Economy* (New York, 1950), p. 449f.
40. Solomon M. Schwarz, *Labor in the Soviet Economy*, pp. 77–83.
41. Himmler's entrepreneurial ambitions are narrated in Speer's study entitled *Infiltration: How Heinrich Himmler Schemed to Build an SS Industrial Empire* (New York, 1981).
42. Jerzy Gliksman, an inmate in the Gulag, gives us this accurate understanding of the Stalinist slave labor system:

   The Soviet *lagers* are in fact institutions practicing slave labor. They are closely tied to various industrial or other enterprises which, in turn, are part of the over-all Soviet economy. They are expected to fulfill their part in the general economic plan, and are a tremendous source of cheap labor for this plan. Openly and cynically, without any trace of concern for appearances, the camp inmate is therefore treated simply as a forced supplier of needed work. (*Tell the West* [New York, 1948], p. 244)

43. Raul Hilberg, *The Destruction of European Jewry* (Chicago, 1967), pp. 334–345, discusses the relation of slave labor to survival in detail. His important conclusion: "The Polish Jews were annihilated in a process in which economic factors were truly secondary" (p. 345).
44. R. Conquest, *Kolyma*, p. 47.
45. On these events see ibid., pp. 49–66.
46. Ibid., p. 58.
47. By comparison the Nazis were killing more Jews in one week at Auschwitz in late 1943 and 1944 than is represented by this Gulag total for the entire year 1938.
48. Further details of this deadly activity are provided by R. Conquest, *Kolyma*, pp. 51–52.
49. This conclusion becomes incontrovertible when one examines in detail the-day-to day conditions in the two environments. I.e., matters of "selections," work assignments, health care, living conditions, sex, women, children, and release all reveal fundamental differences.
50. Even Robert Conquest, in his most telling indictment of the Stalinist enterprise, does not claim more than this.

   All in all, these conditions reflected one main truth. In the minds of its creators and organisers the conscious purpose of Kolyma, which had originally been the production of gold, with death as an unplanned by-product, had become the production, with at least equal priority, of gold and death. (*Kolyma*, p. 124)

51. I.e., in the generality of Gulag life itself.
52. Lenin, *Selected Works* (Moscow, 1977), Vol. 1, p. 44.
53. On the role of the Communist party, see first Joseph Stalin's own understanding as presented in his *Problems of Leninism* (Moscow, 1949), pp. 179–80. Julian Towster's *Political Power in the USSR 1917–1947* (New

York, 1948) is a work of considerable merit that repays close study; see also on this important issue Raymond Bauer, et al., *How the Soviet System Works* (Cambridge, 1963); Adam Ulam, *The Bolsheviks* (New York, 1965); Leonard Schapiro, *The Origins of Communist Autocracy* (Cambridge, 1966); and idem, *The Communist Party of the Soviet Union* (New York, 1971); and Philip Selznick, *The Organizational Weapon* (Glencoe, Ill. 1952).

54. Discussed by J. H. Keep, *The Rise of Social Democracy in Russia* (Oxford, 1963); and Dietrich Geyer, *Lenin in der Russichen Sozialdemokratie* (Cologne, 1962). See also Georg Lukács' early essays now collected in *Taktik und Ethik* (Neuwied, 1975).

55. On Article 58 consult R. Conquest, *The Great Terror*, Appendix G; A. Solzhenitsyn, *Gulag* (New York, 1974–75), Vols. I and II, pp. 60–67; and Robert Sharlet, "Stalinism and Soviet Legal Culture," in R. Tucker (ed.), *Stalinism*, pp. 164–165.

56. Lenin as quoted in R. Medvedev, *On Stalin and Stalinism* (Oxford, 1979), p. 185.

57. Lenin as cited by L. Schapiro, *Communist Party*, p. 40. For a wider investigation of this phenomenon, see Otto Kirchheimer, *Political Justice: The Use of Legal Procedure for Political Ends* (Princeton, 1961).

58. Despite this theoretical parallelism, the actual role of the party differed greatly in the two cases. The Nazi party never achieved the power and transformational role of the Bolshevik party. The Bolshevik party has always had a pre-eminence over the state apparatus and bureaucracy that the Nazi party could only envy. See on this complex issue Amos Perlmutter, *Modern Authoritarianism* (New Haven, 1981), pp. 104–107; K. Bracher, *German Dictatorship* (New York, 1970), pp. 235f; D. Orlow, *The History of the Nazi Party: 1933–1945*, 2 vols. (Pittsburgh, 1973), throughout; and L. Schapiro, *Communist Party*, throughout. Conversely, Stalin, even at the height of his "will," was never cast in the same, fully embodied, metaphysical role as was Hitler. Though he may have had as much power in fact (after 1935), in theory the Bolshevik party General Secretary never became *Der Führer*.

59. The often-made comparison specifically of Stalin and Hitler in terms of the "cult of personality" is here significant. Assuredly Stalin's authority was as autocratic and complete as Hitler's. However, having said this, one must still recognize that crucial systemic distinctions exist between Nazism and Stalinism. The *Führerprinzip*, with its metaphysical claims for Hitler has, first of all, no real counterpart in Marxist-Leninist ideology. Secondly, even under Stalin, i.e., even when the "cult of personality" flourished beginning in the 1930's, Stalin was not accorded either the theoretical or ontological role accorded Hitler. The *ad hoc* adulation of Stalin was always at odds, however ignored in practice, with elemental Marxist doctrine and hence always held an "anomolous" status in the Soviet matrix. Indeed it was this tension that allowed Khrushchev to criticize just this "cult of personality" in his "secret speech" to the Twentieth Communist Party Congress in 1956. His speech is reprinted as an appendix in Nikita Khrushchev, *Khrushchev*

Remembers (Boston, 1970). Such a criticism of the Führer would be self-contradictory, in principle, even impossible within the theoretical parameters of Nazism. Hitler, by definition, was beyond such criticism. For fuller exploration of this important issue in terms of the Soviet context see Robert C. Tucker's essay, "Revolutionary Mass Movement Regimes," in his *The Soviet Political Mind* (New York, 1963), pp. 3–19; idem, "The Rise of Stalin's Personality Cult," *American Historical Review*, Vol. 84, No. 2 (1979), pp. 347–366; idem, "The Dictator and the Totalitarian," *World Politics*, Vol. 17, No. 4 (July, 1965), pp. 555–583. For a comparative analysis of this issue within the broader socialist camp see Jeremy T. Paltiel's, "The Cult of Personality and Some Comparative Reflections on Political Culture in Leninist Regimes," in *Studies in Comparative Communism*, Vol. 16, Nos. 1 & 2, (Spring–Summer, 1983), pp. 49–64. Paltiel's essay has much to say, especially about the interesting comparative case of Maoism in China.

60. Lenin, *Collected Works*, Vol. 8, p. 123. See here the informative essay by Robert Sharlet, "Stalinism and Legal Culture," in R. Tucker (ed.), *Stalinism*, pp. 155–179.

61. Stalin, *Collected Works*, Vol. XI, p. 48.

62. The standard work on the show trials and the extraction of confessions, though not without problems in its "explanation" of these events, is R. Conquest, *The Great Terror*.

63. This accounts for the empirical Soviet situation in which—unlike Auschwitz—changes of status can be reversed. For example, the traumatic forced collectivization of late 1929 and early 1930 which saw the percentage of peasant householders rushed into collectivization rise to over 55% was reversed, for a time, in March 1930, falling to 23.6% by June 1, 1930. A. Ulam, *Stalin*, p. 329 [based on the researches of M. L. Bogdenki, "The Collective Movement in Spring and Summer of 1930," *Historical Notes* (Moscow), Vol. 7, No. 76 (1965), p. 31], estimates that 75 million peasants changed their status in this flip flop. It is worth noting that this trend was itself reversed later in 1930–31, during which the figures for collectivization reached 60% by September 1931. As status, not biology, was the issue, Stalin could talk of "*converting* the middle peasant to socialism" (*Collected Works*, Vol. XIII, p. 42 [italics added]). The same obtains for most of the purged Party members, estimated at up to 800,000, purged in 1933. They were not killed—unlike the threatening old Bolshevik leadership, e.g., Kamenev and Zinoviev, etc.—but expunged from their place in the hierarchy, thereby creating "discipline" within the Party as well as a fierce new loyalty on the part of those purged who sought to return to the Party's good graces. Even Zinoviev and Kamenev had been readmitted to the Party for a time in 1933 after suitable acts of contrition and self-abasement. For details of these purges see Robert Conquest, *The Great Terror*. The same considerations apply to the national minorities who survived to be "rehabilitated" by the Soviet State in 1956.

64. Of course, this is *not*—need I say it—to justify the Gulag in any manner

whatsoever. The Gulag caused unbelievable cruelty and excess in every direction. While different from Auschwitz, it is no less open to moral censure. Phenomenological disjunctions do not here entail any difference of moral response.

65. Stalin's instinctive, neurotic fear of the peasantry as a whole is described in A. Ulam, *Stalin,* p. 205. Stalin's concern with the peasantry was justified even if, as some distinguished students of the Russian peasantry argue, the peasantry generally lacked hostility towards the Soviet regime in the period 1917–28. This non-hostile view of peasant attitudes is argued by Otto Schiller, *Die Landwirtschaft des Sowjetunions 1917–1953* (Tübingen, 1954), pp. 19f. Alternatively, however, there is considerable evidence that the peasantry from 1917 on had no great affection for the Bolshevik state, as can be seen in their response to state needs in 1918–19, as well as, and even more so, in the sizeable peasant revolts that occurred at the end of the Civil War in the Ukraine and Tambov, on which see Oliver H. Radkey, *The Unknown Civil War in Russia: A Study of the Green Movement in the Tambov Region 1920–21* (Stanford, 1976). There can be no doubt that after the crisis of 1928 the peasants were increasingly aligned against the Communist leadership. The "Procurement Crisis of 1928," is brilliantly analysed by M. Lewin, *Russian Peasants and Soviet Power,* pp. 214–249.

66. I borrow this expression from M. Lewin, "The Soviet Background of Stalinism," in *The Making of the Soviet System* (New York, 1985), p. 122.

67. Vasily Grossman's remark that: "Just as the Germans proclaimed Jews not human beings, thus did Lenin and Stalin proclaim, 'Kulaks are not human beings,' " cited with at least implicit approval by Robert Conquest, is simply an error. Grossman's remarks are from his *Forever Flowering* (New York, 1972), p. 144, cited by Conquest, *Harvest of Sorrow,* p. 129.

68. I.e., which assumed, however much ignored in practice (though far from completely ignored in practice as we shall see), that one could separate a kulak's status from his person.

69. Consult *The Writings of Leon Trotsky, 1930–1931* (New York, 1971), Vol. IV, pp. 54–64 and 299–308.

70. On the diverse opinions held in this debate see A. Ehrlich, *The Soviet Industrialization Debate* (Cambridge, 1960); E. H. Carr, *A History of Soviet Russia: Socialism in One Country,* Vol. I (London, 1958); H. Ellison, "The Decision to Collectivize Agriculture," *American, Slavic and East European Review,* Vol. 21 (April, 1961), pp. 189–202; and M. Lewin, *Russian Peasants and Soviet Power,* pp. 132–171 and 294–343. The general Bolshevik debate regarding the peasantry and the changes it must be required to undergo are described in T. Shanin, *The Awkward Class. Political Sociology of Peasantry in a Developing Society: Russia 1910–1925* (Oxford, 1972).

7

Defining the Uniqueness of the Holocaust: Preliminary Clarifications and Disclaimers

G iven the confusion, crossed purposes, and misunderstandings that have accumulated around the evidently contentious question of the "uniqueness" of the *Sho'ah* I should like, in this chapter, to clarify six elemental issues that must be understood aright if any real philosophical advance is to be made in the analysis of this matter.

I

In advancing and supporting the position that the destruction of European Jewry between 1933 and 1945 is phenomenologically unique I am not proposing or endorsing any particular theological conclusion(s). It is not at all clear to me that there is a direct, and preferred, theological meaning to be drawn from the exceptionality of this event, at least not as I will describe and interpret this singularity. As I understand the multiple epistemological and metaphysical issues both the theological radicals [1]—e.g., Richard Rubenstein, Arthur Cohen, Emil Fackenheim, Yitzchak Greenberg, and on the Christian side, e.g., such Protestants as A. Roy Eckardt and Alice Eckardt,[2] to a degree Jurgen Moltmann,[3] Franklin Littell,[4] Franklin Sherman,[5] Paul Van Buren,[6] Harry James Cargas,[7] and such Catholics as Karl Thieme, David Tracy, Clemens Thoma, and to some degree John Pawlikowski,[8] as well as the theological conservatives—e.g., Eliezer Berkovits,[9] Jacob Neusner,[10] and the Lubavitcher Rebbe,[11] and on the Christian side, e.g., the Protestant Karl

Reprinted by permission of Sheffield Academic Press.

Barth,[12] and the Catholic theologians D. Judant and Charles Journet,[13] have all run ahead of the available evidence and the extant philosophical-theological argumentation to posit conclusions that are not epistemically or intellectually persuasive. Neither Rubenstein's endorsement of the "death of God" nor the Lubavitcher's Rebbe's conservative kabbalistic pronouncements on the *Sho'ah* as a *tikkun*[14] flow necessarily from the event itself. Both these, and other denominational expositions, are premature and inconclusive. They represent, in essence, *a priori* impositions that are extrinsic to the Death Camps and rooted in deeply held prior theological positions.[15]

Any theological position, at present, is compatible with the singularity of the *Sho'ah*. Religious conservatives who "intuitively" reject the uniqueness of the Holocaust on the, usually implicit, grounds that such an unequivocal conclusion would *necessarily* entail ominous alterations in the inherited normative *Weltanschauung* are simply mistaken. That is, one can, without self-contradiction, adopt an unexceptional conservative theological posture (either Jewish or Christian) while, at the same time, accepting the discrete contention that the destruction of European Jewry was an historical *novum,* given the disciplined understanding of the concept of historical *novum* that I would wish to argue for and employ.[16] Conversely, the theological radicals who hold that the singularity of the *Sho'ah* necessarily entails religious transformations, and within Jewish parameters halachic changes, have not shown this to be the case. They have merely assumed it to be so, positing the "required changes" they take to be obligatory without providing either halachic[17] or philosophical justification for such innovation. It may be that one or other of these alternative positions is true, but so far none has made a convincing case for itself. Therefore, I avoid all theologizing, and encourage others to avoid such theologizing, at this still preliminary stage of enquiry.[18]

2

In defending uniqueness I am *not* simultaneously endorsing the injudicious claim that the Holocaust is *more evil* than alternative occurrences of extensive and systematic persecution, organized violence, and mass death. The character of that uniqueness which I am prepared to champion is not tied to a scale, a hierarchy, of evil, i.e., of an event X being more or less malevolent than another event Y, or all previous events E_l

to E_N. This, of course, is not to deny the compelling fact that the *Sho'ah* was a monumental crime, an astonishing act of cruelty, comprised of millions of acts of cruelty, as great as any that has ever taken place. But in acknowledging this I am not asserting that the *Sho'ah* is *more* evil than certain other specific events, e.g., the centuries-long brutality and dehumanization represented by Greco-Roman and New World slavery, the mass-murder of Armenians in 1915–1917, the vast depopulation of the indigenous peoples of North and South America, the monumental violation of human dignity, the millions of dead, that is the Gulag, or the monstrous transgression that is Cambodia. These other happenings are also morally outrageous, and arguably as outrageous as the *Sho'ah*.[19] The insuperable epistemological dilemma that confronts us is that there is no argument, no method, that will allow for the quantification of evil beyond the simple mathematical. But this, I take it, is not what is meant when the Holocaust is said to be more evil than other incidents, at least not when this formidable proposition is defended by competent authors and speakers possessed of even minimal philosophical sophistication. Moreover, on this measure of numbers alone, the *Sho'ah*, as an empirical matter, is far from the "most evil" event in history. In the absence of convincing criteria for making such absolute comparative judgments, all such judgments become indefensible.[20]

Here I demur from Yehuda Bauer's contention that there

> may be no difference between Holocaust and genocide for the victim of either. But there are gradations of evil, unfortunately. Holocaust was the policy of total, sacral Nazi act of mass murder of all Jews they could lay their hands on. Genocide was horrible enough, but it did not entail *total* murder.[21]

The categorical distinction that Bauer draws between *some* and *all*, between Holocaust and Genocide,[22] is not best, or even properly, under-stood as a moral distinction but rather as a phenomenological and logical one. Seeking to kill all of a group is descriptively, even ontologi-cally, different from seeking to kill part of a group, but it is not *necessar-ily*, morally worse. For example, the killing of some X may be a greater evil, assuming one could measure such things, than killing all Y, where there are more X than Y and the absolute number of X killed exceeds the total number of Y even though the killing of X is not, using a form of Bauer's nomenclature, "Holocaustal." To repeat: this is not to deny that non-Holocaust X *is* different from Holocaust Y but, rather, to assert that the *nature* of this difference is logical and structural not moral. To impute less evil, for example, to Stalin than Hitler because of the categorical distinction between Holocaust and Genocide (Stalin, on Bauer's definition, being guilty of perpetrating the latter but not the former crime, while Hitler perpetrated the former crime) appears unwarranted on its face and undecidable, except by stipulation, in both theory and practice. Again, to judge the Young Turks or the Khmer Rouge less evil than Hitler because they failed to want to kill all Armenians or Cambodians respectively is logically and ethically unconvincing.

Kenneth Seeskin, in commenting on an earlier presentation of my view,[23] has given voice to the elementary confusion we wish to disclaim, as follows:

> To his credit, Katz tries to avoid ethical or theological conclusions. He admits that numbers alone do not tell the full story. In his survey of mass murder, he refrains from judgments of better or worse. Unlike Maier and Aron, he does not get tangled in distinctions between an ideology and its interpretation. His thesis is simply that the uniqueness of the Holocaust consists in its "genocidal intent against the Jewish people." The question is whether he can employ a concept like genocidal intent without falling victim to moral comparisons he does not want to make. If the Nazi extermination of Jews is the first and only case of genocidal intent in history, how can we not conclude that it unleashed a new and previously unimagined form of evil? One cannot refer to a term like genocidal intent without expecting the audience to draw moral inferences for itself — particularly when writing on the Holocaust. So while Katz is anxious to stay clear of these inferences, his language gives him away. This is more than a verbal dispute. Even if Katz were to replace a charged word like intentionality with a neutral one like policy, the same problems would arise.[24]

But this criticism is unpersuasive for it rests on a logical error. There is no logical reason not to maintain the distinction between G, the presence of genocidal intent, in event E, and $\sim$ G, the absence of genocidal intent, in event E_1, and again in every other event E_2 to E_N, while at the same time insisting that this phenomenological difference, between G and $\sim$ G, does not necessarily entail any hierarchy of immoral acts or events. It is true that the *Sho'ah* represents a "new form of evil," but this is not logically or ontologically equivalent to the claim that the *Sho'ah* represents a "new *and higher* level of evil." The separable notions of form and degree, structure and quantity, intent and ethical valence, are not synonymous and should not be employed as if they were. Moreover, there is no incoherence or contradiction in entertaining the possibility that one could produce the same degree of evil through two alternate historic-systemic forms, assuming we could calibrate degrees of evil.

Contra Seeskin, I see no authentic reason why, given the careful disjunctive conditions here indicated, I cannot avoid "falling victim to moral comparisons I do not want to make," indeed that I explicitly repudiate and encourage my readers to repudiate, and why intelligent readers, if requested to do so, cannot distinguish between different *forms* of evil "without drawing [incorrect] moral inferences."

In this connection it is also necessary, especially given the prominence of his work,[25] to reject the criticism of Irving Louis Horowitz, at least insofar as it might be misunderstood to apply to my position. Horowitz writes: "Those who take an exclusive position on the Holocaust [and argue for its uniqueness] are engaging in moral bookkeeping, in which only those who suffer very large numbers of deaths qualify."[26] My understanding, however, is that while the Holocaust is unique, its uniqueness is not related to numbers. While I am concerned to defend the "exclusive position of the Holocaust" I have no interest in, and altogether reject, what Horowitz polemically labels "moral bookkeeping." This dichotomous response to Horowitz's ill-formed critique is possible, and necessary, because the two determinate categories that he erroneously equates, "moral bookkeeping" and "claims for exclusiveness," are in actuality distinct and can, and ought, to be separated. An admirable, supportable desire to empathize with all victims of oppression does not justify a fallacious argument.

3.

The phenomenological character I will associate with the notion of historical incommensurability is to be wholly distinguished from more dramatic metaphysical claims sometimes associated with the concept of uniqueness. Though sympathetic to claims that "the Holocaust has meant an ontological redirecting of the course and fate of history,"[27] and agreeing with Emil Fackenheim that "the Holocaust . . . was indeed a world, and it was dominated by the 'logic of destruction' that left untouched neither God nor man, neither hope nor will, neither faith nor thought,"[28] no one, in my view, has produced *arguments* that demonstrate the transcendental uniqueness of the *Sho'ah*. Therefore, I will resist the strong temptation to employ such seductive meta-historical criteria of uniqueness as my own. A. Roy Eckardt is right to note that the murder of European Jewry "raises the question of *Heilsgeschichte* ('salvation history'), perhaps even the total eclipse of 'salvation history,' " and again that "if it is comparable at all, [it] can only be compared with a very small number of other 'incomparable' events, such as the Exodus and the giving of the Torah or the Crucifixion and the Resurrection."[29] However, it is just the unsettling accuracy of this observation that entails caution, for the Exodus, the giving of the Torah, the Crucifixion and the Resurrection, insofar as one enters into and reclaims their theological or metaphysical meaning, are not givens whose singularity is *proven,* incontrovertible, but rather *realia* whose overpowering mysterious presence is assumed by the believer and affirmed by the transforming experience of faith. The immediate significance of this unremarkable observation in the present context, however, is exacting, for it reminds us that, for example, Jews do not affirm the transhistorical reality of the Resurrection, the essential dogma of Christianity, and no appeal seems able to convince them to abandon this skepticism. Though we must be open to the philosophical possibility that the *Sho'ah* is transcendentally unique, that it may transcend all inherited and established philosophical categories, categories that are unashamedly constructed to deny uniqueness by the very fact of belonging to a group, I will *not* advance this, and like claims as my own.

In particular, my guarded construal of the character of the Holocaust's incomparability is not to be equated with Alice and A. Roy Eckardt's intriguing contention that among the various meanings of the term uniqueness there is one beyond others, "transcending uniqueness,"[30] that peculiarly applies to and individuates the *Sho'ah.* This exceptional category they define as follows:

The concept of transcending uniqueness refers to events that are held to be essentially different from not only ordinary uniqueness but even unique uniqueness. With transcending uniqueness the quality of difference raises itself to the level of absoluteness.[31]

And they go on:

One way to situate the qualitative shift to transcending uniqueness is to speak of a radical leap from objectness to subjectness, a total existential crisis and involvement for the party who makes one or another affirmation of transcending uniqueness. This extraordinary about face is accompanied by a marked transformation in modes of language.[32]

One recognizes that in this odd language the Eckardts are wrestling with the limits of the sayable, are striving to identify a distinctive ontic circumstance whose conceptualization may point to something philosophically fertile, but given the ambiguities of their formulation, the notion of "transcending uniqueness" is unendorsable. To the degree that I understand their meaning, the shifts and modifications they introduce apply to many collective tragedies and do not provide compelling grounds for historical and metaphysical individuation. The Eckardts are correct to note that:

Antisemitism, as it has manifested itself within the entire history of the West, is itself a markedly unique phenomenon. This phenomenon is radically discontinuous with ordinary forms of "prejudice," such as is race and religion, forms that have their occasions and their locales and then atrophy or are superseded. Antisemitism is the one perennial malady of its kind within the history of the Western World, and it is spread universally within the entire geography of the West. Distinctively, it is pervasive in time as in space. Thus is the peculiar generality of antisemitism wedded indissolubly to the peculiar peculiarity of the Holocaust.[33]

But this penetrating judgment, even while being unimpeachable, does not serve to make their larger historiosophical and interpretive claim convincing. The authentic anomalousness of antisemitism, as well as its disquieting endurance over place and time, does not necessarily involve any transcendental correlates. It is true that the antisemitism of the West is rooted primordially in Christian theology, that on Christian grounds Judaeophobia is generated and warranted by meta-historic oppositions, but this intra-Christian dogma is not to be misunderstood, and extrapolated, *per se,* into a genuine transcendental reality, into a legitimate transcendental analysis. We remain, therefore, satisfied with a more modest phenomenological, *contra* transcendental, definition of the historical *novum* that is the *Sho'ah*.

4.

In a recent work that attracted considerable scholarly notice, George Kren and Leon Rappaport attempt to define the uniqueness of the Holocaust in terms of the notion of "historical crisis." According to Kren and Rappaport an "historical crisis" occurs

when events make such a profound impact on the way people think about themselves and the world around them that the apparent continuity of their history seems drastically and permanently changed. In the lives of individuals, such events are usually called life crisis; when they happen to whole societies or civilizations, they must be recognized as historical crisis. Moreover, like a personal life crisis, a historical crisis is compounded by events or situations which render accumulated past experience or learning quite irrelevant. In many respects, the effect of historical crisis is to turn the world upside down, as Dwight Macdonald indicated when he suggested that in post-Holocaust society, it was not those who break the law but those most obedient to the law who would be the greatest threat to humanity.

Societies facing historical crises are usually thrown into a period of chaos until they can replace their traditional but now ineffective modes of conduct with new, more appropriate modes. It is, therefore, possible to define a historical crisis as involving any new situation of sufficient impact or magnitude to require serious, wide, and comparatively rapid changes in the normative behavior of a society. If these normative changes are at least minimally effective, they tend to become institutionalized as relatively fixed patterns of thought and action which resist serious change until another crisis situation occurs.[34]

Now while this proposal is suggestive, it is finally unsatisfactory for rigorous purposes of definition. As Kren and Rappaport themselves note:

Applied to the Holocaust, the concept of historical crisis can as yet only be suggested rather than demonstrated, although the main thrust of the succeeding chapters is to show how the relevant cultural, historical, and psychosocial dimensions converge to require a crisis interpretation. Our thesis is that the Holocaust has been the major historical crisis of the twentieth century—a crisis of human behavior and values. If this has not yet been widely acknowledged, it is because the consequences of such a crisis—unlike economic, political, and ecological crises—tend to be impalpable, especially when they are masked by a language that seems unable to express them and a public rhetoric that seems unwilling to try.[35]

And again:

Yet the Holocaust may be hard to grasp as a historical crisis because the breakdowns of consensus and culturally defined meanings consequent to it are not easily perceived. There were no great changes in ideas concerning government and political power, for example, because the Holocaust was not a revolution. Economic systems and practices were not influenced, for it was not a financial or economic collapse. Furthermore, the Holocaust itself led to no startling changes in national boundaries; it did not generate any sweeping new religious forms or views of human nature; and it had no discernible impact on modern science.[36]

That is, on their criterion the *Sho'ah* is not, except as an article of faith and in contradistinction to their own definition, an "historical crisis." As an empirical matter the world appears little changed morally or otherwise by Auschwitz. As Elie Wiesel has complained: "Nothing has been learned: Auschwitz has not served as a warning. For details consult your daily newspaper,"[37] viz. the tragedies of Ethiopia, Nigeria, Sudan,

Cambodia, Vietnam, Botswana, Burundi, Indonesia, and various parts of South America (to name only a few of the scores of deadly happenings that have occurred since the end of World War II).[38] Reflecting upon this abysmal aggregate historical evidence, ought we not to conclude that the notion of "historical crisis" is just a well-intentioned "wish," a pious hope that the *Sho'ah,* given its monumental depravity, does mean something after all. And this recognized I will refrain from including the category of "historical crisis"[39] in my own efforts at defining the particularity of the *Endlösung der Judenfrage in Europa.*[40]

5

Ismar Schorsch criticizes those who are "obsessed" with uniqueness because such a claim is

politically downright counterproductive. It impedes genuine dialogue, because it introduces an extraneous, contentious issue that alienates potential allies from among other victims of organized human depravity. Similarly, our fixation on uniqueness has prevented us from reaching out by universalizing the lessons of the Holocaust.[41]

But such apologetics, however well intended, however ecumenical, are misplaced. The question "Is the Holocaust unique?" is a legitimate question, a meaningful question, and perhaps even an important question in a variety of ways. To rule it out because of some extraneous political, or even ethical agenda, no matter how virtuous,[42] is to confuse scholarship and homiletics, the often lonely search for truth with the altogether different effort to build practical coalitions or to win popularity contests.[43] Even if claims of incommensurability make enemies, which if properly understood they should not, this conclusion is neither to be avoided nor denied.[44] One could keep silent on this cardinal issue, exercising strict self-censorship, or even lie about one's hard-won conclusions to satisfy, at what high cost, those who object to the implications of the defense of uniqueness, but such behavior would hardly negate the truth of the claim. Moreover, and not inconsequential, it would introduce undesirable elements of "bad faith" into the serious, already difficult discussion of the *Sho'ah* and its meaning, contravening thereby the very effort to create *genuine* dialogue between Jews and non-Jews that Schorsch advocates.[45] Half-truths and purposeful evasions are bad foundations for authentic cross-cultural, inter-communal encounters. Then, too, the interpretive disjunction that Schorsch makes, the distinction that underwrites his entire polemic, between concluding for uniqueness and "universalizing the lessons of the Holocaust" is neither necessary nor necessarily correct. There is no logical or normative reason why the maintenance of the notion of uniqueness *must* "prevent us from reaching out [to other victims]."[46] Knowing that X is not Y does not entail that those who know phenomenological U about X cannot empathize and be *practically* concerned with the victims of Y, even if Y lacks U.[47] There is nothing in warranting phenomenological U that makes a universal care and sympathy, a trans X activism and involvement, impossible. Conversely, knowing X may make one more, not less, concerned with others, if only so as to deny the possibility of the repetition of X.[48]

Likewise, Schorsch's concern that advancing a claim for uniqueness "is to imply or even to indulge in invidious comparisons with earlier or later instances of genocide"[49] does not necessarily follow if, as I insist, the distinction being argued for is phenomenological not moral and entails no diminution of the impossible to quantify existential dimension of each event. (See point 2 above.) Again, Schorsch's objection, until now essentially correct, that the claim for uniqueness "may be a measure of our pain, but it is hardly the conclusion of dispassionate comparative research" is, I believe, no longer viable, given the larger historical and philosophical project of which this essay is a part.

In this methodological context it is also relevant to reject the related claim of Geoff Eley that worries that: "to insist on the uniqueness of the event is a short step to insisting on the exclusiveness of interpretation which asserts an empathetic privilege and even Jewish proprietorship in the subject."[50] This may be an appropriate caution in certain specific interpretive circumstances, but it should not be taken as more than this if one avoids the "short step" of "insisting on the exclusiveness of interpretation." That is, there is no necessary reason to link the historical and phenomenological claim to uniqueness to any Jewish interpretive privilege; and I categorically reject such a tie. My grounds for concluding for uniqueness are public, discussable, and treatable by any scholar without regard to his or her ethnic or religious affiliation or community of origin. There are, in other words, no necessary grounds for requiring the diminution of the universal meaning and significance of my position because I argue for uniqueness. Conversely, the suspicion of *a priori* prejudice would appear to attach itself to any methodological approach to the Holocaust that did not at least in principle admit the possibility that the *Sho'ah* was unique, whether or not it turned out to be so at the conclusion of one's intensive investigation.

6.

My version of uniqueness rejects the mystification of the *Sho'ah*, and this in at least four senses.

First, I reject all efforts at *linguistic* mystification according to which the *Sho'ah* is said to transcend all language. If any event X is described as being "unique" in this *absolute* sense, i.e., in the strict form that: "for X no predicates apply," then X effectively drops out of our language and with its departure any coherent discussion of or reference to X becomes logically impossible.[51] Entailed by such a self-sacrificing logical scenario is the elimination of the notion of "uniqueness" for what is incomprehensible, "that X to which no predicates apply," cannot[52] be said to be "unique." The incomprehensible, the unintelligible, is not "unique"—it is merely incomprehensible and unintelligible.

Though this apophatic status, this numinous being beyond language, would appear to be exactly what proponents of such a radical *via negativa* intend, upon reflection even they must reject this linguistic gambit. And this because it makes the Nazi terror unimaginable and unintelligible as well as irrelevant: unimaginable and unintelligible because this is the logical consequence of such obliterative negations, irrelevant because what can post-Nazi generations understand of[53] and learn from, not least in the arena of morality, an event that, by definition, transcends all language, all appraisals, all normative matrices, and is thus unavailable for transmission from one generation to the next. Apophatic claims deny efforts at both historical understanding and moral evaluation and, on these compelling grounds, are unacceptable.

In truth, rhetoric aside, no one *really* holds to the non-predicative form of the term "uniqueness," because this sense of the term is actually meaningless. To summarize a highly complex philosophical argument, one could not even make sense to oneself regarding the concept of uniqueness or the reality of the Holocaust if one actually employed the concepts "unique" and "uniqueness" in accordance with the rule "For any predicate 0, X is not 0."[54] This is because the present apophatic claim is another, if special, instance of what Wittgenstein labeled the search for "the beetle in the box,"[55] the search for that elusive "private language" that retains its intelligibility even though, by definition, uncommunicable.[56] But such a "language"[57] is self-devouring; the absence of public[58] communicability negating private intelligibility.[59]

Secondly, I reject the *metaphysical* mystification of the *Sho'ah*. For this reason I oppose, for example, the language (and approach) employed by the Eckardts that would draw an analogy between the *Sho'ah* and religious experience, as such experience is described by Rudolf Otto. They write:

> The response that finds in the Holocaust a transcendent, crushing mystery incarnates the dimension of the numinous, as described by Rudolf Otto in *Das Heilige*. The mental state called the numinous by Otto presents itself as *ganz andere*, wholly other, a condition absolutely *sui generis* and incomparable whereby the human being finds himself utterly abashed. There is a feeling of terror before an awe-inspiring mystery, but a mystery that also fascinates infinitely.[60]

But this is to confuse the issue not to clarify it. It must be shown, not merely asserted, that the *Sho'ah* is, in the mystical sense, *ganz andere*, and this, despite their well-intentioned efforts, the Eckardts have not been able to do. They have not been able to do it because the assumed analogy between the *Sho'ah* and God, the *ganz andere*, is wholly misconceived. Whatever else the Holocaust is or isn't, it is *not* beyond spacetime nor does it stand in the same oblique relation to the categories of human understanding and meaning as does the *Eyn Sof*,[61] the Ineffable One, of the mystics.

The *Sho'ah* is not an ontological reality that is necessarily incomprehensible, except when it is so defined, as it often is.[62] But creating incomprehensibility by stipulation does not make for a convincing philosophical argument. Conversely, this is not to claim that we who were not there can "know" the *Sho'ah* like those who were,[63] but this salient epistemological disparity obtains with regard to all historical experiences, indeed it is inherent in the difference between first- and third-person experience as such. The epistemic dilemma is, of course, in its actuality, made far more complex when we are dealing with a multi-dimensional, many person, event like the *Sho'ah,* but the philosophical problem, how can we know that past of which we were not a part, is in no way unique to the experience of the *Sho'ah*.

Thirdly, I reject the *psychological* mystification of the *Sho'ah* according to which the Holocaust is said to be *irrational per se* and therefore beyond discussion and analysis—except by psychoanalysts[64] or psycho-historians[65]—and beyond morality "by virtue of insanity."

Whatever the real contribution of the irrational, the pathological, the insane, to the murder of European Jewry, these psychological elements have to be placed within the larger, encompassing, metaphysical, historical, and socio-political context of the event itself, lest the Holocaust be understood as little more than a Rorschach test. In so contextualizing the psychological one comes to recognize that Nazism had a logic of its own, its own way of organizing the world, that, once its premises were accepted, most especially its racial theory, made its program, however evil on alternative moral and ontological criteria, "reasonable." This is to acknowledge that *racial theory, per se,* is not inherently irrational,[66] even if it is false, and even though its fallacious imperatives led to genocidal enactments. Similarly, Nazism's romantic embrace of völkisch "feeling" is not deranged,[67] but rather a rational, if unacceptable theory of what is fundamental and decisive in individual and group behavior.[68] One may disagree or despair at this conclusion, but it does not violate any canon of reason *per se.*

Saul Friedlander, a sophisticated practitioner of the psychoanalytic analysis of Nazism, has made an important methodological remark about the balance that must exist between the psychoanalytic and other factors whose consideration is vital for understanding Nazism aright:

During crises in which existing interests, norms and certainties collapsed or seemed threatened, the emotional regression experienced by masses of people, the weakening of rational controls, offered vast opportunities to the extreme antisemitic minority. In German society extreme antisemitism, including Hitler's own obsessions, expanded against such a background after World War I. Yet while this very general analysis identifies conditions permitting the rise of Nazi antisemitism, it leaves open the question of the specific relationship between the antisemitic obsessions of the Nazi leadership and the huge bureaucracy industriously implementing the Final Solution. Here our starting point should be, it seems to me, a re-examination of the myth of the Jew in the Nazi world view, and particularly in Hitler's world view.[69]

This embedding of the psychological in the larger historic and ideological context renders psychoanalytic mystification impossible. For it reminds us that to understand why the pathological was let loose cannot be explained by recourse to the pathological. Here it must be remembered that Hitler and his circle were not "insane" in any ordinary sense. They threaten us precisely because, while *unique,* their uniqueness comes from their merciless willingness to pursue a logic, however unconventional, that is recognizably intelligible to others,[70] even though others dared not dream it before they made it real. Having been made manifest, it is now conceivable. What makes Nazism dreadful is not its contended irrationality, but its unlimited rationality, a rationality that devoured all opposition, all morality, all values other than its own and which, because rational, can be replicated. It was a case in which the *Idea* was supreme and would brook no exceptions, no compromises, no limits as a consequence of existing social norms and inherited fellow feelings. Given the incontrovertible assumption that Jews are bacilli, Auschwitz was the logical conclusion: if one's home is infected, one calls the exterminator.[71]

Fourthly, I reject the historiographical mystification of the *Sho'ah* according to which the confused and erroneous claim is made that because we cannot know everything about this event, and-or because we cannot know it like those who lived it knew it, we can know nothing at all about it. Post-Holocaust scholars can, despite their indirect relationship to the horrors, know about the *Sho'ah* even while acknowledging the real epistemological and existential limits, and difficulties, involved in their ability to know. Conversely, given their "distance" from the event, such observers may actually be at an advantage at least as regards certain non-existential types of historical and philosophical knowledge.[72]

A similar, acute, epistemic sensitivity illuminates the discussion, the search, for *causes* in regard to the *Sho'ah*.[73] Insofar as there were undoubtedly multiple causes at work in creating the *Sho'ah,* their complete specification is difficult, in practice even impossible. However, this fact does not justify the argument that because we can only supply a partial and incomplete causal explanation we should resist offering any causal explanation whatsoever. The often-made presumption underpinning this false contention, that causal explanations must be complete explanations, is merely a prejudice. If we can offer partial and incremental explanations that cumulatively build a clearer and clearer account of the Holocaust we should not, on the grounds of some dubious *a priori* principle, reject these explanations or this approach to explanations. It may well be that the logical confusion that reigns in this area stems, at least in part, from the erroneous notion that a unique event E cannot be subjected to causal decipherment, "Why is it the case that P?" without reducing its uniqueness. But this assumption, for it is only that, is indefensible and unwarranted.

The related misconception, that insofar as the *Sho'ah* was not predictable[74] it transcends causal explanation, is likewise to be rejected.

Predictability and causal explanation are two distinct conceptual operations. So, for example, no one could predict the outbreak of AIDS but no biologist or physician would construe this as entailing that AIDS is not subject to causality and not open to causal explanation.[75]

All these subtle ways of obscuring the study of the Holocaust, these multiple methods and forms of mystification, must be rejected. And they must be rejected precisely because we want to maintain, and retain, the singularity of the *Sho'ah* as a meaningful claim. The mystifiers by contrast, and contrary to their intentions, make this objective impossible.

CONCLUSION

The avoidance of the philosophical, methodological, and logical errors here analyzed will not yet produce, in itself, a convincing argument for the incommensurability of the *Sho'ah*. However, if these confusions are not repeated it will at least make it possible to open up the conceptual space in which an exploration of uniqueness might reasonably take place —and even succeed.

NOTES

1. Richard Rubenstein, *After Auschwitz: Radical Theology and Contemporary Judaism* (Indianapolis, 1966); idem, *The Cunning of History: The Holocaust and American Future* (New York, 1975); idem, *The Age of Triage: Fear and Hope in an Overcrowded World* (Boston, 1983); idem, along with John Roth, *Approaches to Auschwitz: The Holocaust and Its Legacy* (Atlanta, 1987); Arthur A. Cohen, *The Tremendum;* Emil Fackenheim, *God's Presence in History: Jewish Affirmations and Philosophical Reflections* (New York, 1972); idem, *The Jewish Return into History: Reflections in the Age of Auschwitz and a New Jerusalem* (New York, 1978); idem, *To Mend the World;* and Yitzchak (Irving) Greenberg, whose publications on this theme are mainly in the form of articles, the most important of which are: (1) "Cloud of Smoke, Pillar of Fire: Judaism, Christianity, and Modernity after the Holocaust," in E. Fleischner (ed.), *Auschwitz: Beginning of an Era?* (New York, 1977), pp. 1–55; (2) "Judaism and History: Historical Events and Religious Change," in Jerry V. Dillen (ed.), *Ancient Roots and Modern Meanings* (New York, 1978), pp. 43–63; (3) "New Revelations and New Patterns in the Relationship of Judaism and Christianity," *Journal of Ecumenical Studies* (Spring, 1979), pp. 249–267; (4) "The Transformation of the Covenant" (not yet published); and (5) "The Third Great Cycle of

Jewish History," printed and circulated by the National Jewish Resource Center (New York, 1981), 44 pages.

2. They have gone so far as to write:

> The Crucifixion and Resurrection are all decisively transfigured because the absolute God-forsakenness of Jewish children renders the ostensible absoluteness of the cross of Jesus nonabsolute and the Resurrection is transfigured because in the Holocaust the intrinsically triumphant nature of the dogma of the Resurrection of Jesus is finally revealed as an absolute seal of hostility and guarantor of the destruction of Jews ("The Holocaust and the Enigma of Uniqueness: A Philosophical Effort at Practical Clarification," *The Annals of the American Academy of Political and Social Science,* Vol. 450 [July, 1980], p. 173).

See also A. Roy Eckardt's essays, "Christian Responses to the Endlösung," *Religion in Life,* Vol. 47, No. 1 (Spring, 1978), pp. 33–45; idem, "Christians and Jews: Along a Theological Frontier," *Encounter,* Vol. 40, No. 2 (Spring, 1979), pp. 89–127; idem, "Is there a Way out of the Christian Crime? The Philosophic Question of the Holocaust," *Holocaust and Genocide Studies,* Vol. 1, No. 1 (1986), pp. 121–126; and his longer study, with Alice L. Eckardt, *Long Night's Journey into Day: A Revised Retrospective on the Holocaust* (Detroit, 1988[2]). For an appreciation of the revisionist efforts of the Eckardts, and Paul Van Buren (see note 1 next page), see B. A. Asbury, "Four Theologians: Revision of Christian Thought after Auschwitz," in Y. Bauer et al. (eds.), *Remembering for the Future* (Oxford, 1989), Vol. 1, pp. 562–570.

3. Jurgen Moltmann, *The Crucified God: The Cross of Christ as the Foundation and Criticism of Christian Theology* (New York, 1974).

4. Franklin Littell, *The Crucifixion of the Jews* (New York, 1985[2]).

5. Franklin Sherman, "Speaking of God after Auschwitz," *Worldview,* Vol. 17, No. 9 (September, 1974), pp. 26–30.

6. Paul Van Buren, *A Christian Theology of the People of Israel,* 3 Vols. (New York, 1980–1988).

7. Harry James Cargas, *A Christian Response to the Holocaust* (Denver, 1981); and idem, *When God and Man Failed: Non-Jewish Views of the Holocaust* (New York, 1982). And on these Christian responses see also Eva Fleischner, *Judaism in German Christian Theology since 1945* (Metuchen, 1975); idem, (ed.), *Auschwitz: Beginning of a New Era?* (New York, 1977); John T. Pawlikowski, *The Challenge of the Holocaust for Christian Theology* (New York, 1978); Michael B. McGarry, *Christology after Auschwitz* (New York, 1977); the highly unusual and provocative study of Eugene Borowitz, *Contemporary Christologies: A Jewish Response* (New York, 1980); Alan T. Davies, *Antisemitism and the Christian Mind: The Crisis of Christian Conscience after Auschwitz* (New York, 1969); and Charlotte Klein, *Anti-Judaism in Christian Theology* (London, 1978). In addition, Volume 1 of *Remembering for the Future* is largely devoted to issues relating to Christian theology and behavior in relationship to the *Sho'ah.* The dozens of essays, of varying quality, give a sense of the many questions the Holocaust raises for Christian life and thought after Auschwitz.

8. See, for example, David Tracy's essay "Religious Values after the Holocaust: A Catholic View," in Abraham J. Peck (ed.), *Jews and Christians after the Holocaust* (Philadelphia, 1982), pp. 87–107; Thoma's very well-intentioned *A Christian Theology of Judaism* (Mahwah, N.J., 1980); John Pawlikowski's, *What Are They Saying about Christian-Jewish Relations?* (New York, 1980); idem, *Christ in the Light of the Christian-Jewish Dialogue* (New York, 1982); idem, *The Challenge of the Holocaust for Christian Theology;* and Franz Mussner, *Tractate on the Jews: The Significance of Judaism for Christian Faith* (Philadelphia, 1984).

9. Eliezer Berkovits, *Faith after the Holocaust* (New York, 1973); idem, *With God in Hell: Judaism in the Ghettos and Death Camps* (New York, 1979); and idem, *Crisis and Faith* (New York, 1976).

10. Jacob Neusner, *Stranger at Home: The "Holocaust," Zionism, and American Judaism* (Chicago, 1981), pp. 6–8.

11. See for more details the printed *Sichot* (talks) of the present Lubavitcher distributed by the Lubavitch movement centered at 770 Eastern Parkway, Brooklyn, New York.

12. Barth's particular Christian understanding of the destruction of European Jewry and its doctrinal valence is woven into his very traditional reflections on the relationship between the "Old Israel" and the Church, i.e., the meaning of the Jewish people's rejection of Christ and the consequences of this act of apostasy, presented primarily in Volumes 2 and 3 of his *Church Dogmatics* (Edinburgh, 1936–77); but see also his essay, "Die Judenfrage und ihre christliche Beantwortung," *Judaica*, Vol. 6 (1952), pp. 67–72. For more on Barth's position see the highly critical appraisal of Alan T. Davies, *Antisemitism and the Christian Mind;* Dieter Kraft, "Israel in der Theologie Karl Barths," in *Communi Viatorum: A Theological Quarterly*, Vol. 27, Nos. 1 and 2 (1984), pp. 59–72; and Hans Jansen, "Antisemitism in the Amiable Guise of Theologica; Philo-Semitism in Karl Barth's Israel Theology before and after Auschwitz," in Y. Bauer et al. (eds.), *Remembering for the Future*, Vol. 1, pp. 72–79. Barth's position regarding the theological significance of the reborn State of Israel, however, did continually develop in a positive direction. For more details of his changing attitude see H. Berkhof, "Israel as a Theological Problem," *Journal of Ecumenical Studies*, Vol. 6, No. 3 (Summer, 1969), pp. 329–347.

13. D. Judant, *Les deux Israël, Essai sur le mystère du salut selon l'économie des deux Testaments* (Paris, 1960); and Charles Journet, *Destinées d'Israël, A propos du Salut par les Juifs* (Paris, 1945).

14. This term is used in kabbalistic thought to refer to acts that have a unifying-restorative effect on the cosmic order. Such acts help to "mend" both the world below and the world above.

15. For further analysis of many of these recent Jewish theological views see my *Post-Holocaust Dialogues: Critical Studies in Modern Jewish Thought* (New York, 1983). I, however, do not discuss the argument of R. Menachem Schneerson, the Lubavitcher Rebbe, in this work.

16. For more on the theological response in certain traditional orthodox Jewish

circles, see William Helmreich, "Understanding the Holocaust: The Yeshiva View," *Transaction/Society,* Vol. 18 (1980–81), pp. 42–59; Rabbi Isaac Hutner, "Holocaust," *The Jewish Observer,* (October, 1977), pp. 3–11; and three responses elicited by Rav Hutner's remarks, the first a defense of Hutner by R. Yaacov Feitman, "Reviewing a Shiur: Rabbi Hutner's 'Holocaust' Seminar," *The Jewish Observer* (January, 1978), pp. 11–14; the second a strong critique by Lawrence Kaplan, "Rabbi Isaac Hutner's 'Dark Torah Perspective' on the Holocaust," *Tradition,* Vol. 18, No. 3 (Fall, 1980), pp. 235–248, and the response to this article by Aaron I. Reichels "Communications," *Tradition,* Vol. 21, No. 2 (Summer, 1983), pp. 180–187; and the third by Shubert Spero in the January 1978 issue of the *Jewish Observer*. Another more recent, tendentious effort to deal with the *Sho'ah* from a right-wing perspective is Bernard Maza, *With Fury Poured Out: The Power of the Powerless during the Holocaust* (New York, 1989).

17. In this connection one immediately thinks of a number of Irving (Yitz) Greenberg's challenging "neo-halachic" claims, for more discussion of which see my essay on his work in the present volume, pp. 225–250, and some of the fallacious arguments that were offered during the debate over "patrilineal descent," i.e., regarding the criteria for Jewish status, in the Reform Movement. In the latter case it was suggested that insofar as having a Jewish father, rather than a Jewish mother, as the *halachah* requires, was enough to condemn one to death in Nazi Germany we ought now to alter the traditional halachic definition of Jewishness to include those who have a Jewish father but not a Jewish mother. But this is a *non sequitur,* for what halachic status do Hitler's racial Nuremberg Laws have? None.

18. This should not be misunderstood as a general criticism of the possibility of doing theology in the face of the *Sho'ah* as such.

19. This, however, does not mean, as for example Paul Robinson holds, that the Holocaust does not represent a "distinct category." The distinctiveness of the *Sho'ah,* as we shall argue, lies elsewhere than in the fact that Jews died —as others have died. And in fact, *contra* Robinson's plea that "we should resist the temptation to make the distinction [between the *Sho'ah* and prior events of mass death] categorical" this is exactly what we must do. Not, I hasten to add, in order to mystify the Holocaust but, rather, to *de*-mystify it. That is, as an historical judgment, given our criteria, the destruction of European Jewry represents a distinctive event in human history. Robinson, a distinguished Stanford University historian, has simply not done the historical research (represented by the detailed case studies in Volumes 1 and 2 of my forthcoming study, *The Holocaust in Historical Context*) to be able to "categorically" deny that the *Sho'ah* was *un*like, for example, the acts of "Alexander the Great, Attila the Hun, the Albigensian Crusade, the Thirty Years War, European Imperialism or black slavery" (p. 63) that he explicitly refers to. Based on the case studies of each of these events, excluding the Thirty Years War, prepared for this project, I, however, deny just such asserted commonality. Not of course for the dead victims—the point emphasized by Robinson—but rather as historical and phenomenological events

that involve more than the common factor that the dead in all such tragedies are equally dead. But to reduce the qualitative debate about uniqueness to this level is misconceived and bypasses the real and important issues at stake in this dialogue. Robinson is correct to find fault with three reasons often given to justify claims to uniqueness:

First, unlike previous horrors, it was "systematic," meaning that it was pursued with all the efficiency accessible to a modern technological society. Second, it had no apparent economic motive, indeed was economically counterproductive, and therefore, unlike an abuse such as slavery, seems "senseless," . . . And finally, it meant not merely pain, humiliation and servitude, but death . . . so do not categorically separate the holocaust from other historical acts of inhumanity." (p. 63)

These contentions are not, as Robinson indicates, logically coercive. My argument for uniqueness, however, while agreeing with Robinson as to the insufficiency of these three arguments offers a different reason turning on the notion of genocide as defined by me and connected to my definition of uniqueness offered in this chapter. And this criterion is not addressed at all by Robinson's position. Moreover, in line with my insistence in this subsection (2) on rejecting moral criteria as criteria relevant to establishing uniqueness, i.e., I do not assert the Holocaust was *more evil* than other events of mass death, I explicitly reject Robinson's assertion, at least for myself and my own studies, that in insisting on the singularity of the *Sho'ah* "we dismiss as relatively trivial all the sins that mankind has to answer for up to 1933." This conclusion is a *non sequitur* vis-à-vis the present work. For Robinson's full remarks see his review entitled "Apologist for the Superego" [Review of Bruno Bettelheim's *Surviving and Other Essays*], *New York Times Book Review* (April 29, 1979), pp. 7 and 63.

20. In light of this I want to explicitly distance my position on the uniqueness of the *Sho'ah*, which I will defend, from Pierre Papazian's charge that:

To claim that the Holocaust was unique can only imply that attempts to annihilate other national or cultural groups are not to be considered genocide, thus diminishing the gravity and moral implications of any genocide anywhere, any time. It also implies that the Jews have a monopoly on genocide, that no matter what misfortune befalls another people, it cannot be as serious or even in the same category as the Holocaust. ("A Unique Uniqueness?" *Midstream*, Vol. 30, No. 4 (April, 1984), p. 18)

Papazian commits the logical error we are here rejecting, if in an inverted way. He holds that Jews in denying the comparability of the Holocaust are advancing a moral claim and diminishing, if only by indirection, the "misfortunes [that] befall another people." I.e., he too equates uniqueness with morality and again uniqueness with "types" or "degrees" of evil. The Armenian tragedy can only be *as evil* as the Holocaust if the Holocaust is not unique. But if we do not commit the basic error of equating uniqueness with levels of moral evil, then we can assert, without either logical contradiction or offensive moral chauvinism, the uniqueness of the Holocaust while at the same time resisting any (unfavorable or diminishing) comparison (or judgment) as to the amount of evil represented by, in this case, the

Armenian massacres and the destruction of European Jewry. This same form of argument, it should be added, applies to the notion of genocide. To identify A as genocide and B as not-genocide is not necessarily to make an ethical argument. A and B can be structurally and phenomenologically different, one a case of genocide the other not a case of genocide, and yet equally evil. As Papazian employs the unsatisfactory and ambiguous notion of "implication" ("implies") twice in the few lines quoted above I here state my position directly so no one will take it, erroneously, as "implying" its converse.

21. Yehuda Bauer, *The Holocaust in Historical Perspective* (Seattle, 1978), p. 36.
22. I also reject, on other grounds, Bauer's idiosyncratic formulation of "Holocaust" versus genocide. My own understanding of these terms, and my reasons for rejecting Bauer's proposals, are set out in Vol. One, chapter 4 of my forthcoming *The Holocaust in Historical Context*.
23. He is referring to the essay entitled "The Unique Intentionality of the Holocaust," in my *Post-Holocaust Dialogues*, pp. 287–317.
24. Kenneth Seeskin, "What Philosophy Can and Cannot Say about Evil," in Alan Rosenberg and Gerald Myers (eds.), *Echoes from the Holocaust* (Philadelphia, 1989), p. 98.
25. See especially his *Taking Lives: Genocide and State Power* (New Brunswick, 1982).
26. Irving Louis Horowitz, "Many Genocides, One Holocaust? The Limits of the Rights of States and the Obligations of Individuals," *Modern Judaism*, Vol. 1, No. 1 (May, 1981), p. 75.
27. A. Roy Eckardt, *Long Night's Journey into Day*, p. 54.
28. Emil Fackenheim, *To Mend the World*, p. 24.
29. A. Roy Eckardt, *Long Night's Journey into Day*, p. 54. Here Eckardt was anticipated by Richard Rubenstein who, in *After Auschwitz*, published in 1966, wrote: "I don't compare [Hiroshima and Auschwitz], Auschwitz was a unique phenomenon, like the revelation at Sinai" (p. 227).
30. Alice Eckardt and A. Roy Eckardt, "The Holocaust and the Enigma of Uniqueness," p. 168.
31. Ibid., p. 169.
32. Ibid., p. 168.
33. Ibid., pp. 170–171.
34. George Kren and Leon Rappaport, *The Holocaust and the Crisis of Human Behavior* (New York, 1980), p. 13.
35. George Kren and Leon Rappaport, *The Holocaust and the Crisis of Human Behavior*, p. 15. Importantly, Emil Fackenheim, the philosopher who has thought about this event more deeply than almost anyone else and whose work is a cornerstone of much theological and philosophical reflection about the Holocaust, has also to admit that despite his assertion that "the world [after Auschwitz] can never be the same" (*Jewish Return into History*, p. 279) "the world has thus far shied away from it [the Holocaust]" (ibid., p. 107). Likewise Henry Feingold, in general a defender of the claim

that the Holocaust is unique, has written in review of Lucy S. Dawidowicz's *War against the Jews:* "Seen on the larger canvas of European history, the holocaust does not have the importance and uniqueness it has on the canvas of Jewish history" (Henry Feingold, review of Dawidowicz, *Jewish Social Studies,* Vol. 38, No. 1 [1976], p. 83). Anson G. Rabinbach and Jack Zipes have gone even further: "It is not only true that the lessons of the Holocaust have not yet been learned, it is doubtful that they have been discovered" ("Lessons of the Holocaust," *New German Critique,* No. 19 [1980], p. 7).

36. George Kren and Leon Rappaport, *The Holocaust and the Crisis of Human Behavior,* p. 129. More recently George Kren has reconfirmed this appraisal of the negligible impact that the Holocaust has had on the consciousness of the post-Holocaust age. Writing of the treatment of the Holocaust by contemporary historians he acknowledges:

> Histories of Europe in the twentieth century assign little space to it, and many textbooks of "Western civilization" all but ignore it. At best it stands as another example that history has always produced victims, and Nazism is seen only as another example of a recurrent "inhumanity of man to man." Contemporary historians of the twentieth century have tended to see the Holocaust as one of the many brutalities of Nazism, proof of the dangers of racism, but hardly as a focal point of modern history. Its consequences were minimal, and, in contrast to other events that have become significant components in philosophical, historical, literary, or theological discourse, it is the subject of few serious discussions. The argument of its centrality must then rest upon reasons other than that it produced visible consequences. Most historians writing on the twentieth century perceive the killing of a substantial portion of Europe's Jews and the destruction of Eastern Europe's Yiddish culture as events of no great significance. An examination of historical accounts documents the thesis that most historians do not regard the Holocaust as particularly important. ("The Holocaust As History," in Alan Rosenberg and Gerald Myers (eds.), *Echoes from the Holocaust,* p. 8)

Supporting evidence for Kren's conclusion can be found in the historiographical investigations of Gerd Korman, "The Holocaust in Historical Writing," *Societas,* Vol. 2, No. 3 (Summer, 1972), pp. 251–270; Henry Friedlander, *On the Holocaust: A Critique of the Treatment of the Holocaust in History Texts* (New York, 1972); and Lucy S. Dawidowicz's highly polemical *The Holocaust and Historians* (Cambridge, 1981).

37. Elie Wiesel, *One Generation After* (New York, 1970), p. 15.

38. Over 100 wars have been fought worldwide since 1945.

39. Kren and Rappaport's description, already quoted, of the Holocaust as an "*impalpable*" crisis raises the elementary logical question: can a crisis that is *impalpable* be a crisis, given the definition of the terms "crisis" and "impalpable." *Websters New World Dictionary of the American Language* (Cleveland, 1956) defines the latter term as: "1. not perceptible to the touch, that cannot be felt; 2. too slight or subtle to be grasped easily by the mind; inappreciable" (p. 727).

40. It might be argued that Kren and Rappaport produce more support than I here indicate in favor of their concept of "historical crisis." That is, while I

have concentrated on their opening methodological stipulations, and their weakness, their entire monograph should be considered as evidence for their view. While there is some marginal truth to this suggestion, my critical judgment, in its totality, remains unaffected by this fact for, in the end, as they themselves admit, as quoted, no real data is available to support their claim. We have finally only their stipulated definition and undefended conjectures.

41. Ismar Schorsch, "The Holocaust and Human Survival," *Midstream*, Vol. 17, No. 1 (January, 1981), p. 39.
42. Alan Rosenberg also falls into this trap when he contends:

    We cannot accept the simple situation of the Jews and the special "intention" of the Nazis with respect to their total extinction. This emphasis . . . obscures the more universal implications for the future of *all* mankind that the Holocaust raises. ("Was the Holocaust Unique? A Peculiar Question?" in Isidor Wallimann and Michael N. Dobkowski (eds.), *Genocide and the Modern State* (New York, 1987), p. 157)

    This argument is misconceived. The universal implications for the future of *all* mankind that the Holocaust raises can have no logical standing at all in deciding the prior question: Is what happened to the Jews an event without precedent or parallel? Then, too, Rosenberg errs in failing to recognize that particularity, even radical particularity, can have universal significance.
43. As Max Weber recognized, truth telling is "inconvenient" for "party opinions," Hans Gerth and C. Wright Mills (eds.), *From Max Weber: Essays in Sociology* (New York, 1946), p. 147.
44. I would note that even Schorsch has need to speak, if not of uniqueness, then of "centrality," and explicitly endorses the claim that

    the unadorned truth is that the Jews were the only victims of genocide in World War II and that grisly fact is enough to warrant attention. The mass murder of Polish intellectuals, Russian prisoners-of-war, and Gypsies was equally final, but not the implementation of a policy of genocide. ("The Holocaust and Human Survival," p. 39)

    I wonder aloud if those critical of Jewish claims to uniqueness and its supposedly negative political implications would find Schorsch's assertions of "centrality" (entailing by definition the "marginality" or "non-centrality" of others) and the above-cited limited claim to uniqueness at least within the context of World War II any more appealing and politically (and otherwise) useful than the more general claim Schorsch is critical of.
45. Schorsch's additional contention that the claim for (or against) uniqueness adds nothing substantive to the larger decoding of the *Sho'ah* is mistaken.
46. Ismar Schorsch, "The Holocaust and Human Survival," p. 39.
47. I would agree with Schorsch that it is important that "we translate our [Jewish] experience into existential and political symbols meaningful to non-Jews." But I do not see that this necessarily entails the denial of the uniqueness of that experience which is, in fact, essential to it. Or put another way, to deny the uniqueness of the experience in order to allow us to "translate our experience . . . to non-Jews" would negate the very meaning of the

experience we wish to translate, i.e., what we would convey to others would be a *different* experience.

48. Note: On my definition of "uniqueness" the notion of uniqueness means not that X cannot happen again but that to this point it has only happened once. Alan Montefiore has observed that:

> the peculiar uniqueness of the Holocaust may, if one so chooses (for there is always that important element of choice involved in one's reading of symbols), be perceived as lying in significant part in the way in which it is indeed peculiarly fitted to stand as a unique symbol for all human genocides, whether actual or "only" possible; and, indeed, of all such abasement and denial of man by man—of individuals whether because of their name or their anonymity, as of whole peoples or of man in the mass. It is thus right that the Holocaust should be felt, and felt deeply, to be unique; for it is thus that it may stand also to remind us that everything which happens, happens to human beings who are each in their own particularity unique, and that only through the recognition of that uniqueness, that untranscendable particularity, is human self-awareness, the awareness of what it is to be human, made possible. ("Jewish Identity: The Interplay between the Universal and the Particular," *Remembering for the Future*, Vol. 2, p. 1933)

This sensitive yet unsophisticated exegesis of the notion of particularity, of the universality of particularity, is one among several possible routes that are open with regard to a nondisjunctive reading of uniqueness, i.e., a reading that does not create false dichotomies for reasons of apologetics but rather comes to grips with the logical and ethical issues raised by the issue of singularity in a manner that manifests the appropriate sensibility and seriousness to the scholarly conversation of which this narrow issue is a subset. Schorsch's suggestion that Lurianic kabbalah did something similar in response to the Spanish Expulsion is also suggestive, though I would caution that Schorsch's exegesis of the self-understanding of Lurianic kabbalah, pp. 41–42, is somewhat inexact and underestimates, to use his term, the "centrality" of the Jew and Torah in the process of *Tikkun Olam,* the repair of the world and cosmic order.

49. I. Schorsch, "The Holocaust and Human Survival," p. 39.

50. Geoff Eley, "Holocaust History," *London Review of Books* (March 17, 1982), p. 6.

51. This view has also been well expressed in the idiom of the historian by the distinguished English medievalist G. Elton:

> No historian really treats all facts as unique; he treats them as particular. He cannot —no one can—deal in unique fact, because facts and events require reference to common experience, to conventional frameworks, to (in short) the general before they acquire meaning. The unique event is a freak and a frustration; if it is really unique—can never recur in meaning or implication—it lacks every measurable dimension and cannot be assessed. But to the historian, facts and events (and people) must be individual and particular: like other entities of a similar kind, but never entirely identical with them. That is to say, they are to be treated as peculiar to themselves and not as indistinguishable statistical units or elements in an equation; but they are linked and rendered comprehensible by kinship, by common possessions,

by universal qualities present in differing proportions and arrangements. (G. R. Elton, *The Practice of History* [New York, 1967], p. 11)

The significance of this recognition for sociological and historical investigations has been emphasized by Pitirim A. Sorokin, *Social and Cultural Dynamics* (New York, 1937), Vol. 1, pp. 167–173.

52. This is a logical "cannot."

53. Louis Gottschalk has well understood the complexity of the relationship between claims to historical uniqueness and generalization:

> The writers of the articles that precede and follow this one agree that adherents of the school of the unique are likely to be beguiled if they think they can avoid generalization. The arguments in support of this agreement seem to run essentially as follows: (1) language consists largely of verbal and written symbols which by their very nature must have general denotations and connotations; (2) the method by which the historian examines testimony and other evidence to arrive at the unique historical fact comprises in itself a set of rules (i.e., generalizations); (3) what is special, segregate, or unique cannot be understood except by comparison with the average, the normal, the aggregate, or the general (and vice versa). Even if a member of the school of the unique were to make a most strenuous effort to avoid generalization, he would first have to test his evidence for its authenticity and credibility by some set of recognized general rules such as are set forth from time to time in manuals of historical method. Then, to avoid using words or other symbols freighted with general meaning, he would be obliged to present only the duly tested evidence itself and in a strictly chronological order without comparisons, interrelations, reflections, or interpretations. (Louis Gottschalk, [ed.], *Generalization in the Writing of History* [Chicago, 1963] p. 114)

Or as Aristotle already recognized, "it is necessary to discern similarities even in the most different objects," *Rhetoric,* III, XI, 5.

54. The logic of this absolute sense, or rather its incoherence, can be exposed by considering the implications of Wittgenstein's parable of the "beetle in the box" in his *Philosophical Investigations,* ed. G. E. M. Anscombe and R. Rhees (Oxford 1967), section 293, and his example of "The Diary," section 258ff. There is also much that bears on this issue in Wittgenstein's *Zettel,* edited by G. E. M. Anscombe and G. H. Von Wright (Oxford, 1967); idem, "Notes for Lectures on 'Private Experience' and 'Sense Data,' " edited by Rush Rhees, *Philosophical Review,* Vol. 77 (1968), pp. 275–320; and idem, *On Certainty,* edited by G. E. M. Anscombe and G. H. Von Wright (Oxford, 1969). I am indebted to Prof. G. E. M. Anscombe, one of the supervisors of my doctoral dissertation, who helped me understand the full complexity of these issues. They have been much discussed in the secondary literature under the rubric of "private languages." See G. Hallett, *A Companion to Wittgenstein's "Philosophical Investigations"* (Ithaca, N.Y., 1977); A. J. Ayer, "Can There Be a Private Language?" reprinted in G. Pitcher (ed.), *Wittgenstein, The Philosophical Investigations* (Garden City, N.Y., 1966), an unsuccessful attempt to defend the notion of "private language"; R. Rhees and J. Cook also have articles on this topic in the Pitcher *Wittgenstein* collection, which also contains a bibliography for further research up

to 1965. See also on this topic the papers collected together in O. R. Jones (ed.), *The Private Language Argument* (London, 1971). For more recent studies up to 1977 see the bibliography in G. Hallett, *A Companion;* and for still more recent discussions see S. Kripke, *Wittgenstein on Rules and Private Language* (Oxford, 1982); C. Wright, "Does *Philosophical Investigations* I, 258–260, Suggest a Cogent Argument against Private Language?" in P. Pettit and J. McDowell (eds.), *Subject Thought and Context* (Oxford, 1986), pp. 209–266; Charles Travis, *The Uses of Sense: Wittgenstein's Philosophy of Language* (Oxford, 1989); David Pears, *The False Prison: A Study of the Development of Wittgenstein's Philosophy* (Oxford, 1988), Vol. 2, pp. 328–422; and Colin McGinn, *Wittgenstein on Meaning* (Oxford, 1984).

55. Sources listed in note 54.

56. I have explored some of the peculiar and unintended consequences of this linguistic claim in the context of mystical reports and the study of mysticism in my essay, "Language, Epistemology and Mystical Pluralism," in Steven T. Katz (ed.), *Mysticism and Philosophical Analysis* (New York, 1978), pp. 22–74; see also my paper entitled "Utterance and Ineffability in Jewish Neoplatonism," in Lenn Goodman (ed.), *Jewish Neoplatonism* (Albany, 1991), pp. 279–298; and idem, "The Varieties of Mystical Language," in Steven T. Katz (ed.), *Mysticism and Language* (New York, 1992), pp. 3–50.

57. The extraordinarily difficult issue of the accuracy of linguistic descriptions of experience, i.e., of how language and experience "make a fit," is raised by this exploration, though we shall not pursue it. However, we are mindful of Elie Wiesel's warning that even in the case of survivors like himself, "Perhaps, what we tell about what happened and what really happened have nothing to do one with the other." "Jewish Values in the Post Holocaust Future," *Judaism,* Vol. 16, No. 3 (Summer, 1967), p. 283. In this profound hermeneutical reflection Wiesel raises elemental issues in the theory of language and meaning that bear directly upon all writing and speaking about the Holocaust, including narratives and reports of the survivors no less than upon the writings of those like myself who were fortunate to be born in a different place though not a different time.

58. Wittgenstein makes a brilliant comment about this in the *Philosophical Investigations.*

When one says, "He gave a name to his sensation," one forgets that a great deal of stage-setting in the language is presupposed *[schon viel in der Sprache vorbereitet sein muss]* if the mere act of naming is to make sense. And when we speak of someone's having given a name to pain, what is presupposed is the existence of the grammar of the word "pain"; it shows the post where the new word is stationed. (Section 257)

In the case of the *Sho'ah,* too, we require this public grammar, even when we deny that we require it or attempt, at our peril, to avoid or transcend it.

59. Here the separate, but related issue, first raised by Theodor Adorno, of

whether the *Sho'ah* can become the proper occasion for literary and other "aesthetic" works, needs to be evaluated. As Adorno wrote:

After Auschwitz to write a poem is barbaric. . . . Through aesthetic principles or stylization . . . the unimaginable ordeal still appears as if it had some ulterior purpose. It is transfigured and stripped of some of its horror, and with this, injustice is already done to the victims. (*Gesammelte Schriften* [Frankfurt a.M., 1974], p. 422)

Like Adorno, other than for first-person reports, i.e., survivor testimony, including "fictionalized" forms of such testimony, e.g., and most famously, Elie Wiesel's *Night,* the works of Primo Levi, Charlotte Delbo, Tadeusz Borowski, and André Schwarz-Bart, or in poetic form Yitzchak Katznelson's *Song of the Murdered Jewish People,* I am not at all confident that this is a proper subject for literature. And, it should be added explicitly, for myself, and I believe for most other readers, the significance of Wiesel's or Levi's work does not lie in its "literariness," but in its significance as reportage and authentic memoir. Compare Piotr Rawicz's powerful, even savage comment, regarding Holocaust literature: "The literary manner is an obscenity. Literature is the art, occasionally remunerative of rummaging in vomit" (*Blood from the Sky,* [New York, 1964]). For more on this difficult normative-aesthetic question, see the important studies by such informed literary critics as Lawrence Langer, *The Holocaust and the Literary Imagination* (New Haven, 1975); idem, *The Age of Atrocity* (Boston, 1978); idem, *Versions of Survival: The Holocaust and the Human Spirit* (Albany, 1982); Alvin Rosenfeld, *A Double Dying: Reflections on Holocaust Literature* (Bloomington, 1980); Sidra Ezrahi, *By Words Alone: The Holocaust in Literature* (Chicago, 1980); Alan Berger, *Crisis and Covenant: The Holocaust in American Jewish Fiction* (Albany, 1985); George Steiner, *Language and Silence: Essays on Language, Literature and the Inhuman* (New York, 1972); idem, *In Bluebeard's Castle: Some Notes on the Redefinition of Culture* (New Haven, 1971); Ruth Angress, "Discussing Holocaust Literature," *Simon Wiesenthal Center Annual,* Vol. 2 (1985), pp. 179–192; James Young, *Writing and Rewriting the Holocaust: Narrative of the Consequences of Interpretation* (Bloomington, 1988), contains a valuable bibliography of primary and secondary sources; and the recent philosophically informed comments of Berel Lang in his *Act and Idea in the Nazi Genocide* (Chicago, 1990), pp. 103–164. Lang calls to notice in this connection Adorno's later reconsideration of this issue: "Perennial suffering has as much right to expression as a tortured man has to scream; hence it may have been wrong to say that after Auschwitz you could no longer write poems" (Theodor Adorno, *Negative Dialectics* [New York, 1973], p. 362, cited by Lang, *Act and Idea,* p. 125 n. 8).

60. "The Holocaust and the Enigma of Uniqueness," p. 169.
61. The term applied by Kabbalists to God as He is in Himself and beyond all human comprehension.
62. Though having reservations about particular arguments made by Dan Ma-

gurshak in his essay, "The 'Incomprehensibility' of the Holocaust: Tightening Up Some Loose Usage," in Alan Rosenberg and Gerald E. Myers (eds.), *Echoes from the Holocaust,* pp. 421–431, his sorting and critique of the various meanings of the term "incomprehensible" as applied to the Holocaust does help in the clarification of the issue.

63. This epistemological dilemma is further complicated as a consequence of Emil Fackenheim's salient methodological caution regarding survivor reports:

It is normally assumed that, with all due allowance for bias of perception and memory, the eyewitness is the most reliable source of "what actually happened." When the eyewitness is caught in a scheme of things systematically calculated to deceive him, subsequent reflection is necessary if truth is to be given to his testimony. (*The Jewish Return into History,* p. 58)

Fackenheim's remark is cited from Alan Rosenberg, "The Crisis in Knowing and Understanding the Holocaust," in Alan Rosenberg and Gerald E. Myers (eds.), *Echoes from the Holocaust,* p. 388, wherein Rosenberg offers some pertinent glosses on this point.

64. See, for example, the psychoanalytical efforts to explain Nazism of W. Reich, *Mass Psychology of Fascism* (New York, 1970); E. Fromm, *Escape from Freedom* (New York, 1941); R. Loewenstein, *Christians and Jews: A Psychoanalytic Study* (New York, 1952); B. Bettelheim, *The Informed Heart: Autonomy in a Mass Age* (Glencoe, Ill., 1960); Nathan Ackermann and Marie Jahooda, *Antisemitism and Emotional Disorder* (New York, 1950); T. Adorno et al., *The Authoritarian Personality* (New York, 1950); Nevitt Sanford and Craig Comstock (eds.) *Sanctions for Evil* (San Francisco, 1971); Frederic Wertham, *A Sign of Cain: An Exploration of Human Violence* (New York, 1966); Henry V. Dicks, *Licensed Mass Murder: A Socio-Psychological Study of Some SS Killers* (London, 1972); Erich Fromm, *The Anatomy of Human Destructiveness* (New York, 1973); Israel Charny, *How Can We Commit the Unthinkable? Genocide the Human Cancer* (Boulder, 1982); Wendy Stellar Flory, "The Psychology of Antisemitism," in Michael Curtis (ed.), *Antisemitism in the Contemporary World* (Boulder, 1986); John Sabini and Maury Silver, "Destroying the Innocent with a Clear Conscience: A Sociopsychology of the Holocaust," in Joel E. Dimsdale (ed.), *Survivors, Victims and Perpetrators: Essays on the Nazi Holocaust* (Washington, 1980), pp. 329–358.

Of real importance are the sober, skeptical conclusions regarding what the psychological data reveal offered by Gerald L. Borofsky and Don J. Brand in their paper, "Personality Organization and Psychological Functioning of the Nuremberg War Criminals: The Rorschach Data," in Joel Dimsdale (ed.), *Survivors, Victims and Perpetrators,* pp. 359–403. Also relevant, if that is the correct term, are the more general psychohistorical studies of group behavior and social pathology that have been written with a knowledge of the Holocaust in mind, e.g., Fred Weinstein and Gerald Platt, *The Wish to Be Free* (Berkeley, 1969); Harry Levinson, *Organiza-*

tional Diagnosis (Cambridge, 1972); Elliott Jaquls, "Social Systems as a Defense against Persecutory and Depressive Anxiety," in M. Klein (ed.), *New Directions in Psychoanalysis* (New York, 1955); S. Milgrom, *Obedience to Authority: An Experimental View* (New York, 1974); R. A. Baron, *Human Aggression* (New York, 1977); Lloyd de Mause's phantasy, "Historical Group Phantasies," *Journal of Psychohistory*, Vol. 7 (1979), pp. 1– 70; and most recently, Ervin Staub's very derivative, *The Roots of Evil: The Origins of Genocide and Other Group Violence* (Cambridge [England], 1989). See also R. Rubenstein's work connecting the psychoanalytic and the theological, *After Auschwitz*. My reservations about these efforts will be set out in detail in Volume 3 of my study, *The Holocaust in Historical Context* (forthcoming).

65. On psycho-historical efforts to deal with Nazism, see R. Binion, *Hitler among the Germans* (New York, 1976); and Peter Loewenberg's review of Binion's approach in the *Journal of Modern History*, Vol. 47, No. 2 (1975), pp. 241–244; Robert G. L. Waite's influential though deeply flawed work, *The Psychopathic God: Adolf Hitler* (New York, 1977); and the review of Peter Loewenberg in *Central European History*, No. 3 (September, 1974), pp. 265–272; George M. Kren, "Psychohistorical Interpretations of National Socialism," *German Studies Review*, Vols. 1 & 2 (May, 1978); Peter Loewenberg, "Nixon, Hitler and Power: An Ego Psychological Study," *Psychoanalytic Inquiry*, Vol. 6, No. 1 (1986), pp. 27–48; idem, "The Psychohistorical Origins of the Nazi Youth Cohort," *American Historical Review*, Vol. 76 (1971), pp. 1457–1502; idem, "Psychohistorical Perspectives on Modern German History," *Journal of Modern History*, Vol. 47 (1975), pp. 229–279; and idem, "Psychohistory," in M. Kammen (ed.), *The Past Before Us: Contemporary Historical Writing in the United States* (Ithaca, 1980). A bibliography on the subject is provided by Terry Mensch, "Psychohistory of the Third Reich," *Journal of Psychohistory*, Vol. 7, No. 3 (1979–1980), pp. 331–354; and see also the review essay of work in this area by Geoffrey Cocks, "The Hitler Controversy," *Political Psychology*, Vol. 1, No. 2 (Autumn, 1979), pp. 67–81.

George M. Kren and Leon Rappaport, *The Holocaust and the Crisis of Human Behavior*, also engage in psychohistory, with only marginal success, at various important junctures in their argument. They do, however, provide a useful summary of some of the psycho-historical literature in their "Bibliographic Essay," in *The Holocaust and the Crisis of Human Behavior*, pp. 165–169. George Kren has also made a more recent, equally marginal foray into the debate, "Psychohistory, Psychobiography and the Holocaust," *Psychohistory Review*, Vol. 13, No. 1 (1984), pp. 40–45. This approach has been reviewed by Saul Friedlander in his *History and Psychoanalysis* (New York, 1978); and severely criticized by Jacques Barzun in his *Clio and the Doctors: Psycho-History, Quanto-History, and History* (Chicago, 1974). Barzun's "Seven Regretful Objections [to psychohistory]" given on pp. 39– 41 are indeed, despite their lack of development, and their highly aggressive tone, telling objections.

More recently Gertrude Himmelfarb has also made an undeveloped but significant critique of psychohistory in her *The New History and the Old* (Cambridge, 1987). Other critics of psychohistory who have made important analyses of the subject are: D. E. Stannard, *Shrinking History: On Freud and the Failure of Psychohistory* (New York, 1980), the most radical, at times excessive, critique to date; Oscar Handlin, *Truth in History* (Cambridge, 1979), esp. pp. 14–15; A. Marwick, *The Nature of History* (London, 1981²), pp. 111–115; and Lawrence Stone, *The Past and the Present* (Boston, 1981), pp. 40–41 and 220–229. Two additional sets of papers that explore the methodological issues raised by psychohistory in interesting ways are R. J. Lifton and E. Olson (eds.), *Explorations in Psychohistory: The Wellfleet Papers* (New York, 1974); and the recent volume edited by William McKenley Runyan, *Psychology and Historical Interpretation* (New York, 1988). The essays in this latter collection contain very complete and up-to-date bibliographies on various aspects of the subject. For further bibliographical assistance see also W. J. Gilmore, *Psychohistorical Inquiry: A Comprehensive Research Bibliography* (New York, 1984).

66. A crude, erroneous presentation of the contrary view is argued by Ronald Aronson in his essay, "Social Madness," in I. Walliman and M. Dobkowski (eds.), *Genocide in the Modern Age*, pp. 125–141, esp. pp. 129–132. Aronson asks: "Why is it not enough simply to label as *mistakes* the man who sees the devil or the Nazi who sees the Jew as devil?" And he replies as follows:

> After all, we are first of all talking about a mistake. The problem is that to call misperception a mistake locates it within the realm of reason and evidence we presume in all discourse and indeed perception. Within that realm a mistake may be corrected, for example, by demonstrating it to be false. But to call it madness underscores on the one hand its depth and seriousness, on the other its psychological roots and quality of being beyond reason and demonstration. If we regard a belief as mad we see it as being both willful *and* beyond reach. (p. 129)

But Aronson is simply wrong here. Consider the actual historical case in which entire segments of European society saw the devil everywhere, especially in league with old single women (for more details see chapter 5 of the present volume on the witch craze). This belief was *false* and, in time, counter-arguments demonstrated its incorrectness and the witch craze came to a halt. That is to say, the belief in the devil and his putative involvement with humankind was not "beyond reach." The decline of *theologically* grounded antisemitism since the seventeenth century, especially in twentieth-century liberal democracies, supports this argument, i.e., antisemitism is certainly not "beyond reach." It only becomes so when it becomes the prisoner of a bad Aronson-like theory about madness. Here one recognizes that at least one of the key sources of Aronson's profound confusion is his failure to distinguish between metaphysical doctrines (including myths) and beliefs and madness, i.e., metaphysical doctrines and beliefs and madness may all be beyond "demonstration," that is disconfirmation, but the two categories are not to be conflated and reduced to the psychological without remainder. For example, the execrable role assigned to the "Jew" by Christian theology is not open to disconfirmation and in this lies the recurring tragedy of Jewish-Christian relations, but Christians, who on classical New Testament theological grounds are anti-Jewish, are not *mad,* however evil, in any clinical sense of madness. (I remind readers again of conservative Christian theologians such as Karl Barth who saw the Death Camps as a confirmation of their classical theological world-view, i.e., who did not allow the million slaughtered Jewish children to alter their theology at all. Yet one would hardly classify Barth as "mad.") This same judgment applies to Crusader murderers, Black Death mobs, and medieval Inquisitors, all of whom held false views of Jews and Judaism but who in pursuing the often deadly logic of their beliefs were not insane. A fuller, equally unsatisfactory, presentation of Aronson's views is to be found in his *The Dialectics of Disaster* (London, 1983), a book one is tempted to retitle *The Disaster of Dialectics.*

67. Uriel Tal has collected some early citations on Nazism as irrational. See his "Political Theology and Myth Prior to the Holocaust," in Y. Bauer and N. Rotenstreich (eds.), *The Holocaust as Historical Experience* (New York, 1981), pp. 44–49. Unfortunately, Tal, a profound student of the intellectual foundations of Nazism, does not analyze the use of the term "irrational" in the sources he reproduces.

68. Consider here, for example, the views of Richard Wagner as expressed in his *Das Judentum in der Musik, Gesammelte Schriften* (Leipzig, 1869). His views are false but not irrational. Wagner's views on Jews and Judaism have been studied by Jacob Katz, *The Darker Side of Genius: Richard Wagner's Antisemitism* (Hanover, 1986).

69. S. Friedlander, "On the Possibility of the Holocaust," in Y. Bauer and N. Rotenstreich (eds.), *The Holocaust as Historical Experience,* p. 7.

70. "The trouble with Eichmann," Hannah Arendt suggested in one of her few correct observations on the Eichmann trial, "was precisely that so many were like him and that the many were neither perverted nor sadistic, that they were and still are terribly and terrifyingly normal. . . . This normality was much more terrifying than all the atrocities put together" (*Eichmann in Jerusalem: A Report on the Banality of Evil* [New York, 1964], p. 276). My serious, extensive reservations about Arendt's analysis of the Eichmann trial, including her much-discussed *non sequitur* between the banality of Eichmann the man and the purported "banality" of the evil he perpetrated, will be provided in detail in Volume 3 of my forthcoming study, *The Holocaust in Historical Context,* in the context of a fuller discussion of the *Judenräte.*

71. This microbial view is rooted in a metaphysical thesis that provides its frame of reference. Saul Friedlander, who sees this parasitological conception of "The Jews" as the mediating link between the pathological and the technological elements within Nazism, writes of this inter-relationship:

> The fuzzy racial ideology could not have been the "prime mover," but it was the "transmission belt," the mediating element between the murderous pathological drive

and the bureaucratic and technological organization of the extermination. ("On the Possibility of the Holocaust," p. 9)

But this is a mistaken description, for the "murderous pathological drive" is itself grounded in a distinctive ideological foundation, a *Weltanschauung*. The "murderous pathological drive" against Jews, despite its pervasiveness in the last 1700 years of Western history, is not a "natural" state of nature; it rests upon and is encouraged by a complex, though quite definite set of metaphysical ideas. Thus the "pathological drive" should be recognized as the "transmission belt" of the racial (and related) metaphysic rather than the reverse. As a consequence, it is again recognized that the *irrational* is not the decisive category, but one of the subordinate factors in a complex socio-ideological mix.

72. Here the philosophical distinction between "knowledge by acquaintance" and "knowledge by description," i.e., existential vs. propositional knowing, should be recalled and applied.

73. John P. Fox, "The Holocaust: A 'Non-Unique' Event for all Humanity?" in Y. Bauer et al. (eds.), *Remembering for the Future*, Vol. 2, pp. 1863–1878, errs in arguing that the need for historicizing and contextualizing the *Sho'ah*, including the need for an investigation of its causes, is incompatible with a claim for uniqueness. He holds that such a claim short-circuits real and full investigation. However, why is it improper to conclude for uniqueness *after* all such needed historical enquiry has taken place just as one reaches other apposite and informed conclusions at the end of one's labors? That is, "uniqueness" need not be, and is not employed by me, as an *a priori* stipulation, nor as a "mystical" notion, but rather as a legitimate phenomenological judgment arrived at as a *consequence* of standard, sharable historical research, the full character of which is open to scrutiny in the comparative case studies that comprise Volumes 1 and 2 of my forthcoming study, *The Holocaust in Historical Context,* and in the more narrow investigation of modern antisemitism and the *Sho'ah* that constitutes Volume 3 of this work.

74. Jacob Katz has written very wisely on some of the historiographical and moral issues related to this difficult question, "Was the Holocaust Predictable?" in Y. Bauer and N. Rotenstreich (eds.), *The Holocaust as Historical Experience*, pp. 23–42.

75. Though C. Hempel initially equated predictions with explanations, he no longer holds this view as a result of the work by Wesley Salmon and others. For more details of this important debate see Hempel's paper "Aspects of Scientific Explanation," in his *Aspects of Scientific Explanation and Other Essays in the Philosophy of Science* (New York, 1965), Ch. 12; idem, "Maximal Specificity and Lawlikeness in Probabilistic Explanation," *Philosophy of Science*, Vol. 35 (1968), pp. 116–133; and W. Salmon, *Scientific Explanation and the Causal Structure of the World* (Princeton, 1984).

8

Technology and Genocide: Technology as a "Form of Life"

Technology is a determinative, metaphysical factor requiring consideration in any analytic probe of the uniqueness of the *Shoah*. Though the technological element has been recognized as salient from the inception of the debate over Nazism, it is important for analytic purposes to give it heightened prominence as a "normative" category. The quintessence of this designation lies in the recognition that the dominating reality of technology is not merely a matter of a consuming mechanics, but is tied to a larger uncompromising cultural-ideological process that needs to be described through such modalities as "dehumanization," "rationalization," "disenchantment," bureaucracy, and totalitarianism —all transformative categories that have as one of their seemingly necessary corollaries a growing unconcern with individuals. That is, we need to learn that the role of technology in the mass killings is ontologically significant.

In analyzing the machinery of killing per se, we need to begin by making a distinction between: (1) a given technology per se as representing a "unique" method or technique of killing, and (2) technology as a servant of, a facilitator of, a "unique" goal. Let us examine these two possibilities, beginning with the former; was the technology qua technology used by the Nazis to annihilate Jewry unique? The answer is "no." That is to say, Jewish deaths were caused in three main ways: (1) until 1941 through starvation and the diseases that came in its wake in the ghettos.[1] The death rate in the ghettos was so high that estimates indi-

Reprinted by permission of Temple University Press.

cate that without any further specific killing operations all Jews would have disappeared in twenty-five years under these conditions. The ghetto inhabitants put it this way: "When we had nothing to eat they gave us a turnip, they gave us a beet—here have some grub, have some fleas, have some typhus, die of disease." (2) At the hands of the *Einsatzgruppen* (murder squads) that accompanied the Nazi invasion into Russia from late 1941 to 1943.[2] Estimates suggest that these groups killed between 1.5 and 2 million Jews. Their method of execution was simple. The *Einsatzgruppen*

would enter a village or city and order the prominent Jewish citizens to call together all Jews for the purpose of resettlement. They were requested to hand over their valuables to the leaders of the unit, and shortly before the execution to surrender their outer clothing. The men, women and children were led to a place of execution which in most cases was located next to a more deeply excavated anti-tank ditch. Then they were shot, kneeling or standing, and the corpses thrown into the ditch.[3]

No great technological feat. (3) Through the workings of the death camps, especially the newest, most advanced camp, Auschwitz.[4] In these camps, the preferred method of murder was gas. The process has been described by an eyewitness as follows:

Outside, says Nyiszli, the men on night-shift were handling a convoy of Jews, some 3,000 men, women and children, who had been led from their train into the hall 200 yards long and prominently labelled in various languages, "Baths and Disinfecting Room." Here they had been told to strip, supervised by the S.S. and men of the Sonderkommando. They were then led into a second hall, where the S.S. and Sonderkommando left them. Meanwhile, vans painted with the insignia of the Red Cross had brought up supplies of Cyclon [Zyklon] B crystals. The 3,000 were then sealed in and gassed.

Twenty minutes later the patented mechanical ventilators were turned on to dispel the remaining fumes. Men of the Sonderkommando, wearing gas masks and rubber boots, entered the gas chamber. They found the naked bodies piled in a pyramid that revealed the last collective struggle of the dying to reach clean air near the ceiling; the weakest lay crushed at the bottom while the strongest bestrode the rest at the top. The struggling mass, stilled only by death, lay now inert like some fearful monument to the memory of their suffering. The gas had risen slowly from the floor, forcing the prisoners to climb on each other's bodies in a ruthless endeavor to snatch the last remaining lungfuls of clean air. The corpses were fouled, and the masked men washed them down with hoses before the labour of separating and transporting the entwined bodies could begin. They were dragged to the elevators, lowered to the crematoria, their gold teeth removed with pliers and thrown into buckets filled with acid, and the women's hair shaved from their heads. The desecrated dead were then loaded in batches of three on carts of sheet metal and fed automatically into one of the fifteen ovens with which each crematorium was equipped. A single crematorium consumed 45 bodies every 20 minutes; the capacity of destruction at Auschwitz was little short of 200 bodies an hour. No wonder Hoess was proud. The ashes were removed and spilled into the swift tide of the river Vistula, a mile or so away. The valuables—clothes, jewels, gold and hair—were sent to Germany, less what the S.S. and the Sonderkommando managed to steal. Nyiszli estimates each crematorium amassed some eighteen to twenty pounds of gold a day. It was melted into small ingots and sent to swell the resources of the Reich in Berlin.[5]

While it is true that the Nazis refined the use of the gas Zyklon B, to do the job more effectively, death by gas was not a major technological advance as compared with, say, the jet engine, radar, and sonar, the Nazis' own V1 and V2 rockets, or, above all else as a qualitative breakthrough, the atomic bomb. Though the Germans were unprecedentedly disciplined in their application of these methods of mass murder, the technology of death employed by the Nazis already existed, though of course in a less refined state, by the end of the First World War. While Auschwitz may represent a quantum leap in the domain of evil, it has no corresponding significance in the realm of technology in the narrow sense. Technology qua technology does *not* seem an essential mark of Nazi uniqueness.

There is, however, another more sinister side to the consideration of technology, technology in its broader sense as a fundamental transformative category of modern life. That is, though the techniques of murder per se were not unique, the general societal function of technology as employed by the Nazis may well have been. For has there ever been a comparable example of so much disciplined planning and modern technological know-how, so much specialization and concern with efficiency, being harnessed and used solely to murder a noncombatant civil population, where a technology came into being and had as its sole raison d'être the murder of a segment of one's own, and then one's subject (through conquest) population? An entire, sophisticated industry, and much of the energy of the German nation and its allies, was devoted solely to the production of corpses. Everything, from the making of trains to carry the victims, to the making of gas chambers to gas the victims, to ovens to burn the victims, to the communications that controlled the entire process, was the end product of a technologically advanced civilization that decided to turn its economy, as well as its inmost soul, over to manufacturing death.

Still more fundamental is the fact that it was advances in the general state of technology that made the "Kingdom of Night" possible.[6] The sheer size of the European Jewish community and the enormous geographical span of its places of habitation had until the twentieth century been a source of protection, even being often cited in theological discourses as a blessing that preserved the Jewish people "in their sojourn among the nations."[7] Technology, including modern communications, obviated this prophylaxis, though not simply, and not without enormous bureaucratic planning, technological organization, and social manipulation. The large number of Jews to be killed required a novel *plan* (as distinguished from the actual performance of the murderous deeds discussed above, which lacked originality) for it required the efficient "processing" of millions of Jews and the disposal, as well as exploitation, of their remains. An SS officer, it was reported at his trial, "stopped the wild shooting of the Lithuanian auxiliary police, but he substituted for it the routine mechanical slaughter of the Chicago stockyards at the rate of 500 [Jews] a day."[8] Such behavior, in turn, necessarily involved a technological and bureaucratic reconstruction that implicated all segments of German society, all levels of the military-industrial hierarchy.[9]

Raul Hilberg's[10] classic studies of the collusion of German railways, Benjamin Ferencz's[11] and Joseph Borkin's[12] researches into the appalling behavior of German industry, Telford Taylor's study of the complicity of the legal profession,[13] Richard Rubenstein's[14] and Robert J. Lifton's[15] of the ghoulish activities of the medical profession, and the many studies of the eager participation in the slaughter of the churches[16] and academics,[17] are all salient cases that collectively represent the totality of the bureaucratic-technological mosaic of the Nazi machine of destruction. The Final Solution required an army of collaborators.

The substantive impact of technology on the murderers can serve as our starting point.[18] To understand it, the most significant factor to grasp is the anesthetizing properties of modern technology. Technology aims to produce more "things" more efficiently, that is, more cheaply and in less time, than other forms of production. In the immediacy of the workplace, it is not concerned, in theory, with the larger metaproductive, ideological issues with which it interconnects, focusing instead on the "object" and its manufacture. In reality, of course, technology is never so pure, never so narrowly situated, for the "objects" produced are, as perceived from the top down, subservient to a larger "good," medical products, for example, to healing as well as profit, and missiles for war and politics as well as profit, but these "ends" do not often intrude into the prosaic elements of the process itself as performed by the technocrats, certainly not the functioning technocrats at lower echelons of control and authority. Their job is meeting schedules, maximizing that particular productive stage in which they are involved. Moreover, larger insidious questions of value, private pieties, *are* irrelevant to the actual task at hand. Murder is not limited by the parameters of passion, death defined by self-interest. Adolf Eichmann could still preen himself in Jerusalem about the smooth operation of his department.[19] Building "a better mousetrap," or gas chamber, is a technical advance into which one can pour all one's energies without either making a moral statement or reflecting on morality. Thus Albert Speer writes to Hitler: "The task which I have to fulfill is an unpolitical one. I felt comfortable in my work as long as my person and also my work were valued solely according to my specialist achievement."[20] Rudolf Höss told his interrogators: "We could only execute orders without thinking about it."[21] The inherently alienated process, and the continual striving to improve the process and its end product, are carried on autonomously and independently of nontechnological normative categories.[22]

A senior SS officer, cited in his trial for exceptional brutality, described a meeting he had attended that had been called to discuss how best to kill several hundred Russian Army political commissars. At the meeting he noted that "there were five SS generals and one civilian, whom he took to be an Army general incognito. . . . The five SS generals vied with each other in ingenuity. Only ways and means were debated; no one expressed any misgivings on the principle of preparing this slaughter."[23] Likewise, Speer defended himself against charges of violence against slave labor not on moral but utilitarian grounds: It would have been imprudent policy counterproductive to productivity goals.[24] If morality means anything in such a setting, it is not a concern with traditional ethical categories, which involve the abuse and harm inflicted on the human victims, but rather issues arising out of the categories of fidelity and obedience, function, and hierarchy. As such, virtue has been reconceptualized as loyalty, loyalty to the system, to one's senior officers who entrusted you with a given task, to the Führer to whom one has sworn ultimate fealty. In this reconstructed environment a selective axiological schizophrenia allows technocrats to kill by day and sleep by night.

Parenthetically, it should be recognized that this extreme alienation at work creates intensified desires for self-fulfillment and "belonging outside of work" and thereby reinforces, for example, the romantic, racial group identity incessantly preached by the Nazi state. Accordingly, the pervasive anomie of one aspect of daily life under the Reich, paradoxically, encouraged heightened self-identification with the Reich on a second, yet more fundamental level.[25]

These many participants involved themselves in varied and complex ways. On the one hand, there were those who, like Reinhard Heydrich or Martin Heidegger, threw themselves into the fray, while on the other hand many, if not most, of the participants are best understood as manifesting a mode of consciousness that has been instructively described as that of "adaptation," adaptation being understood as "a process whose advance is only in part willed and controlled, and to a much larger extent unconscious."[26] This definition has the virtue of reminding us that the object of the technological modality, of the ideological superstructure, is a transformation of behavior, in the case of the Nazis, murderous, sadistic behavior, such that specific acts are performed "automatically," without reference to the domains of morality and subjective freedom. What Nazism, like all *Weltanschauungen* that aspire to totalitarian absoluteness, seeks to do is to reorient, reconceive, the forms of knowing and acting so that the material content of knowledge and action is "arbitrarily," that is, ideologically, prearranged, though the perception of such knowledge and such action is received as a "given," as a *natural* phenomenon, whose reality and authority is unquestioned. Technology creates, in this broader sense, an a priori form of consciousness analogous to, for example, language, which mediates in fundamental ways our awareness of reality. As a formative epistemic element, it defines not only what we know but how we know, with this mediating effect also, dialectically, in turn, defining what we know— that is, how something is known creates the *what* known. Technology is, in this cognitive, epistemological manner, an instance of that sort of category that Kant, in his Transcendental Analytic, defined as a "rule for the organization of the manifold of sensibility."[27] Consciousness, at least empirical consciousness, under the form of technology organizes the world into a quite specific, though neither necessary or absolute unity governed by its own synthesizing, prioritizing awareness, a synthesis operative most elementally on the level of "near instinctive" adaptation, that is, nonreflexively, as an unquestioned regularity. Such a category, even if contingent and alterable (as against Kant's claims for his categories), posits its own rules which establish the order of reality that governs, to the degree to which one's consciousness is such a consciousness, one's individual life. As such, that is, operating under this sort of conceptual structure, its entrepreneurs, including most assuredly those who use it for ideological purposes, intend from the outset that its employment should produce effects, style of behavior, a hierarchy of values and perceptions, that are predictable, hence exploitable.

"Specific brands of learning," it has been correctly observed, in one application of this epistemological insight, "originate and condition specific modes of thinking, develop and adhere to categories through which they can best express their content and by means of which they can further progress."[28] Applied to technology, this logic suggests that technocrats develop those specific, formidable skills relevant to their immediate, often recalcitrant technical concern, narrowing down, as it were, the wider context of any issue to the particular project they wish to improve. Surveyors concentrate on perfecting accuracy, and civil engineers on durability, and mechanical engineers on efficiency (or other related and overlapping utilitarian values that are content as well as job specific).[29] Hence technology as such helps shape consciousness into a "semi-autonomous cognitive domain."[30] It helps to redirect, to close off, the mind from larger, perennial considerations of the equation of ends and means, of objects and their use. This, in turn, produces a reconditioned mentality that is conventionally amoral (not necessarily immoral) vis-à-vis the composition of the workplace, its operating "system," and its products. In such rites of labor there is an operative rationality that has "goals" but not "ends." Yet it is a ritual not without attraction, for the power and appeal of the "goals" are quite sufficient in their compensatory possibilities to allow the system to operate.[31]

The idiom of means, ends, and "rewards" is repercussive, for it reminds us that technology allows an individual to control singular forms of power (and other human beings subject to that power) while, at the same time being, in turn, an object of manipulation by others elsewhere in the bureaucracy. The Nazi official uses technology to destroy Jews while he is himself manipulated by the more general, often subliminal, though always coercive technology of Nazi propaganda and fear.[32] In an odd, surprising way, the SS man is no less an abstraction for Nazism than is the Jew.[33]

Technology thus, even paradigmatically, redefines the landscape of the technocrats' reality in terms not improperly described, using Buber's vocabulary, as *I-IT*.[34] In this living space the concern is with others as "things" not persons, with an impersonal and utilitarian calculus that measures (and sometimes murders!) rather than relates and cares. Through technology the Nazi vis-à-vis Nazism, no less than the Jew vis-à-vis Nazism, is in his or her own concrete, inordinately alternative ways turned into an object in relationship to the reigning system. This anonymous, impersonal aspect of technology is not by definition always and everywhere undesirable, for there is much of humane significance accomplished by this manner of organization. But distorted, odiously manifest in the service of a totalitarian dictatorship, exploited as the means of a brutish presentness made into the stuff of daily life, such modes of relationship, such collective exercises in alienation, become the environment in which mass murder, even genocide, becomes realizable.

Technology, moreover, in particular as a consequence of its drive toward efficiency, embodies a modality of abstraction and a calculus of abstract entities that are at variance with the affirmation of individualized, existentially instantiated human dignity. To be is only to be as a number—at its most diabolical—tattooed on the arm of an Auschwitz inmate. People are translated into *units of production,* values into quantities that can be plotted on a graph. The technocrats' task is to maximize production, not moral value, and in this metamorphosis of the rules governing human intersubjectivity, which transforms moral imperatives into the mathematics of quantity, the humanity of both the technocrat and the "other," now passionlessly understood as a reified "unit," is lost. Viewing the remains of charred Jewish corpses at Treblinka, Christian Wirth asked, "What shall we do with this *garbage?*"[35] Jews were only a problem in the logistics of refuse disposal.

When technology is grounded in an ontological context of freedom, the consequences of its inherent, amoral, mathematical nature are controlled and tempered in, and through, the dialectical mediation exercised by the ruling, constitutive, sociopolitical arrangement. Ecological laws, child-labor laws, union legislation are all examples of such ethical mediation by the body politic. When, however, such countervailing moral tendencies are consciously obliterated and all dialogue between the grammar of compassion and that of "productivity" vehemently sundered, when technology's "unit" mentality is not only exploited but unreservedly exacerbated in the service of a radical totalitarian state, a unique type of human behavior results. An SS sergeant who murdered many in cold blood as part of his "duty" as a camp sick-bay "charge nurse," tells his jury: The murdered "were of no further *use*," "there were too many *useless* mouths," and, finally, "those aren't people—they have to be handled quite differently." And they were.

This meant merciless beating of people who were sick or had to be admitted into the over-filled hospital barrack. A particularly cruel incident occurred when 15 young Slovak Resistance fighters were brought to his camp by the Gestapo. All were wounded. GM had them thrown naked into a bare room without windows, their wounds not dressed, and starving. Here he beat them daily until successively they died. He had admitted in court that he had helped a batch of inmates by giving them ropes with which to hang themselves. Eleven had done so, but in three cases he admitted "he had helped a bit" *(nachgeholfen)*, by hanging them on bedposts. A young Russian trying to escape had been run down by a pursuit car, and his leg was broken. When sent into the sick bay, GM had thrown him into a cellar among the already dead where the Russian expired.

Some of GM's atrocities, verified in the court, were such that I hesitate to record them here. Essentially they showed that his greatest venom went to persons who suffered from diarrhoea and were incontinent. His favourite site for beatings were mens' buttocks, but there was much evidence to show that his habitual method of killing was by manual throttling; though he would also use his jack boots to trample prisoners, whom he had floored, to death.[36]

After all this, as a final irony: "A Hungarian physician survivor described in court how the SS 'nurse' had made him draw up the official daily returns of deaths. The doctor was forced to enter fancy diagnoses and even append faked temperature charts that fitted. The monstrous last column entry was 'the body had to be cremated for reasons of hygiene.' "[37]

The sentiment and behavior of the killers who callously operated the Death Camps in their various phases, and others involved in related stages of the *Endlösung*, provide invaluable evidence of this insistent, yet removed mentality. Begin with the *Reichsbahn* (railway) workers who had to figure the schedules and also the fee payment for Jews transported to "the East": groups of 400 traveled at 50 percent of third-class rail fare with 50 percent of regular fare for children.[38] This quick, brutal movement of millions of civilians across Europe in the midst of war was a vast undertaking unique to modern technological enterprise. In all, 1,400,000 people worked for the *Reichsbahn* in Germany, another 400,000 in Poland and Russia,[39] and all must have known of the palpable cruelty, many of the actual stench of death, inseparable from these journeys. Yet not one *Reichsbahn* official resigned or protested. "All treated the Jewish cattle-car transports as a special business problem that they took pride in solving so well."[40] For the *Reichsbahn* this was a challenge of logistics, not a moral dilemma. Hilberg has cynically, but accurately, summarized the reality: "Despite difficulties and delays, no Jew was left alive for lack of transport."[41] There is in the logic of the transport authorities a consummate utilitarian resolution. It was not their task, as assignments and roles were allocated by the state, to consider the *why* of the project of annihilation as a whole, or even the *why* of their segment of its implementation. In the lived structure in which they made judgments and under which they worked, the concordance between values and facts had been altogether obliterated, and it was not in their self-interest, nor in the interest of the system, nor part of the obligations placed upon them by the public regime in order to reap its rewards, to make such inquiries. Just the reverse: One did one's job best if one did not ask about overriding policy, about where the trains were going and why; one was rewarded, praised, promoted, for allowing the system to run with one's mute collaboration, to operate by making oneself an instrument, a tool, of its design, just as it made Jews into corpses by decree. The profoundest aspect of this relationship between German and Polish workers and the Nazi state is therefore only grasped when one recognizes the contours of the compulsive context in which they operated. The lines of power between individuals and the systemic order need to be read, that is, as flowing from the totality of the political domain downward: the Nazi order runs the *Reichsbahn* officers rather than the reverse.[42] The bureaucratic arrangement[43] of the totality is conceived with just this end in mind. There was no moral collision between individual conscience and state murder because the state had already organized itself through the medium provided by a "rationalized" technological order in just such a way as to usurp all moral autonomy and hence censure, while at the same time ensuring the maximum, unobstructed implementation of its grotesque Manichaean prerogatives.

Now move on with the "cargo" to the camps themselves. At least four technological factors and phases of camp operation require deciphering. They are (1) the working of the industrial slave-labors units operated by I.G. Farben and other industrial giants at several of the death camps; (2) the medical experiments on camp inmates; (3) the "efficiency" of the killing operations per se; and (4) the technological exploitation of the dead.

The employment of Jewish labor for industrial production in the slave empire allied to the death camps was predicated on unprecedented, though precise calculations of a kind possible only in a technological domain operating under Nazi racial principles. Consider the following situation regarding the maltreatment of Jewish slave workers as reported by a Farben agent:

We have ... drawn the attention of the officials of the concentration camp to the fact that in the last few weeks the inmates are being severely flogged on the construction site by the Capos in increasing measure, and this always applies to the weakest inmates who really cannot work harder. The exceedingly unpleasant scenes that occur on the construction site because of this are beginning to have a demoralizing effect on the free workers [Poles], as well as on the Germans. We have therefore asked that they should refrain from carrying out this flogging on the construction site and transfer it to ... the concentration camp.[44]

For the I.G. Farben executive in charge of camp production, the dilemma posed by the sadism of the Capos was not a moral one. His assignment was to guarantee that the construction plans agreed upon by his company and the SS be completed on time and within cost estimates. He had not made these plans, raised the capital, recruited the labor, chosen the Capos, or signed any agreements of principle or purpose. His responsibility was that of a good employee seeking to ensure the economic results of his firm's obligations undertaken in "good faith." If the construction work went smoothly, he did his job and was rewarded; at that point his role functions ceased. The atomization of his moral consciousness precedes, as it were, his appointment; it is a requisite component of his technical role to which he acquiesces usually only tacitly or subconsciously, when he takes up this employment. In time this fragmentation becomes internalized, the technocratic self-awareness is reshaped to conform to the arrangement of his living external reality. When he introspectively searches his conscience for guidance, he finds as his primary resource the categories of moral responsibility he had been taught, and assumed, of being a loyal, honest, hard-working employee; of "following orders." His substantive morality has become a "product" of his employment; he has internalized the ethical contradictions of the human tragedy, of technological murder.

Given I.G. Farben's economic interests and its obligation to its shareholders, its imperative was to protect its investment. Yet "Auschwitz" was, in Joseph Borkin's phrase, "approaching a financial and technical crisis" in 1942.[45] The reasons were obvious: "sickness, malnutrition, the work tempo and sadistic SS guards and Capos all took their toll."[46] What was to be done? The conundrum, as perceived by Farben's board, was technical: how to expropriate more effective labor under death-camp conditions. They had not created Nazism, nor Auschwitz; they only sought to serve their Führer and make a profit, as they were obligated to do by the state and encouraged to do by their legal-economic role. Petroleum and rubber, dividends and salaries were their responsibility, not compassion. They therefore solved this problem in this most rational way open to them: They created their own concentration camp (called Monowitz). In so doing, the board members did not make what can be described as a *personal* decision, or individual choice, nor was their judgment predicated on any moral passion. Rather this conclusion was a further collective, necessarily fragmented, structurally directed step along the prearranged path created by the employment of technology in the service of Hitler's phantasmagoria. From within, from where they sat, given their problems—efficiency, productivity, profit— it was an obvious solution.

Under the circumstances an I.G. concentration camp had obvious advantages to recommend it. Inmates would not be drained of their already limited energy by the long marches from the main concentration camp to the construction site. Security would improve and fewer of the scarce S.S. guards would be required. Discipline and punishment would be more effective, and I.G. would also have greater and more immediate control over the use of the inmates. Of no small consequence, costs would be reduced.[47]

A corporate-sponsored slave-labor camp would make it possible for Farben to reach its limited goals; goals that, *ab initio,* systematically did not include moral decisions, for all their fateful ramifications. The ethical equation had already been made at a different, higher level—the transcendental *Führerprinzip.* What remained was an unreflexive, delimited merciless, technocratic decision. It was not a matter of who should live and who should die, but given that Hitler had decreed that all must die, how their death could be most usefully arranged. Such a circumstance was not meant to entail agonizing soul searching, to involve questions of guilt and innocence, even good and evil; its only challenge was cost effectiveness within the operating limits permitted by the general death sentence hanging over every Jew.[48] As Hitler told Admiral Horthy: "[Jews] who could not work had to be treated like tuberculosis bacilli."[49] This attitude was nakedly in evidence at Monowitz: R. E. Waitz, a Jewish physician imprisoned there, recalled at Nuremberg: "I heard an

SS officer in Monowitz saying to the prisoners: You are all condemned to die, but the execution of your sentence will take a little while."[50] It was preordained, with all the theological implications of this term, that "in the administration of Monowitz, I.G. adopted the principle enunciated by Fritz Sauckel, plenipotentiary for labor allocation in the four-year plan: 'All the inmates must be fed, sheltered and treated in such a way as to exploit them to the highest possible extent, at the lowest conceivable degree of expenditure.'"[51] The results:

Starvation was a permanent guest at Auschwitz. The diet fed to I.G. Auschwitz inmates, which included the famous "Buna soup"—a nutritional aid not available to other prisoners—resulted in an average weight loss for each individual of about six and a half to nine pounds a week. At the end of a month, the change in the prisoner's appearance was marked; at the end of two months, the immates were not recognizable except as caricatures formed of skin, bones, and practically no flesh; after three months they were either dead or so unfit for work that they were marked for release to the gas chambers at Birkenau. Two physicians who studied the effect of the I.G. diet on the inmates noticed that "the normally nourished prisoner at Buna could make up the deficiency by his own body for a period of three months. . . . The prisoners were condemned to burn up their own body weight while working and, providing no infections occurred, finally died of exhaustion."[52]

What is not simple, what is not apparent, is the meaning of such tragedy.

There was, in addition, of course, culpable, gratuitous brutality in the dominion of the technocrats, as there was in that of the SS. No "justification" or "rationality" exists for it in technology *simpliciter*. It was unoriginal, pedestrian sadism on the part of industrial employees:

During the third week of September 1943, a Director of the Krupp installation at Fuenfteichen, Germany, arrived a the Birkenau quarantine Lager of Auschwitz to select able-bodied inmates of the KZ [concentration camp] to work at his plant. The prisoners, completely naked, were paraded before him. . . . I was one of those chosen and thus became separated from my father. . . . I was 16 years old. . . . I remember very distinctly how . . . at a motion from the Krupp representative the SS man, standing nearby, hit my father across the face with force that broke his eye-glasses. This is how I left my father and made my acquaintance with the Krupp enterprises for which I was destined to work for 15 terrible months. . . . . I was always hungry, sleepy, filthy, tired beyond any normal human comparison, and most of the time by any normal human standards, seriously ill. . . . Whenever a prisoner sneaked closer [to the oven] to warm his stiff hands, he was chased away and usually beaten by the Krupp people. Beating and torture administered by the Krupp charges. . . . Hungry, cold, stiff from hard labor, lack of sleep and beating, and in constant fear of our masters we were forced to exert all of our remaining energies to make guns for our oppressors. We worked until we dropped.[53]

Yet even for these acts, if they are to be understood, not exonerated, the ideological norms under which they became possible need to be recalled. The Nazis taught others that Jews were nonpeople upon whom any degradation could be inflicted, in dealing with whom no restraint need be exercised. Sadism was acceptable when its victims were Jews. The camp industrial environments were created to permit, even encourage, through the "signals" emitted in every possible way by the ruling apparatus, such abuse.[54] Moreover, the camp structures emphasized that in the dominant calculus under which the slave-labor industries operated the only value was production; thus no account of the means taken to achieve such industrial quotas need be given, nor any self-reflection on the inherent, endemic, "spontaneous" brutalities entered into. The liberty of Aryan self-awareness becomes the freedom to immediately disregard, then ignore, the implications of one's behavior. It is the freedom to act without guilt. For the conceptual component that defines authentic, autonomous, moral action and its abuses has been removed; Nazism, the Führer, has thought through the *Judenfrage* and offered its, his, devastating resolution, making further critical self-reflection not only unnecessary but even treasonous (for such continued scrutiny and uncertainty implies that the dominant structure may have limitations, even immoral foundations). In such a matrix, to act aggressively against Jews was not a wholly "individual," that is, a free action, but the living out of the collective will through a particular agent whose own volition the system hoped to absorb into its collective self. The governing equation is not the identification of the individual self with an autonomous moral conscience, but the coalescence of the particular agent with the aims of the state, or in Nazi Europe the will of the Führer mediated through the state apparatus.

The technocrat's behavior manifests three criteria: (1) the negation of inherited nontechnological values; (2) a reduction in the status of acts that, under other circumstances, involve autonomy and the requisite ingredients of full moral deeds—would-be moral actions—to the status of technique; and (3) an emphasis on the acquisition of high levels of objective knowledge while, simultaneously, eliminating a concern with the effect of such an acquisition on oneself. This is the equivalent phenomenon in the ethical realm of the reduction from policy formulation to procedure in the political-economic sphere. For in both the movement is radically delimited, exorcising the requirements of authentic freedom. In neither domain does the actor transcend the external limits posited by the empirical political gestalt; he or she only *re*acts, and this in ways that are wholly immanent and non-self-reflexive, ways that secure their life and material political well-being at the cost of their human essence. This is the exact inversion of the goal sought by classical theistic and non-theistic moral systems alike. Nor is this turn to be equated with that privatization of conscience that began with the Reformation and Wars of Religion, and that became such a noble virtue in liberal political traditions stemming from Grotius and Locke. What is being advanced in this totalitarian circumstance is the altogether different thesis that there is no valid claim to be made on the public political domain by the individual conscience. The self need not seek, nor the state provide, the means for bringing personal and public, subjective and objective, into line other than to cut through the dilemma by effectively denying or negating one pole of it. Ideally the Nazi technocrat will sense no tension between these alternative, competing realms; he or she will have abdicated any sense of self-direction, self-valuation, self-criticism, conscience, before the inexorable, uncompromising, objective servitude characteristic of the new order.

After lively competition the contract for the construction of crematoria was finally given to J. A. Topf and Sons, manufacturers of heating equipment. On February 12, 1943, Topf wrote to Auschwitz regarding Crematorias Two and Three: "We acknowledge receipt of your order for five triple furnaces, including two electric elevators for raising the corpses and one emergency elevator." Installations for stoking coal and one for transporting ashes were also on order. But other German businessmen continued to compete for the business of corpse disposal. One of the oldest companies in that field offered its drawing for other crematoria. They suggested using a metal fork moving on cylinders to get the bodies into the furnace. Another firm, Kori, seeking the Belgrade business, emphasized its great experience in the field; it had constructed furnaces at Dachau and Majdanek, and given "full satisfaction in practice."[55]

At the very highest level the collaboration between the SS and German industry was more involved and less "mechanical," with many an industrial baron an enthusiastic supporter of Nazi policy, some even sincere devotees of its racial illusions. Yet even at this rarefied remove, the power relationship was wholly asymmetrical, though it did allow as all bureaucracy allows, for individual initiative to improve the working of that slice of the overall policy that fell to one's lot, at times even straining to the limit the meaning of such initiative.[56] As reflective of the fundamental dynamics involved, consider Dr. Carl Krauch's suggestion to Heinrich Himmler, in a top secret memo sent in July 1943, to establish another synthetic rubber plant "in a similar way as was done at Auschwitz, by making available inmates of your camps, if necessary."[57] Krauch is certainly guilty of flagrant inhumanity and immorality, but is he not still operating within the bounds of that technocratic logic presently of concern, within, in this case, the overriding policy of war production and genocide?[58] Certainly there is one major difference between the situation of these few top Nazi technocrats and most others: They knew the entire plan for the annihilation of Jews. Thus they could not plead ignorance, nor were they in as totally schizophrenic a position to render moral judgments. But then, alternatively, this knowledge was *after* the fact; that is, it did not generate policy, only procedure in the execution of policy.[59] For the elite, it was still only an elite within a dynamic, operative, *Weltanschauung* in which its members were, as individuals, dispensable. For example, they had the power to "rationalize" Auschwitz's slave labor by building a more efficient Monowitz camp, but Auschwitz as such did not come into being, continue to operate, or disappear as a result of any intrinsic power residing in I.G. Farben hands.[60] Conversely, any attempt to hinder the existence or operation of Auschwitz would have occasioned great personal risk.[61] In this context the "defense of necessity" plea is not without some truth.[62] This is *not* an exoneration of the behavior of leading German industrialists—the moral issues are extraordinarily difficult in these and related cases—it is rather an attempt to establish a phenomenological deconstruction of their operating matrix, that is, the nature of technocracy's power to influence, even transform, the field of moral vision within the lived reality of a totalitarian technocracy. At a minimum, it can be said with confidence that the character of the problems concerned, their construction, perception, and constellation, are dialectically altered by the power exerted by the medium out of which, in which, and through which, they come to be.

Nowhere is this more evident than in the Nazi perversion of medical science.

Consider first the question of sterilization of Jewish women. The issue, as raised by Himmler, was how to maximize the process, how, that is, to sterilize the greatest number of women in the shortest possible time.[63] Himmler, in presenting the problem to Aryan science, used the arbitrary, not inconsiderable figure of 1,000 Jewish women as the sample case.[64] After a year's experimentation, Carl Clauberg, the SS physician in charge of the project, reported that 1,000 women could be sterilized by one doctor and ten assistants in one day.[65] But Clauberg's was not the only experimental attempt to "perfect" this process. Interest in the logic of the situation created an escalator effect in Nazi scientific circles which drove them to seek a program capable of ever-increasing utility. A competing X-ray sterilization program was therefore begun:

The experiments were carried out in Auschwitz by Dr. Horst Schumann, on women and men. As Schumann moved into Auschwitz, competition in the experimental blocks was shifted into high gear. Schumann and Clauberg were joined by the chief camp doctor, Wirtz, who started his own experimental series, performing operations on girls seventeen and eighteen and on mothers in their thirties. A Jewish inmate doctor from Germany, Dr. Samuel, was also impressed into the experiments. Another camp doctor, Mengele, confined his studies to twins, for it was his ambition to multiply the German nation. All these experiments, which consumed many hundreds of victims, led to nothing. Not one of the rivals succeeded. One day Brack's deputy, Blankenburg, admitted failure of the experiments conducted on men: the X-rays were less reliable and less speedy than operative castration. In other words, it had taken three years to find out what was known in the beginning.[66]

This is the technological mentality unbridled, the technological consciousness at its purest: technology at the service of an obscene racial doctrine, technology without limits and without parallel in a situation in which the efficiency of murder is *the* only value. The intuitive sense that technology must transcend itself normatively, that it must consider right and wrong, still more good and evil, when in operation has itself been subscended in these experiments. There is no contraposition of facts and values, of inquiry and goals, of data and ideals; there is no juxtaposition of performance and truth. Facts, inquiry, data, performance have become undialectical, supreme. It is also undialectical in yet a second sense: Such acts are premised on the belief that the physician's final, inmost, self-consciousness is not a recognition of human reciprocity between doctor and patient. What takes its place is a mutual, desolate isolation of *things*. Even while alive, the patient-experimentee is dead for the German doctor, the physician's role is already that of coroner, or actuarial interrogator. Technology has created this fateful silence only so it can garner that firm statistical information of which, for no humane reason, it has a desire.

Consider the details of this third experiment related to high altitude research conducted by a Dr. Sigmund Rascher.

> The third experiment developed in such an extraordinary way that, since I was doing these experiments on my own, I called in an S.S. doctor of the camp to witness it. This was a prolonged oxygen-less experiment at an altitude of seven and a half miles on a 37-year-old Jew whose general condition was good. Respiration continued for thirty minutes. After 4 minutes the subject began to perspire and wag his head. After 5 minutes, cramp set in; between 6 and 7 minutes, respiration quickened, the subject lost consciousness; between 11 and 30 minutes, respiration slowed to 3 per minute and then stopped completely. In the meantime a strong cyanosis set in and the subject began to foam at the mouth.[67]

Note the clinical tone, the technical precision, the scientific objectivity, the detachment. Note, too, the categorical absence of any sense of ineradicable evil, the absence of any need for denial. The events were even preserved on film and shown in various quarters.[68]

Again, listen to the aseptic clinical report of the laboratory results of the experiments at "supercooling" in low temperatures: "generally speaking (in 6 cases) death supervenes when the temperature is lowered to between 24.2 deg. and 25.7 deg."[69] One would never suspect by the tone or language that what is being described is the murder of six human beings. There is no horror, no remorse, not a hint of the outrage against all decency that these statistics "report." The very prose conjures an image of unfeeling objects: "6 cases," "death supervenes," "temperature is lowered," "between 24.2 degrees and 25.7 degrees." The vocabulary shields the inmost self of the Nazi scientist as it reduces the Jewish victim to an abstraction. It permits the murderer to forget at once that he has murdered, to hide his degeneracy by recasting it as "science." Techno-cratese is created not least for just this reason. It flattens out the contingent, immediate pain of the victim; it allows a macabre sadism to be called research and thereby legitimates it. This transference from one realm to another also simultaneously shifts the value schemata operative in the mind of the technician-murderer. The norms that are apposite to scientific inquiry are the universal, the mathematical, the dispassionate, the quantitative, all of which measure and describe but do not judge. The Nazi technocrat is required only to perform his studies and report, not to betray himself by leaping into the misplaced syntax of existential communication. To exaggerate, but not to distort, the existence of the cooly disinterested jargon of science makes technological mass murder possible because it facilitates the creation of technological mass murderers.

With some reason, therefore, physicians and other "racial" scientists felt betrayed after the war when they were accused of war crimes. *Rasse und Siedlungs Hauptamt* (Main Office of Race and Settlement) officials, for example, whose judgments on one's racial pedigree actually were a death (or life) sentence, could nonetheless claim that they were not murderers but racial experts merely offering a "scientific" judgment on racial criteria;[70] what became of those classified as *Untermenschen* (inferior races) was neither their idea nor their responsibility. Race, after all, was a biological, not a moral category.[71] Moreover, "the logic of experimental procedure entails that exact cognition already comprises the mastery of effects ... the cognitive process is, itself, a technical process."[72]

If this implacable instrumental indifference has one especial monument, it is the gas chambers, their conception, creation, and efficient utilization.

To begin with, it is important to recognize the magnitude of the enterprise. Land had to be acquired and cleared,[73] communication and railroad connections established, financing arranged, chains of command formed, a camp hierarchy selected and put in place, and, of course, an efficient machinery of murder and disposal created. At Auschwitz, the greatest of the killing centers, this process involved two "improvements" introduced for the sake of maximizing the facility's utility. The first was the original design of the "killing area," which concentrated in one combined space an anteroom, the gas chambers, and the ovens. The second was the use of Zyklon B gas because it was, in Commandant Höss's words, more "efficient."[74] The use of Zyklon B, in turn, created novel technical problems of manufacture, shipment, and storage because its "useful life" was only three months.[75] These novelties in the manufacture of corpses also set off fierce competition between different camp commanders, a confrontational attitude that continued to exist right through the Nuremberg trials, with each officer vying for the dubious title of "most efficient" mass murderer.[76]

For those not immediately sent to "the showers," the camp managers had made another refined calculation: starvation.

According to the calculations of the SS chiefs of staff, a prisoner could survive on the daily portion of food he received for about three months. After this time he was supposed to waste away and perish. The calculations of the SS were correct, although in my opinion applied only to young or younger middle-aged prisoners, who arrived in camp well-nourished and in good health. For others it was difficult to survive even the three months, especially in the winter and at hard labor.[77]

The absolute concreteness of this slow, terrible death is "raised" to an abstraction, to categories that effectively and affectively divide the macabre deed from its cognitive conceptualization. The pain of hunger has become a substantively empty, that is, a formal, theoretical determination. The matter is conceived in terms of lawlike sequences and material causality rather than the suffering of people. This is not murder done out of passion or as the result of hubris; the rhetoric of emotion and commitment is inapposite. What he or she is doing is solving an intellectual puzzle rather than responding to visceral, emotional, intuitive, or other human feelings. Genocide has become a logistical challenge; it has ceased being an overwhelming ethical dilemma.

This instrumental, amoral, technological, positivistic mind-set did not exhaust itself in its "suggestion" of a "solution" to the challenges presented by gassing and induced starvation. For these "institutions" generated a further, major problem: The bodies of the dead had to be disposed of. An inmate eyewitness recounts the following tale of how experts from Topf and Sons, the builders of the crematoria, experimented with differing loads of lifeless bodies in order to gauge the most efficient way to use the ovens:

In the course of these experiments corpses were selected according to different criteria and then cremated. Thus the corpses of two *Mussulmans* were cremated together with those of two children or the bodies of two well-nourished men together with that of an emaciated woman, each load consisting of three, or sometimes, four bodies. Members of these groups were especially interested in the amount of coke required to burn corpses of any particular category, and in the time it took to cremate them. During these macabre experiments different kinds of coke were used and the results carefully recorded.

Afterwards, all corpses were divided into the above-mentioned four categories, the criterion being the amount of coke required to reduce them to ashes. Thus it was decreed that the most economical and fuel-saving procedure would be to burn the bodies of a well-nourished man and an emaciated woman, or vice versa, together with that of a child, because, as the experiments had established, in this combination, once they had caught fire, the dead would continue to burn without any further coke being required.[78]

Mechanics is the issue. The physical laws of weight and force, freed from the immediate material particularity of what is being weighed, lifted, burned, are the focus. There is no recognition of any special normative dimension, no adaptation to the claims of human life and death. For the engineers from Topf and Sons the problematic is divorced from the teleological, or rather what is at issue is a self-contained empirical reality whose decoding is its own, internally justifying, nonreflexive finality. That such normative opacity, with its willed and savage schizophrenia, has become more than an idiosyncratic contingency, is evident in a description regarding the construction of Treblinka, itself a repetition of the Auschwitz account:

In Treblinka, as in other such places, significant advances were made in the science of annihilation, such as the highly original discovery that the bodies of women burned better than those of men.

"Men won't burn without women."

This is not an inelegant joke, a bad pun with a macabre theme. It is an authentic quotation from conversations actually conducted at Treblinka. The statement was based on fact.

It is all very simple. In women the layer of subcutaneous fat is better developed than in men. For this reason, the bodies of women were used to kindle, or, more accurately put, to build the fires among the piles of corpses, much as coals are utilized to get coke to burn. . . . Blood, too, was found to be first-class combustion material.

Another discovery in this field: Young corpses burn up quicker than old ones. Obviously, their flesh is softer. The difference between young humans and older ones is the same as that between veal and beef. But it took the German corpse industry to make us aware of this fact.

It took some time for the technology and terminology of this new industry to reach full development, and for specialists to complete their training in the annihilation of humans, and in the destruction of the dead bodies. One Treblinka document stated: "The burning of corpses received the proper incentive only after an instructor had come down from Auschwitz." The specialists in this new profession were businesslike, practical and conscientious. The instructor in incineration at Treblinka was nicknamed by the Jews as "Tadellos" (perfect); that was his favorite expression. "Thank God, now the fire's perfect," he used to say when, with the help of gasoline and the bodies of the fatter females, the pile of corpses finally burst into flames.[79]

Systematic negation of human worth arising not from betrayal but from annihilatory indifference to the claims of human particularity has now become encoded in the archetypical grammar of the totalitarian technocratic consciousness. The tragic fate of Jewish children under the tyranny of this imperious logic reveals, above all else, the unforgiving, because unconcerned, monstrousness of this mechanistic environment.

Children, too, were often liquidated in the *lazaret* rather than in the gas chambers. These were the toddlers too little to be able to run, children who had no mothers to undress them and lead them by the hand on their "trip to Heaven," or children of large families whose mothers had their hands full. These children were separated from those bound for the gas chambers—in order to "make things easier on the way to the bathhouses." All children of this category were processed in the *lazaret*. If the "caretaker" was kind, he would smash the child's head against the wall before throwing him into the burning ditch; if not, he would toss him straight in alive. There was no danger that small children would climb out of the ditch and would have to be dealt with all over again. Therefore, in Treblinka as in other places, children were often thrown live into the fire, or into the regular mass grave. The most important consideration was to conserve bullets or gas wherever possible. It was also believed that children did not die as easily and quickly from a bullet or from gas as adults did. Doctors had given some thought to this matter, and they had concluded that children have better circulation because their blood vessels were not yet hardened.[80]

And what of the dead? Their "processing" was not yet over. The engineers of Hitler's Reich pushed utilitarianism to its obscene limits, organizing one final stage in their productive program. This entailed the abysmal exploitation of corpses now treated as "raw materials." The procedure was simple, unrestrained, simultaneously dispassionate, "rational," and craven. Before women entered the "showers" their hair was shaved off for blankets and other war needs.[81] Twenty-five carloads of hair packed in balls were sent from Treblinka alone.[82] Hair sold at 50 pfennig a kilogram.[83] After "processing," the victims' still warm bodies were searched for concealed gems and valuables, then their gold teeth were extracted, and their body fat utilized—even their bones, skin, and ashes were used for various "ends." Hilberg has given an appropriately distanced summary of the whole chain:

Let us examine how the system actually worked. We have said that the confiscations were a catchall operation, but they were more than that. They were a model of conservation. Everything was collected, and nothing was wasted.

How was it possible to be so thorough? The answer lies in the assembly line, a method which was foolproof. Inmate work parties picked up the luggage left in the freight cars of the transports and on the platform. Other inmate Kommandos collected clothes and valuable in the dressing rooms. Women's hair was cut off in the barber shops near the gas chambers. Gold teeth were extracted from the mouths of the corpses, and the human fat escaping from the burning bodies was poured back into the flames to speed the cremations. Thus the two organic processes of the death camp, confiscations and killings, were fused and synchronized into a single procedure which guaranteed the absolute success of both operations.

A corollary to the thoroughness of the collections was the care with which the inventory was conducted. Every item of foreign currency was counted; watches were sorted and valuable ones repaired; unusable clothes and rags were weighed. Receipts were passed back and forth, and everything was accounted for. All this was done in accordance with Himmler's wish for "painstaking exactness" *(die grösste Genauigkeit)*. "We cannot be accurate enough." [84]

An intimate participant provides a perhaps yet more informative recollection:

" 'Cargo,' [Stangl] said tonelessly. 'They were cargo.' I think it started the day I first saw the *Totenlager* in Treblinka. I remember Wirth standing there, next to the pits full of blue-black corpses. It had nothing to do with humanity—it couldn't have; it was a mass—a mass of rotting flesh. Wirth said, 'What shall we do with this garbage?' I think unconsciously that started me thinking of them as cargo." [85]

All these instances, while they leave us horror struck, should also inform us of the mode of consciousness operative throughout the Nazi technological universe. In every case we experience that mentality called by German technocrats *Machbarkeit,* the fluid possibility that nothing is given, all is open to novel forms of arrangement, original constellations of relationships, unprecedented usages. Nothing, including Jewish bodies living or dead, has innate worth, only instrumental, extrinsic value. Driven by this original modern technocratic consciousness, the physicians, engineers, builders, scientists seek to discover what is possible when operating without moral restraints in their areas of expertise, to push to the limit their research under the motive of discovery rather than virtue. The method has its own primordial dynamism; its subject matter, its "content," is only a contingency. What the modern planner asks is, Will it work, is it efficient, will it produce the desired effect? If the answer to these queries is affirmative, then the procedure is justified in the regnant axiology. Quantifiable, abstract, measurable, the "end" is the whole. The *Prinzip der Konzentration auf den Effekt* (the principle of the concentration of the effect), as Arnold Gehlen notes, "exercises a literally compulsive hold upon the men of a technical age." [86] When asked could he "not have stopped the nakedness, the whips, the horror of the cattle pens [areas leading to gas chambers]," Franz Stangl replied with all the integrity he could muster: "No, no no. This was the system. Wirth had invented it. It worked. And because it worked, it was irreversible." [87]

NOTES

1. The literature on life and conditions in the ghettos is vast. Among the more accessible works, see Raul Hilberg, *The Destruction of European Jewry* (Chicago, 1961); Lucy Dawidowicz, *The War against the Jews, 1933–1945* (New York, 1975); Jacob Apenszlak (ed.) *The Black Book of Polish Jewry* (reprinted New York, 1982), produced by the World Jewish Congress and other organizations in 1946, contains important material on these events; G. Reitlinger, *The Final Solution* (London, 1968²); Philip Friedman, "The Jewish Ghettos of the Nazi Era," in Friedman (ed.), *Roads to Extinction* (New York, 1980), pp. 59–87. See also in this same volume his interesting essay in social history relating to life in the ghettos, "Social Conflict in the Ghetto," pp. 131–152. See also Emil Apfelbaum (ed.), *Maladie de famine: recherches cliniques sur la famine exécutée dans le ghetto de Varsovie en 1942* (Warsaw, 1946); Raul Hilberg et al. (eds.), *The Diary of Adam Czerniakow: Prelude to Doom* (New York, 1979); Emanuel Ringelblum, *Notes from the Warsaw Ghetto* (New York, 1958); Yisrael Gutman, *The Jews of Warsaw: Ghetto, Underground, Revolt* (Bloomington, 1982); Isaiah Trunk, *Judenrat: The Jewish Councils in Eastern Europe under Nazi Occupation* (New York, 1972). For discussion of Trunk's book and the issue of the *Judenrat* see Yehuda Bauer and Nathan Rotenstreich (eds.), *The Holocaust as Historical Experience* (New York, 1981), Part III, pp. 155–272. There are also a considerable number of further diaries. Now see also Lucjan Dobroszycki (ed.), *The Chronicle of the Lodz Ghetto, 1941–1944* (New Haven, 1984).

2. The horrific details of the action of the *Einsatzgruppen* are described in R. Hilberg, *Destruction*, pp. 182ff.

3. Cited in L. Dawidowicz, *War*, p. 127.

4. The literature on the concentration camps is by now extensive. The most recent and wide-ranging historical review is Konnilyn G. Feig, *Hitler's Death Camps: The Sanity of Madness* (New York, 1981). Feig's volume also contains 25 pages of bibliography relating to all aspects of the history and running of the camps, both in general and for each camp individually. I would add only one further item too recent to have been included in Feig's bibliography, the essay by Henry Friedlander, "The Nazi Concentration Camps," in Michael D. Ryan (ed.), *Human Responses to the Holocaust: Perpetrators and Victims, Bystanders and Resisters* (New York, 1981), pp. 33–70.

5. Leo Kuper, *Genocide* (New Haven, 1981), pp. 133–134, quoting Miklos Nyiszli, *Auschwitz: A Doctor's Eyewitness Account* (New York, 1960), Ch. 7.

6. Many important students of Nazism, since at least Franz Neumann, fail to give due weight to this because they one-sidedly overemphasize the romantic, reactionary ideological content of the movement, failing to recognize that Hitler's success lay in his ability to bring together the most advanced

technology and the most reactionary, nostalgic axiology. Though for many 19th and even 20th century men of the right, technology was the enemy responsible for the ills of modern society, Hitler and his coterie, e.g., Fritz Todd and especially Speer, adopted a more dialectical, integrationist approach based on the correct recognition that without the power made available by the control and adaptation of technology, Germany would remain forever a weak, second-rate state. Recent German studies have made this fact increasingly evident. See Herbert Mehrtens and Steffen Richter, *Naturwissenschaft, Technik und NS-Ideologie* (Frankfurt, 1980); Karl-Heinz Ludwig, *Technik und Ingenieure im Dritten Reich* (Düsseldorf, 1979); Timothy Mason, "Zur Entstehung des Gesetzes zur Ordnung der nationalen Arbeit, vom 20. Januar 1934 . . . ," in Hans Mommsen et al. (eds.), *Industrielles System und politische Entwicklung in der Weimarer Republik* (Düsseldorf, 1974), pp. 323–351. Especially central are the views of Ernst Jünger which have been analyzed in context and data in Karl-Heinz Bohrer's distinguished study, *Die Ästhetik des Schreckens: Die pessimistische Romantik und Ernst Jüngers Frühwerk* (Vienna, 1978). On the political views of Jünger see also Klaus-Frieder Bastian, *Das Politische für Ernst Jünger: Non Konformismus und Kompromiss der Innerlichter* (Freiburg, 1962); and Hans-Peter Schwartz, *Der konservative Anarchist: Politik und Zeitkritik Ernst Jünger* (Freiburg, 1962). There are three works in English that are also of value: J. P. Stern, *Ernst Jünger: A Writer of Our Time* (New Haven, 1953); the discussion of Jünger in Walter Struve, *Elites against Democracy* (Princeton, 1973); and the chapter on Jünger in Jeffrey Herf, *Reactionary Modernism: Technology, Culture and Politics in Weimar and the Third Reich* (New York, 1984), pp. 70–108.

7. Also suggested by scholars such as Elias Bickerman, *Ezra to the Last of the Maccabees* (New York, 1962), p. 3.

8. Cited in Henry V. Dicks, *Licensed Mass Murder* (New York, 1972), p. 206.

9. Göring's order to Heydrich of July 31, 1941, issued in his role as Chairman of the Ministerial Committee for Defense of the Reich, makes this clear: "make all necessary organizational, technical and material preparations for an overall solution of the Jewish Problem in Germany's sphere of influence. Other central authorities will co-operate insofar as their responsibilities are affected." This was, in effect, the beginning of the practical translation of the decision earlier arrived at by Hitler and shared with others at the Wannsee Conference of January 1941.

10. R. Hilberg, *Destruction*, Index; and his essay "German Railroads—Jewish Souls," in *Transaction, Social Science and Modern Society*, Vol. 14 (1976), pp. 60–74.

11. Benjamin Ferencz, *Less Than Slaves* (Cambridge, 1979).

12. Joseph Borkin, *The Crime and Punishment of I. G. Farben* (New York, 1978).

13. Telford Taylor, "The Legal Profession," in Henry Friedlander and Sybil Milton (eds.), *The Holocaust: Ideology, Bureaucracy and Genocide* (New York, 1980), pp. 133–140.

14. See Richard Rubenstein's chapter on "The Health Professions and Corporate Enterprise at Auschwitz," in his *Cunning of History* (New York, 1975); see also Alexander Mitscherlich and Fred Mielke, *The Death Doctors* (London, 1962).

15. Robert Jay Lifton, *Nazi Doctors* (New York, 1986).

16. On this highly controversial issue, see Richard Gutteridge, *Open Thy Mouth for the Dumb: The German Evangelical Church and the Jews 1879–1950* (New York, 1976); Frank Littell and Hubert Locke (eds.), *The German Church Struggle and the Holocaust* (Detroit, 1974); Frank Littell, *The Crucifixion of the Jews* (New York, 1975); Guenther Lewy, *The Catholic Church and Nazi Germany* (New York, 1965); Saul Friedlander, *Pius XII and the Third Reich: A Documentation* (New York, 1966); Arthur C. Cochrane, *The Church's Confession under Hitler* (Philadelphia, 1962); and Gordon C. Zahn, *German Catholics and Hitler's Wars: A Study in Social Control* (New York, 1962).

17. One of the most depressing aspects of the Nazi period is the near total capitulation of German (and European) academics and intellectuals. On this see Fritz K. Ringer, *The Decline of the German Mandarins: The German Academic Communities, 1890–1933* (Cambridge, 1969); Edward Hartshorne, *The German Universities and National Socialism* (London, 1937); Karl Bracher et al., *Die Nationalsozialistische Machtergreifung. Studien zur Errichtung der totalitären Herrschaftssystems in Deutschland 1933/34* (Cologne, 1960); Alan Beyerchen, *Scientists under Hitler: Politics and Physics Community in the Third Reich* (New Haven, 1977); Julien Benda, *The Treason of the Intellectuals* (New York, 1969); Max Weinreich, *Hitler's Professors: The Part of Scholarship in Germany's Crimes against the Jewish People* (New York, 1946). Perhaps the two most famous incidents involve the psychoanalyst Carl Gustav Jung and Martin Heidegger, Germany's greatest philosopher, and acclaimed, incorrectly in my view, as the greatest philosopher of the century in many quarters.

On Heidegger see now especially Emil Fackenheim's penetrating critique in his *To Mend the World* (New York, 1982), p. 166. See also Christian Graf von Krockow, *Die Entscheidung: Eine Untersuchung über Ernst Jünger, Carl Schmitt, Martin Heidegger* (Stuttgart, 1958); George Steiner, *Martin Heidegger* (New York, 1978); A. Schwan, *Politische Philosophie im Denken Heideggers* (Cologne, 1965); the series of essays by F. F[dier]in *Critique*, No. 234 (Paris, 1966), No. 242 (Paris, 1967), No. 251 (Paris, 1967); David Novak, "Buber's Critique of Heidegger," *Modern Judaism*, Vol. 5, No. 2 (1985), pp. 125–140; Victor Farias, *Heidegger et le nazisme* (Paris, 1987), also available in English translation from Temple University Press (Philadelphia, 1989); Richard Rubenstein, "Heidegger and the Jews," *Modern Judaism*, Vol. 9, No. 2 (1989), pp. 179–196; and Jean François Lyotard, *Heidegger et les juifs* (Paris, 1988). For what this meant in the sciences, see the "Introduction" to Nobel Prize winner (no less) Philipp Lenard's four-volume study entitled *Deutsche Physik in vier Bänden* (Munich, 1938), Vol. 1, pp. ix–x. On the growth of antisemitism in German universities in the pre-Hitler period see George Mosse, *The Crisis of German Ideology* (New York, 1964), pp. 190–203; and Peter G. J. Pulzer, *The Rise of Political Anti-Semitism in Germany and Austria* (New York, 1964), pp. 247–258. Ernst Waymar's important study *Das Selbstverständnis der Deutschen. Ein Bericht über den Geist des Geshichtsunterrichts der höheren Schulen im 19. Jahrhundert* (Stuttgart, 1963), is a valuable introduction to still earlier German educational attitudes.

18. What will be described in this chapter must, of necessity, be cast in the form of an "Ideal-type," a maximum account, of the technological consciousness. It will apply to different individuals, in varying circumstances, in variegated, uneven ways. Also, of course, it will be contradicted by other factors at work in the Nazi state which mitigate its actualization.

19. See Eichmann's testimony in Jochen Von Lang (ed.), *Eichmann Interrogated* (New York, 1983).

20. Cited by J. Fest, *The Face of the Third Reich* (New York, 1970), p. 198.

21. R. Höss as cited in ibid., p. 280.

22. By this I mean non-moral, non-philosophical, non-aesthetic values relevant particularly to technology, e.g., efficiency, economy, durability, reliability, etc. For more on this see T. Kotarbinski, *Praxiology—An Introduction to the Science of Efficient Action* (Oxford, 1965); H. Skolimowski, "Praxiology—The Science of Accomplished Action," *The Personalist* (Summer, 1965); idem, "The Structure of Thinking in Technology," *Technology and Culture,* Vol. 7, No. 3 (Summer, 1966), pp. 371–383.

23. H. Dicks, *Licensed Mass Murder,* p. 102.

24. See *Trials of Major War Criminals* (Nuremberg, 1948), Vol. 16.

25. This seems a general characteristic of technological society. Katherine Archibald's study of blue-collar workers in American shipyards during World War II made the point that the workers organized themselves around, and accentuated, ethnic factors. *Wartime Shipyard: A Study in Social Disunity* [Berkeley, 1947]. Thankfully the meaning of ethnicity in 1940s' America was not that of 1940s' Germany, i.e., a decision on life or death.

26. Arnold Gehlen, *Man in the Age of Technology* (New York, 1980), pp. 47–48.

27. I. Kant, *Critique of Pure Reason,* section II A.

28. Ibid., p. 378.

29. I take these examples from H. Skolimowski, "Praxiology," pp. 380–381.

30. Ibid., p. 382.

31. Studies of industrial workers show that they are not dissatisfied with their repetitive jobs, even though they are "self-estranged" through its performance. Robert Blauner's study of this phenomenon suggests that between 75 and 90 percent of industrial workers are "reasonably satisfied" with their work. See Robert Blauner, "Work Satisfaction and Industrial Trends in Modern Society," in Walter Galenson and Seymor Martin Lipset (eds.), *Labor and Trade Unionism* (New York, 1960). See also Blauner's *Alienation and Freedom: The Factory Worker and His Industry* (Chicago, 1964), pp. 24ff.

32. It is not unimportant that there was a hard core of SS officers who manned the Death Camps throughout the war. For as Robert Koehl has correctly observed, "a kind of common denominator did develop in the war years among a few hundred officers and men who stayed in the camp administration; since preference for remaining implied disinterest in the front, there was an additional ingredient of ruthlessness in the determination to become indispensable in the productive efforts of the camps." Robert Lewis Koehl, *The Black Corps: The Structure and Power Struggles of the Nazi SS* (Madison, 1983), p. 167.

33. It is notable that Henry Dicks concludes his reflections on his series of interviews with SS murderers with this significant judgment:

    The first thing that needs to be said, when we leave the individual predisposition to murder and turn to the conditions of its release or instigation, is to stress the great difference in this regard between the killers investigated by the forensic psychologists cited and my SS men. With the dubious exception of Captain A and KW none of these SS men would have been likely to become "common murderers" in normal conditions. Their instigatory triggering was not a sudden, solitary experience, but a process extending over time, shared with team mates in a facilitating group setting. It was, as we saw in S2 and the relevant quotation from Hoess's autobiography (Chapter Five) a *conditioning* process which in this context we can term *brutalization*. (*Licensed Mass Murder*, pp. 253–254)

34. Martin Buber, *I and Thou* (E.T. [New edition by Walter Kaufmann], New York, 1970).

35. G. Sereny, *Into That Darkness: From Mercy Killing to Mass Murder* (New York, 1974) p. 201.

36. H. Dicks, *Licensed Mass Murder*, p. 163.

37. Ibid., p. 164.

38. R. Hilberg, *Destruction*, pp. 297–298; and K. Feig, *Hitler's Camps*, p. 37. See also Hilberg's pioneering articles "In Search of Special Trains," *Midstream* (October, 1979), pp. 32–38; and idem, "German Railroads—Jewish Souls." See also Adalbert Ruckerl, *NS-Prozesse* (Karlsruhe, 1972), pp. 112–117.

39. Figure given in K. Feig, *Hitler's Camps*, p. 36.

40. Ibid., p. 37.

41. R. Hilberg, "In Search of Special Trains," pp. 37–38.

42. I differ here with Raul Hilberg who emphasizes the individual roles of the *Reichsbahn* officials and who stresses, according to his, I believe erroneous, understanding, that the power flow upwards, i.e., the individuals run the system, no more no less. His contention appears to me to lose sight of the unique mechanics of modern technology and bureaucracy.

43. Analyzed more fully by me in a larger, three-volume study of the *Sho'ah* to be published by Oxford University Press beginning in 1992, *The Holocaust in Historical Context*.

44. J. Borkin, *Crime*, pp. 118–119.

45. Ibid., p. 120.

46. Ibid.

47. Named Monowitz.
48. J. Borkin, *Crime*, p. 120.
49. On the especially brutal treatment of Jews at Monowitz see B. Ferencz, *Less Than Slaves*, pp. 24–25, and *Trials of War Criminals*, Vol. 8, p. 583 and again p. 618. The Nuremberg Tribunal referred to Jews at Monowitz and Buna as "living and laboring under the shadow of experimentation." *Trials of War Criminals*, Vol. 8, p. 1184.
50. Cited in *Nazi Conspiracy and Aggression*, (Washington D.C., 1946), Vol. 7, p. 190. See also the report of the *Judenreferenten* group meeting held at Krummhübel on April 3–4, 1944, at which no minutes were taken because the Nazi goal was still the total elimination of Jewry. *Nazi Conspiracy*, Vol. 6, pp. 4–38.
51. NI-12373, cited in J. Borkin, *Crime*, p. 143.
52. Ibid., p. 121. Saukel's order is found in *Trials of War Criminals*, Vol. 1, p. 197; and *Nazi Conspiracy*, Vol. 3, p. 57.
53. J. Borkin, *Crime*, p. 125. Quote of physician from *Trials of War Criminals*, Preliminary Brief, Part III, p. 97, NI 4830.
54. B. Ferencz, *Less Than Slaves*, pp. 24–25, 77–78.
55. Robert L. Koehl's observation regarding SS sadism and abuses in the death camps applies, *pari passu*, to the industrial technocrats as well: "It was not the kind of SS man which was decisive; it was the situation SS bureaucrats had created in the camps which made these excesses possible. Indeed the excesses were more (normal) than the *fact* of the death factories itself." *Black Corps*, p. 176. See also R. Hilberg, *Destruction*, pp. 575ff.
56. Cited from K. Feig, *Hitler's Camps*, p. 356.
57. The taking of initiative is a somewhat more "autonomous" act, though it is, as a rule, still action taken within the highly circumscribed limits of the whole. However, on rare occasions the Nuremberg Court, for example, found otherwise, as when it found Ter Meer guilty of the crime of mass murder for "taking the initiative." *Trials of War Criminals*, Vol. 8, pp. 1191–92.
58. Krauch was chairman of I.G. Krupp at this time.
59. *Trials of War Criminals*, Vol. 8, p. 532.
60. The Nuremberg Court was certainly correct to find Krauch guilty of count three, "slavery and mass murder," in his indictment. *Trials of War Criminals*, Vol. 8, p. 1190.
61. Krauch's actions are still, in my sense, procedural, for the war policy requiring synthetic rubber, and its consequent charge to Krupp to produce such rubber, was not caused by Krauch or his industrial superiors. But given the synthetic rubber mandate, Krauch sought to maximize Krupp's (and his own) role in meeting the national need.
62. I.G. Farben and other industrial giants undoubtedly supported Hitler's rise to power, but this is *not* yet a support for his actual murderous activity against Jewry. Few (Germans or Jews) envisioned this would be the actual end of Hitler's antisemitic rhetoric. Thus, I.G. Board members such as Carl Bosch actively sought to deter Hitler from his antisemitic policies, though

without success, while a Jew, Carl von Weinberg, Deputy Chairman of I.G. Farben's supervisory board, was, at least publicly, an enthusiastic supporter of Hitler on nationalist and economic grounds. For details of this complex story see J. Borkin, *Crime*, pp. 53–75; the fate of the Weinbergs under the Nazis is described in Borkin, *Crime*, pp. 145–46. On the larger, complex issue of big business support for Hitler, see also the recent important study by Henry Ashby Turner, Jr., *German Big Business and the Rise of Hitler* (New York, 1985).

63. The Nuremberg Tribunal accepted the defense contention that, in conforming to the slave-labor program, its defendants had "no other choice than to comply with the mandate of the Hitler government." And the Court went on, "The defiant refusal of a Farben executive to carry out the Reich production schedule or to use slave labor to achieve that end would have been treated as treasonous sabotage and would have resulted in prompt and drastic retaliation." *Trials of War Criminals*, Vol. 8, p. 1175.

64. See *Trials of War Criminals*, Vol. 7, pp. 414f., as introduced by the defense counsels for I.G. Farben officials at Nuremberg. On the Court's evaluation of this plea, *Trials of War Criminals*, Vol. 8, pp. 1179ff.

65. K. Feig, *Hitler's Camps*, pp. 356–357.

66. R. Hilberg, *Destruction*, p. 606.

67. Letter of Claubey to Himmler of June 7, 1943, cited in R. Hilberg, *Destruction*, p. 606.

68. Hilberg, *Destruction*, p. 607.

69. P. Berben, *Dachau 1933–1945* (London, 1975), p. 128.

70. Ibid., pp. 129–130.

71. Berben, *Dachau*, p. 131.

72. Main Office of Race and Settlement of the SS. One should also include here the medical experts from the *Gemeinnützige Stiftung für Heil und Anstaltspflege* (The General Foundation for Institutional Care), which carried out the earlier euthanasia program.

73. On the work of the *RuSha (Rasse-und Siedlungs-Hauptamt* [Race and Settlement main office of the SS]) see Robert L. Koehl, *Black Corps,* pp. 188–189; and his more extended study of the RFKDV (*Reichs-Kommisar für die Festigung Deutschen Volkstums* [Reich Commissioner for the Strengthening of Germandom]) System concerned with German settlement in the East, *RFKDV: German Resettlement and Population Policy 1939–1945* (Cambridge, 1957).

74. A. Gehlen, *Age of Technology*, p. 70.

75. This proved to be considerably more complicated than one might think. For details see R. Hilberg, *Destruction*, pp. 564f.

76. This summary follows R. Hilberg's description, *Destruction*, p. 565. The quote from Höss's affidavit of April 5, 1946, is also cited by Hilberg, ibid.

The gassing was a short process in Auschwitz. As soon as the victims were trapped in the Badeanstalt or Leichenkeller, they recognize in a flash the whole pattern of the destruction process. The imitation shower facilities did not work. Outside, a central switch was thrown to turn off the lights. A Red Cross car drove up with the Zyklon, and a masked SS-man lifted the glass shutter over the lattice, emptying one can after another into the gas chamber. Untersturmführer Grabner, political chief of the camp, stood ready with stop watch in hand. As the first pellets sublimated on the floor of the chamber, the law of the jungle took over. To escape from the rapidly rising gas, the stronger knocked down the weaker, stepping on the prostrate victims in order to prolong their life by reaching the gas-free layers of air. The agony lasted for about two minutes; then the shrieking subsided, the dying men slumping over. Within four minutes everybody in the gas chamber was dead. The gas was now allowed to escape, and after about a half-hour the doors were opened. The bodies were found in tower-like heaps, some in sitting or half-sitting position under the doors. The corpses were pink in color, with green spots. Some had foam on their lips; others bled through the nose. (P. 627)

77. L. Dawidowicz has described the use of gas in early Nazi euthanasia programs in detail in *War*, pp. 132–134.

78. On the issue of the difficult technical aspects concerning the production of Zyklon B, see J. Borkin, *Crime*, pp. 122–123. Borkin's review includes the following detail, apposite to a close scrutiny of the technological (and bureaucratic) character of the Nazi onslaught:

> There was still another episode that gave the officials of Degesch more than a hint of the dread purpose to which their Zyklon B was being put by the S.S. When manufactured as a pesticide Zyklon B contained a special odor, or indicator, to warn human beings of its lethal presence. The inclusion of such a warning odor was required by German law. When the S.S. demanded that the new, large order of Zyklon B omit the indicator, no one familiar with the workings of the S.S. could have failed to realize the purpose behind the strange request. The Degesch executives at first were unwilling to comply. But compassion was not behind their refusal. What troubled them was the fact that the S.S. request endangered Degesch's monopoly position. The patent on Zyklon B had long since expired. However, Degesch retained its monopoly by a patent on the warning odor. To remove the indicator was bad business, opening up the possibility of unwelcome competition. The S.S. made short shrift of this objection and the company removed the warning odor. Now the doomed would not even know it was Degesch's Zyklon B. (P. 123)

79. Note in this context, Höss's comment: "Another improvement we made over Treblinka was that we built our gas chambers to accommodate 2,000 people at one time whereas at Treblinka their ten gas chambers only accommodated 200 people each." *Trials of War Criminals*, Vol. 11, p. 417. See also the account of the acrimonious competition between Höss and Wirth recounted in R. Hilberg, *Destruction*, pp. 571–572.

80. Anna Pawelczynska, *Values and Violence in Auschwitz: A Sociological Analysis* (Berkeley, 1979), p. 76.

81. Filip Mueller, *Auschwitz: Three Years in the Gas Chambers* (New York, 1979), pp. 99–100.

82. A. Donat (ed.), *The Death Camp Treblinka* (New York, 1979), pp. 38–39.

83. Ibid., pp. 37–38.

84. Ibid., pp. 51ff.

85. Ibid., p. 57.
86. K. Feig, *Hitler's Camps,* p. 351. Seven thousand kilos of hair were still at Auschwitz awaiting shipment when Auschwitz was liberated.
87. R. Hilberg, *Destruction,* pp. 611–612. See also J. Borkin, *Crime,* pp. 186f., for another description of the entire process.

9

"Voluntary Covenant": Irving Greenberg on Faith after the Holocaust

One of the most widely discussed recent theological responses to the Holocaust is to be found in Irving (Yitz) Greenberg's challenging and provocative writings on this theme. In this chapter I would like to review and critique Greenberg's analysis of this difficult matter.

I. THE HOLOCAUST AND ITS IMPLICATIONS: EXEGESIS OF GREENBERG'S POSITION

In a series of five articles[1] to date, Greenberg has sketched (I use this term in its literal meaning) his evolving view of the meaning of the *Shoah* and its consequences. His first[2] and, I believe, still most important statement on the subject was made in the 1973 Symposium on the Holocaust held at St. John of the Divine in New York City. Here he began to articulate his belief that the Holocaust radically challenges the essence of the existing theological frameworks of *both* Judaism and Christianity[3]—i.e., it challenges belief in the God of Sinai, the God of redemption. "The cruelty and killing raise the question whether even those who believe after such an event [as the Holocaust] dare talk about [a] God who loves and cares without making a mockery of those who suffered."[4] Moreover, as Greenberg acutely intuits, not only are the traditional theological schemata called to answer, but even more so is modernity itself, that substitute "God" in whose name Europe marched forward from the Enlightenment to the rise of Hitler. "There is the shock of recognition that the humanistic revolt, celebrated as the liberation of humankind in freeing man from centuries of dependence upon God and nature, is now revealed—at the very heart of the enterprise—to sustain a capacity for death and demonic evil."[5]

The multiple consequences of this dual recognition are, as Greenberg contends: (1) that one must respond to this new situation in some direct way for "not to respond is to collaborate in the repetition";[6] (2) "Never Again!"[7], i.e., such a possibility must not be allowed to repeat itself. Every position and group that "failed" the test of the *Shoah* "must be challenged, shaken up, rethought" if they wish to have any right to survive; (3) "The Holocaust challenges the claims of all the standards that compete for modern man's loyalties." All invented orthodoxies are suspect. "[The Holocaust] does not give simple, clear answers or definitive solutions. To claim that it does is not to take burning children seriously. This would—and should—undercut the ultimate adequacy of any category, unless there were one (religious, political, intellectual) that consistently produced the proper response of resistance and horror at the Holocaust. No such category exists to my knowledge." Thus, Greenberg, concludes, "to use the catastrophe to uphold the univocal validity of any category is to turn it into grist for propaganda mills."[8] (4) "The Holocaust offers us only dialectical moves and understandings," dialectical here being defined as "moves that stretch our capacity to the limit and torment us with their irresolvable tensions."[9] Moreover, this "dialectical response" is not one option among others; "it is," rather, "the only morally tenable way for survivors and those guilty of bystanding to live."[10] This dialectical factor issues forth, accordingly, in the following stark principle of theological meaning and validity: "No statement, theological or otherwise should be made that would not be credible in the presence of the burning children."[11]

Translated into a specific theological program, Greenberg understands these imperatives as undermining all security and all dogmatic certitude. Even one's "relationship to the God of the Covenant cannot be unaffected."[12] Out of this ambiguous circumstance the new, post-Holocaust "response," if there is to be a "response" at all, must arise. It means that:

after Auschwitz, faith means there are times when faith is overcome. Buber has spoken of "moment gods": God is known only at the moment when Presence and awareness are fused in vital life. This knowledge is interspersed with moments when only natural, self-contained, routine existence is present. We now have to speak of "moment faiths," moments when Redeemer and vision of redemption are present, interspersed with times when the flames and smoke of burning children blot out faith—though it flickers again. [13]

And such "moment faith" entails that:

the easy dichotomy of atheist/theist, the confusion of faith with doctrine or demonstration is at an end. It makes clear that faith is a life response of the whole person to the Presence in life and history. Like life, this response ebbs and flows. The difference between the skeptic and the believer is frequency of faith, and not certitude of position. The rejection of the unbeliever by the believer is literally the denial or attempted suppression of what is within oneself. The ability to live with moment faith is the ability to live with pluralism and without the self-flattering, ethnocentric solutions which warp religion, or make it a source of hatred for the other. [14]

Greenberg is quick to recognize that given the horrors of Auschwitz even to speak of "moment faiths" is not self-evident. For what makes faith possible at all, even flickering, wavering, uncertain, and anguished faith? "Why is it not a permanent destruction of faith," he rhetorically asks, "to be in the presence of the murdered children?" [15] His reply to this all-important question is given in a series of four arguments. The substance of each can be summarized as follows:

(1) "There are still moments when the reality of the Exodus is reenacted and present." [16] That is to say both that the original Exodus event is still available to us, especially in its yearly Passover [17] re-enactment, and that reality is not one, uninterrupted, unmitigated series of tragic occurrences. The evidence of our life's journey reveals moments of despair as well as moments of redemption.

(2) Secondly, "the Breakdown of the Secular Absolute," [18] as Greenberg calls the dark side of modern humanistic relativism, demands that we not "jump to a conclusion that retrospectively makes the covenant they [the victims] lived an illusion and their deaths a gigantic travesty." [19] We must be open to at least the possibility of transcendence. Because "the Secular Absolute," i.e., modernity, denied God, we must obstinately explore this alternative. [20]

(3) The third argument is a corollary and extension of the second. "It is enough," Greenberg writes," that this [Western] civilization is the locus of the Holocaust. The Holocaust calls on Jews, Christians, and others to absolutely resist the total authority of this cultural moment." [21] The Holocaust destroyed the belief system of modernity, thereby opening up conceptual space for other axiological and normative claims, including "the possibilities of Exodus and Immortality." [22]

(4) Last, and most important, is "the Revelation in the Redemption of Israel."[23] Greenberg is here willing, as a corollary of his basic and deepest belief that Judaism is a religion of and in history, to posit direct theological weight to the recreation of a Jewish State. He wisely proposes that "if the experience of Auschwitz symbolizes that we are cut off from God and hope, and the covenant may be destroyed, then the experience of Jerusalem symbolizes that God's promises are faithful and His people live on."[24]

If these arguments for belief, especially the last, are convincing, why then only "moment faith"? Here Greenberg's commitment to the provisional, uncertain character of our times, as heirs of *both* Auschwitz and the Western Wall, comes again to the fore. "Faith is a moment truth, but there are moments when it is not true."[25]

If this is so, what exactly is to be the substance of our faith-commitment, after Auschwitz, after Jerusalem, when each of these *realia* cries out over against the other? Greenberg appeals to three classical theological paradigms for help: Job, the "Suffering Servant" of Isaiah, and what Greenberg calls the model of Lamentations III, i.e., entering into debate with the Almighty. From Job we might learn "the rejection of easy pieties or denials and the dialectical response of looking for, expecting, further revelations of the Presence."[26] For, as Job of old, "when suffering had all but overwhelmed Jews and all but blocked out God's Presence, a sign out of the whirlwind [e.g. the rebirth of Israel] gave us strength to go on, and the right to speak authentically of God's Presence still."[27] From Isaiah we might learn that the "Suffering Servant is a kind of early warning system of the sins intrinsic in the culture but often not seen until later." As such, "the Holocaust was an advance warning system of the demonic potential of modern culture . . . a kind of last warning that if man will perceive and overcome the demonism unleashed in modern culture, the world may survive. Otherwise, the next Holocaust will embrace the whole world."[28] From Lamentations III we might learn "to justify human beings, not God. It suggests a total and thoroughgoing self-criticism that would purge the emotional dependency and self-abasement of traditional religion and its false crutch of certainty and security."[29]

But these biblical paradigms provide only partial answers in our time and therefore Greenberg climaxes the presentation of his view by asserting:

In the silence of God and of theology, there is one fundamental testimony that can still be given—the testimony of human life itself. This was always the basic evidence, but after Auschwitz its import is incredibly heightened. In fact, it is the only testimony that can still be heard.

The vast number of dead and morally destroyed is the phenomenology of absurdity and radical evil, the continuing statement of human worthlessness and meaninglessness that shouts down all talk of God and human worth. The Holocaust is even model and pedagogy for future generations that genocide can be carried out with impunity—one need fear neither God nor man. There is one response to such overwhelming tragedy: the reaffirmation of meaningfulness, worth, and life—through acts of love and life-giving. The act of creating a life or enhancing its dignity is the counter-testimony to Auschwitz. To talk of love and of a God who cares in the presence of the burning children is obscene and incredible, to leap in and pull a child out of a pit, to clean its face and heal its body, is to make the most powerful statement—the only statement that counts. . . . Each act of creating a life, each act of enhancing or holding people responsible for human life, becomes multiplied in its resonance, because it contradicts the mass graves of . . . Treblinka.[30]

Greenberg here intimates a provocative thesis: we are now responsible for our world as well as for God's "Name" in history. "The religious enterprise after [the Holocaust] must see itself as a desperate attempt to create, save, and heal the image of God wherever it still exists—lest further evidence of meaninglessness finally fill the scale irreversibly. Before this calling, all other 'religious' activity is dwarfed."[31] For the Jewish people this act of life, this act of affirmation, is first and foremost witnessed to in the reborn State of Israel. "To fail to grasp that inextricable connection and response is to utterly fail to comprehend the theological significance of Israel."[32] But the command to a new life, even to resurrection, if one likes, goes beyond the facts of the State of Israel, beyond the narrowly Jewish context. It requires that:

We also face the urgent call to eliminate every stereotype discrimination that reduces—and denies—this image in the other. It was the ability to distinguish some people as human and others as not that enabled the Nazis to segregate and then destroy the 'subhumans. . . .' The indivisibility of human dignity and equality becomes an essential bulwark against the repetition of another Holocaust. It is the command rising out of Auschwitz.

This means a vigorous self-criticism, and review of every cultural or religious framework that may sustain some devaluation or denial of the absolute and equal dignity of the other. This is the overriding command and the essential criterion for religious existence, to whoever walks by the light of the flames. Without this testimony and the creation of facts that give it persuasiveness, the act of the religious enterprise simply lacks credibility. To the extent that religion may extend or justify the evils of dignity denied, it becomes the devil's testimony. Whoever joins in the work of creation and rehabilitation of the image of God is, therefore, participating in "restoring to God his scepter and crown." Whoever does not support—or opposes—this process is seeking to complete the attack on God's presence in the world. These must be seen as the central religious acts. They shed a pitiless light on popes who deny birth control to starving millions because of a need to uphold the religious authority of the magisterium; or rabbis who deny women's dignity out of loyalty to divinely given traditions.[33]

Three further lessons are also to be learned from the Luciferian reality of the Death camps. The first is that the older secular-religious dichotomy must be transcended. "Illumined by the light of the crematoria, these categories are dissolved and not infrequently turned inside out."[34] The second lesson has to do with power. Greenberg puts it succinctly:

Out of the Holocaust experience comes the demand for redistribution of power. The principle is simple. No one should ever have to depend again on anyone else's goodwill or respect for their basic security and right to exist. . . . No one should ever be equipped with less power than is necessary to assure one's dignity. To argue dependence on law, or human goodness, or universal equality is to join the ranks of those who would like to repeat the Holocaust. Anyone who wants to prevent a repetition must support a redistribution of power.[35]

The third deals with Jewish-Christian relations.[36] Here Greenberg asserts that "Jews have not appreciated Christianity enough."[37] He explains:

There is a general Jewish tendency to underestimate Christianity's redemptive contribution to the world, due to the bad experience Jews have had with it. Anger at Christian mistreatment has obscured the ambivalence and importance of Judaism in Christianity, which meant that Christians persecuted, but also kept alive and protected, Jews. Even persecuting Christians gave Jews the option of converting, rather than styling the Jew as intrinsically demonic and beyond the right to exist. Rebuking the widespread, almost stereotyped Jewish identification with secular, liberal modernity and against Christianity, the Holocaust suggests that modern values created a milieu as dangerous as—more dangerous than—Christianity at its worst. Indeed, Jews have a vested interest in Christianity's existence. Russia, the society of secularism triumphant, has demonstrated again that secular absolutism is just as dangerous to Judaism as is an abusive Christianity, unchecked.[38]

This new appreciation of Christianity, moreover, is not merely based on the relative superiority of Christianity to Nazism and Stalinism. Deeper theological revaluations are now, in light of Auschwitz, both possible and necessary. Greenberg calls upon Jews, as he calls upon Christians, to open an unprecedented dialogue on the spiritual meaning of Christianity (and of Christians on Judaism). Not to do so is to risk indifference to a future Holocaust built upon the old, now recycled stereotypes. He goes so far as to propose that:

Confirmed now in its resumed redemption [State of Israel], shaken by the Holocaust's challenge not to put down others, Judaism can no longer give patronizing answers. It must explore the possibility that the covenant grafted onto it is a way whereby God has called Gentiles to God.[39]

At the same time this Jewish response is predicated on a reconsideration of Christian attitudes towards Judaism. Hence, Greenberg adds:

Of course, this invokes the principle, "by their fruits, you shall know them." When Jesus' Messianism led to hatred, exclusion, pogrom, it could only be judged false. If it now leads to responsibility, *mitgefuhl,* sharing of risk and love, then its phenomenology becomes radically different. Suffice it to say—without irony—Christians have an extraordinary opportunity in this age: of showing the power of love and concern for Jews and the embattled beginnings of Jewish redemption, the State of Israel. Such a demonstration would give new seriousness among Jews to Christianity's own perception that it is a vehicle of divine presence and redemption in the world.[40]

II. THE DIALECTIC OF JEWISH HISTORY: OR HOW THE COVENANT BECAME "VOLUNTARY"

Having begun with these relatively preliminary and unfinished remarks, Greenberg recognizes that he has only initiated the necessary theological task of clarifying the significance of the Holocaust for contemporary Jewish thought. To proceed further he must return and re-engage, now in a more detailed way, the meaning of historical experience in Judaism —i.e., in what sense is Judaism a "historical religion" and hence what difference do historical events (such as the *Shoah* and re-creation of the State of Israel) make to the Jewish view of reality? All of Greenberg's thought deals, either directly or obliquely, now in one way, now in another, with this question. History is his main concern. (And one perhaps ought to add that, for Greenberg, history is never neutral. It either challenges or confirms covenantal theology.)

The premise of his analysis is that Judaism is a uniquely historical religion. Since the experience of the Patriarchs and the time of the Exodus, Judaism has been shaped by God's actions in history. History is the primary milieu for the Divine–human encounter, "at once the scene of human activity and divine redemption."[41] As such it is also the laboratory of verification, the test of all theology. One learns of God, His ways, and what appears to be His absence through the historical experiences of the Jewish, and other, peoples.[42] Greenberg even allows for the possibility of the "refutation"[43] of God's existence as a consequence of historical events. But this affirmation, too, is "dialectical." That is to say:

Faith is not pure abstraction, unaffected or unshaken by contradictory events; it is subject to "refutation." Yet it is not simply empirical either. A purely empirical faith would be subject to immediate refutation, but in fact the people of Israel may continue to testify in exile and after defeat. It may see or hope beyond the present moment to the redemption which will inevitably follow. Thereby, it continues to testify despite the contradiction in the present moment. In fact, when the redemption comes, it will be all the greater proof of the assertions of faith and of the reliability of God's promises because it will overcome the present hopeless reality. On the other hand, if redemption never came or if Israel lost hope while waiting for redemption, then the status quo would win and Jewish testimony would come to an end. Thus, faith is neither a simple product of history nor insulated from history. It is testimony anchored in history, in constant tension with it, subject to revision and understanding as well as to fluctuation in credibility due to the unfolding events.[44]

Israel's faith, however, is not groundless. It is rooted in Israel's formative national experience of Exodus and Covenant. Having known God's redemptive and revelatory acts in times past, it has grounds for hope in their continued reality. And this, Greenberg re-emphasizes, is the particularly historical thrust of Judaism. "God's mighty acts of redemption *are* in history. In taking this stand, Jewish tradition promises to move history forward and at the same time leaves itself vulnerable to being shattered on the rock of that very history."[45]

What follows necessarily from this emphasis on the vulnerability of Judaism to historical disconfirmation is the theological significance of national tragedies that seem to be weighty counter-evidence to the claims of the Exodus and Sinai. For "unless the facts of suffering and defeat are reconciled with the claims, in fact the ability to make them, is overthrown."[46] Prior to the Holocaust, such response to national tragedy was to be found particularly in three classic forms. First, the tradition of *mipnei chata'eynu*—"for our sins we are punished," i.e., that such punishment is proof of God's continued concern with even a wayward Israel. This was the primary, though not the only, explanation of the

Destruction of the First Temple. And, of course, it was connected with a doctrine of the redemption of Israel that was sure because it was grounded in God's promise that the Exile was *not* forever. Secondly, in reaction to national catastrophe, there was a transformation in "the understanding of the nature of God."[47] This, Greenberg contends, is the major feature of the response to the destruction of the Second Temple:

God was no longer going to be as available, as directly or dramatically involved in history, as He had been until then. Rather, God had withdrawn and the human involvement in history, both in tragedy and redemption, was much greater than had been realized before. This is the dynamic behind the triumph of the Halakhic method and the conclusion that prophecy no longer existed. This is the validation of the rejection of heavenly voices as the arbiter in legal disagreements.[48]

Thirdly, there have been those Jews like Elisha ben Abuya who have taken Israel's fateful negative experiences as decisive proof that existence is meaningless, "leth din v'leth dayan"[49] ("there is no judgment and no judge"), life has no transcendent meaning.

In Greenberg's estimation, consistent with most modern rabbinic scholarship, the second type of response became normative for Judaism after 70 c.e. It is "the one given by Rabbi Yohanan Ben Zakkai and the rabbis. It became the dominant post-Destruction [70 c.e.] form of Judaism. . . . The crucial development is the shift from the revealed intervening God of the biblical period to the relatively hidden Deity of the exilic period. God is close now as *Presence*, as *Shechinah*, not as automatic intervenor who brings victory to the deserving."[50] Greenberg goes on to describe this *re*-interpretation of God's character in a powerful way. Reflecting on the *aggadic* text in the talmudic treatise *Yoma* 60a, he writes:

Moses had spoken of God as "great, mighty, and awesome." Jeremiah, the prophet of destruction, declined to speak of God's might. If Gentiles cavort in His sanctuary, where is His might? Daniel declined to speak of God as awesome. If Gentiles enslave and oppress his People, where is His awesomeness? The men of the Great Assembly restored this praise by *reinterpretation*. They answered: This is His might—that He controls His urges. When the wicked flourish (for example, the Temple is destroyed). He is patient with them (that is, He gives them time and freedom to act; He does not intervene and stop them). And this is God's awesomeness—were it not for awe of God, how could this one people,—the Jewish people—exist among all the other nations that are out to destroy it? How is it known that God is, in fact, present after the Destruction? Only by a radical reinterpretation of His presence in the world: He controls Himself. He is the hidden presence, not the intervening presence. The only other way we know of His presence is that His people continue to exist in defiance of all logic and all force. This proves that behind it all there is a God who keeps the Jewish people alive.[51]

But what of the Holocaust? Can the model of R. Yohanan also be satisfactorily applied to it? Or does it break asunder the rabbinic reformulation of God's *Presence?* Greenberg's answer to this has undergone a two-step development. In the first stage, as given expression in his essay on "Judaism and History," published in 1978, he argued for the radicalizing[52] of the traditional rabbinic response. What is required is the deliberate radicalizing of tendencies already at work within the *halachic* tradition. For example, what is characterized as the "secularizing" tendency needs encouragement as well as a new prominence, especially because of the secular, though profoundly religious character of the State of Israel. Secondly, and as a corollary of this secularizing tendency, the increasing shift from rabbinic to lay leadership in the contemporary Jewish community is to be welcomed. Thirdly, the redefinition of God's "self-control" in the face of evil, already begun at *Yavneh,* needs further accentuation in the light of God's "silence" at Auschwitz. Fourth, and as a corollary of God's "silence," we need to understand the fact "that the human role in redemption is more central and dramatic than that emphasized in the grandest speculation of rabbinic tradition."[53]

At this juncture Greenberg knows the right question to ask: "Why is this not simply a suggestion that Judaism is entering an atheist or purely natural period?" To his own interrogative, he answers as follows. The Holocaust has bankrupted humanism, just as radically as it has challenged theism. Secondly, "Jewish secularism" after Auschwitz is theologically "awesome" in its willingness to continue as an identifiably Jewish phenomenon. Thirdly, "the rebirth of Israel does speak (as Isaiah suggested) of redemption, purpose and fulfillment in history."[54]

The second, more recent, more radical stage in Greenberg's theological vision turns not on a deepening of the Yavnean response, but on its dramatic extension (Greenberg himself would favor more reciprocal terms here that still retain certain overtones of the dialectic of continuity and discontinuity), which leads to a transformation through the creation of a new pattern. This new metaphysical configuration speaks explicitly not only of continuity with the past but of a unique beginning, a new era of Jewish covenantal history. Greenberg explicates his meaning in this way. There are three major periods in the covenantal history of Israel. The first is the biblical era. What characterizes this first covenantal stage is the asymmetry of the relationship between God and Israel. The biblical encounter may be a covenant but it is clearly a covenant in which "God is the initiator, the senior partner, who punishes, rewards and enforces the partnership if the Jews slacken."[55] This type of relationship culminated in the crisis engendered by the destruction of the First Temple in 586 B.C.E. To this tragedy Israel, through the Prophets, in keeping with the "logic" of this position, responded primarily with and through the doctrine of self-chastisement. The destruction indicated Divine punishment rather than God's rejection of Israel or proof of God's non-existence.[56] The second phase in the transformation of the covenant idea is marked by the destruction of the Second Temple. The "meaning" adduced from this event, the response of the Rabbis, was that now Jews must take a more equal role in the covenant, becoming true partners with the Almighty.[57] "The manifest divine presence and activity was being reduced but the covenant was actually being renewed."[58] For the destruction signalled the initiation of an age in which God would be less manifest though still present. "The Divine Presence becomes more shielded and more present. The Jewish role more active."[59] Moreover, after 70 C.E., the Sages began to think again about the meaning of the destruction and God's role in it. According to Greenberg, they now began to recognize

that explaining the Destruction as divine punishment for sins is not as adequate an explanation as before. Although this remains the dominant explanation—it is also an important defense against the claim that the Destruction is a rejection of Israel as covenant partner. There is significant expansion of an alternate interpretation. The Divine Presence does not so much punish Israel in the Destruction as it suffers alongside Israel. "Since the Temple was destroyed, there is no laughter before the Holy One Blessed Be He." (*Yalkut Shimoni*, Section 454)[60]

And again, and seminally, "that God's might is expressed in allowing human freedom instead of punishing the wicked."[61] The essential thesis that Greenberg is concerned to develop *vis-à-vis* the rabbis of the Mishnah is that they were conscious of *both* their continuity with the inherited tradition as well as of their own innovative role in further interpreting the meaning of the covenant.[62] As a consequence the very status of the covenantal relationship was re-oriented. Previously it had come into being essentially because of God's will and power; now it was reconfirmed "on 'new' terms, knowing that destruction can take place, that the Sea will not be split for them, that the Divine has self-limited and they (Israel) have additional responsibilities."[63] This further "hiding" of the Divine is described by Greenberg as a process of the increasing secularization[64] of history. In such an era it becomes both appropriate and necessary for human beings to take a more active role in history, to fill the gap left by the absenting God. In a strikingly suggestive analysis of the new post-70 C.E. situation, Greenberg notes that for the mishnaic sages Purim rather than Passover becomes the "redemptive paradigm."[65] Only through this transformation can covenantal existence continue after 70 C.E.[66]

This brings us to what is decisive and novel in Greenberg's more recent ruminations, what he has termed the "Third Great Cycle in Jewish History," that has come about as a consequence of the Holocaust. Where previously he saw our contemporary form of covenantal relationship as a continuous, if extreme stage in the rabbinic understanding of covenantal partnership, now he presents it in a new light.[67] The *Shoah* marks a new era in which the Sinaitic covenant was shattered. Thus, if there is to be any covenantal relationship at all today it must assume new and unprecedented forms.[68] In this context Greenberg insists that the covenant always implied further human development. The natural outcome of the covenant is full human responsibility. "In retrospect," he argues, paraphrasing A. Roy Eckardt,

it is now clear that the divine assignment to the Jews was untenable. In the Covenant, Jews were called to witness to the world for God and for a final perfection. After the Holocaust, it is obvious that this role opened the Jews to a total murderous fury from which there was no escape. Yet the divine could not or would not save them from this fate.

Therefore, morally speaking, God must repent of the covenant, i.e., do Teshuvah for having given his chosen people a task that was unbearably cruel and dangerous without having provided for their protection. Morally speaking, then, God can have no claims on the Jews by dint of the Covenant.[69]

What this means is that the covenant

can no longer be commanded and subject to a serious external enforcement. It can not be commanded because morally speaking—covenantally speaking—one cannot *order* another to step forward to die. One can give an order like this to an enemy, but in a moral relationship, I cannot demand giving up one's life. I can ask for it or plead for it—but I cannot order it. To put it again in Wiesel's words: when God gave us a mission, that was all right. But God failed to tell us that it was suicide mission.[70]

Moreover, having witnessed the horrors of the *Endlösung* nothing God could threaten for breach of the covenant would be frightening, hence the covenant cannot be enforced by the threat of punishment any longer.[71]

Out of this complex of considerations, Greenberg pronounces the fateful judgment: *The Covenant is now voluntary!* After Auschwitz Jews have, quite miraculously, chosen to continue to live Jewish lives and collectively to build a Jewish State, the ultimate symbol of Jewish continuity, but these acts are, now, the result of the free choice of the Jewish people. "I submit that the covenant was broken but the Jewish people, released from its obligations, chose voluntarily to take it on again and renew it. God was in no position to command anymore but the Jewish people was so in love with the dream of redemption that it volunteered to carry on with its mission."[72] The consequence of this voluntary action transforms the existing covenantal order. First Israel was a junior partner, than an equal partner, now after Auschwitz it becomes "the senior partner in action. In effect, God was saying to humans: you stop the Holocaust. You bring the redemption. You act to insure: never again. I will be with you totally in whatever you do, wherever you go, whatever happens but you must do it."[73]

In turn, Israel's voluntary acceptance of the covenant and continued will to survive suggest three corollaries. First, they point, if obliquely, to the continued existence of the God of Israel. By creating the State of Israel, by having Jewish children, Israel shows that "covenantal hope is not in vain."[74] Secondly, and very importantly, in an age of autonomy rather than coercion, living Jewishly under the covenant can no longer be interpreted monolithically, i.e., only in strict *halachic* fashion. A genuine Jewish pluralism,[75] a Judaism of differing options and interpretations, is the only legitimate foundation in the age of Auschwitz. Orthodox observance, no less than Reform, Conservative, or "secular" practices are freely adopted—none can claim either automatic authority or exclusive priority in the contemporary Jewish world.[76] Thirdly, and repeating a theme sounded several times in earlier essays, Greenberg offers that:

the urgency of closing any gap between the covenantal methods and goals is greater in light of the overwhelming countertestimony of evil in this generation. The credibility of the Covenant is so troubled and so hanging in the balance that any internal element that disrupts or contravenes its affirmations must be eliminated. So savage was the attack on the image of God that any models or behavior patterns within the tradition that demean the image of God of people must be cleansed and corrected at once.[77]

A note of caution in pushing this dramatic statement of a "voluntary covenant" too far is, however, now required because of Greenberg's further, mediating remarks on this provocative thesis. He writes: "We are at the opening of a major new transformation of the covenant in which Jewish loyalty and commitment manifests itself by Jews taking action and responsibility for the achievement of its goals. This is not a radical break with the past. In retrospect, this move is intrinsic in the very concept of covenant."[78] And Greenberg goes on: "The Rabbis [of the Talmud] put forth Purim, with its hidden, human agency and flawed redemption, as *the* new redemptive model to which the Jews gave assent in upholding the covenant. *Today we can say that the covenant validated at Purim is also coercive, for then the genocide was foiled, and it is less binding in a world that saw Hitler's murder of six millions Jews.*"

III. THE *HALACHAH* AS A THEOLOGY OF HISTORY

Here a brief, focused description of Greenberg's recent book-length study of the yearly cycle of Jewish festivals entitled *The Jewish Way*[79] will help clarify his understanding of the historicity of Judaism. Though the overt theme of this book is the character of the Jewish holidays, the real meaning of the book, if I may put it this way, is to vindicate its author's view that Judaism sees redemption as occurring within history. In this connection the two stages in the overall pattern of redemption are, first, the Exodus and, secondly, mankind's subsequent efforts to perfect historical existence. In this complex drama humankind is seen as playing an essential role, re-enforcing Greenberg's more general thesis regarding the dominant role that humankind must now assume in the post-Holocaust age. "The ultimate goal," Greenberg writes, "will be achieved through human participation. The whole process of transformation will take place on a human scale. Human models, not supernatural beings will instruct and inspire mankind as it works toward the final redemption."[80] And this redemption, the messianic completion, will include, and effect, all peoples. The Jewish task is therefore the universal task, and Israel's redemption is the world's perfection. The cycle of the Jewish year, expressive as it is of the larger *halachic Weltan-*

schauung, incarnates these repercussive themes and gives them temporal and spatial reality. It provides substance to Jewish theology and the rhythm of Jewish existence. Still more, it offers a perennial history lesson teaching each Jew the record of Israel's past and "in an annual cycle, every Jew lives through all of Jewish history and makes it his or her personal experience. The holidays generate the sense of community by making the story of all, the possession of each one."[81]

The holidays are of two types, those of biblical origin, Passover, Shavuot, Sukkot, Sabbath, and the Days of Awe, "present a stationary model of Judaism coherent, revealed, structured."[82] Over against these are a series of festivals and remembrances, Purim, Chanukah, Tisha B'av, that emerged from the fact that "Judaism opens itself to further historical events that can challenge or confirm its message."[83] Today again Judaism is challenged by the *Shoah* and the re-creation of the State of Israel and as in the past the Jewish people are attempting to find the means through which to confront the meaning of these extraordinary events without permitting them to destroy the overall character of Jewish faith. *Yom Ha Atzmaut,* Israeli Independence Day, and *Yom Ha Shoah,* Holocaust Remembrance Day, reflect these struggles in concrete forms. Indeed, it might fairly be said that Greenberg's discussion of these two contemporary events forms the core of *The Jewish Way* for here such elemental Greenbergian themes as the meaningfulness of life after the Holocaust, the renewal of the covenant essentially through human energy, and the redemption of history microcosmically represented by the "resurrection and redemption"[84] that is the State of Israel find expression. Of the latter he asserts: "the creation of the State was an act of redemption of biblical stature . . . in the 1940's after Auschwitz. The redemption then was nothing less than renewed witness in a world where all transcendence seemed to have collapsed."[85] For Greenberg, this event is the source and confirmation of his more general thesis regarding the meaning of a "Third Era in Jewish History," of the now-voluntary covenant and the heroic stature of the Jewish People in carrying on with the work of redemption. He tells us: "In the case of the State of Israel . . . the human role is dominant and self-assertive. This secularism should not be confused with atheism or celebration of the death of God. . . . Rather, . . . the creation of the State of Israel takes place in the context of a new era in Jewish history. In this new era, God becomes even more hidden, the circumstances even more ambiguous. This ambiguity serves a twofold function: It allows those who prefer to interpret the activity as purely secular to do so, it permits the religious soul to recognize the divine role out of mature understanding and free will rather than out of 'coerced' yielding to divine *force majeure*."[86] Thus *Yom Ha Atzmaut* is the perfect paradigm for Greenberg's new/old vision of Jewish existence.

IV. CRITIQUE

As the critical remarks that I am now about to offer are meant to be suggestive rather than exhaustive I shall present them *seriatim*.

(1) In responding to the many genuinely interesting philosophical and theological positions Greenberg has advanced there is, to begin, a certain unease that one has not quite captured his meaning completely. The source of this disquiet lies not only in the limits of one's own understanding but also in Greenberg's imprecise use of essential terms and ideas. Such elemental terms as "revelation," "messianic," "messianism," "history," "redemption," "real," "secular," "religious," are all used in a multiplicity of ways, aimed at a spectrum of differently informed listeners, and all are employed (perhaps in part intentionally) without any precising definitions being offered. Then again, his work suffers from a certain lack of logical rigor. This is evident both in the construction of particular arguments as well as in certain underlying architectonic features of Greenberg's thought as a whole. The most notable of these lapses, which is present so consistently that it should be seen as a structural flaw, is located in his hermeneutical overemployment of the notions "dialectic" and "dialectical" and in his unsatisfactory usage of the interrelated notion of "paradox." Merely holding, or claiming to believe, two contradictory propositions simultaneously is *not* a fruitful theological procedure.

(2) Greenberg offers two seminal criteria of verification for theological discourse in our time. The first criterion is strikingly powerful in its directness and simplicity. It states: "No statement, theological or otherwise, should be made that would not be credible in the presence of burning children."[87] The second criterion, more philosophically sculpted and no doubt shaped in response to the Positivist verificationist challenge, reads as follows:

Faith is not pure abstraction, unaffected or unshaken by contradictory events; it is subject to "refutation." Yet it is not simply empirical either. A purely empirical faith would be subject to immediate refutation, but in fact the people of Israel may continue to testify in exile and after defeat. It may see or hope beyond the present moment to the redemption which will inevitably follow. Thereby, it continues to testify despite the contradiction in the present moment. In fact, when the redemption comes, it will be all the greater proof of the assertions of faith and of the reliability of God's promises because it will overcome the present hopeless reality. On the other hand, if redemption never came or if Israel lost hope while waiting for redemption, then the status quo would win and Jewish testimony would come to an end. Thus, faith is neither a simple product of history nor insulated from history. It is a testimony anchored in history, in constant tension with it, subject to revision and understanding as well as to fluctuation in credibility due to the unfolding events.[88]

While modern Jewish philosophers have tended to ignore the all-important challenge raised by requests for verification, here Greenberg, astutely as well as courageously, meets it head-on. The question to be put to him, however, is whether his two formulations are adequate as principles of verification. Begin with the first formulation. It does not set out a straightforward empirical criterion. Empirical evidence will neither simply confirm it, nor as it is phrased in the negative, simply disconfirm it. There is no empirical statement E with which it is incompatible. That is, it is not, finally, a statement of an empirical sort. But this need not matter *decisively,* for it is not put as an empirical criterion; rather, its appeal is to the broader category of "credibility" and many things are credible that are not empirical. In this way, the task before us transforms itself into showing that "credible" is not used trivially, but this is a far more ambiguous and uncertain task than at first appears to be the case. Consider, for example, the remarks of the German Protestant Pastor Dean Grüber that had such a profound impact on Richard Rubenstein.[89] The Dean honestly held that Jewish children died for the crime of deicide committed by their First Century ancestors. Such "good" Christian theology was obviously "credible" to the Dean in the face of the Holocaust. Likewise, Satmar Hasidim and other right-wing orthodox Jews who continue to account for the Holocaust through recourse to the doctrine of "for our sins we are punished" *(mipnei chata'eynu)*, remembering, for example, the terrible fate of the children of Jerusalem of old recounted in Lamentations which is credited to "our sins," also believe that their propositions are "credible." It thus becomes evident that *credible* is not a self-explanatory category of judgment. What is credible to Dean Grüber and the Satmar Rebbe is *incredible* to Greenberg—and the dispute between them is not resolved by appeal to the criterion Greenberg has established, as it would be were it a viable criterion. It turns out that what is "credible" depends on one's prior theological commitments, the very issue at stake. Accordingly, the argument becomes circular.

Consider now the second, more formal, criterion. It is attested to be falsifiable, "subject to refutation," yet it is not, at the same time, a "simply empirical" proposition. The two conditions of "refutation" established are: (a) "Redemption never comes"; or (b) "if Israel lost hope while waiting for redemption, then the status quo would win." The first criterion appears, at least in what has been called a "weak" sense, to be empirically verifiable—i.e., it states a specific empirical condition under which it would, in principle, be disconfirmed. However, the established thesis is inadequate as a criterion because it turns on the temporal notion "never comes." Logically, we could not make any use of this norm until world history ended, in redemption or otherwise. At any time prior to the end of history an appeal could be made to "wait a minute more," hence putting off the empirical disconfirmation indefinitely. It certainly is not, *contra* Greenberg, a "testimony anchored in history . . ." in any strong sense, as immediate and available historical evidence, e.g., the obscene reality of the Death Camps, is deflected by appeal to the end that never is.

The second condition offered is of more interest. But it, too, is not sufficient for two reasons. First, the continued and continuing status of Israel's faith *qua* subjective affirmation is not a logical or ontological warrant for any proposition regarding "God's mighty Acts in History," Greenberg's claim to the contrary notwithstanding. What is disconfirmed "if Israel loses hope" is, of course, Israel's faith—i.e., the strength of its commitment—but the ontological content of the commitment is unaffected. Propositions such as "there is a God," or "God Redeems," or "History reveals a loving Providence," are neither confirmed by Israel's faith nor disconfirmed by Israel's apostasy.

Given the weak verification procedures proposed by Greenberg, his advocacy of faith in God after the *Shoah* would seem compatible with any empirical set of conditions. That is, there seems no empirical state of affairs that is actually incompatible with theism, especially Greenberg's particular exposition of theism.

(3) What is the relationship, if any, between the *Shoah* and *halachah*? Does the *Shoah* justify *halachic* transvaluations? Here one needs to go slowly. As a preliminary conclusion subject to revision it appears to me that the *Shoah* does *not* legitimate either wholesale *halachic* change or a transformation in the fundamental structures of the *halachic Weltan-*

schauung.[90] Greenberg's extremely well-intentioned call for widespread and dramatic *halachic* innovation, for a *voluntary covenant* and the rest, even if made with enormous *ahavat Yisroel,* "love of Israel," may well be misguided. In any case, there seems no certain methodological or metaphysical bridge between Auschwitz and *halachah,* between Nazis killing Jews and the need for a Jewish-re-definition of *halachah.*

To avoid any misunderstanding let me repeat that this conclusion is not based on the denial of the 'uniqueness' of the Holocaust as is usually the case with more *halachic* orientations. Indeed I am convinced of the historical uniqueness, both in Jewish and in world-historical terms, of the *Shoah.*[91] However, having come to this conclusion, which I share, for various reasons, with Greenberg and the other post-Holocaust theologians such as Richard Rubenstein and Emil Fackenheim, I do not see any compelling logical or theological reason for equating this historical judgment with a mandate for *halachic* change. Historical uniqueness is one thing, the legitimating criteria for *halachic* change are something else and I am yet to see, or to have been shown, the bridge from one to the other.

(4) Revelation is a technical and awe/ful term. A term not heard often enough today even in theological circles yet, ironically, at times overused and almost always employed too loosely and imprecisely in contemporary discourse. These several thoughts are sparked by Greenberg's recurring, often imprecise or ambiguous theological employment of this theme, especially as it becomes decisive in relation to claims made by him for the putative revelatory character of the *Shoah* and the reborn State of Israel. From a narrowly Jewish theological perspective nothing rivals these assertions in importance, for no category is as elemental as revelation. All that Judaism is flows from revelatory claims, is predicated on a specific understanding of what revelation is and is not. The structure as well as the content of Judaism presumes a delimited and defined hermeneutic of the revelatory event as well as of the way the content of revelation is unfolded, expounded, applied. Because the stakes are so high, insisting, *contra* Greenberg, on a careful employment of this term is required lest the possibility arise that any claim might be advanced as a revelatory one.

(5) The structure of Greenberg's three covenantal eras, his many propositions about a "saving God," his talk of revelation and redemption, and his radical proposition that the Almighty is increasingly a "silent partner" in Jewish and world history, all these ideas cannot be

advanced without pondering their consequences for the "God of Abraham, Isaac and Jacob."

To put it directly, what happens to the God of Judaism in Greenberg's theology? *Prima facie* the God of all the traditional omni-predicates does not fit easily with a "God" who is a "silent partner." This may not be a telling criticism, though I think it is, because Greenberg is free to redefine "God" for the purposes of theological reflection. But having redefined "God" however he feels it appropriate, Greenberg must attend to the myriad metaphysical and theological consequences of such an action. It is therefore incumbent to require that whatever Greenberg's "God-idea," its character and implications be explained fully and carefully. On the one hand, this means that the ontological entailments of treating God as a "silent partner" have to be spelled out. On the other hand, the implication of such a metaphysical principle (God as a "silent partner") for such traditional and essential Jewish concerns as covenant, reward and punishment, morality, Torah, Mitzvot, redemption, and other eschatological matters, have to be attended to. For example, is a God who is a "silent partner" capable of being the author and guarantor of moral value both in human relations as well as in history and nature more generally? Or is the axiological role traditionally occupied by God largely evacuated?[92] Likewise, is there a possibility of sin, in a substantive and not merely a metaphorical sense, in this perspective? Again, is God as a "silent partner" capable of being the God of salvation both personal and historic? And lastly, is God as a "silent partner" the God to whom we pray on Yom Kippur and to whom we confess our sins and ask forgiveness? If my skepticism regarding the ability of Greenberg's "God-idea" to answer to these challenges is misplaced, this has to be demonstrated. For it would appear that while this revised "God-idea" allows him to unfold the logic of the "Third Era" as he desires, it in turn generates more theological problems than it solves.

(6) This brings us to the most dramatic, most consequential, of Greenberg's affirmations—his espousal, in our post-Holocaust era, of a "voluntary covenant." According to Greenberg, as already explicated in detail above, the Sinaitic covenant was shattered in the *Shoah*. As a consequence he pronounces the fateful judgment: *the Covenant is now voluntary!* Jews have, quite miraculously, chosen after Auschwitz to continue to live Jewish lives and collectively to build a Jewish State, the ultimate symbol of Jewish continuity, but these acts are, post-*Shoah*, the result of the free choice of the Jewish people.

Logically and theologically the key issue that arises at this central juncture, given Greenberg's reconstruction, is this: if there was ever a valid covenant[93], i.e., there is a God who entered into such a relationship with Israel, then can this covenant be "shattered" by a Hitler? Or put the other way round, if Hitler can be said to have "shattered" the covenant, was there ever such a covenant, despite traditional Jewish pieties, in the first place? The reasons for raising these repercussive questions are metaphysical in kind and are related to the nature of the biblical God and the meaning of His attributes and activities, including His revelations and promises, which are immune, by definition, from destruction by the likes of a Hitler. If Hitler could break God's covenantal promises, God would not be God and Hitler would indeed be central to Jewish belief.

V. CONCLUSION

The nature of this chapter, and the character of my critique, reflect the seriousness with which I believe one must take Greenberg's theological position. Its sensitivity to the right issues, its commitment to the Jewish people, its learning and intelligence, its concerns with the interfacing of *halachah* and history, its profound affirmation of the meaning of the State of Israel, are all attributes that recommend it to those truly concerned with the present condition of the people Israel and the viability of Jewish belief in the post-Holocaust age. Alternatively, however, much of its argumentation is unconvincing, its use of sources open to question, and its "method" often lacking in method. Paradoxes are admitted too easily, and the notions of dialectic and dialectical are far too casually employed, often to avoid facing real and pressing logical contradictions. For these reasons, Greenberg's work must be judged unfinished, still in the stage of development and completion. A judgment Greenberg himself would agree with. This conclusion, however, should not be misunderstood. It does not negate the value of Greenberg's provocative conceptual efforts, but rather challenges all of us to re-engage still more deeply the rudimentary theological matters that he has the courage to address.

NOTES

1. The five articles by Greenberg I will be concerned with in this section are: (1) "Cloud of Smoke, Pillar of Fire: Judaism, Christianity, and Modernity

after the Holocaust," in E. Fleischner (ed.), *Auschwitz: Beginning of a New Era?* (New York, 1977), pp. 1–55 (hereafter cited as *Cloud*); (2) "Judaism and History: Historical Events and Religious Change," in Jerry V. Dillen (ed.), *Ancient Roots and Modern Meanings* (New York, 1978), pp. 43–63 (hereafter cited as *JH*); (3) "New Revelations and New Patterns in the Relationship of Judaism and Christianity," *Journal of Ecumenical Studies* (Spring, 1979), pp. 249–267 (hereafter cited as *New Revelations*); (4) "the Transformation of the Covenant" (not yet published) (hereafter *Transformation*); and (5) "The Third Great Cycle in Jewish History," printed and circulated by the National Jewish Resource Center (New York, 1981), 44 pages (hereafter *TGC*).

2. It is important to add here both for purposes of chronology as well as conceptual clarity that Greenberg's essay "Cloud of Smoke, Pillar of Fire," while the first essay we will be concerned with, was not his first effort to articulate the meaning of history for Judaism, i.e., the relevance of seeing Judaism as an historical religion. This is clear from his very early publication entitled "Yavneh: Looking Ahead, Values and Goals," that appeared in *Yavneh Studies*, Vol. 1, No. 1 (Fall, 1962), pp. 46–55.

3. I will not discuss Greenberg's understanding of the significance and challenge of the Holocaust for Christian theology, most of which I agree with, as our concern here is his account of the way the Holocaust has impacted on post-1945 Jewish life and thought.

4. *Cloud*, p. 11. It should be noted here, however, so as not to distort Greenberg's position by over-concentration on its radical or novel elements, that he begins this powerful essay with the traditional affirmation that "Judaism and Christianity are religions of redemption" (p. 1). Moreover, this element of continuity is more evident in his later essay "Judaism and History" that was, unlike "Cloud," addressed to an internal Jewish audience and which, in this context, concerns itself more with Jewish historical links between past and present.

5. Ibid., p. 15.

6. *Cloud*, p. 20. I have reversed the order of Greenberg's presentation—i.e., my second "consequence" is actually stated first in the text of Greenberg's paper.

7. Ibid., p. 20.

8. Ibid., p. 23.

9. Ibid., p. 22.

10. Ibid., p. 22.

11. Ibid., p. 23. Here it might clarify the picture Greenberg was portraying, the argument he was making, if we suggest that already in this early essay he was proposing, however obliquely, that there is something essentially revelatory about the Holocaust and that therefore new theological understandings, by all groups, will be required to decipher it and to respond to it appropriately.

12. *Cloud*, p. 27.

13. Ibid., p. 27.

14. Ibid., p. 27.

15. Ibid., p. 27.
16. Ibid., p. 28.
17. Spelled out now much more fully in his *The Jewish Way: Living the Holidays* (New York, 1988).
18. *Cloud,* p. 28ff.
19. Ibid., p. 29.
20. Greenberg's full statement of this argument is found in the bottom paragraph on pp. 29f.
21. Ibid., p. 31.
22. Ibid. To be exact on what Greenberg holds this post-modernist move to entail I quote him: "This new era will not turn its back on many aspects of modernity but clearly will be free to reject some of its elements, and to take from the past (and future) much more fully" (p. 31).
23. Ibid., p. 32.
24. Ibid.
25. Ibid., p. 33.
26. Ibid., p. 35.
27. Ibid.
28. Ibid., p. 37.
29. Ibid., p. 40.
30. Ibid., pp. 41f.
31. Ibid., p. 42. In *Cloud,* Greenberg was more concerned with people taking political and military power than revising the meaning of power *vis-à-vis* the covenant. This latter theological notion only becomes really important in his later work. See now, also, his further thoughts on this central issue in *The Jewish Way,* pp. 18ff., 127ff. and 370ff.
32. *Cloud,* p. 43.
33. Ibid., p. 44.
34. Ibid., p. 45.
35. Ibid., p. 50.
36. *New Revelations.*
37. Ibid., p. 259.
38. Ibid.
39. Ibid., p. 265.
40. Ibid.
41. *JH,* p. 47. See also section I of Greenberg's "Third Great Cycle in Jewish History."
42. See the discussion in *JH,* p. 47.
43. *JH,* p. 47.
44. Ibid.
45. Ibid., p. 48.
46. Ibid., p. 49.
47. Ibid., p. 50.
48. Ibid., p. 51.
49. This is the declaration of Elisha ben Abuya, the most famous heretic of the Talmudic tradition.

50. Ibid., p. 55.
51. Ibid., p. 57.
52. See ibid., pp. 61ff. Greenberg uses the word "projection" for this project. He entitles this section of his paper: "The Model Projected: The Case of the Holocaust."
53. *JH*, p. 62.
54. Ibid.
55. *TGC*, p. 6. Greenberg correctly cites the telling prophetic word of Ezekiel 20:32–33 in support of this exegesis, with which I concur.
56. *Transformation*, pp. 7ff. in typescript. See also *TGC*, pp. 3–6.
57. *TGC*, p. 7.
58. Ibid., pp. 9ff. in typescript. Greenberg's detailed discussion of the Rabbinic responses is full of interest. For our present purposes, however, we need not review all the elements sketched and analyzed by him as corollaries of this greater equality of Israel in the covenantal relationship. See also *TGC*, pp. 6–12, which presents additional exegesis of this view.
59. Ibid., p. 12. See also p. 8.
60. *Transformation*, p. 11.
61. *TGC*, p. 8. Here Greenberg touches on the theme that Eliezer Berkovits has particularly emphasized in his reflections on the Holocaust. Consult his *Faith after the Holocaust* (New York, 1973). For a discussion of Berkovits's position see my paper "Eliezer Berkovits's Post-Holocaust Jewish Theodicy," in my *Post-Holocaust Dialogues: Critical Studies in Modern Jewish Thought* (New York, 1983), pp. 268–286.
62. In the name of Rav Soloveitchik he states: "The scholar is the co-creator of the Torah (cf. *Ish Hahalacha* [by Rav Soloveitchik])," ibid., p. 14. Whether Rav Soloveitchik would concur with the use of his argument as employed by Greenberg is open to conjecture.
63. Ibid., p. 17. In *TGC* Greenberg recalls a teaching of R. Joshua ben Levi that he paraphrases as follows: "R. Joshua ben Levi said that God's might, shown in Biblical times by destroying the wicked, is now manifest in self control" (p. 8).
64. See *TGC*, p. 8. In this connection he correctly calls attention to the fact that "Rabbis were a more secular leadership than priests and prophets" (ibid., p. 9). I would, however, prefer a different adjective to "secular." But, in any case, it must be understood that Greenberg's use of the term "secularism" is not equivalent to atheism. He explicitly tells us: "In the Temple, God was manifest. Visible holiness was concentrated in one place. A more hidden God can be encountered everywhere. But one must look and find" (ibid., p. 5). And again, and very explicitly, "This secularism must not be confused with atheism or the celebration of the death of God" (ibid., p. 10).
65. Ibid., p. 10.
66. Note here his full explanation of this shift to Purim as the "redemptive paradigm" in ibid., p. 10.
67. In *TGC*, Greenberg makes it clear that he does not want this new position of his to be understood as representing a wholly discontinuous view of the

covenant after Auschwitz. In fact he explicitly states that his new view is "not a radical break from the past. In retrospect this move is intrinsic in the very concept of the covenant" (p. 18). This claim, however, is subject to doubt, though the issue is a very complex one. Greenberg continues to wrestle with the meaning of "voluntary" as in "voluntary covenant" in his ongoing theological work and is, as far as one can tell, not happy with either his original formulation of this idea or any new reading of it.

68. We must, Greenberg recognizes, even take seriously the possibility that the covenant is at an end. Ibid., p. 23.

69. Ibid., p. 23. Here it is to be noted, as already indicated, that in this paragraph Greenberg is paraphrasing a remark by A. Roy Eckardt and there may be some differences between Eckardt's position and Greenberg's over the final understanding of this seminal issue.

70. Ibid., p. 23.

71. Ibid., pp. 23–24.

72. Ibid., p. 25.

73. Ibid., p. 27. Because of the importance of this doctrine and its apparent radicalness, it is important that we understand Greenberg's position correctly. In further correspondence with this author he has given the following explication that I quote in full:

> It is true that I go on to describe "the shattering of the Covenant" and "the Assumption of the Covenant." However, in the light of this whole essay the human taking charge, i.e., full responsibility for the covenant is God's calling to them. "If the message of the destruction of the Temple was that the Jews were called to greater partnership and responsibility in the covenant, then the Holocaust is an even more drastic call for total Jewish responsibility for the covenant" (ibid., p. 36). The more I reflected upon this insight, I grew more and more convinced that this third stage was an inevitable and necessary stage of the covenant. The covenant always intended that humans ultimately must become fully responsible. In retrospect, the voluntary stage is implicit in the covenantal model from the very beginning. Once God self-limits out of respect for human dignity, once human free will is accepted, the ultimate logic is a voluntary covenant. (Personal correspondence from Dr. Greenberg to the author, January 3, 1989)

74. *TGC*, p. 30.

75. See ibid., p. 33. For further adumbration of Greenberg's position on pluralism and its many implications, cf. also his more recent essay "Toward a Principled Pluralism," *Perspectives* (National Jewish Center for Learning and Leadership, New York, March, 1986).

76. These ideas are more fully described in *TGC*, pp. 37ff. For Greenberg this means that it is God's will that humans take full responsibility for the outcome of the covenant. Such a grant of autonomy entails that even if the actual policy decisions reached and acted upon are erroneous, the error is, in some real sense, a legitimate error within the broader confines of the covenant rather than a wholly illegitimate form of religious behavior.

77. Ibid., pp. 37–38. See also p. 16ff.

78. *TGC*, p. 18.

79. *The Jewish Way: Living the Holidays* (New York, 1988).
80. Ibid., p. 18.
81. Ibid., p. 22.
82. Ibid., p. 28.
83. Ibid., p. 29.
84. Greenberg's title for his treatment of *Yom Ha-Atzmaut,* p. 385.
85. *The Jewish Way,* p. 393.
86. Ibid., pp. 393–439.
87. *Cloud,* p. 23.
88. *JH,* p. 47.
89. On the details of this encounter see R. Rubenstein's article in *After Ausch-witz* (Indianapolis, 1966), pp. 47–58.
90. Here a clarification made by Dr. Greenberg, in response to this criticism, deserves citing. He replies to my argument as follows:

    It is not that Holocaust validates halachic change but that it makes more urgent the accomplishment of the redemptive goals; it calls for a "messianic" breakthrough in this generation. This expresses itself in coming closer to the ideal norms of the tradition in such areas as women, Gentiles, etc. . . . This is not to be confused, however, with faddishness or trying to be on the right side of currently trendy values and issues. (Private communication from Dr. Greenberg, January 3, 1989)

91. I have made a detailed study of this central issue in my forthcoming three-volume study, *The Holocaust in Historical Context,* to be published by Oxford University Press beginning in 1992.
92. Here a further nuance must be noted. Greenberg insists that though God is intentionally more self-limited in the "Third Era," this should not be mis-understood as positing either God's absence or weakness. God is still active, though He is more hidden. In a private correspondence Greenberg argued that in his view God is still seen as possessing, at least, the following four classical attributes of "calling," "accompanying," "judging," and "sustaining" men and women, as well as of the world as a whole. Whether Greenberg has a right to maintain these attributes for his "God-idea," given the other characteristics of his theology, is open to question.
93. An open question on independent philosophical grounds.

10

"The Tremendum": Arthur Cohen's Understanding of Faith after the Holocaust

Among the most sustained recent Jewish theological discussions of the *Sho'ah* is Arthur A. Cohen's *The Tremendum: A Theological Interpretation of the Holocaust*.[1] Though a relatively short book, 110 pages in all, it attacks this immense conceptual issue with all of Cohen's customary verve and intelligence. No school theologian, either in the dogmatic or systematic sense, Cohen here makes a prodigious effort to strike out in a new, more radical metaphysical direction as a necessary response to the Event with which he deals.

I

Four highly ramified theses lie at the root of Cohen's philosophical reflections. They are: (1) the Holocaust is unique and this uniqueness entails particular theological concomitants; (2) thought is unable to grasp the reality of Auschwitz; (3) no "meaning" is to be found in this genocidal carnage; and (4) evil is more real, more consequential, than Cohen had heretofore allowed. These four intellectually radical presuppositions lead Cohen to recognize the need to return, with a new uncertainty, to the traditional questions of theology. To ask again concerning "the reality of evil and the existence of God, the extremity of evil and the freedom of man, the presentness of evil and the power of God."[2] To ask still more concretely if "like our ancestors we are obliged

to decide whether (national) catastrophies are compatible with our traditional notions of a beneficent and providential God. The past generations of Israel decided that they were. The question today is whether the
same conclusion may be wrung from the data of the *tremendum*." [3]

If this is, and I agree that it is, the essential question, what is Cohen's
answer? If "there is no end until the end is final. Until that moment, it is
only caesura and new beginning," [4] what is the substance of the new,
post-*tremendum* beginning? Cohen presents the following schematic formulation of its defining and necessary characteristics:

"Any constructive theology after the *tremendum* must be marked by the following characteristics: first, the God who is affirmed must abide in a universe whose
human history is scarred by genuine evil without making the evil empty or
illusory nor disallowing the real presence of God before, even if not within,
history; second, the relation of God to creation and its creatures, including, as
both now include, demonic structure and unredeemable events, must be seen,
nonetheless, as meaningful and valuable despite the fact that the justification
that God's presence renders to the worthwhileness of life and struggle is now
intensified and anguished by the contrast and opposition that evil supplies; third,
the reality of God in his selfhood and person can no longer be isolated, other
than as a strategy of clarification, from God's real involvement with the life of
creation. Were any of these characteristics to be denied or, worse, proved untrue
and unneeded, as strict and unyielding orthodox theism appears to require,
creation disappears as fact into mere metaphor or, in the face of an obdurate
and ineffaceable reality such as the *tremendum,* God ceases to be more than a
metaphor for the inexplicable." [5]

What these three theological requirements entail for Cohen is the
bringing together of two seemingly opposite traditional theological strategies. One is that "of the kabbalistic counter history of Judaism" [6] by
reference to which Cohen intends to call attention to the kabbalistic
doctrine of the *Eyn Sof* and the related doctrine of creation in which:

"God, in the immensity of his being, was trapped by both its absoluteness and
necessity into a constriction of utter passivity which would have excluded both
the means in will and the reality in act of the creation. Only by the spark of
nonbeing (the interior apposition of being, the contradiction of being, the premise of otherhood, the void that is not vacuous) was the being of God enlivened
and vivified." [7]

And this cosmogonic speculation has now to be linked to a second
cosmological tradition, that associated with Schelling and Rosenzweig.
This Cohen describes as follows:

" 'What is necessary in God,' Schelling argues, 'is God's nature,' his 'own-ness.' Love—that antithetic energy of the universe—negates 'own-ness' for love cannot exist without the other, indeed, according to its nature as love, it must deny itself that the other might be (contracting itself that the other might be, setting limits to itself). However, since the divine nature as *esse* cannot have personality without the outpouring, the self-giving of love to define those limits, it must be postulated that within God are two directions (not principles, as Schelling says): one which is necessary selfhood, interiority, self-containment and another, vital, electric, spontaneous that is divine *posse,* the abundant and overflowing. There arises from all this the dialectic of necessity and freedom, the enmeshment of divine egoity and person, divine self-love and free love, divine narcissism and the created image, the sufficient nothing of the world and the creation of being. The human affect is toward the overflowing, the loving in God; his containment, however, the abyss of his nature, is as crucial as is his abundance and plenitude. These are the fundamental antithesis of the divine essence without which the abyss would be unknown or all else would be regarded as plenitude. ... the quiet God is as indispensable as the revealing God, the abyss as much as the plenitude, the constrained, self-contained, deep divinity as the the plenteous and generous." [8]

What the synthesis of these kabbalistic and Schellingian conceptions means for Cohen is that: (a) there is an elemental side of God that is necessarily hidden, but still necessary, in the process of creation and relation; (b) conversely, reciprocally, creation, which is continuous and ongoing, is a necessary outcome of God's loving nature; (c) God's nature requires our freedom; and lastly, (d) we require a "dipolar" [9] theological vision which admits that things and events look different from God's perspective, and to God as He is in Himself, than they do from our vantage point and vis-à-vis our relation to the transcendent.

On the basis of these complex theological foundations Cohen goes on to fashion what in fairness can be called a new, if dramatic, version of the "Free-Will defense," i.e., an articulated theodicy that turns on the necessity for, as well as on the abuse of, human freedom in creation. Framed in Cohen's unique idiom, this ambitious defense is described as "an enduring strife and tension (in man), enlarged and made threatening by our finitude, in which freedom enhances when it is marked and contained by reason, but when reason fails to find language, freedom is destructively cut loose or bends toward untruth or succumbs to sheer willfulness." [10]

What this means as specifically applied to the *Sho'ah* is, Cohen argues, that we require a new understanding of God's work in the world that insistently differs elementally from that taught by traditional theism.

The understanding of the traditionalists issues forth in the putatively "unanswerable" question: "How could it be that God witnessed the holocaust and remained silent?"[11] Alternatively, Cohen's recommendation would free us of this causal understanding of the need for direct Divine intervention and allow us to see: "that which is taken as God's speech is really always man's hearing, that God is not the strategist of our particularities or of our historical condition, but rather the mystery of our futurity, always our *posse,* never our acts."[12]

If we can acquire this alternative understanding of what divine action allows—as well as of what it does not allow—we will "have won a sense of God whom we may love and honor, but whom we no longer fear and from whom we no longer demand."[13] This argument, with its redefinition of God and its emphasis on human freedom, emerges as the center-piece of Cohen's revisionist "response" to the *tremendum.*

Exegesis of Cohen's position, however, would not be complete without brief comment on one further aspect of his argument, his critique of Zionism. Whereas most of the other major thinkers[14] who have discussed the *Sho'ah* in theological terms have embraced the re-creation of the State of Israel as a positive event, even while understanding its value in a variety of ways, e.g., in terms of Richard Rubenstein's naturalism or Yitzchak Greenberg's incipient messianism, Cohen remains wedded to a non-Zionist (which must be scrupulously distinguished from an anti-Zionist) theological outlook. Cohen's reservation stems from his continuing understanding, indebted as it is to Rosenzweig, of the Jewish people's "peculiar" role in history, or rather, as Cohen describes it, "to the side of history."[15]

"It may well be the case that the full entrance of the Jewish people into the lists of the historical is more threatening even than genocide has been, for in no way is the Jew allowed any longer to retire to the wings of history, to repeat his exile amid the nations, to disperse himself once again in order to survive. One perceives that when history endangers it cannot be mitigated. This we know certainly from the *tremendum,* but we know it no less from the auguries of nationhood, that every structure of history in which an eternal people takes refuge is ominous."[16]

This reserve, this mooted pessimism as regards the State of Israel is the product of Cohen's transcendental theology coupled, it must be said, with a not inconsiderable degree of historical realism. While I do not agree with his formulation of the meaning of Israel among the nations, nor his explication of Israel's mission, nor again his reserve about the return to Zion as positive theological fact, I do recognize a certain real wisdom in his caution, for the Jewish people and the Jewish State have not yet arrived at the *eschaton*. At most, we are at "the beginning of the dawn of our redemption," as the prayer for the State of Israel composed by the Israeli Chief Rabbinate has phrased it. Perhaps even more accurately, if sceptically, one ought to refer to "the hope that this is the beginning of the dawn of our redemption," and reserve further judgment. In any case, however, Cohen's a-Zionist dogmatics raise an important, if unfashionable, issue for consideration. We ignore his challenge at great cost to ourselves.

II

There is much to agree with in Cohen's novel formulation of the theological implications of the *tremendum*. One is impressed by his bold attempt to shift the angle of vision for the discussion as a whole, as well as of individual elements within the whole. And one is even more impressed by his willingness, even passion, to do theology—a rare passion-flower in this a-theological era. Cohen is correct in his belief that Jewish thinkers cannot, ultimately, eschew theology. Then again, his willingness to strike unpopular positions, e.g., his stance on the theological, or one might more accurately say the non-theological, significance of the State of Israel, is commendable, even if one seriously disagrees with it, for theologians should not theologize to win friends but for the sake of Truth. Lastly, one recognizes in Cohen's difficult style, for all its obscurity, authentic theological seriousness that is being stretched on the rack of the most intractable, the most basic, theological issues. Having oneself experienced the need to seek out new, more elastic resources in language in order to address these matters, one recognizes that Cohen is trying to say what seems *a fortiori* unsayable. In short, there is a good deal to be learnt, if most notably of a deconstructive sort, from Cohen.

Acknowledging all this, and much else of value in Cohen's work, I remain unpersuaded by his main theological claims, his most essential doctrinal affirmations. Indeed, where theological fundamentals, or rather *the* theological fundamental—namely God—is at issue, I am in basic disagreement with what Cohen has described as "dipolar" theism and its implications for thinking about, and responding to, the *Sho'ah*. In what remains of this chapter I would like to set out my particular reservations and the reasons that lie behind them.

(1) Let us begin our critique where Cohen begins his constructive theological endeavor, i.e., with his invoking and employment of the theological systems of the Kabbalah and Schelling. Cohen argues for the need to rediscover the value of each of these "counter-history" traditions and then to bring them together in a larger, original theological synthesis. However, even before proceeding to Cohen's exegesis of the substantive content of these respective systems a seminal fact needs to be recognized about their structure and context and it is this: neither account stands independently of a broader intellectual environment. For Kabbalah this larger environment is the Jewish halachic tradition in all its breadth and diversity as well as certain gnostic trends which it adapted and re-worked according to its own genius. For example, its doctrine of *tzimtzum,* Divine Contraction, to which Cohen appeals for the initial half of his *dipolar* theism, is inseparably part and parcel of a larger "mythos" (not myth in the pejorative sense) that was grounded, in particular, in the then (medieval) shared traditional Jewish dogma regarding the absoluteness and literalness of the Sinaitic revelation. Added to this were a wide range of metaphysical and theological concepts and beliefs, for example, the belief in the ontic status of the Hebrew alphabet, or again, very specific theories of emanation drawn from neo-Platonism, and a host of notions regarding creation. It was only out of, and on the grounds of, these seminal propositions that the Kabbalists could offer their celebrated cosmogonic speculations—and believe them.[17] But Cohen, especially as becomes clear in his technical discussion of miracles,[18] and his sharp critique of what he calls fundamentalism[19]— something which all the classical Kabbalists were in that sense of the term which he criticizes—does not share any of these primal beliefs and therefore it is hard to see how he can recommend and defend the theory of *tzimtzum* torn out of its original context. Gershom Scholem's work, and his deserved prestige, referred to by Cohen in this connection does not alter this fact for Scholem is a historian of Kabbalah not its advocate.[20] One simply cannot base a contemporary theological reconstruction on Scholem's work without additional argument that moves the creative discussion from the historical and descriptive to the theological and prescriptive—but this additional, independent link has not been supplied.

While the theory of Divine Contraction sounds plausible in its kabbalistic context, the grounds of its plausibility in a modern non-kabbalistic philosophical setting need to be worked through and argued for.

Here it is explicitly to be recognized that Cohen would certainly not subscribe to the traditional kabbalistic gnosis, interlaced with neoplatonic metaphysical premises, cum *halachah,* that gives the original doctrine it conceptual foundation and hence one would think that for Cohen the doctrine should lose its coherence even in its uniquely kabbalistic modality. Cohen ignores altogether the fact that the kabbalistic account also seeks to assure the continued and direct interaction between above and below, between God as *Eyn Sof* after the act of *tzimtzum* and the emanated world, through the action of the *sefirot* (divine pleroma). This is a necessary, unbreakable, causal connection rooted in the metaphysics and logic of emanation. This link is of the essence for the *mekubbalim* (the mystics), for it is this relationship that allows the entire dialectical process of the system to function, including the ultimate aims of *devekut* (personal adhesion to God in mystical relation), and *tikkun olam* (repairing the world) by the messianic action of reversing the downward and negative flow of reality, i.e., raising the *nitzozot* (the sparks of holiness) in things and thereby restoring the broken primordial harmony in the upper realm. It is this ontic reciprocity that also gives Torah and *mitzvot* their cosmological status and power—*mitzvot* are the lever by which the Jew moves the world, uniting even God Himself in the process ("kivyachol," as if we can say this). Cohen's metaphysics, built putatively on this kabbalistic (and Schellingian) tradition, and on which more below, explicitly denies, and is designed so as to deny, just such causal ontological relationships. Alternatively, if Cohen wishes to eschew this claimed kabbalistic inheritance and to argue instead for the more open-ended thesis that creation requires some limitation of God, he can do so just as well, probably even better, without invoking technical kabbalistic notions whose meaning has been negated by the negation of their context. Such a non-kabbalistic doctrine of Divine limitation would, of course, still require justification but it would now come to us on independent grounds for assessment and verification. And it would not raise all sorts of historic and ideological associations and meanings Cohen wishes to have no part of. In such revised circumstances it would certainly lack the prestige of Kabbalah, that emotional and exotic seductiveness that Kabbalah has come to acquire in our time thanks in large part to Scholem's work,[21] but it would also come to us in a more accurate way.

A similar demurral must also be voiced against Cohen's recourse to Schelling as the grounds for his argument for the di-polarity of God. For again, Schelling's thought comes to us from a context that is a murky admixture of misunderstood Enlightenment natural science, doses of gnosticism and mythology, and overwhelming quantities of German Idealism, even if an Idealism in tension with the reigning Idealist conception of Hegel and earlier of Fichte. Hence it *means* in a very particular context—but can this idealist-cum-gnostic context be defended today? Or rather, has it not been thoroughly discredited, making appeal to it less than convincing. While Schelling, for all his contradictoriness and tendency to the obscure, is a thinker of genius, and Cohen's use of him is, in places, theologically intriguing, one is hard pressed to credit the introduction of his theism *per se* as providing any substantive part of a contemporary theology. Certainly one cannot merely adopt segments, fragments, of his world-view without finding convincing ways to defend them on more secure and independent philosophical grounds than Schelling himself provided. However, Cohen does not enter into such a protracted and technical transcendental discussion, nor does he provide such autonomous legitimating grounds. Rather, he naively assumes, and I choose this characterization with great care, the usefulness of Schelling's account and employs it accordingly. But all this is too direct, too unconvincing a procedure under the intellectual circumstances.

There is also a second, even more telling, hermeneutical difficulty connected with Cohen's reliance on Kabbalah, Schelling and Rosenzweig, and it is this. The *caesura* marked by the *tremendum* has, on Cohen's own definitions of *caesura* and *tremendum,* broken the continuity of Jewish and world history into *pre-tremendum* and *post-tremendum* epochs. The philosophical and theological systems that served to make sense of the world before Auschwitz—understanding "system" here in its broadest sense—are no longer viable after Auschwitz. The Holocaust has changed everything. This being so, indeed it is the primal assumption of Cohen's whole mode of reflection, how can either the *pre-tremendum* mythos of the Kabbalah or the *pre-tremendum* idealism, or anti-idealism if you wish,[22] of Schelling or Rosenzweig, be retrievable as the appropriate structural bases for the post-*Sho'ah* moment. It is true that these exemplary intellectual and spiritual traditions can be classed as subterranean and proclaimed, with some justification, as "counter-history," but by what inventive logic do we say that the *tremendum* invalidated only the orthodoxies of the *pre-tremendum* era. Surely, if Cohen's explicit root premise is correct, then it forces drastic revision, if not outright rejection, of all *pre-tremendum* thinking, whether such thought is diagnosed as mainline or underground, acclaimed or suppressed, history or "counter-history." One would think, given what has here been assumed *a priori,* that Kabbalah and Schelling-Rosenzweig are outdistanced no less so than other *pre-tremendum* theologies. Alternatively, if this is not the case, then a convincing argument for the unique retrievability of just this specific material must be provided.

David Tracy in his Foreword to the work before us described Cohen's intended procedure as follows:

"—To understand any tradition after the *tremendum* is to retrieve its genius through a retrieval that is also a suspicion. Through that kind of hermeneutics, we may find hidden, forgotten, even repressed aspects of the tradition for thought now. A hermeneutical enterprise like this occurs in the powerful theological reflections of the final chapter of this work. There the reader will find Arthur Cohen's own constructive rethinking of the reality of God in a post-*tremendum* age. Unless I misread him, Arthur Cohen moves in this section through a powerful hermeneutics of suspicion to an equally powerful hermeneutics of retrieval. By that dangerous route he retrieves for thought the deconstructive mode of thinking of the Jewish kabbalistic tradition historically retrieved by Scholem, the negative theology in the gnostic-kabbalistic tradition from Boehme through Schelling, and, above all, the unthought that must now be thought in the mystic epistemology and ontology of the incomparable Franz Rosenzweig.

Cohen does not allow himself simply to "repeat" the solutions of his chosen classics, those defamiliarizing trajectories of the tradition. The choice of these particular classics is both liberating and courageous. For precisely these classic modes of deconstructive thought, let us recall, were and are still often despised when not altogether forgotten or repressed by both Jewish and Christian theologians in favor of some "clearer" or "more orthodox" aspect of the traditions. As Cohen's creative rethinking of the position of Franz Rosenzweig makes especially clear, he understands this subterranean tradition of negative deconstructive theological reflection on God only by understanding it differently. He must so understand it for Cohen understands it post-*tremendum.* Traditional deconstruction must itself now be deconstructed in order to be retrieved at all."[23]

Here Tracy indicates his theological and methodological sophistication. He knows that all *pre-tremendum* theology, even that of a "negative deconstructive" sort, can only be retrieved, if retrievable at all, *differently* than in the past because it is now retrieved *post-tremendum.* If Cohen had accomplished through his analysis what Tracy attributes to it, it would indeed be of the greatest importance and our present critical remarks would be in error. However, while the conscious design behind the work might be as Tracy describes it, it is difficult to discern any real "deconstruction" of Kabbalah and very little of Schelling in the actual working out of its argument. There is some in respect of Rosenzweig, though not of Rosenzweig's account of creation but rather, in a modest way, of his view of history and the Jewish presence in, or in Cohen's phrase "on the side of" history. At the same time, the explication of a radical hermeneutics of suspicion is not provided beyond the banal assertion of traditional theology's inadequacy in the face of the Death Camps while the deeper, more substantive retrieval desired through the deconstruction of the deconstructive tradition is very little advanced. There are, at best, only intimations of what could be adjudged a thorough deconstructive exploration prior to any mature theological retrieval. Therefore, we ought to characterize Cohen's presentation as a *stipulated* hermeneutics of suspicion followed by a *stipulated* retrieval for, in its generality, the "unthought that now must be thought" has not been thought. As a consequence, Cohen's conclusions never progress beyond the level of assertions.

(2) This first preliminary observation concerning method brings into focus a related epistemological question that Cohen does not address. What is the *status* of his radical theological remarks? Are his theological recommendations, drawn from Kabbalah, Schelling and Franz Rosenzweig, to be understood as *hypotheses,* and if so, how are they to be tested and against what and how? Are they *proofs* à la Anselm or Aquinas? Are they tautologies? Are they necessary *a priori* synthetic propositions? Are they first principles as in a mathematical-deductive system? If so, what governs their confirmation and possible revision? These are questions to which Cohen supplies no answers.

(3) Let us now move to the very center of Cohen's response to the *tremendum,* his dipolar account of God. The subtle intention that lies behind this transformative re-description of God is two-fold. On the one hand it seeks to assure the reality of human freedom and hence to facilitate a simultaneous re-employment of a sophisticated version of a "Free-Will" theodicy. On the other hand, and reciprocally, it redefines the transcendent nature of God's being such that He is not directly responsible for the discrete events of human history and hence cannot be held responsible for the *Sho'ah* or other acts of human evil. This is a very intriguing two-sided ontological strategy. Our question therefore must be: does Cohen defend it adequately? If so, at what theological price?

Let us explore these questions by deciphering first Cohen's second thesis as to God's re-defined role in history. The clearest statement of

Cohen's revised God-idea in respect of Divine accountability for the *Sho'ah* comes in his discussion of God's putative silence and what Cohen takes to be the mistaken tradition-based expectation of miraculous intervention.

"The most penetrating of post-*tremendum* assaults upon God has been the attack upon divine silence. Silence is surely in such a usage a metaphor for inaction: passivity, affectlessness, indeed, at its worst and most extreme, indifference and ultimate malignity. Only a malign God would be silent when speech would terrify and stay the fall of the uplifted arm. And if God spoke once (or many times as scripture avers), why has he not spoken since? What is it with a God who speaks only to the ears of the earliest and the oldest and for millennia thereafter keeps silence and speaks not. In all this there is concealed a variety of assumptions about the nature and efficacy of divine speech that needs to be examined. The first is that the divine speech of old is to be construed literally, that is, God actually spoke in the language of man, adapting speech to the styles of the Patriarchs and the Prophets, and was heard speaking and was transmitted as having spoken. God's speech was accompanied by the racket of the heavens so that even if the speech was not heard by more than the prophetic ear, the marks and signals of divine immensity were observed. As well, there is the interpretive conviction that God's speech is action, that God's words act. Lastly, and most relevantly to the matter before us, God's speech enacts and therefore confutes the projects of murderers and tyrants—he saves Israel, he ransoms Jews, he is forbearing and loving. God's speech is thus consequential to the historical cause of justice and mercy. Evidently, then, divine silence is reproof and punishment, the reversal of his works of speech, and hence God's silence is divine acquiescence in the work of murder and destruction."[24]

As opposed to this older view Cohen recommends an alternative:

"Can it not be argued no less persuasively that what is taken as God's speech is really always man's hearing, that God is not the strategist of our particularities or of our historical condition, but rather the mystery of our futurity, always our *posse,* never our acts. If we can begin to see God less as the interferer whose insertion is welcome (when it accords with our needs) and more as the immensity whose reality is our prefiguration, whose speech and silence are metaphors for our language and distortion, whose plenitude and unfolding are the hope of our futurity, we shall have won a sense of God whom we may love and honor, but whom we no longer fear and from whom we no longer demand."[25]

In response to this reconstruction of the God-idea four critical observations are in order. First, it need not be belabored that there is truth in the proposition that "what is taken as God's speech is really always man's hearing."[26] But at the same time, it is only a half-truth as stated. For our hearing the word of revelation does not create "God's speech"

—this would be illusion and self-projection. Certainly we can *mis*hear God, or not hear what there is to hear at all—but these qualifications do not erase the dialogical nature of Divine speech, i.e., the requirement that there be a Speaker as well as a Hearer. And if revelation requires this two-sidedness, then we have to reject Cohen's revisionism because it fails to address the full circumstance of the reality of revelation and God's role in it. Alternatively, if Cohen's description is taken at face value, revelation as such disappears, in any meaningful sense, from the theological vocabulary, for what content can we ultimately give to "man's hearing" as revelation? And specifically from a Jewish point of view, anything recognizable as *Torah* and *mitzvot* would be negated altogether.

Secondly, this deconstruction of classical theism and its substitution by theological di-polarity fails to deal with the problem of Divine attributes. Is God still God if He is no longer the providential agency in history? Is God still God if He lacks the power to enter history vertically to perform the miraculous? Is such a dipolar Absolute still the God to whom one prays, the God of salvation? Put the other way round, Cohen's divinity is certainly not the God of the covenant,[27] nor again the God of Exodus-Sinai, nor yet again the God of the Prophets and the *Churban Bayit Rishon* (Destruction of the First Temple) and the *Churban Bayit Sheni* (Destruction of the Second Temple). Now, none of these objections, the failure to account for the very building blocks of Jewish theology, count *logically* against Cohen's theism as an independent speculative exercise. However, they do suggest that Cohen's God is *not* the God of the Bible and Jewish tradition and that if Cohen is right, indeed, particularly if Cohen is right, there is no real meaning left to Judaism and to the God-idea of Jewish tradition. Cohen's deconstruction in this particular area is so radical that it sweeps away the biblical and rabbinic ground of Jewish faith and allows the biblical and other classical evidence to count not at all against his own speculative metaphysical hypotheses.

The dipolar ontological schema is certainly logically neater and sharper than its "normative" biblical and rabbinic predecessor, but one questions whether this precision has not been purchased at the price of adequacy, i.e., an inadequate grappling with the multiple evidences and variegated problems that need to be addressed in any attempt, however bold, to fashion a defensible definition and description of God and His relations to humankind. Logical precision must not be achieved here too easily, nor given too high a priority, in the sifting and sorting, the phenomenological decipherment and re-arranging, of God's reality and our own.

Third, is the dipolar, non-interfering God "whom we no longer fear and from whom we no longer demand" yet worthy of our "love and honor?"[28] This God seems closer, say, to Plato's *Demiurgos* or perhaps closer still to the innocuous and irrelevant God of the Deists. Such a God does not count in how we act, nor in how history devolves or transpires. After all "God is not," Cohen asserts, "the strategist of our particularities or of our historical condition." But if this is so, if God is indeed so absent from our life and the historical record, what difference for us between this God and no God at all? Again, is such a God who remains uninvolved while Auschwitz is generating its corpses any more worthy of being called a "God whom we may love," especially if this is His metaphysical essence, than the God of tradition?[29] A God who we can only see as the "immensity whose reality is our prefiguration" while rhetorically provocative, will not advance the theological discussion for it provides negations and evasions just where substantive analysis is required.

In this connection let me add a relevant historical observation. In the medieval era Jewish theologians and philosophers conducted a constant and ongoing debate with Platonists and Aristotelians regarding creation. The "deep structure" of the debate turned on the desire of Jewish thinkers to defend God's will, i.e., to defend creation as an act of God's will rather than as a result of the necessity of His nature, which they recognized was essential to the maintenance of Judaism, for only a God with a will could make covenants and give the Torah. The *locus classicus* of this view is found in Maimonides' *Guide* II:25. Here Maimonides argues as follows:

"Know that with a belief in the creation of the world in time, all the miracles become possible and the Law becomes possible, and all questions that may be asked on this subject, vanish. Thus it might be said: Why did God give prophetic revelation to this one and not to that? Why did God give this Law to this particular nation, and why did He not legislate to the others? Why did He legislate at this particular time, and why did He not legislate before it or after? Why did He impose these commandments and these prohibitions? Why did He privilege the prophet with the miracles mentioned in relation to him and not with some others? What was God's aim in giving this Law? Why did He not, if such was His purpose, put the accomplishment of the commandments and the nontransgression of the prohibitions into our nature? If this were said, the answer to all these questions would be that it would be said: He wanted it this way; or His wisdom required it this way. And just as He brought the world into existence, having the form it has, when He wanted to, without our knowing His will with regard to this or in what respect there was wisdom in His particularizing the forms of the world and the time of its creation—in the same way we do not know His will or the exigency of His wisdom that caused all the matters, about which questions have been posed above, to be particularized. If, however, someone says that the world is as it is in virtue of necessity, it would be a necessary obligation to ask all those questions; and there would be no way out of them except through a recourse to unseemly answers in which there would be combined the giving the lie to, and the annulment of, all the external meanings of the Law with regard to which no intelligent man has any doubt that they are to be taken in their external meanings. It is then because of this that this opinion is shunned and that the lives of virtuous men have been and will be spent in investigating this question. For if creation in time were demonstrated—if only as Plato understands creation—all the overhasty claims made to us on this point by the philosophers would become void. In the same way, if the philosophers would succeed in demonstrating eternity as Aristotle understands it, the Law as a whole would become void, and a shift to other opinions would take place. I have thus explained to you that everything is bound up with this problem. Know this."[30]

Ironically, Cohen's present metaphysical suggestion for redescribing the nature of God again raises this same issue of Divine volition. That is, its determinate account of creation as a necessity of God's nature à la Schelling, rather than as an act of God's free will, makes it impossible, now for yet another reason, to sustain Torah and Covenant, i.e., Judaism.

Lastly, this proposed metaphysical reconstruction is not founded upon any direct phenomenological procedure *per se*. Though fashioned in response to the *Sho'ah,* belief in such a dipolar God requires just as great a "leap of faith"—maybe even greater as it lacks the support of the Jewish past—as do the theistic affirmations of the tradition. Phenomenologically, it is difficult to discern why one would move in the direction of dipolar theism, given the negativity of the *Sho'ah,* unless one were committed at a minimum to theism, if not dipolar theism, to start with. Cohen is correct that both Schelling and Rosenzweig begin "by *assuming* that human natures are created and therefore dependent upon the operative analogue of divine nature."[31] But why should we, or he, begin with this assumption? Especially given his negation of much of the theistic inheritance that both Schelling and Rosenzweig retained, even if not always consciously. It is surely not enough to introduce this as an argument from authority, i.e., to hold this view on the claimed authority of Schelling and Rosenzweig; some better reason(s) for even introducing the dipolar God into the present conversation is required—but remains always absent.

(4) The second major aspect of Cohen's account turns on what I have called his revised "Free-Will" theodicy. He advances the familiar thesis that God gave mankind freedom as an integral part of creation and, of necessity, this freedom can be variously misused, *ergo* the *tremendum*.

"The bridge that I have, not casually but I fear insubstantially, cast over the abyss is one that sinks its pylons into the deep soil of human freedom and rationality, recognizing no less candidly now than before that freedom without the containment of reason returns to caprice and reason without the imagination of freedom is supineness and passivity." [32]

In response to this proposal two reservations must be entered. The first is evoked by the particular form that the reconstructed Cohenian version of this classic theodicy takes. The second concerns itself with the "Free-Will" defense in its generality.

(a) It is not clear why we need dipolar theism to produce the "Free-Will" defense; or that the "defense" is any more or any less sound in a dipolar than a traditional theistic context. That is, given Cohen's metaphysical dependence on Kabbalah and Schelling it is hard to see why or how their thinking makes any effective difference to the correctness, or otherwise, of the "Free-Will" position.

Cohen, in attempting to justify recourse to these sources in this context, i.e., in relation to the reality of authentic human freedom, criticizes traditional theism, what he chooses to call "fundamental theism," for holding that:

"God (is) respondent to extremity, the greater the human need the greater the certainty of his assistance, with the result that human life denies its essential freedom returning to ethical passivity and quietism in which everything is compelled to be God's direct work." [33]

But this criticism is inaccurate and establishes a "straw man" to be demolished by Cohenian di-polarity. "Fundamentalist" theologians have championed the "Free-Will" defense as vigorously and as "successfully" as Cohen; see, for example, Eliezer Berkovits' recent theological response to the Holocaust. [34] *Contra* Cohen, the pressing, gnawing problematic for the "fundamentalist" does not arise from the side of human freedom but rather from the belief in a Saving God, a belief radically challenged by the Holocaust. That is to say, the "fundamentalist" knows the evil of humankind to be a striking challenge to its elemental doctrine(s) regarding the character of the Creator. In comparison, Cohen's position is specifically structured in such a way so as not to have to grapple with this extreme difficulty. Indeed, this is the very reason for his particular theological reconstruction, i.e., the world's evil does not, cannot, impinge in a dipolar system upon God's being or status. But while this metaphysical redescription succeeds in solving, or dissolving, certain tensions—not allowing the evil of the world to count against God—it raises others of equal or greater force, especially regarding the Divine attributes, in particular, those relating to the categories of omnipotence and omniscience. Of course, Cohen wants to redefine these cardinal attributes, this is, if I understand his call for a renewal of a kabbalistic-Schelling model of Creation-Revelation aright, exactly what he intends. But in so doing does his dipolar God still remain God-like? Or has Cohen actually capitulated to those critics who deny God's meaningful reality, by whatever name, while attempting to make a virtue of this covert capitulation.

Then, too, the moral dimension of theodicy remains to be dealt with even after Cohen's ontological reconstructions, if for something of a new reason. For the moral, or rather, amoral corollary of the dipolar schematization of God is deeply disquieting. Cohen's dipolar God appears, of necessity, morally indifferent to human suffering and historical acts of evil,[35] factors of no small consequence for, in the end, the most sensitive as well as the most telling objections to theodicy arise from the side of the ethical.

(b) Elsewhere (in my *Post-Holocaust Dialogues*, pp. 270–283) I have analyzed the logical weaknesses inherent in attempting to meet the theological problems raised by the *Sho'ah* through recourse to the "Free-Will" argument. Though this analysis needs to be modified in certain specific respects given the total construction of Cohen's theodicy, the general negative conclusion there argued—that this defense is inadequate to the immense task at hand—applies in the case of *The Tremendum* as well. Rather than setting out my views again in full here let me add just one additional summary comment. Of all the "moves" made in the theodicy debate, the "Free-Will" gambit is as sober, intelligent and persuasive as any proposed alternative. However, it is, on the one hand, altogether too emaciated an "explanation" of the experience of the *victims,* while on the other hand, it vindicates God's morality, in Cohen's system God's indifference, too easily. Insofar as this argument has real strengths, and it does have such strengths, I think Cohen's employment of it shares in these residual virtues,[36] while insofar as it remains incomplete, Cohen's version of the argument does not materially improve it or remedy its incompleteness.

(5) Cohen recognizes that his programmatic reconstruction impacts upon the fundamental question of God's relation to history. In explicating his understanding of this vexing relationship he writes:

"God and the life of God exist neither in conjunction with nor disjunction from the historical, but rather in continuous community and nexus. God is neither a function nor a cause of the historical nor wholly other and indifferent to the historical."[37]

If God then is unrelated to the historical in any of these more usual ways, as "neither a function nor a cause," how then is He present, i.e., not "wholly other and indifferent," and what difference does He make in this redefined and not wholly unambiguous role:

"I understand divine life," Cohen tells us, "to be rather a filament within the historical, but never the filament that we can identify and ignite according to our requirements, for in this and all other respects God remains God. As filament, the divine element of the historical is a precarious conductor always intimately linked to the historical—its presence securing the implicative and exponential significance of the historical—and always separate from it, since the historical is the domain of human freedom."[38]

But this advocacy of an "implicit" but non-causal nexus will not do.

In the final reckoning, this impressionistic articulation of the problem must collapse in upon itself for at some level of analysis the reciprocal notions of "causality" and "function" cannot be avoided. One can talk lyrically of God as a "filament" and a "conductor" in history as if these were not causal or connective concepts but upon deeper probing it will be revealed that they are. For talk of God as "filament" and "conductor" to retain its coherence, for it not to evaporate into empty metaphor, we have to know what it means to refer to God as a "filament," as a "conductor," no matter how precarious. To rescue these instrumental concepts from complete intellectual dissolution we need also to know something of how God is present in the world in these ways—what evidence can we point to in defense of these images.[39] For example, and deserving of a concrete answer, is the question: What of God is conducted? His love? Grace? Salvation? And if so, how? Wherein, against the darkness of the *tremendum,* do we experience His love, His grace, His salvation? To anticipate this objection as well as to attempt to deflect it by arguing that God is a "filament" but "never the filament that we can identify . . ."[40] is a recourse to "mystery"[41] in the obfuscatory rather than the explanatory sense. For as explanation it means simply: "I claim God is somehow present or related to history but don't ask me how." Alternatively, to come at this thesis from the other side, the analogies of "filament" and "conductor" are disquieting as analogs of the relation of God and history because they so strongly suggest passivity and inertness. If they are the proper analogs for God's activity or Presence in history, all our earlier concrete concerns about maintaining the integral vitality of Judaism re-surface. For the God of creation, covenants, Sinai and redemption is altogether different, i.e., qualitatively, metaphysically and morally other, than a "conductor" or "filament."

Given the dispassionate, disinterested, amoral nature of Cohen's deity, it is not surprising that the conclusion drawn from this descriptive recasting of God's role in "community and nexus" is, vis-à-vis the *Sho'ah,* finally, trivial (in the technical sense).

"Given these assumptions, it would follow that the *tremendum* does not alter the relation of God to himself, nor the relation in which God exists to the historical, nor the reality of creation to the process of eternal beginning within God, but it does mean that man—not God—renders the filament of the divine incandescent or burns it out. There is, in the dialectic of man and God amid history, the indispensable recognition that man can obscure, eclipse, burn out the divine filament, grounding its natural movement of transcendence by a sufficient and oppository chthonic subscension. It is this which is meant by an abyss of the historical, the demonic, the *tremendum.*"[42]

That the Holocaust makes no difference to God's relation to Himself we can grant *in principle* for the purposes of this analysis. And, logically and structurally, i.e., ontologically, we can allow for the purposes of argument Cohen's conclusion that "the *tremendum* does not alter the relation in which God exists to the historical." But, having granted both these premises it is necessary to conclude, *contra* Cohen, that the *tremendum* is not, and *in principle* could not be, a theological problem. It is, on its own premises, irrelevant to God's existence, irrelevant to God's relation to history and, on these criteria, irrelevant to God's relation to mankind—whatever mankind's relation to God.

The *tremendum* is seen by Cohen to be crucially relevant to man's recognition of a Creator, but this is anthropology for it perceives the *tremendum* only as human event with *no* consequences for God other than our indifference to Him. And our indifference does not appear to matter in any transcendental sense, for God apparently does not make any response to it. This is the logic of the "Free-Will" position driven to its "nth" degree. To a degree that makes God all but irrelevant. This remarkable implication flows, ironically, from Cohen's consummate attempt to redefine and reconstruct the theological landscape in order to *protect the viability of some* (not the traditional) *God-idea* in the face of the *tremendum*. An end it accomplishes through the total disconnection of God and the *tremendum*.

Talk of God's involvement in history in terms of "community"[43] after the manner of Cohen becomes unintelligible at this juncture. When God joins in the classic covenantal community of Israel He speaks of being together with His people, *Emo anochi B'tzarah* ("I will be with them in their troubles"),[44] i.e., God shares in the suffering of Israel. This doctrine is the root of the haunting midrashic image of the "Exile of the Shechinah" *(Galut ha-Shechinah)* that expresses the idea that the Divine Presence wanders along with exiled Israel.[45] However, in Cohen's projected "community" such an image of God's participation, as any representation of active participation on His part, is disallowed and unavailable. But then what sort of community can be said to exist between God and Israel, especially in light of the Death Camps—when six million of one's community are murdered, and it makes no difference to one's essential self, "God's relation to Himself," or to one's relations with the decimated community, "God's relation to the historical." Community is not an apt analogy or description of such unrelatedness.

(6) The a-Zionism[46] which is the complement of this ontology is logically consistent. If God is not the causal agent of Auschwitz He is not the causal agent of the Return to the Land. Hence Zionism becomes, if not theologically problematic, then certainly theologically irrelevant. And yet Cohen's formulation of his view is so gnomic, so sibylline, that I think, in fairness, it should be quoted rather than paraphrased.

"Earlier in this discussion I expressed a provisional pessimism. I spoke darkly in the language of history about the Jewish people taking up the arms of history to come before it. For those who caught my gloom, it may well have sounded like the trope of one who stood outside not only the Jewish State but also *propter hoc* outside the Jewish people. Not at all. In fact, at this juncture, quite the contrary. Outside the Jewish State, any state for that matter, but never outside the Jewish people. Indeed, it is precisely because the Jewish people constitutes the eternal speaking of revelation to the Jew of history, the turn of that people into the winds of history, its taking up of the arms of the nations, is a turning of its guardianship of the word towards the nations, rather than its traditional posture as merely concerned observer. The being of the Jewish people is always behind the becoming of the nations, its reformulation as State coming at a moment when the states of the nations are weary and declining, but this is the way of Being—imponderable slowness, because its renewals and conservations are outside life and death, but always changes rung on eternal scales."[47]

In these cryptic remarks about the relation of Israel's Being to the "becoming" of the nations, Cohen seems to want to say something positive about the importance, theologically rendered, of the State of Israel, but does not know how and so falls back on a Rosenzweigian-like vocabulary and ideology. Yet, this will not do. Neither its obscurity nor its espousals recommend it. Indeed, its positive ideology claims too much given Cohen's stringent earlier ontological commitments while, on the other hand, it clearly does not dare enough, from a Jewish theological perspective, where the State of Israel is concerned. And this not least because after Auschwitz, and after more than forty years of the existence of the State of Israel, one cannot so easily dissociate the nature and fate of the Jewish people from that of the Jewish State in which about thirty percent of the Jewish people now live, an ever-increasing percentage, and in which more than forty percent of Jewish infants world wide are born. A theology in which this does not matter, as the *Sho'ah* does not matter theologically, cannot speak meaningfully to the Jewish condition after Auschwitz.[48]

III

The Tremendum is an important work, though at times stylistically and theologically infuriating. Important because it forces us to do theology, a rare occurrence in modern Jewish circles; important because it is saturated with and grows out of an intense concern with the people of Israel; important because it knows, despite its intellectual roots, its conceptual dogmatics, that something has happened in the *tremendum* (and in the State of Israel) that stretches us to the limits as human beings as well as theologians. We therefore need to learn those things that Cohen can teach us. And then having learnt them, we need to go beyond them, beyond Cohen's deeply problematical dipolar theism and its profoundly unsatisfactory corollaries, in search of a more comprehensive, more Jewishly satisfying response to the problematics of Jewish life and thought after, and in the face of, the *tremendum*.

NOTES

1. Published in New York in 1981.
2. Ibid., p. 38.
3. Ibid., p. 50.
4. Ibid., p. 58.
5. Ibid., p. 86. It should be noted that Cohen is very, and rightly, critical of liberal theology after the *tremendum,* see pp. 45 and 46. He is also correct in his critical judgment of what he terms "the varieties of neo-orthodoxy" (p. 55) which he scores as follows: "Neo-orthodoxy does not cope adequately since its situates the *tremendum* as the dialectic counter of an absent or hidden God, enabling the immensity of the one to pass the mystery of the other in the dark night of this century without compelling them to their dreadful confrontation" (Ibid., pp. 85–86).
6. Ibid., p. 86.
7. Ibid., pp 86f.
8. Ibid., pp 89f.
9. Cohen's term, ibid., p. 91.
10. Ibid., p. 92.
11. Ibid., p. 95f.
12. Ibid., p. 97.
13. Ibid., p. 97.
14. Ignaz Maybaum tried haltingly to deal positively with the State of Israel though he was unable to do much with it theologically because of the nature of his thought as a whole.
15. Ibid., p. 103. This is Cohen's phrase.
16. Ibid., p. 101.
17. On the significance of these issues see Steven T. Katz, "The Conservative Character of Mystical Experience," in Steven T. Katz (ed.), *Mysticism and Religious Traditions* (New York, 1983); and my more recent essay "Mystical Speech and Mystical Meaning," in Steven T. Katz (ed.), *Mysticism and Language* (about to be published by Oxford University Press, New York).
18. See *The Tremendum,* p. 95ff.
19. See ibid., p. 96f.
20. David Biale's suggestion that Scholem is also something of a Kabbalist himself is hard to accept; see Biale's comments in his *Gershom Scholem* (Cambridge, 1979).
21. The influence of Martin Buber's hasidic work is also a seminal, if more oblique factor, here tied up as it is with the widespread interest in "mysticism" in our time. In fact, Gershom Scholem credits Buber with being the

first modern Jewish thinker to take mysticism seriously as an integral part of Judaism and hence opening the kabbalistic tradition as a legitimate resource for others, including himself. See G. Scholem, "Martin Bubers Auffassung des Judentums," in *Eranos-Jahrbuch* XXV (Zurich, 1967), pp. 9–55. Available in an English translation as "Martin Buber's Conception of Judaism," in G. Scholem, *On Jews and Judaism in Crisis* (New York, 1976), pp. 126–171.

22. Debates about the historical and philosophical nature of Schelling's and Rosenzweig's relation to idealism need not detain us here.

23. *The Tremendum*, "Foreward" (by David Tracy), pp. x–xi.

24. Ibid., p. 96f.

25. Ibid., p. 97.

26. Ibid., p. 97.

27. Cf. here my comments on Yitzchak Greenberg's redefinition of God and his notion of a "voluntary covenant" in Chapter 9 of this volume.

28. Ibid., p. 97.

29. It is worth comparing Cohen's present description and understanding of the Divine as dipolar with his comments made in conversation with Mordecai Kaplan over the idea of God in Kaplan's reconstructionism and printed in the volume entitled *If Not Now, When?* (New York, 1973). There Cohen offered:

"I think it also implies a rather fundamental distinction within the tradition between God as creator and God as revealer. One of the things that I particularly love in Rosenzweig's discussion of the reality of God in his *The Star of Redemption* is the recognition that the distinction between God the creator and God the revealer is rather too sharp in traditional theology. The assumption that the creating God is not also a revealing God and that the revealing God is not also a creating God at one and the same time is mistaken. The God who brought the people of Israel out of the land of Egypt to be their God was not only revealing himself to the people and calling the people to himself, convoking the people as the object of the act, but at the same time was exhibiting an undisclosed aspect of himself. The notion in classical theology (which I dislike as much as you do) that God is *being* alone, *ens entissimus,* and that history is somehow oppositive to the divine nature; that God concedes to history, condescends himself to it, seems to me meaningless and defeating.

God needs history. God needs his creatures. God as creator requires as much the thing that he creates as does the capacity to create.

The creation of the universe and the giving of the Torah are part of the same continuum of self-expression. God's nature demands self-expression as profoundly as his creatures demand it."

Cohen's presentation here seems more satisfying and closer to the reality of Jewish views of God than his statement in his new work. It is instructive to follow the whole of Cohen's debate with Kaplan. Also of interest is a comparison of his present views as to the nature of God with those voiced in his earlier, *The Natural and the Supernatural Jew* (New York, 1962).

30. Maimonides, *Guide of the Perplexed*, English translation by S. Pines (Chicago, 1963), II, 25.

31. *The Tremendum,* p. 90. The emphasis of "assumed" is supplied by me.
32. Ibid., p. 94.
33. Ibid., p. 96.
34. Compare in particular Eliezar Berkovits, *Faith after the Holocaust* (New York, 1973), and *With God in Hell* (New York, 1978). See also my critical discussion of Berkovits' views in *Post-Holocaust Dialogues* (New York, 1983), pp. 268–286.
35. For more on the issue of the relation of God and History see section (5) below.
36. Cohen's reliance on this argument attests to his theological sensibilities.
37. Cohen, *The Tremendum,* p. 97.
38. Ibid., p. 97–98.
39. Here, that is, we raise issues as to meaning and related, but separate, questions as to verification, i.e., not conflating the two but asking about both.
40. Ibid., p. 97f.
41. See my paper on the "Logic and Language of Mystery," in S. Sykes and J. Clayton (eds.), *Christ, Faith and History* (Cambridge, England, 1972), pp. 239–262, for a fuller criticism of this common theological gambit.
42. Cohen, *The Tremendum,* p. 98.
43. This is the term Cohen uses to describe the relation of God to history, see ibid., p. 97. I have quoted this passage above.
44. Rav Joseph Soloveitchik has emphasized this text and its meaning for an understanding of covenantal existence and relationship in his classic article, "The Lonely Man of Faith," in *Tradition,* Vol. 7, No. 2 (Summer, 1965), pp. 5–67.
45. Eliezer Berkovits has also expanded upon and utilized this notion in connection with the *Sho'ah;* see, for example, his *With God in Hell,* final chapter.
46. Stated in Cohen, *The Tremendum,* p. 101ff.
47. Ibid., p. 109.
48. The single exception to this generalization is to be found in right-wing ultra-orthodox circles, e.g., Satmar Hasidism and among the *Naturei Karta* of Jerusalem, who can carry on a meaningful Jewish existence because of their profound commitment to traditional Torah observance and study. Outside of these very small, very specially constituted groups, however, my judgment stands.

11

Criteria for a Contemporary Zionist Ideology

I

Exile and return, the twin premises of Zionism, are co-extensive on one fundamental, substantive level with classical rabbinic Judaism. Both are rooted in the negative, empirical odyssey of the Jewish people inside and outside the land of Israel after the *Churban Bayit Sheni* (the destruction of the Second Temple in 70 C.E.); both perceive the historic status quo as a temporary estrangement (if for how long?), that must necessarily be opposed, finally to be negated and overcome. Moreover, the influence of the latter upon the former, of millennial old Jewish hopes upon modern Zionism, cannot à la, e.g., Amos Elon, be ignored or denied without radical historical, conceptual and psychological distortion. The passionate, inherited yearning for Zion as *Eretz Yisroel*, rather than, for example Uganda, made itself felt with a palpable presentness first in Zionist ideology, viz. the 1903 Zionist Congress as well as the struggle with the Bundists and Autonoments, and then in much that is concretely embodied in the *Medinah* (the State). It is this authentic-symbiosis that is seized upon by many, from Harold Fisch to segments of *Gush Emunim* (Block of the Faithful) and even elements of the *Agudah* community, in order to reduce modern Zionism, in its essence, to some variant of classical theology, to some 're-experiencing' of the primal facticity of covenantal intimacy. And, let us not be impatient with

This chapter was first prepared for a conference on "Zionist Ideology" held in Jerusalem in 1985.

those who, within the parameters of the Zionist achievement, sense, even share, this metaphysical exaltation. Yet, at the same time let us not make the consequential error of conceiving this sharing as a statement of phenomenological identity.

Zionism is to be differentiated from theology, from messianism, for all its indebtedness to these generative and sustaining conceptual categories, through its dissociation from their a-historical, a-political teleology. Zionism affirms that the tragic current of Israel's exilic condition is not to be overcome by the intervention of meta-historical agencies, at least not in the guise of meta-historic syntheses that abort the historical process, but rather that the required solution lies in and through history, and still more particularly through the spatio-temporal agency of a corporate political body, a state. To this extent Zionism is a uniquely modern phenomenon insofar as it insists on the necessary reciprocity of the personal and collective, on the necessary linkage of private and historical existence, on the unavoidable presence of the political domain in all areas of human and group relations.

The intellectual founders of modern Zionism understood that the category of a state creates, literally, unique and particular epistemological, moral and social realities. Indeed the body politic creates, in varying degrees, the integral human personality and all attempts to find unity and authenticity independently of the political fabric are illusions, dangerous and costly illusions. Certainly the Jewish people can, and have, constructed lesser political instrumentalities, other forms of community, but none can rival the state as a medium for collective organization and transformation, not least because all other arrangements are predicated on the relative, in varying degrees, absence of power. Insofar as the negative conditions of Jewish life stem directly, if not only, from the absence of such public power, the only remedy that begins to manifest the required potency is that of statehood. By definition—on the Zionist reading—only a state can "cure" the alienation, division and vulnerability of the Jewish people. This is the center, as well as the challenge, of Zionism. Those who deny this perception, whether for autistic or apocalyptic reasons, are not Zionists. Conversely, to identify with Zionism, to be a Zionist, is to conceive the 'aloneness' of the Jewish people and its overcoming in rigorously statist terms.

Yet this specific decoding of the modern Jewish situation should not be mis-understood as entailing that once the State of Israel was created Zionism ceased, especially in Israel, to be relevant. For the Jewish State makes reference to an ideal, as well as to an empirical, construct, certainly as long as the Jewish people remain "unhealed," as manifestly they are. Perceived in this way, Zionism after 1948 is the *Ombudsman* of the normative condition of the State of Israel, as it was of the *Yishuv* before 1948. It is, arrogant as this may sound, the judge of its own success—the concrete socio-political arrangements that are the State of Israel. The embodied State is not yet, and short of the ecstasies of *yemei mashiach* will not be, the perfect cure for the internal and external maladies that confront world Jewry. At every interval the State of Israel requires the matching of its presentness with its own aspirations. Zionism is charged with the actualization of this didactic, constantly self-revising, radical obligation. The seemingly paradoxical, though only seemingly paradoxical, consequence of this broad and encompassing reflection can be stated so: Zionism insists both that the State of Israel is absolutely necessary for the meaningful reconstitution of the Jewish people, and simultaneously, that the State as existent reality is not ultimate *per se*. Or put in a converse way, the State is not *per se* ultimate, though it is only through it that our ultimate object, the maintenance and healthy growth of the Jewish people, can be realized. To go a step further, Zionism is predicated on the premise that the State belongs to and is an instrument, a necessary instrument, of the Jewish people. This is the defining difference between Zionism and all other modern nationalist movements. Zionism does not culminate merely in Statehood.

This last, elemental remark should make it pellucid that when I raise the idiom of critique, of Zionist critique, I am not advocating the tense, exterior posture that one might equate with the situation of American or more broadly *galut* Jewry criticizing Israel, always an unpleasant, if at times legitimate prospect, but rather a subtler, if more comprehensive dissent from within the Zionist movement itself, i.e., the Zionist movement centered in Jerusalem as the nerve center of world Jewry, critiquing its own "first born and beloved child."

What this entails is that Zionism must have a vision of the State, must constantly monitor the real against the ideal, and must act to bring the two into ever-closer harmony.

II

Amidst the many versions, often incoherent and opaque, of Zionism that would claim our loyalty today I would contend that an authentic, as well as viable Zionist ideology must include, and be in harmony with, a set of propositions now to be specified. At the outset, however, if parenthetically, let me suggest that my formulation may not be fully adequate not only as a result of subjective factors but as a consequence of the fact that the condition of the Jewish people today is so complex and revolutionary that we lack the full vocabulary, the adequate syntax, to express the ideological needs of the moment. Nonetheless, and all countervailing difficulties duly acknowledged, let me suggest eight criteria on the basis of which to begin to make the Zionist critique so urgently required.

(1) The Politics of Idiosyncrasy

One must grant the 'mystery' of Israel, at least as an unprecedented historical reality that gave rise to unique circumstances, if one is to come to grips with Zionism, i.e., political Zionism. The sense of the Jewish 'problematic,' the notion of *kibbutz ha-Galuyot,* the 'ingathering of the exiles,' specific details of the Israeli Constitution, the Law of Return, the need for this land and no other, all emanate from this historico-theological legacy. For Jewry all these elements point to quite specific existential factors in the Jewish past and present. Yet, precisely because they press so forcefully upon us, we must counterpose them *qua* state morality and political consciousness, with an alternative, dialectical logic. Under the imperative of political equilibrium we, as Zionists, must assert that Zionism, rooted though it is in the 'uniqueness' of felt Jewish consciousness, cannot be conceived, i.e., translated into formal and structural compulsions, through rudimentary categories that are, in essence, appeals to idiosyncrasy. Though Zionism is not equivalent, nor reducible without remainder, to modern nationalism, insofar as it seeks to provide a contemporary national-statist solution to the problematic of Israel's homeward journey, the overcoming of existential and collective inauthenticity and distortion, it must strive to do so within the contours of the contemporary democratic, legal-political consensus. Even if one conceded *in extremis* that, to use the vocabulary of *Agudat Yisroel,* "Torah-true Judaism" is the primordial stasis of the Jewish people, such a positivity cannot be of service politically, for once adopted it will destroy, both internally and externally, the State of Israel. Such Agudist-like sentiments enacted as national policy will have at least three dire consequences:

A) They will produce a coercive internal milieu predicated on a world of religious values and images that will pulverize the pragmatic base of the state. Here one must recognize that the issue is not primarily one of halachic man vs. non-halachic man, of halachic community vs. non-halachic community, though this is the way the collision is usually presented by secularists on the one hand and *haredim* (ultra-orthodox) on the other. Rather the dilemma is based on a philosophical controversy as much within the orthodox community as between the orthodox and secular segments of the population. The root issue is whether one conceives of the *halachah* as implicated in historical experience and responsive to it; and again, and related, whether one perceives the demands of the *halachah* as intensive or extensive, that is recognizing or denying the legitimacy of, even the need for, alternative and complementary forms of understanding. The conflicting *Weltanschauungen* collide most intensively and meaningfully, not surprisingly, in the broad areas of education, i.e., over the legitimacy of, and the requisite value of, modern education and its many ramifications, and politics, i.e., the recognition of authority other than that exercised by the *Gedolei ha-Dor,* the rabbinical elite of the *haredi* quarter of the traditional community. The politics of idiosyncrasy is therefore to be understood as the outgrowth of a specific and limited halachic orientation, one not necessarily co-extensive, except to its advocates, with halachic Judaism as such. The position should also be recognized as a pre-eminently political position, that is, one concerning authority and power.

B) They will jeopardize the standing, dire and under constant threat as it is, of the State *qua* state in the international forum. Such pragmatic considerations are not to be lightly dismissed within the arena of international politics.

C) They will legitimize the politics of idiosyncrasy as the modality of the Jewish State's relations to other states. Or more precisely, they will justify the authenticity of alternative claims to idiosyncrasy as the basis of international actionability, e.g., that of Khomeini's Iran, Ghaddafi's Libya, and more recently, Saddam Hussein's Iraq. To Khomeini and Ghaddafi, as Hitler a generation ago, the existence of Israel, among many other things, is incompatible, irreconcilable, with what they affirm to be the metaphysical impartiality of their Koranic (or Aryan) canonic gloss, and this, they claim, is sufficient warrant for their anti-Israel behavior. In Nazism the elemental appeal was to an idiosyncratic antimodernism that triumphed in an "hour of authoritarian biology."

In Iran and Libya the idiosyncratic antimodernism has triumphed in an "era of authoritarian theology." To appeal for alliances to resist these motives, to affirm an altogether different destiny, requires a shared, mutually constraining, mutually activating, international normative ethic.

A further clarifying remark is required in respect of this contention for I do not want to be misunderstood regarding it. Sovereign states and diverse cultures co-exist and transact affairs in the international arena, this pluralism being most clearly manifest in communist-capitalist state relations. However, the point to be emphasized is that, vis-à-vis their relationships they appeal to, and within broad (even very broad) parameters respect, an established international code of political behavior. Neither side appeals to God, much as American Presidents favor such rhetoric, nor alternatively, the "necessities" of history, much as such "necessities" form the faith of Communist Commissars, as the basis for international discussion, negotiation and compromise. For the Jewish State to make metaphysical doctrines of "special providence" the basis of its international policy is to court disaster. The Talmudic counsel "not to rely on miracles" is sound advice in the world of *realpolitik*.

(2) The Primacy of Politics

The Zionist movement must advocate, support and provide criteria of worth for high Jewish politics—politics in the Aristotelian not the party sense. It must possess, and encourage the State of Israel and world Jewry to possess, a strategy that transcends class, ethnic and party divisions; it must also resist a too narrow interpretation of national self-interest at the expense of the larger world Jewish polity. Zionist politics ought to be rooted, idealistic though it sounds, in an explicit commitment to national action that embodies collective values. Put another way, Zionism must intend national politics as being different from national administration. It must also hold politics above economics, and further, not allow political action to be the consequence of a semi-autonomous sphere of economic competition (and this independently of questions of which economic system is in place). In a strong sense, this entails Zionism's critique of the bourgeoisification of the state polity (whether based on a socialist or capitalist model). The events leading up to the 1973 war are one example of the dangers of such contrary economic supremacy, the nature of much West Bank settlement another (independently of issues arising from the debate over the correctness of this settlement and development). Again, this means holding the autonomy of the collective above party politics and self-interested sub-sections of the populace. In a generalization, Zionist politics must contend for national actuality as the measure of value above other realms. (As a practical first step this would mean the radical re-organization of the World Zionist Organization; the re-consideration of the procedures used in order to discern the mandate under which the WZO operates; and not least the re-evaluation of the norms used by the WZO to measure its performance.)

Four current areas where the need for such a parallelism between politicized consciousness, "the primacy of politics," and national deed are uncompromisingly called for are:

A) The West Bank and the so-called "Territories," or, in a different idiom, Judea and Samaria. Here the Government of Israel, unflinchingly, relentlessly, must dictate policy—whatever policy that will be in practice —and not capitulate to segments of its own population who usurp the prerogatives of the state. Zionist politics, as presently being advocated, entails a posture of non-negotiation under such circumstances; a state does not negotiate its boundaries with its own citizenry, whatever those boundaries are or may become. I remind you of the Begin Government's structurally and conceptually correct stand on this issue in its negotiations with Egypt. That is, the government acted properly, independently of one's judgment on the terms of the Egyptian peace treaty. Nor again does a state negotiate security with any segment of its people. Citizens have channels for expressing their support or dissent of governmental policies, but extra-parliamentary tactics are not to be countenanced, certainly not capitulated to or the entire civil fabric begins to fray.

B) The state does not divide and delimit its elemental political autonomy through a welter of fiercely competitive extra-parliamentary minorities. This means it does not treat the *Moetzei Gedolei Hatorah* (the rabbinic leaders of *Agudah*), for example, as an independent "government in exile." The *daat Torah,* the earliest mention of which I know being an 1883 essay of R. Israel Salanter,[1] is not, for all its authority among its own *gemeinschaft* community, a national-political, or Zionist-political category. In explaining the discourtesy of not extending an invitation to the President of Israel to address its *Kenessiah Gedolah* the *Agudah* press wrote: "The Agudah possesses the Crown of the Torah and has no need for the Crown of the State." So be it: let the Zionist leadership together with the National leadership fully exercise the *Keter Malchut,* the 'Crown of the State.' In any case, and programmatically, let the Zionist constituency understand its own imperatives and act accordingly, even to the point of censoring the government of Israel when it fails to do less. What the Zionist political dialogue must insist upon, what it must treat with sacerdotal reverence, is the axiological requirement of parliamentary political structures and procedures (recognizing the differing forms such parliamentary arrangements can take within logically coherent and sociologically required limits).

C) The state must control the economy. Just as it must resist the mendacity of the *Agudah* so it must have independence from the *Histadrut* as well as mastery over its free-capitalist elements. It must do this not least because earlier theoretical presumptions about the causal connection between economic development and political transformations rooted in Marxist doctrines of the relationship between political structures and the economy and then broadly adapted and adopted by all the functionalist theories of modernization and state development are unproved, or rather disconfirmed by a wide variety of hard contemporary political evidence. Then, too, even if mindful only of the level of economic efficiency, recognizing the significance of economic matters for the larger policies of the Zionist state, e.g., *aliyah,* (and today specifically the vast Russian *aliyah*), it is sad to note that since the days of the *Yishuv* the state apparatus has never fully mastered the economy. The result has been the nation's continual vulnerability, and mixed legacy of accomplishment and ruin. In concrete terms this means that we require a Zionist analysis of: taxation, and marginal rates of taxation, exchange rates, dollar and other foreign currency controls (or their absence), the balance of payments, land policy, cola's (cost of living adjustment wage arrangements), and much more. Yet, despite the foundational nature of this issue, there is almost no Zionist analysis of this matter to be found in the extensive contemporary literature. Certainly no Zionist critique of state fiscal and economic policies.

D) The Zionist leadership must insist that the national political leadership obstinately and unreservedly control the policy, the decisions, regarding war and peace. This entails that it not be the prisoner of one of its ministers (or factions) on the one hand, nor capitulate to contrary factions at the other end of the political spectrum. The debacle of Lebanon incarnates both these failures of political control (or its absence). Alternatively, the recent behavior of the Israeli government in response to the Iraq crisis is a brilliant example of how Israeli national policy should be conducted.

(3) Zionism as Anti-Romanticism

Romantic longings as well as romantic rhetoric fill the pages of Zionist ideological history. And both the longings and the rhetoric made a real contribution to Zionism's dynamic evolution, for there is something authentically romantic about the cry for national renewal, about the Dionysian call for the transcendence of Israel's tragic exilic existence through the radiant autonomy of self-realization, of vital, energizing actions emerging from one's deepest, undamaged, individual and collective intuitions. Yet in the era of the Zionist State such intense, sincerely felt convictions must not be allowed to serve as the sole basis of the national political ethic. For such self-authenticating energies, asserted most often in the name of the mystery of kinship, produce a morality of immediacy, a morality of conviction, that if unrestrained must consume all ethical balance, all notions of other-directed ethical responsibility, all possibility of rational debate, checks and balances, limits and repair.

'Organic' is the term that repeatedly appears in the classical Zionist sources to describe the desired end of the rebirth of Jewry in its own land. The reasons for this choice are easily recognized: the alienation attendant upon and through the *galut* condition has eviscerated, so the recurrent chorus, the Jewish *neshamah* (soul) both individually and collectively. Yet the more I reflect upon the needs of this hour, of the post-state moment, the more I am fearful of using this metaphor as the reigning symbolism of Zionist and Israeli political life. And this not least because it has been the rallying thesis for fascism and reaction everywhere. In opposition, i.e., not only over-against romanticism *per se,* but in order to be in a position to legitimately oppose ideologies of "blood," Zionism must be a politics or rationality, of *recht,* of law, of accountability, of reconciliation between means and ends, an advocate of the imposed sophistications of the civilizing process.

There can be no denial of the power of feelings in the origin and continuation of the Zionist enterprise. Yet Zionism is not primarily about feelings but about justice. Its primal generative and sustaining context is the criminality of the majority population (both Christian and Muslim) among whom the Jewish sojourned for the past two millennia.

Justice demanded an end to that excessive Jewish powerlessness that was at the root of this barbarism, this continual terrorization of the Jewish people. Zionism instantiated this high aspiration. Zionism must continue to do so, and in my view, has continued to do so, most recently with regard to the Ethiopian and Russian *aliyah*. But it can continue to do so, given the visible power of romantic sensibilities and the politics established upon them, only if it is willing to counterpose contractual and rational juridical and ethical norms over against the excesses of this romanticism, if it is prepared to assert the legal and moral foundation of its enterprise on non-romantic grounds. The collision with, and rejection of, Kahanaism is a particularly significant example of just what is at stake here.

(4) For and Against Normalization

Classical Zionist ideologues of the non-religious camp made the value, the condition, of *normality* supreme. Natan Rotenstreich has correctly summarized this position and called our attention to an important nuance in the usage of this term, by noting that the expression has at least two meanings. (1) The first entails "bringing Jewish existence closer to what was normal in the life of other nations. This was, first and foremost, territorial existence." (2) The second indicates "normalization as the fulfillment of a 'norm.' " Hence "the life of other peoples is taken as a yardstick with which to measure the progress of the State of Israel."[2] Because world history organizes its space, shapes it contours and distributes power according to the calculus of national units, the first interpretation of normalization proposed by Rotenstreich, "bringing Jewish existence closer to that of the nations," has dominated the history of Zionism. Zionism has, however, also, at various times and in various ways, attempted to normalize itself in the second sense outlined above. And here it must exercise supreme caution. That is, it should resist Jewish assimilation now under the guise of national reconstruction. For even though the national political forms that Zionism and the State of Israel have replicated and made their own are shared products of the post-Enlightenment landscape, the inner cultural-spiritual immediacies of the Zionist State need not be, ought not to be, clones of gentile European, post-Enlightenment culture *per se*. For if they are, then the inner core of the Zionist revolution has been a failure, an illusory self-reconciliation, a mere transposition of alienation from one geographical locus, *galut,* to another *Eretz Yisroel.*

The expansion and re-weighting of the significant occasions on the Hebrew calendar, the remarkable renaissance of the Hebrew language, aspects of education both religious and secular, the recovery of hidden or obscured dimensions of our history, the control of our public space, have all been revivifying elements in a varied program of renewed Jewish cultural creativity and sensibility; but, as yet, this program is fragmentary and inchoate. Yet even as we fumble for suitable expression of such a re-imagining of a contemporary Zionist canon we can assert this much with confidence: only the State of Israel provides the circumstance for the collective, comprehensive reconstitution of a specific Jewish hermeneutic in all spheres of personal and group activity. Insofar as social context, in its broadest sense, is epistemologically formative even for the most intimate of endeavors, a regnant Jewish-Hebrew collective is, of necessity, bound to be transformative; it may even be profoundly constructive—and this must be encouraged, though the verdict is still out.

(5) Zionist Morality as a Morality of Relations not Reifications

The two preceding reflections are inseparable from a third: Zionist morality cannot remain in the realm of lifeless abstractions, reifications that exist platonically above and separate from social relations. A distinctive Zionist ethic ought not to be conceived of as the exchange relationship between things, nor again between independent, idealized types or classes. Rather political morality, Zionist political morality, must emerge from, and apply concretely to, the embodied, contingent, diverse, pluralistic relation between groups and classes and crucially between peoples.

(6) The Manipulation of Violence as an Ideological Weapon

I isolate this as a separate rubric, though it is a direct corollary of the theme of the primacy of politics, as a consequence of its seminal, and temporally apposite, importance. Zionism must, as one of its dominant, unambiguous imperatives control violence within the Jewish State, as well as within those other territorial loci it governs. Recognizing the distinction between force and violence, the State, with Zionist endorsement, must, if necessary, use all the force at its disposal to eliminate violence within its operational parameters, co-incident with a principled declaration against the recognition of violence as an instrument of political dialogue. Whatever ambiguity might exist in the conflict at hand, the existence of a State means that law must prevail over barbaric innocence, over passions no matter how well intended, over self-justifying bias, over extra-legal normative mechanisms of inspiration and legitimacy.

It is not appropriate for me, in this context, to enter into an analysis of the detailed political divisions within the current Israeli circumstance. On one topic only I am compelled to speak in some specificity. Working as I have been for many years on the issue of comparative mass murder in relation to the *Sho'ah,* it would be intellectually and morally irresponsible of me not to call to attention one overriding fact: evil of all forms can be perpetrated by the most "selfless," "idealistic," "committed" individuals. The "idealism" of the terrorist, however, except in the rarest of instances, does not justify his terror. Certainly terrorism carried out by those with power and influence against those without it is never justified.

This profound ethical issue, this complex dilemma regarding the relationship of power and the proper use of force, provides a quintessential example of the *Ombudsman* role, that squaring of ideal vision and ambiguous reality, that Zionist ideology cannot avoid.

(7) On Destiny and Decision

The Jewish people is a tiny people, a weak people, an exposed people. Zionism sought to provide some protection from this powerlessness, and has succeeded, if not completely. As a consequence, three reflections can be justified. The first is the obvious banality that we, the Jewish people, are in the grasp of powerful historical forces stronger than ourselves. The second is that what we do does affect how these external forces relate to, and dominate, us. This latter truth is not only a confessional mark of Zionist faith, but an evident, exact, historic disclosure, if not one totally devoid of that dark humorous irony that marks Jewish history. The third, following upon the second, is that Zionism must be: (a) activist, i.e., a manifestation of the inherent resonances of the notions of 'autoemancipation' and 'halutziut'; (b) open to the future and future directed; (c) unafraid of action that is not wholly pure, i.e., willing "to move," as Weizmann argued before the Anglo-American Enquiry Commission, "on the line of least injustice," but obligated at the same time to reach for the highest ethical standards available within the confines of the dialectical ambiguities of real life; (d) not paralyzed by that special form of self-hate and egocentricity that holds the Jewish people to an illusory standard of moral perfection if a deed is to be undertaken in the name of Jewry. Zionism aims at ideal reality but it does not insist that if we cannot live unadulterated lives we must continue to be *korbanot* (sacrifices) on the altars of the nations. Zionism is not a form of utopianism; (e) opposed in logic to determinism of all sorts—economic, historical or metaphysical; (f) and anti-eschatological. Even if one concurred in the metaphysical presumption that history were the veil behind which suprahistorical forces existed, that the external world were the incarnation of genuinely transcendental powers, as a Zionist one must insist that these ontological agencies are open to persuasion by human behavior. Zionism grows from the belief that the hermeneutic of history opposes closure. For those of different opinion let it be recalled that according to the *Tanach* (the Hebrew Bible) even God changes His mind as a consequence of, and in response to, human intercession, while the logic of *Teshuvah* (Repentance, Return), so fundamental to Jewish life and theology, means, remarkably, that not only the future, but, as it were, even the past is not fixed.

(8) The Golah

To this point my analysis has centered on the relationship of Zionism and Zion, but Zionism holds a self-imposed responsibility for the Jewish people both inside the State of Israel as well as in the *Golah*. The peculiar originality of Zionism as a nationalist movement lies in its wholly instrumental character: the State is only the means of healing the Jewish people. In Usshiskin's phrase, "If the Jewish people will redeem the land the land will redeem the Jewish people." It is always *Klal Yisroel* that has priority; any alternative rendering of Zionism is not consonant with mainstream classical Zionism across the spectrum. In light of this larger responsibility for the Jewish people, and given the already extended nature of this essay, let me raise for consideration only two points relative to the status of the *Golah*, and then only schematically.

(A) The ultimate paradox of the present Zionist circumstance is that the creation of the State of Israel has partly solved the "Judenfrage" while at the same time recreating it, i.e., it has engendered new and intense forms of antisemitism. This is a fact not faced frontally by Zionist theoreticians, yet it is an issue that calls for urgent analysis.

(B) American Jewry, and other western Jewries to lesser extents, are not the classical *galut* Jewries of Zionist understanding. The Zionist "solution" therefore no longer exactly or self-evidently fits the "problem."

In a nutshell, for these post-Holocaust western Jewish communities the problem is not antisemitism but assimilation—not oppression but success—the inner unconcern of Jews with their Jewishness to the point of the uncoerced, casual extinction of that Jewishness. It is this malaise, this emptiness, that makes the corporate, the collective embodiment of Jewry in the State all the more urgent and significant.

In this unprecedented historic situation Zionism, and the Zionist State, must look to world Jewry with help that is adequate to its current crisis. They must seek to bolster Jewish life in the *Golah,* not merely lament its "inevitable" demise. Thus, as much as money, energy and support must flow from periphery to center, from *galut* to Zion, from secondary to primary Jewries, so there must be a reconsideration of that flow and of the possibility of a complementary system of support in the opposite direction. Let this brief mention of a very large and complex problem suffice for the moment.

This ideological inventory centering on the Zionism of Zion makes no pretense as to descriptive completeness or analytical refinement. Yet the elements here adumbrated are, I believe, central to any and all serious discussion of contemporary, relevant, Zionist ideology. My intention is to open up the conceptual conversation so *urgently* required rather than to immobilize or anesthetize it. I say *urgently* because ultimately one cannot separate a state from its "first principles"; in the biography of its citizens the values of a state are encoded. For those who would voluntarily conjoin their destinies with the destiny of the State of Israel what kind of state it is matters intensely—this is just as true today for Russian Jews as French and American Jews. For those who pay the highest price for the maintenance of the State of Israel—young and not-so-young Israelis who serve the State and the whole Jewish people in the army—the normative issues are still more consequential, for in resolving them to their satisfaction they, and they alone, will decide whether Zionism is a reality worth fighting, and dying, for or whether the dream is empty and life in Los Angeles or Toronto is equally defensible, and much less immediately anxious and difficult.

NOTES

1. R. Israel Salanter, *Or Yisrael* (Vilnius, 1900), No. 62, 1883.
2. Natan Rotenstreich, *Essays on Zionism and the Contemporary Jewish Condition* (New York, 1980), p. 24.

12

Zionism as an Expression of Jewish Freedom

Zionism is the momentous Jewish response to modernity. Amid all the diverse and alternating reactions to the unprecedented situation of the Jewish people after 1750, Zionism and Zionism alone insisted, and rightly, that the unresolved and tragically unresolvable tensions, the painful ambiguities, and the dark ironies of the post-Enlightenment landscape required both a political and a fully national response. In the context of 20th century European history, where the optimism of the *Haskalah* and *The Enlightenment,* where the nationalist loyalties of assimilated and Reform Jews, where the insurrectional naivete of the socialists, Bundists, and Marxists, were all devoured in the ritual immo-lation of the Jewish people at Auschwitz and Treblinka, this contention needs little defending. Even if understood only in the most skeletal Herzlian modality, in the barest defensive political-emigratory terms, the luminous correctness of Herzl's dialectical prognosis is now unarguable. Even for those whose ideological commitments run in other directions, who would prefer a Kantian teleology or a non-nationalist universalism predicated upon an aversion to ethnicity and religious particularism, the brute, barbarous realities of the murderous *Einsatzgruppen* and the genocidal imperatives of Himmler's SS silences their conceptual, princi-pled, but abstract representations. If less than an ideal, if short of a utopian solution, if not a total panacea, if mired in the weaknesses of human behavior, in the crosscurrents of human volition, in the unavoid-

This essay was first delivered as the 1986–87 Sol Feinstein Memorial Lecture on the Meaning of Freedom at Gratz College, Philadelphia. Reprinted by permission.

able complexities of historical existence, Zionism, in the 20th century context, that is for those who could realize its promise, meant life not death: dignity rather than despoliation; an open future brimming with possibilities rather than a funereal end to all hope and to all meaning. On the collective, the national level, it meant that the sepulcher that Hitler had planned for the Jewish people would yet remain empty; that they would survive to continue their struggle with seemingly recalcitrant reality in order to bring out of it a perfected creation. Those few who have continued to demur from the Zionist project even in the face of the crematoria, on the putative metaphysical grounds that Zionism was falsifying the messianic, that it was guilty of the sin of *Dehikat ha-ketz,* of "forcing the end," through its overturning, in hubris, of Israel's divinely ordained exilic status, have sinned against both God and man in what can only be construed as the arrogant blindness of their own confused self-righteousness.

Against American Jewry too this savage history exerts a claim. By one or two generations we or our parents and grandparents escaped the inferno. If not for ourselves then for the "remnant," the Zionist actuality, whatever our ideological construction of its obligations and character, must be defended, encouraged, supported. And so it has been, to the eternal credit of our American community, since at least the 1940's. If American Jewry before the war failed, in its generality, to grasp the demand of the hour its fault, though real, is understandable. In more recent decades, by contrast, almost all American Jews have been, in the minimalist sense of financial and political support, if not Zionists, then at least pro-Israel. They have not failed to grasp, despite their privileged situation, the meaning, the obligation, of providing a refuge.

To this elemental degree then, Zionism as embodied in the *Yishuv* and thereafter in the State of Israel is the ultimate expression of Jewish freedom, defining freedom here in its most rudimentary form as the ability to survive. As one would be hard pressed to find another people whose very physical existence has been marked out for annihilation, whose enemies actively sought nothing less than its full extermination, who stood alone, targeted for nothing short of genocide in its technical sense of the utter physical eradication of every man, woman, and child who belonged to its rank, this rejoinder—survival—is no small matter. After Auschwitz Jewish existence is never "mere existence," and thus to the considerable degree that Zionism facilitates Jewish continuity it incarnates freedom. For what freedom transcends the freedom to be?

But Zionism has always willed to be more than haven, though if it were only this, given our recent blood-stained past, we ought still to say *dayenu*. For Zionism has a fuller, deeper grasp of the resonances of freedom. And it is with these that we must occupy ourselves, however schematically, for the remainder of this chapter.

Ten elements, no kabbalistic *gematria* or *notarikon* intended, require elucidation. All ten deal with what, in the vocabulary of classical Zionism, are known as the twin problems of the "status of the Jews" and the "condition of the Jews."

1. Zionism is rooted in the repercussive recognition that real freedom, both individualistically and communally, is not only freedom of thought but freedom of the will. "If you will it," Herzl argued, "it is not a dream." The full expression of such freedom, that which substantively makes it more than a mere wish,[1] is the purposive activity that intends its realization, that structured process that must be empirically, existentially exemplified in *all* of life's concrete situations. It must be performance not only pronouncement. As such Zionism insists, requires, that it make a real difference to the way Jews, and others, live out their daily lives. By controlling the political domain, and only by controlling the political domain, does this axiom become actionable. This is especially true insofar as Zionism understands that the personal and collective cannot be fully divided into sealed compartments. Rather the two realms intermingle, with the political domain exerting a ubiquitous presence in all the covert and overt spheres of human and group relations. Put another complementary way, the activism of Zionism wills that there be no division between ideals and reality. Volition, guided by principles, translates the *ought* into the *is*. The public arena, through willed behavior, becomes the embodied *loci* of the normative, the prescriptive.

A word of further explanation is here required in light of the degenerate history that the notion of national will has had in our time. Since Nazism exalted its diabolic racial violence as "the triumph of the will," morally sensitive individuals have recognized the dangers inherent in extreme national manifestations of this notion. Therefore, it is required to draw a clear division between Zionism as the incarnation of national will, and those movements that draw upon, but thoroughly debase, this fecund idea. In Zionism the national will is, in consonance with its own deepest principles, never self-sufficient, never an end in itself, never the autonomous bearer of value to the degree that it can trample morality underfoot. The national will as expressed in Zionism, that is conscious of itself as a movement of liberation, entails openness, accessibility, malleability, and accountability. The national will, *contra* fascism or, and especially, Nazism, is not conceived of as a blind, destructive, ultimately suicidal reality. Committed irrevocably, in principle, to libertarian and democratic norms, it does not seek to usurp individual autonomy but to encourage it, it does not desire to manipulate its people but to unshackle them, it does not intend to delimit their access to ideas and information but to encourage the free and lively interchange of information. Its *raison d'être* is to justly open up the political process, to encourage access to the sources of power, to distribute the reality of power to its people, rather than to narrow down these political opportunities to the few, or in the extreme case of Nazism, the Führer alone.

2. Zionism perceived that the moral equation requires that the Jewish People become *subject,* become the author of their own destiny. Morality, both individual and even more collective, national, requires that subjectivity, that self-determination shaped by subjects in dialogue that no a-symmetrical utilitarian exchange can possess. Morality cannot maintain itself when the "other" is perceived as *object* only. Jews had, the Zionists intuited, to transform fate into destiny; to raise their lamentable status by initiating action rather than merely reacting to the initiative of others.

3. As such, in its deepest inspiration, Zionism's primal energy is derived from its desire to actualize a profound moral vision. For Zionism freedom is not only, and minimally, the power to execute one's intentions, the capacity to satisfy one's desire,[2] however worthy or otherwise one's intentions and desires are. Rather, in contradistinction to this classical liberal rendering of the notion of freedom, Zionism necessarily associates freedom with goodness, the absence of coercion with the attainment of noble purposes, the capacity to will with the compassionate desire to will the ennobling, even the sublime. Seen in this way, Zionism is a dynamic attempt to correlate the ethical with the actual. At its heart it is a moral crusade that addresses Jews and non-Jews with a moral demand.

4. The expression of this ethical valence, this normative design, in the requirement that the Jewish People have a state of their own is therefore not intended to be the expression of a naturalistic chauvinism. Rather, this imperative flows from the transcendent recognition that only such a reconstructed political arrangement can assure that both Jews and non-Jews will act towards each other with the requisite, minimal decency.

Jewish powerlessness creates the immoral relationship that has governed Jewish life in the Diaspora. To end this asymmetry and its evil consequences a state is needed. It is, however, simultaneously, the recognition of this meta-political normativity, this attempt to create a moral dialogue between Jews and others as the vital, rudimentary fact of Jewish existence, that results in the dialectical judgment that while there must be a Jewish state this state can be allowed always and only to possess instrumental value; that is the Jewish state is subordinate to both the needs of the Jewish People as well as, or even more so, to those axiological stringencies that condition and define the existence of this people Israel.

This defining instrumental circumstance is what decisively individuates Zionism from the broad run of modern nationalist movements. Insofar as Zionism is never an end, *contra* all fascist and statist movements, but always a servant, in that the Zionist movement came into being only to serve the Jewish People, it knows that the correct expression of freedom in this context must be consistent with Israel's nonnegotiable ethical center.

Accordingly Zionist freedom, as Jewish freedom more generally as experienced in the Exodus which culminated in the revelatory moment of Sinai, is never merely negative freedom, freedom from x or y where x or y are prescriptions or principles of juridical or normative behavior. Zionist freedom is not anarchic but disciplined, not only freedom from but, necessarily, freedom for, not only the absence of coercion or restraint but also the recognition of obligations and responsibilities, the acknowledgment not only of means but also of ends, the use of power as well as the control of its misuse.

5. Power, for Zionism, though elemental, indeed the fundamental factor in its analysis of the Jewish people's concrete situation, is, accordingly *never* intended to by tyrannical. The common thread that runs from Callicles' argument in Plato's *Gorgias* (484a), to Nietzsche's *Übermensch,* allowing for qualifications that are necessary here, to the *Führerprinzip* that claims a transcendental immunity from positive law, are the antithesis of Zionist self-definition. Accordingly, while one cannot, and should not, ignore or deny the passionate romantic longings and inspirations active in the milieu out of which Zionism emerged, the freedom that Zionism envisions should not be deciphered as being elementally about feelings but about justice under law. Justice demanded an end to Jewish powerlessness, and Zionism instantiated this ethical demand. Freedom in the State of Israel, for both Jew and non-Jew,

means adhering to these rational juridical and ethical imperatives. Whatever the specific ambiguities that might and do exist in the various competitive and conflict-laden circumstances of the State of Israel, the Zionist credo requires that law must prevail over all barbarism, even when emerging from innocence or passion. The "commitment" of the dogmatist, no less than the "idealism" of the terrorist, whether Arab, European, or Jewish, must be opposed precisely because of the foundational principles upon which Zionism is predicated. Again, and as a corollary, violence in its myriad forms, as a mode of Jewish politics within the state, is unacceptable.

In reflecting on the ethics of politics, on the responsibilities that national freedom entails, a further corollary is to be highlighted. Jews, the Jewish People, are now a majority somewhere and, as such, the "minority mentality" has begun, to what degree we could argue, to give way to a new form of collective consciousness. Integral to this transformation is the significant inescapable challenge, unknown for two millennia, of how to exercise the freedom of the majority while protecting the rights and dignity of "minorities."[3] Since 1948 a whole new extraordinary experience has unfolded. Not since 70 C.E. have we, the Jewish People, been tested by the control of power; now we are. The seminal debates over the West Bank, the Arab minority in Israel, the Druze, the Palestinians, as well as the intra-Jewish dialogue over the non-Orthodox rabbinate, the role of women, the State's relations with the non-Zionist Jewish Orthodox right, are all part and parcel of this complex discussion. So too are internal matters of social and economic justice, of the *edot mizrach,* of the Falasha's. Our profoundest activity as a free people is now inseparable from the *exercise* of political power.

6. Zionist freedom envisioned as well a second complementary type of transformation. A transmogrification of the Jewish *condition.* This was to be an *inner* mutation of the Jewish circumstance, for which a state was the pre-eminent facilitator, given its unrivaled possibilities as a channel, a structure, for collective action and reform. As Ahad Ha'Am wrote in reflecting on the first Zionist Congress in *Ha-Shilo'ah* in September 1897: "The Congress [was] a great public statement before all the world that the Jewish people was still alive and wished to go on living . . . [it was important not] so that other nations hear it and grant us our desire but . . . so that *we ourselves* hear the echo of our voice in the depths of our own soul which might then awake and shake off its degradation."[4] Put differently, Zionism recognized that exile, *galut,* was

not only a state of external pressure, of public and juridical debasement, but that it also necessarily involved the mirroring of this political distortion in the inner life of the Jew and Judaism. Exile, then, was not only a territorial and political relationship but also a psychological and spiritual one. Exile meant a crippling psychological dependence, an absolute, suicidal inauthenticity. In its minimalist rendering then, Zionism as interior catharsis meant overcoming the ability to be shamed by non-Jews merely because of one's Jewishness. This shame, so widespread a phenomenon in modern times, the extreme expression of which is the pervasive phenomenon of Jewish self-hatred found in violent forms in individuals such as Karl Marx and Otto Weininger, and in still potent, loathsome, subtle forms in Jews such as Philip Roth and Norman Mailer, is the result of the internalization of that hatred which the anamalous situation of the Jew creates and which Zionism intends to decisively overcome. In its maximal expression Zionist freedom means the recreation of autonomous Jewish creativity out of the sources of Judaism. In between these two extremes it aims to heal the schizophrenia that characterizes the Jewish soul in exile even, or especially, the exilic soul that benefits so markedly from freedom in the western democracies, especially America. To this degree it shares in the wisdom of the Hasidic Rebbe who taught that the deepest exile occurs when one is no longer aware that one is in exile. Rooted in a judicious decipherment of the very real success of western Jewry, Zionism recognizes that individual economic and material success, however considerable, does not fully alleviate the inner tensions of the Jewish psyche.

This psychic burden need not manifest itself as fear, it is enough that it manifest itself as felt difference. For in this awareness of difference lies the radical recognition that the individual is more than a self-creating being, that he is the residue of a millennial-old, national history from which, however devoutly he may wish it, he cannot be completely free. Just as psychoanalysis discovers that the child is the father of the man and through this discovery makes the healing of the adult possible, so Zionism contends that the nation is the father of the individual, however much most Jews feel orphans, and, by analogy, that only this structural diagnosis can provide the cure for that divisive self-identity which is so prevalent, and so potent a reality in the post-emancipation Jew.

Seen thus, even for those who tie their destiny to the *Golah,* as for example, the great majority of American Jews, Zionism provides a creative operative principle that frees them from both indignity and passivity. As an empirical observation, the manifest pride of the American Jewish community in its Jewishness, and its political activism on behalf of world Jewry, as well as other oppressed peoples is no accident; it is rather, in large measure, the practical consequence of the Zionization of the American Jewish community. Here I talk not of achievements, real as they are, but rather of attitudes, of a regnant sensibility regarding the unashamed moral wholeness of united Jewish activism. The dominant anxiety of the previous era not "to appear too Jewish," to support Jewish causes only furtively or anonymously, to falsely juxtapose Jewish and human ends, to labor under the dichotomous typology of particular versus universal, all transparent expressions of the corrosive schizophrenia that Zionism was sensitive to, to which it willed to be an antidote, are now, if not wholly, being transcended by a new, Zionist-inspired, if not fully Zionist, Jewish self-awareness that has no better name than true freedom.

There is a profound, necessary corollary of this vision which is integral to it, though very little understood. The realization of freedom from this perspective means transforming not only the Jewish but also the non-Jewish situation. Insofar as the oppression of Jewry is the consequence of non-Jewish attitudes, Zionism's aim, in one primal sense, is to radically alter these causative attitudes; to if you like, liberate the non-Jew from his anti-semitism. As such, Zionism is therefore as equally dedicated, in principle, to the liberation of the oppressor as it is to the liberation of the Jew whose ruinously disadvantaged plight is the dialectical consequence of the alienated, negative consciousness under which he is subordinated. In self-interest the Zionist is committed to the ethical reconstruction of his enemy. Squaring self-interest and altruism he does not want merely to invert roles with his victimizer and become the oppressor.

7. A child does not choose the language he will speak. Yet his language, which holds him prisoner, is the medium for his discovery of the world, for whatever freedom of thought and experience he will come to know. When the child learns to order his world, to express himself through the mysteries of the inbuilt syntactic and grammatical structure of language, he comes to construct his speech by rules not of his making, yet when he conforms to them we do not call him slave and when he breaks them we do not call him free. The real challenge, the authentic test of freedom, is to learn to use the rules to create new possibilities as did a Shakespeare or Agnon. So, by analogy, are the circumstances of

national belonging. We do not choose our national identity nor by moving within its parameters, by exercising the options therein open, do we become slaves. Rather, in the naturalness of identity, the individual expresses the deepest unity of his or her personality.

As a further expression of such natural contextual and familial freedom, Mordecai Kaplan's insight into the rights of parents and of discrete cultural communities is to be recalled. He reminds us that: "if we deny to any group," in this case specifically the Jewish people, "the right to transmit its language, its experiences, its *sancta,* its beliefs and its desiderata, we rob all its members of the elementary right to exercise their most human, as distinct from subhuman, function—that of eliciting the humanity inherent in the child,"[5] that is their children. Justice requires that Jews have the freedom to teach their children to be Jews. To surrender this right, as modernity has demanded of the Jewish people as the price of its admission to citizenship, is immoral. Or put differently, assimilation to the majoritarian culture is an extreme form of unfreedom. To the degree then that Zionism has reversed this pattern of cultural, axiological surrender; to the extent that it has facilitated the renewal of "natural" Jewish identity, it has been a liberating force. Consider, to make this point more clearly, a number of actual examples of the changes it has wrought in contemporary Jewish life even in the *golah.* First, reflect upon the revaluation of our calendar, a decisive element in any group's self-identity, which Zionism has caused. Chanukah has emerged as more important than ever before, while *Tish'a BèAv* and *Lag Ba'Omer,* two very different sorts of occasions, have been transformed, all because they are subject to a Zionist revisioning. Compare this to the "decline" of the importance of *Purim* in all but orthodox circles. Again, new festivals such as *Yom Ha-Atzmaut* and *Yom Yerushalayim* have been added to the calendar. Secondly, the role of Hebrew in our communal and educational concerns at all levels has again become, in both old and especially new ways, an essential part of our sense of self and community. Thirdly, consider the psychological, social, and historic meaning of the new use of Hebrew names as one's primary name. Remember that the midrash attributes the redemption from Egypt to the fact that Jewish mothers continued to give their children Hebrew names. Such attributions are a sign of Jewish pride and of Jewish cultural freedom.

8. In decoding the meaning of freedom one, as a rule, as in Locke and Montesquieu, and again in Herzl and Jabotinsky, tends to define free-

dom, both personal and civil, in terms of security. In a succinct and weighty definition, Montesquieu describes freedom in these words: "the political liberty of a subject is the tranquility of mind arising from the opinion each person has of his safety. In order to have this liberty, it is requisite the government be so constituted as one man need not be afraid of another."[6] So the repercussive matter of civil status and equality before the law. But Zionism, through its intuitive colloquy with values intends again to transmute the condition of Jewry by posing the systematic problematic of freedom not only as one of juridical and constitutional structure but also as one of metaphysical possibility, of unbounded horizons, in a word perceiving freedom as bold adventure. The Zionist imperative requires that the Jewish People must be open, as a people, to the present.

It is on this fundamental normative level that Zionism came, and continues to come, into profoundest conflict with elements of the classical halachic *Weltanschauung*. The orthodox who opposed Zionism sensed rightly, its revolutionary implications just here in the realm of aspiration and correctly grasped its transcendence of that exalted a-historicity encouraged by traditional piety. Aside from those few who like Rav Kook, armed with his evolutionary kabbalistic cosmology, could find ways of reconciling this polemical tension, this collision lies at the very heart of both the ideological relation of Zionism to Jewish tradition, as well as the practical, threatening, tragic, unresolved dialogue between various factions within the Jewish People in our time. There are no easy solutions here. This very fact, more than any other, witnesses to the radical novelty of Zionism's conceptualization of freedom.

Alternatively, the magnetic attraction that the Zionist enterprise concretely realized in, but has not yet exhausted through, the actuality of the State of Israel is grounded, in large measure, in its futurity. We, the entire Jewish People, are seduced by our desire to participate in the shaping of Israel's future destiny, to be a partner in the momentous adventure which is the State of Israel.

9. Zionism creates, as a concrete corollary of this implication of freedom, novelty. As a consequence of the possibilities it engenders, new forms of Jewish life, new spiritual centers, and new modes of Jewish expression have come into being.

Not only the Kibbutz but *Tsahal* and the *Knesset* have a profound spiritual dimension that affects all Jews in terms of who we are and what we dream we might become. The very possibilities that we might return to the land after the fashion of the kibbutznik or fly a phantom, or be Prime Minister of a Jewish Commonwealth are only three of the myriad possibilities for self-realization that Zionism has made possible.

The horizons of all our imaginations are that much broader than ever before. Old ideals have been refurbished and revived, new ones created. Another way of summing this up is to say that there are now new and unprecedented types of Jewish heroes. Even the idea of new Jewish heroes is itself, in the modern world, a striking novelty:

> "The old will become new/ And the new will be consecrated
> Old and new together/ Will be torches of light over Zion."[7]

10. Tenth and last, Zionism is the assertion that real freedom entails the freedom to be different. Zionism makes it possible for the Jewish people to live a life, to create a civilization, that is not only an alternative to the patterns of social life dominant in non-Jewish society at large, but also one that is different as well from the historic pattern of Jewish life in the *golah*. It provides the opportunity to remove ourselves from exile and to remove the exile that is within ourselves. It challenges us, as nothing else can, to exercise our existential freedom and to make *aliyah;* or, conversely, if we choose to remain in the *golah* to do so as a matter of authentic choice rather than as a result of other people's necessity. In sum, it offers a supreme test of our Jewish substance and a quintessential engagement of our human potentialities. Zionism sets us free.

NOTES

1. As Kant said in *The Fundamental Principles of the Metaphysics of Morals,* "[The good will is not] . . . a mere wish, but the summoning of all means in our power." (Indianapolis, 1948), Section 1.
2. See J. S. Mills' definition: "freedom . . . is . . . pursuing our own good in our own way. . . . Liberty consists in doing what one desires . . ." *On Liberty* (New York, 1910), pp. 75 and 152.
3. As the King in Judah Halevi's *Juzari* already points out, it is easy to be "moral" when one lacks the power to effect the outcome of events. Would, he asks, the Jews do better in this respect than other communities if they controlled the state? Let us hope so!

4. Cited from David Vital, *Zionism: The Formative Years* (Oxford, 1982), p. 24.
5. *Judaism as a Civilization* (Philadelphia, 1934; I cite this quote from the 1981 edition), p. 246.
6. Montesquieu, *Spirit of the Laws* (Cambridge [England], 1989).
7. Rav Kook, *Letters* (Jerusalem, 1961) [in Hebrew].

Index